Grant at 200

Reconsidering the Life and Legacy
of Ulysses S. Grant

Edited by

Chris Mackowski

and

Frank J. Scaturro

SB

Savas Beatie
California

First edition, first printing

ISBN-13: 978-1-61121-614-1 (hardcover)
ISBN-13: 978-1-61121-615-8 (ebook)

Library of Congress Cataloging-in-Publication Data

Names: Mackowski, Chris, editor. | Scaturro, Frank J., editor.
Title: Grant at 200 : reconsidering the life and legacy of Ulysses S. Grant
    / edited by Chris Mackowski and Frank Scaturro.
Other titles: Grant at two hundred
Description: El Dorado Hills, CA : Savas Beatie, [2022] | Summary: "Grant
    at 200: Reconsidering the Life and Legacy of Ulysses S. Grant celebrates
    the bicentennial of the birth of a man whose towering impact on American
    history has often been overshadowed and even ignored. This collection of
    essays by some of today's best Grant scholars offers fresh perspectives
    on Grant's military career and presidency, as well as underexplored
    personal topics including his faith and family life"-- Provided by
    publisher.
Identifiers: LCCN 2022011298 | ISBN 9781611216141 (hardcover) | ISBN
    9781611216158 (ebook)
Subjects: LCSH: Grant, Ulysses S. (Ulysses Simpson), 1822-1885. |
    Presidents--United States--Biography. | Generals--United
    States--Biography. | United States--Politics and government--1869-1877.
    | United States--History--Civil War, 1861-1865--Biography. | United
    States. Army--Biography .
Classification: LCC E672 .G753 2022 | DDC 973.8/2092 [B]--dc23/eng/20220323
LC record available at https://lccn.loc.gov/2022011298

Savas Beatie
989 Governor Drive, Suite 102
El Dorado Hills, CA 95762
916-941-6896 / sales@savasbeatie.com / www.savasbeatie.com

All of our titles are available at special discount rates for bulk purchases in the United States. Contact us for information.

Proudly published, printed, and warehoused in the United States of America.

Dedications

Frank: To Kathleen and John

Chris: To my favorite Illinoisians,
my Aunt Marney Bess and Uncle Buck

We jointly dedicate this book to the faithful stewards of Ulysses S. Grant's memory at historic sites and in archives across the country, who have kept the flame for two centuries and who will carry it forward for many more.

With respect to General Grant, I confess to being an admirer of his tremendous ability to fashion a path to success despite adversity along the way. The chief lessons I draw from Grant's generalship are the value of bold initiative and the absolute necessity for calm in the middle of danger, uncertainty, and the inevitable fog of war. In my view his most brilliant campaign came at Vicksburg. There, after several setbacks, he maneuvered completely around the city, isolated the fortress from reinforcements and won a decisive victory. Throughout that campaign and the Virginia campaign of 1864–65, his unflappable leadership steadied the Union Army and turned tactical setbacks into operational triumphs.

Colin L. Powell
Chairman
Joint Chiefs of Staff

From a 28 June 1991 letter to Frank Scaturro

Table of Contents

Table of Contents
(continued)

Table of Contents

(continued)

*Proceeds from this volume will go to support
the Ulysses S. Grant Association
and the Grant Monument Association.*

Acknowledgments

The Ulysses S. Grant Association (USGA) and Grant Monument Association (GMA) are grateful to their members and supporters over many years leading to 2022's bicentennial of Grant's birth. They also extend their deepest appreciation to the contributors of this volume for their time and generosity in engaging in this labor for the benefit of the USGA and GMA.

This volume would not have been possible without the assistance of John F. Marszalek, the tireless former executive director of the USGA, who drew contributors to this project and helped coordinate its successful completion from beginning to end. The support of former USGA President Emeritus Frank J. Williams was likewise invaluable. Both have since used the bicentennial as an opportunity to retire from their longtime positions, and we wish them all the best (and knowing neither will ever be far from Grant's story).

The editors also thank Al Felzenberg and Ryan P. Semmes for their guidance and help with research and review even as they were working on their own essays for this book. Al would like to add his thanks to Emily Greenhouse, editor, The New York Review of Books, and journalist Judith Miller for their assistance during the course of his research.

Special thanks to the staff of the USGA and Mississippi State University for their support; to Jimmy Kemp of the Jack Kemp Foundation; the Civil War Institute at Gettysburg College; and Tamara Elliott of the Senate Library, Senate Judiciary Committee archivist Amanda Ray, Stephen Spence and Alexandra Villaseran of the National Archives, and Stuart Fraser of the Newberry Library for their help identifying and navigating source materials. The editors also thank Emily Morris and Jon Schmitz of the Chautauqua Institution, current USGA President James Bultema, and Karen Needles for their help with several photo-related questions.

Thanks, too, to Theodore P. Savas and his staff at Savas Beatie, LLC, for their willingness to take on this project. Of particular help were Veronica Kane and Patrick McCormick.

Chris offers his thanks to St. Bonaventure University's Jandoli School of Communication for the professional support his institution provides for writing and research, with a particular nod to Dean Aaron Chimbel. He also thanks his wife, Jennifer, and his kids, Stephanie and Thomas (and Sophie Marie), Jackson, and Maxwell for their ongoing inspiration.

Finally, Kathleen Scaturro's support of her husband's work and her editorial prowess have been an immeasurable help.

Ulysses S. Grant at 200
Foreword | *Frank J. Williams*

Momentous events during a president's term, and his response thereto, define his legacy. Theodore Roosevelt acknowledged this fact, as he said, "a man has to take advantage of his opportunities; but the opportunities have to come. If there is not the war, you don't get the great general; if there is not a great occasion you don't get the great statesman; if Lincoln had lived in times of peace no one would have known his name now."[1] That the circumstances of a presidency define the president in the eyes of future generations is exemplified by our nation's collective memory of Ulysses S. Grant.

Momentous events surrounded Ulysses S. Grant's life. During the Civil War, Grant earned President Abraham Lincoln's complete confidence. The general made his fair share of mistakes during the Civil War, but he was a great wartime leader. He learned from his mistakes, listening to and asking questions of his advisors.

During the Civil War, he and President Lincoln directed the war effort in concert. By 1864, Grant had become a respected strategist and tactician. His efforts led to the creation of one of his most enduring legacies: the modern command system the military still uses.

The modern command system developed by Grant and Lincoln was led by the commander-in-chief, President Lincoln himself, who set overall strategy for the prosecution of the war. Grant, as general-in-chief, executed President Lincoln's overall strategy. His function was to plan and direct the movements of the entirety of the Union army. Between them was a chief of staff, Maj. Gen. Henry Halleck, who relayed information to both Grant and Lincoln. Grant may not have known it at the time, but this relationship with Lincoln set a precedent that the executive branch and the United States military still follow to this day.

When Congress reauthorized the rank of lieutenant general with Grant in mind, Lincoln feared that Grant might get the political bug and challenge him for the Republican Party presidential nomination in 1864. When he was assured this was not the case, Lincoln promoted Grant. Grant's leadership justified Lincoln's

---

1   Theodore Roosevelt, *African and European Addresses* (New York: G.P. Putnam's Sons, 1910), 151.

belief in his capacity and abilities. Grant possessed the ability to see the "whole picture" of the military conflict. He worked to harmonize his strategic thinking with the overall strategy Lincoln prescribed. Grant directed the Union to confront Confederate armies from all sides, attempting to punish those armies—not Confederate cities—with strong and decisive coordinated attacks. He submitted to Lincoln broad outlines of his battle plans. Lincoln trusted Grant's analysis and approved the plans without seeking details.

Although Grant's achievements during the Civil War may not be considered as part of his presidential legacy, those momentous events shaped Grant and the nation as a whole. The military model he spawned is a brilliant illustration of simplicity. Military leaders to this day continue to study that system and his leadership that ended the Civil War.

Little more than three years after the Civil War, the Republican Party nominated Grant as its candidate for president. Grant reluctantly accepted the nomination, writing to William T. Sherman on June 21, 1868, that "[i]t is [a position] I would not occupy for any mere personal consideration, but, from the nature of the contest since the close of active hostilities, I have been forced into it in spite of myself."[2]

Grant's reluctance to become president did not render him an ineffective national leader. In fact, as recently as 2021, C-SPAN's Presidential Historians Survey rated Grant number 20 out of the 44 U.S. presidents who had served (excluding the incumbent).[3] He ranked highest under the poll's "pursued equal justice for all" category as the sixth highest, while his administrative skills were ranked at number 36. Yet, to this day, Grant's presidency seems to be overshadowed by the surrounding events of his life.

With the rise of the media relations profession and the twenty-four-hour news cycle in the late twentieth and early twenty-first centuries, not to mention the omnipresence of the internet, public figures—from politicians to athletes, CEOs to celebrities—are shaped and preened by professionals in the hopes of capturing the nation's attention in a positive manner. For celebrities, the electorate appears to tolerate misrepresentations by the press for the sake of human interest; however, coverage of the government demands rigorous honesty (sometimes lost amid the turmoil in current political news coverage). This news is consumed by a ravenous public, always hoping for more information, from newspaper articles to social media. Nineteenth-century Americans were as hungry for information about

---

2   USG to William T. Sherman, 21 June 1868, John Y. Simon, ed., *The Papers of Ulysses S. Grant*, 32 vols. (Carbondale, IL: Southern Illinois University Press, 1967–2012), 18:292.

3   "Presidential Historians Survey 2021, Total Scores/Overall Rankings," C-SPAN, accessed 15 February 2022, https://www.c-span.org/presidentsurvey2021/?page=overall.

prominent individuals as we are today. However, sources of that information were less widely or quickly available.

Grant was one of those prominent individuals. By the end of the Civil War, Americans knew him, and most considered him a hero who helped to save the Union. His luster may even have surpassed that of Lincoln, as shown by the throngs of Americans who paid their respects during Grant's funeral, the many photographs taken of Grant as compared with Lincoln, and various other metrics.

After being elected president, Grant planned his time in office with self-confidence and independence. He believed that he understood the American people and their wants. Republican members of Congress—having been victorious over Grant's predecessor, President Andrew Johnson—had no intention of yielding to President Grant their legislative agenda, prerogatives, and supplies of patronage opportunities. However, when Grant took office, he was determined to enforce civil rights legislation, reform Indian policy, and maintain a transparent government. He was met with obstacles and criticism for this agenda, not only from Democrats, but also from members of his own party.

President Grant maintained a stoic silence when criticized. He thought that answering these criticisms would simply lead to more. He opted to leave approval of his performance to the people.

But even before Grant's second term, scandals from his administration began to unfold in the press. None involved Grant directly, nor his honesty or integrity, yet each scandal diminished Grant's administration in the American people's eyes. However, individual Americans continued to embrace Grant and his leadership. He was also challenged, as any president would have been, by the Panic of 1873, which forced Grant to confront an economic crisis for which he had little experience and fewer solutions.

Many have written about General Grant, ending their narratives at Appomattox, seemingly wishing he had accepted President Lincoln's invitation to the theater. In fact, since it was taken over by the National Park Service in 1959, Grant's resting place has been officially named the "General Grant National Memorial." But biographies such as Ronald C. White's *American Ulysses*, Ron Chernow's *Grant*, Charles W. Calhoun's *The Presidency of Ulysses S. Grant*, and Joan Waugh's *U.S. Grant: American Hero, American Myth* have done much to reconcile the disparate opinions regarding Grant's generalship and presidency.

Until recently, colleges and universities with American history survey courses seemed almost uniformly to end the first semester with the close of the Civil War. This meant that college students learned of Grant's skill and success as a general in the fall semester and returned after winter break to study Grant's supposedly "inept" presidency. But as American history has itself continued to grow, more

American history courses are divided at 1877 or later. Nevertheless, American college students are introduced to two different, and at odds, Grants.

These differing portraits of General Grant and President Grant may lead to an inability to understand Ulysses S. Grant as a complex but consequential president. These misunderstandings show a broader misunderstanding of the crucial period of American history that many have to this day. Yet, today, we must strive to understand him as one individual who helped shape the nation we live in today— just as the essays in this book accomplish.

Frank J. Williams
President, Ulysses S. Grant Presidential Library and Association

Library of Congress

In honor of Ulysses S. Grant's two-hundredth birthday, all six living U.S. presidents issued commemorative messages, shared here courtesy of the Grant Monument Association. The original documents are at Grant's Tomb in New York City. The presidents' messages appear on the following pages in the order in which each chief executive served:

- Jimmy Carter
- William Jefferson Clinton
- George W. Bush
- Barack Obama
- Donald J. Trump
- Joseph Biden

In 1866, after receiving a promotion to full general and a fourth star, Ulysses S. Grant became the highest-ranking soldier in American history up to that point, surpassing even George Washington. The highest-ranking soldier of our own time, General Mark A. Milley, chairman of the Joint Chiefs of Staff, has also shared a message with us in honor of Grant's bicentennial; it follows the messages from the president.

JIMMY CARTER

April 27, 2022

As a boy growing up in Georgia, I was not taught to admire Union General Ulysses S. Grant. In latter years, I learned to appreciate him. His military skill and leadership were vital in saving the Union. When he became President, he worked both to restore and to transform the South. He advocated amnesty for Confederate soldiers but insisted that they must accept the full citizenship of African Americans. Celebrating the ratification of the Fifteenth Amendment, he sought to protect the right of African Americans to vote and hold public office, to be educated, and to live free from violence.

I also admire him for signing the act establishing Yellowstone as the first national park. Rosalynn and I are pleased to join our fellow citizens in celebrating the 200th birthday of President Ulysses S. Grant.

Sincerely,

Jimmy Carter

WILLIAM JEFFERSON CLINTON

April 27, 2022

Warm greetings to all those gathered to celebrate
the 200th birthday of our nation's 18th President,
Ulysses S. Grant.

This bicentennial gives all Americans the
opportunity to reflect on Grant's enduring legacy of
saving our Union on the battlefield, then making it
more perfect in his two terms as President.

Grant faithfully worked to carry forward Lincoln's
vision of Reconstruction, oversaw the passage of the
15th Amendment, and soundly defeated the Ku Klux
Klan. In a time of growing divisive tribalism, his
actions to heal our nation and defend the
foundations of our democracy are more important than
ever.

Thank you for your efforts to share more broadly the
legacy of President Grant, who I am glad is finally
beginning to receive the historic recognition he so
richly deserves. I wish you all a wonderful
celebration at his final resting place.

Bill Clinton

GEORGE W. BUSH

April 27, 2022

Happy 200th birthday to President Ulysses S. Grant.

As Commanding Army General, President Grant helped lead our country through one of its darkest periods. As President, he restored faith in a unified nation. President Grant worked hard to create a just society and protect the civil liberties and human rights of its citizens. I'm grateful for all he did to promote peace, unity, and equality in America.

Laura and I appreciate all the Ulysses S. Grant Association has done over the years to preserve the history of our country's 18th President. May his legacy inspire us to fight for what is right, lead with integrity, and create a more hopeful tomorrow for our fellow citizens. God bless the memory of President Ulysses S. Grant, and may He continue to bless America.

BARACK OBAMA

July 23, 2022

It's an honor to join the Ulysses S. Grant Association and Americans across the country in celebrating President Grant's 200th birthday.

On the battlefield, President Grant kept our Union intact with remarkable courage and perseverance. In the White House, he took on the Ku Klux Klan, championed the 15th Amendment, and established the Department of Justice. With these actions and more, he laid the groundwork for equal rights for Black Americans and strengthened a fractured nation.

In the years following his presidency, forces of division and hate have threatened these achievements, but the Union he fought so hard to preserve has held. This bicentennial provides us all an opportunity to recommit ourselves to President Grant's vision of a more equal and just America. Continuing to nurture and protect our democracy is the most powerful tribute we can pay to his legacy.

Sincerely,

DONALD J. TRUMP

April 27, 2022

I am pleased to join the Ulysses S. Grant Library, the Ulysses S. Grant Association, and all Americans in observing the 200th birthday of our 18th President.

President Grant believed in and embodied the American spirit of determination, courage, loyalty, and honor. From modest beginnings in Point Pleasant, Ohio, Hiram Ulysses Grant would grow to change the course of American history. Quiet and unassuming but regarded as highly intelligent, Grant trained in the great military tradition of West Point, where he steadily rose through the ranks to become one of our Nation's most emblematic heroes. His chronicle of military accomplishments shaped his political doctrine. History remembers the iconic images of General Robert E. Lee surrendering his sword to General Grant at the Appomattox Court House. Still, little is retold of President Grant's many political achievements—the achievements that moved our war-torn and tormented country forward after the end of a bloody civil war and the assassination of a beloved president.

As President, Grant set his sights on not only rebuilding America, but renewing her broken soul. At 46, the youngest President in our Nation's comparatively young history, Grant envisioned and worked tirelessly toward peace and unity. Ever a champion for the civil rights of African Americans, he fortified the 14th Amendment, assuring citizenship and equality, and secured the ratification of the 15th Amendment granting Black Americans the right to vote.

As a consummate statesman, President Grant promoted goodwill and unity both at home and abroad. His diplomatic agreements with Spain and Great Britain reduced the threat of war at a time when our country desperately needed peace and healing, and the Treaty of Washington set the framework for future conflict resolution—instituting his legacy as a conservative tactician and advocate for peace and prosperity. At home, his conservation and preservation of our lands remind Americans of the infinite beauty of our great country and the immeasurable value and splendor of our natural resources and national parks.

History is long overdue in the commendation of President Grant. Our country must never be timid in telling the story of our Nation's great warriors. They deserve honor, recognition, and lasting tribute for the battles they won, the ideas they championed, and the freedom they secured. We must always remember their hopeful vision passed down to all of us—that united as one American people trusting in God, there is no challenge too great and no dream beyond our reach.

Melania joins me in sending our very best wishes as you celebrate the bicentennial of Ulysses S. Grant's extraordinary life and legacy.

May God bless you, and may He bless the United States of America.

THE WHITE HOUSE
WASHINGTON

April 27, 2022

The First Lady and I are pleased to help celebrate President Ulysses S. Grant's 200th birthday.

As commanding general, President Grant led our Nation through the most trying time in our history, the Civil War and its aftermath. For generations, we have admired his brilliance as a military tactician, his courage on the battlefield, his values as a defender of rights for Black Americans, and his leadership as a President who helped unite a divided people.

President Grant lived many lives. Born and raised in Ohio, he went on to attend the United States Military Academy at West Point and command hundreds of thousands of men in the Union Army. Once a struggling farmer, he went on to serve two terms as President of the United States. Once a slaveowner, he helped to emancipate the South, beat back the first Ku Klux Klan, and establish the Justice Department to protect the civil rights of all Americans, rebuilding our country as it emerged from the long shadow of slavery. President Grant rose to the occasion in one of our darkest periods to preserve our Union, defend our democracy, and pursue justice and unity.

As we observe the bicentennial of his birth, let us honor his legacy by carrying forward his charge to pursue hope over fear and unity over division and forever setting our sights on the more just Nation we know we can and must be.

CHAIRMAN OF THE JOINT CHIEFS OF STAFF
WASHINGTON, D.C. 20318-9999

27 April 2022

**A MESSAGE IN HONOR OF PRESIDENT
ULYSSES S. GRANT BICENTENNIAL**

As the Chairman of the Joint Chiefs of Staff, I am pleased to join the Grant Monument Association (GMA) and our country in celebration of the Ulysses S. Grant Bicentennial—a momentous occasion honoring the 200th birthday of America's 18th U.S. President. Since its inception more than 100 years ago, the GMA has been dedicated to commemorating the life and legacy of this highly regarded statesman, Army General, and American hero.

We acknowledge President Grant's extraordinary bravery and commitment to our national values and principles embedded in the U.S. Constitution. His critical role in guiding and leading our country through some of the most turbulent times turned the tides of war in the face of merciless opposition and strong resistance. He willingly shouldered great responsibility, and made a profound impact on the course of our country's history through his tactical ability and strategic brilliance on the battlefield. He stood to preserve the freedoms and liberties we now enjoy.

In this country, in these United States, every single one of us is born free and equal—and all of us, each generation, must continue to aspire to that ideal. President Grant understood this and dedicated his life to this belief. He continues to be an inspiration for all of us that wear the cloth of our Nation.

On behalf of the men and women of the U.S. Armed Forces, we respect and pay homage to President Grant, and his long storied history of triumph over unimaginable adversity. We are humbled by his selfless service, compassion, and commitment to his fellow Americans and this country. Hollyanne and I join all of our Service members and Veterans, past and present, in recognizing and celebrating President Ulysses S. Grant's 200th birthday.

Sincerely,

MARK A. MILLEY
General, U.S. Army

To the very end, Grant was interested in words. This photo of Grant, reading on the porch of the cottage at Mt. McGregor, was taken on July 19, 1885, just four days before his death. It is the last-known photograph taken of the most-photographed man of the nineteenth century.

Grant Cottage Collection

The Myth of Grant's Silence
Introduction | *Chris Mackowski*

On May 4, 1864, Ulysses S. Grant led Federal forces across the Rapidan River in central Virginia in an attempt to bring Robert E. Lee's Army of Northern Virginia to heel once and for all. He vowed there would be "no turning back," and he stayed true to his word. On May 5, the two armies clashed in the Wilderness, but rather than withdraw when a decisive tactical victory seemed unlikely, Grant maneuvered around Lee's position. Fighting resumed immediately outside Spotsylvania Court House. After two weeks there, Grant maneuvered around Lee again, shifting the fight to the banks of the North Anna River. And from there, on to Totopotomoy Creek and Bethesda Church and Cold Harbor.

Lee's failure to strike a blow at North Anna, coupled with a series of successes through June 1, led Grant to believe he needed just one more strong assault to break his foe. "Lee's army is really whipped," he wrote to Washington following the fight at North Anna. "The prisoners we now take show it, and the action of his army shows it unmistakably."[1]

And so it was, on the morning of June 3, 1864, Grant launched a series of attacks against heavily fortified Confederate positions at Cold Harbor. As the story goes, he lost as many as 6,000 men in a half an hour as the result of a single fruitless charge. In reality, he lost closer to 3,500 men over the course of the entire day, all along the line, not just during the morning's charge, but the inflated casualty figure remains a central lynchpin in anti-Grant mythology.[2]

"I have always regretted that the last assault at Cold Harbor was ever made, ..."

---

1   *The War of the Rebellion: A Compilation of the Official Records of the Union and Confederate Armies*, 128 vols. (Washington, D.C.: U.S. Government Printing Office, 1880–1901), Series 1, vol. 36, Part 3, 206.

2   Gordon Rhea offers an excellent breakdown and analysis of Federal and Confederate losses at Cold Harbor. "When viewed in the war's larger context, the June 3 attack falls short of its popular reputation for slaughter," he concludes. Gordon Rhea, *Cold Harbor: Grant and Lee, May 26–June 3, 1864* (Baton Rouge, LA: Louisiana State University Press, 2002), 385-86.

A photo of Grant at Cold Harbor has become one of the most iconic images of the war, just as his comment about regretting the last Union charge at Cold Harbor has become one of the most iconic lines from the battle. That last charge was used by Grant's Lost Cause critics to tatter his reputation.

Library of Congress

Grant famously wrote in his *Personal Memoirs.* "[N]o advantage whatever was gained to compensate for the heavy loss we sustained."[3]

It's an oft-quoted line, in part because Grant did not write much about Cold Harbor, despite the staggering losses. Historians have tended to accept his relative silence about the incident as tacit acknowledgment that he made a mistake, and Lost Cause mythologizers have exploited such silences to vilify him as "Grant the Butcher." It's worth noting, however, that Robert E. Lee lost a similar number of men during Pickett's Charge at Gettysburg—some 6,555 men—as Grant did in total at Cold Harbor. In Lee's case, that amounted to a decisive defeat, while Grant was able to maintain his strategic momentum by changing tactics after the battle.[4] But rather than condemn "Lee the Butcher," the same Southern partisans who butchered Grant's reputation romanticized Lee's, holding up his casualties as examples of Southern manly virtue. Writing more about Cold Harbor certainly would not have spared Grant from his Lost Cause critics, who had a vested interest in besmirching him no matter what, but Grant's omissions have, at times, been devastating to his historical reputation because they have given his detractors further space to control the narrative right up through the twentieth century.

It's easy to make assumptions about Grant's relative silence on Cold Harbor because it fits neatly in line with widely known stories of his stoicism in times of

---

3   Ulysses S. Grant, *Personal Memoirs of U.S. Grant*, 2 vols. (New York: Charles L. Webster & Co., 1885–1886), 2:276, hereafter cited as *PMUSG*.

4   For a breakdown of Lee's numbers on July 3 during Pickett's Charge, see "Pickett's Charge: That July Afternoon in 1863," American Battlefield Trust, accessed 31 January 2022, https://www.battlefields.org/learn/articles/picketts-charge.

calamity. Think of Grant in the rain after the first disastrous day at Shiloh, ready to "Lick 'em tomorrow." Or his quiet whittling under a tree on that awful first day in the Wilderness. Or the quiet attentiveness he gave Ferdinand Ward when his business partner first hinted at the financial trouble their investment firm was facing. "[T]he general was always silent, Mrs. Grant," William T. Sherman once reminded Grant's wife, Julia, during the winter of Grant's final illness. "Even at the worst times of strain, during the war, I used to go to see him at his headquarters, and he would sit perfectly still . . . ."[5]

Furthermore, there is Grant's well-documented reticence for public speaking. Ronald C. White's essay in this volume, for example, offers several accounts where Grant makes a quick greeting but then turns the spotlight over to a friend or colleague "to tell you how happy I am to be with you."[6]

Robert Underwood Johnson, an editor with *Century Magazine* tasked with convincing Grant to write about his wartime experiences, referred to "The myth of his [Grant's] silence."[7] Grant's silence was very much a part of the great man's public persona, but as Johnson found out when he met Grant for the first time, in June 1884, "the impressions I had of his personality and character had been at second hand, and were, as it proved, for the most part erroneous." Johnson admitted Grant was "a much misrepresented man."

What was, to Johnson, a discovery was something well known to Grant's intimates. "We considered him more than commonly talkative," said Brig. Gen. William Hillyer, once a member of Grant's wartime staff, speaking to a newspaper reporter around the time of Grant's inauguration as president. "So he is now: he won't talk for effect, nor before strangers freely. This reticence of Grant, so much talked of, is partly discrimination and partly the form of an old bashfulness he had when a boy. Anybody whom he knows can hear him speak at any time."[8] Johnson's diligent work with Grant would earn him this privilege.

It fell to Johnson to mentor Grant in what the editor described as "the untried field of authorship"—a series of battle articles for *Century* that would eventually lead to the memoirs. Grant first tried, and struggled, with an account of the battle of Shiloh. It was "dry," Johnson privately noted, and suffered from "the blight of the deadly official report." As Johnson later explained, "The General, of course, did

---

5   Charles Bracelen Flood, *Grant's Final Victory: Ulysses S. Grant's Heroic Last Year* (Cambridge, MA: Da Capo Press, 2011), 120-21.

6   See page 14 in this volume.

7   This and all quotes from Johnson come from Robert Underwood Johnson, *Remembered Yesterdays* (Boston: Little, Brown, and Company, 1923), 210-15.

8   Edward Chauncey Marshall, *The Ancestry of General Grant, and Their Contemporaries* (New York: Sheldon & Co., 1869), 77-8.

Grant's memoirs would become one of the most important documents in the war of words that veterans engaged in—often viciously—into the twentieth century that shaped future generations' understanding of the Civil War. Grant Cottage displays some of the writing tools used by Grant and his editing team.

Chris Mackowski

not realize the requirements of a popular publication on the war, and it was for me to help him turn this new disaster of Shiloh into a signal success."

His follow-up discussion with Grant proved especially illuminating. "General Grant, instead of being a 'silent man'[,]was positively loquacious . . .'"

Johnson marveled. "He spoke rapidly and long . . . and in the frankest manner" and, Johnson importantly added, Grant exhibited "no cocksureness, no desire to make a perfect record or to live up to a later reputation."

In conversation, Grant "revealed the human side of his experience," and it was this approach Johnson urged him to take with his writing: "such a talk as he would make to friends after dinner." Grant grasped the idea at once and set to work on a revision that worked admirably. "I am positively enjoying the work," Grant admitted, a bit surprised.

If we can eavesdrop on the outskirts of these interactions for a moment, we gain important clues into Grant's silences and the limits of our ability to assume anything from them. As Johnson discovered, Grant had plenty to say but just needed to figure out the best way to say it for his audience. Grant had never thought of himself as a "writer" before and so felt intimidated by the very idea. Once he got past that mystification, though, he discovered he wasn't nearly the stranger to the pen he initially thought he was. "I have been very much employed in writing," he one day wrote to former staff officer Adam Badeau:

> As a soldier I wrote my own orders, directions and reports. They were not edited nor assistance rendered. As President I wrote every official document, I believe, bearing my name. . . . All these have been published and widely circulated. The public has become accustomed to them and know my style of writing. They know that it is not even an attempt to imitate either a literary or clas[s]ical style and that it is just what it is pure and simple and nothing else. If I succeed in telling my story so that others can see, as I do, what I attempt to sh[o]w, I will be satisfied. The

reader must also be satisfied . . . for he knew from the begin[n]ing just what to expect.[9]

By the time Grant got around to writing about the Overland Campaign in his memoirs, he was in his last weeks of life. Fighting excruciating pain from throat cancer—not to mention the mind-addling effects of painkillers and exhaustion—his attempt to finish the second volume of his memoirs represents a Herculean effort. All three of his sons were aiding him by that point, as well as stenographer Noble Dawson.

"If I could have two weeks of strength I could improve it very much," he wrote to his publisher, Mark Twain, around June 30, 1885. "As I am, however, it will have to go about as it is, with verifications and corrections by the boys, and by suggestions which will enable me to make a point clear here and there."[10]

As it would happen, Grant would get three weeks, not two. He would die on July 23, 1885. The clock was ticking.

Grant was satisfied with most of what he had written concerning the last year of the war. "It seemed to me that I got the campaign about Petersburg, and the move to Appomattox pretty good on the last attempt," he told his son Fred, who worked as his primary editorial assistant.[11] Grant was also pleased with the Wilderness. He was less pleased, though, with the rest of the Overland Campaign. "I should change Spotts if I was able," he told Fred in early July, "and could improve N. An[n]a and Cold Harbor."[12]

But he was *not* able, of course. The clock was ticking loudly by that point.

"If I could read it [the manuscript] over myself many little matters of anecdote and incident would suggest themselves to me," he had told Twain.[13] And indeed, his daughters-in-law read the manuscript back to him in the afternoons and evenings even as his sons and Dawson continued with their editing and fact-checking. "Tell Mr. Dawson to punctuate," he added.[14]

---

9   John Y. Simon, ed., *The Papers of Ulysses S. Grant*, 32 vols. (Carbondale, IL: Southern Illinois University Press, 1967–2012), 31:355-56, hereafter cited as *PUSG*. (Brackets omitted for content that is not in Grant's hand.) "The last two sentences of this paragraph add up to excellent advice for any budding writer," points out historian Bruce Catton in "U.S. Grant: Man of Letters," *American Heritage* (June 1968), No. 4, 19:98.

10   *PUSG*, 31:391.

11   *PUSG*, 31:411.

12   Ibid.

13   Ibid., 31:390.

14   Ibid., 31:411.

"As a soldier I wrote my own orders, directions and reports," Grant said. That daily practice helped him develop a clear, concise voice as a writer, although he never fully realized its impact until he was nearly done writing his memoirs.

Grant Cottage

Grant was generally unable to speak by this point because his throat cancer had ravaged his voice and sapped his strength so badly. He held conversations and passed out instructions by writing on slips of paper. His scrawlings show a dozen aspects of the book all competing for his attention:

- "We will consider whether [or] not to leave out the appendix."
- "Is that entitled 'preface' or 'introduction'?"
- "What are you engaged at now?"
- "Does what I have written fit the case."
- "Are you reviewing or copying?"
- "I think I am a little mixed in my statement . . . ."
- Mentions of Chattanooga, Knoxville, and Generals Sherman, Burnside, Longstreet.
- "Have I left out many points." (a question without a question mark—no wonder he needed Dawson to punctuate)[15]

"I begin to feel anxious about the review of the second volume," he admitted around July 10. "There may be more difficulty in placing all the parts than we think. It has been written in a very detached way."[16]

It is no wonder, in this maelstrom of edits, that Grant did not have time to do all he wished, although he tried mightily. Even as Twain sent him printed galley proofs of volume one, Grant kept making handwritten corrections on the sheets. Twain fretted that the editing on the first volume would prohibit Grant from finishing the second.

15   The bulleted examples all come from *PUSG*, 31:411.

16   Ibid., 31:426.

"I would have more hope of satisfying the expectation of the public if I could have allowed myself more time," Grant admitted in his introduction to the memoirs.[17]

Imagine: If he'd had more time, what more might he have said?

As someone who has been telling the story of the Overland Campaign for nearly two decades, on the battlefield and in writing, this notion tantalizes me. *"I should change Spotts if I was able, and could improve N. Anna and Cold Harbor."* How would Grant have retold those stories? What changes would he have made? What was he feeling at the time? What did he *really* think about that last charge at Cold Harbor? He always regretted it, he said, but we students of the Civil War have always regretted he didn't say more.

Had he the time, what else did Grant wish he could improve, change, expand upon, or illuminate? What other anecdotes and incidents would have suggested themselves to him? What else might he have told us?

Consider how such first-person revelations might have altered our understanding of Grant or changed the way history has remembered him. Remember, Johnson's second-hand impressions of Grant had proven erroneous. How erroneous are our own impressions of Grant in the absence of his own testimony and in the face of hostile Lost Cause critics?

For three-quarters of a century after Grant's death, historians complained about an "almost complete lack" of Grant resources to look at: no compiled letters, no journals, no collected works. Just the memoir. Grant wrote "as little as possible," one of them groused.[18] There was, in a sense, a documentary "silence" from Grant keeping in line with the in-person "myth of his silence," as Johnson called it.

This speaks to one of the great paradoxes of Grant's legacy. His memoirs, which have never gone out of print, consisted of 291,000 words over 1,231 pages in two volumes. Recent annotated editions have shed additional light on the text. Beyond Grant's masterwork, *The Papers of Ulysses S. Grant*, edited under the auspices of the Ulysses S. Grant Association and published by Southern Illinois University Press, fill thirty-two volumes, and his written orders from the war are sprinkled throughout the *Official Records of the War of the Rebellion*.

Grant really wasn't all that silent after all, even if he didn't get the chance to say quite everything he wanted to.

Grant's silences, then, were both real and imagined—this is the true "myth of his silence." Lost Causers have exploited those silences, and historians have often made

---

17   *PMUSG*, 1:8.

18   See John Y. Simon's introduction to the *Papers of Ulysses S. Grant's* first volume for the story of the dearth, and then plentitude, of Grant documents. *PUSG*, 1:xxviii.

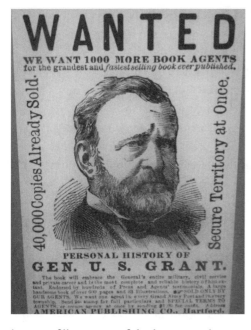

Grant's publisher, Mark Twain, was convinced America—and history—wanted to hear what Grant had to say. "[H]ere was a book that was morally bound to sell several hundred thousand copies in its first year of publication . . ." Twain predicted. He nonetheless hedged his bets by selling Grant's memoirs by subscription.

Chris Mackowski

wholly inadequate assumptions about them. But Grant's silences contain a rich landscape of unexpressed ideas, untold stories, and unshared insights that Grant sought to articulate to, literally, his dying day during a time when he hardly had any cancer-ravaged voice left at all.

In this collection of essays, we hope to fill in some of the long-standing gaps in Grant historiography, offering our own illuminations of his life and legacy. In doing so, we cannot speak for Grant, but we can draw on this new wealth of documentary richness to offer a fuller, fairer, and more balanced view of this so-called "silent man."

Ronald C. White offers the fullest-yet examination of the impact of Methodism on Grant, from his boyhood along the Ohio River through his final days on Mount McGregor.

Ulysses Grant Dietz offers some "insider's" insights about Grant's family life. Dietz is the youngest surviving great-great-grandchild—out of forty-one—of Ulysses and Julia Grant. The legendary general and president is a familiar figure to everyone in the family, but also a stranger from long-ago who still casts a long shadow.

Curt Fields also shares a unique perspective in his essay. As a living historian, Fields has walked in Grant's shoes in a way few other historians have, bringing Grant to life through first-person portrayals. Exploring Grant's life in such a unique way has given Fields unique insights that he shares in his essay.

As advocates of the idea that places can offer us important insights into the people who live in and occupy those places, we have pieces from Nick Sacco at the Ulysses S. Grant National Historic Site in St. Louis, Missouri, and Ben Kemp of the Ulysses S. Grant Cottage National Historic Landmark in Mt. McGregor, New York. In St. Louis, Grant and his wife lived in a home called White Haven, which became the centerpiece of a small national park in 1989. At Mt. McGregor, Grant spent the last six weeks of his life completing his memoirs. A state historic site for decades, Grant Cottage was designated as a National Historic Landmark in 2021.

Grant's Tomb, meanwhile, despite being a national park since 1959, fell victim to desecration and neglect until its restoration during the 1990s. Frank Scaturro, my co-editor, was instrumental in that restoration and shares some of his insights as he explores the Tomb's history.

John F. Marszalek recounts Grant's time at West Point, a formative period in Grant's life. "A military life had no charms for me, and I had not the faintest idea of staying in the army even if I should be graduated, which I did not expect," Grant wrote in his memoirs.[19] As Marszalek recounts, Grant's West Point experience gave the young man a sense of direction.

Few have imagined Grant would attain military greatness. Timothy Smith argues that Grant had an intuitive grasp of how to conduct effective warfare at a time when technology, tactics, and politics were changing all the traditional rules. Grant, in effect, presaged the principles outlined by the great military theorist Carl von Clausewitz, whose German writings had not yet made the rounds in English.

For all the intuitive skill, Grant's military success was hardly inevitable. In reality, the so-called "Rise of Grant" consisted of a string of contingencies. In a later essay in this volume, I argue that examining the many ways things could have turned out differently can help us better appreciate exactly what Grant accomplished on the battlefield.

General Grant had a very human side, too, though. As Joan Waugh's essay points out, his sense of humanity sat at the center of his efforts to bring about peace following the surrender of the Army of Northern Virginia at Appomattox. Lincoln and Grant were very much in simpatico about malice toward none and charity for all.

Following the Civil War, Grant made his shift into politics. It was not a natural transition, says Charles W. Calhoun, although it became practically inevitable. In a time of postwar tumult, Grant became an "adept politician and a civilian leader of great consequence," Calhoun contends.

Two additional essays look at specific components of Grant's political life. Alvin S. Felzenberg looks closely at Grant's significant contributions to civil rights—efforts that rank Grant with Lincoln and Lyndon B. Johnson as the most important civil rights presidents in American history. Grant, of late, has been getting more recognition for those efforts; Felzenberg rightly argues that Grant can't get too much.

19   *PMUSG*, 1:38.

Meanwhile, Ryan P. Semmes looks at Grant's many foreign policy achievements. Grant's philosophy for foreign relations, Semmes points out, stemmed directly from the same philosophy that guided the president's Reconstruction policies. However, as Semmes notes, international concerns and other roadblocks prevented Grant from exporting republicanism even as he successfully resolved disputes with European powers.

For decades, Frank J. Scaturro has advocated a fuller reexamination of Grant's entire presidency. Grant belongs as a rightful member of the pantheon of presidential greats, his essay argues, but his ascension will only happen when we can overcome generations of built-up confirmation bias.

As the man who won the Civil War and then spent eight consequential years in the White House, Grant traced a trajectory from humble beginnings to the heights of fame. Gary Gallagher traces Grant's trajectory since, from Union hero to corrupt drunk butcher to the current new appreciation Grant is enjoying.

Like other Grant mythology—corruption, drunkenness, callous butchery—Grant's silence is a story of complexity and nuance. That he has often been reduced to such bullet points, though, probably would not have surprised Grant, even if it would have disappointed him. He also understood the power of myth. "Wars produce many stories of fiction, some of which are told until they are believed to be true," he wrote in his memoir.[20] Pound the drum often enough and loud enough, and even that one note will start to sound like a song. He had waded through enough partisan political battles and dealt with enough unreconstructed rebels to know there would be an audience for that kind of music.

That didn't keep Grant, ever an optimist, from hoping for more. "I would like to see truthful history written," he said. "Such history will do full credit to the courage, endurance and soldierly ability of the American citizen, no matter what section of the country he hailed from, or in what ranks he fought."[21]

The Civil War and Reconstruction combine to form the most complicated and important period of American history. As the man who won that war and then presided over the Union he saved, Grant deserves better than reductionism and misrepresentation (not to mention outright vilification). Doing justice to his story is part of doing justice to such a formative and misunderstood period.

As he hits his 200th birthday, we are pleased to do our part to fill in some of the silences of Grant's story in a way that helps tell the truthful history.

Imagine what he would say.

---

20   Ibid., 2:488.

21   Ibid., 1:170.

U.S. Grant: The Reluctant Cadet at West Point

Chapter One | *John F. Marszalek*

Of all the stories passed o'er I'll say,
You can believe as few or as many as you may.
Perhaps he did things both foolish and thin,
But it's foolish to believe all that's told of him.[1]

He was never thought of as a West Point possibility. He was a short and pudgy seventeen-year-old who never felt called to the military. His father, Jesse, brought up the idea of the young man going to West Point, mainly because it would cost the father nothing, and the son would either become an army officer or complete his course work and join the engineers who were rebuilding the nation.

Hiram Ulysses Grant never seemed to want to do anything that smacked of the military, and he always seemed to stay in the background when the corps assigned cadets to leadership posts at West Point. Before he went to the Military Academy, his father wanted him to join in the leather tanning industry, but the young man hated the sounds and smells of the tannery, so he found ways to avoid that work.[2]

The Grant family came from Connecticut Yankee stock, by way of Scotland, a distant relative having commanded a part of the Scottish army in a major battle in 1333.[3] In his famous memoirs, Grant wrote that "My family is American, and has been for generations, in all its branches, direct and collateral."[4]

---

1   Adrian Hilt, *The Grant Poem* (New York: Nassau Publishing Co., 1886), 37.

2   Ron Chernow, *Grant* (New York: Penguin Press, 2017), 15.

3   James F. Boyd, *Military and Civilian Life of Gen. Ulysses S. Grant* (Philadelphia: P.W. Ziegler & Co., 1885), 17.

4   Ulysses S. Grant, *The Personal Memoirs of Ulysses S. Grant: The Complete Annotated Edition*, John F. Marszalek with David S. Nolen & Louie P. Gallo, eds. (Cambridge, Massachusetts: The Belknap Press of Harvard University Press, 2017), 5, hereafter cited as *PMUSG-Annotated*.

The first relative to reach what was to become New England was Matthew Grant, who settled there in 1630. A grandfather, who was called Noah, fought in the Revolutionary War and eventually settled in Deerfield, Ohio, in 1799 with his wife and seven children.[5]

One of these children, born in 1794, was Ulysses Grant's father, Jesse. Tragically, when Jesse was but eleven years old, his mother died, and his father sent him to live with the family of George Tod, who would later become an Ohio Supreme Court justice. Tod and his wife gave Jesse the home he needed, and when he was sixteen, Jesse became a tanner, working for his half-brother, Peter, in Kentucky. He then resided with the family of Owen Brown, whose son, John, later became the famous Kansas abolitionist. Jesse was greatly influenced by Brown, and he always said that he moved to anti-slavery Point Pleasant, Ohio, because of Brown's abolitionist influence. And so, in 1820, Jesse Grant took residence as a tanner some 25 miles southeast of Cincinnati on the Ohio River, near where Big Indian Creek poured into that body of water.[6]

Jesse Grant was an ambitious man and determined to make a success in the world. Already 26 years old, he decided that he had better find a wife and begin a family and business. He encountered the family of John and Sarah Simpson, who lived some ten miles away on land purchased from Jesse's boss, Thomas Page. Jesse regularly traveled to the region to get hides for the business, spending time in the process with one of the Simpson children, Hannah, and her mother. The latter was a voracious reader and loaned Jesse books. Over time, Jesse began to see Hannah as a possible wife, and after a whirlwind courtship of several months, they were married on June 24, 1821.[7]

Hannah, who was twenty-two years old when she first met Jesse, was a devout Methodist.[8] The couple settled into a happy relationship, he reaching out to practice local politics and she growing ever more tied to her local church. She was no beauty, and he was not handsome, but their marriage was stable. He held on to his anti-slavery views and even wrote pieces for a local anti-slavery newspaper, the *Castigator*.[9] She was popular in the neighborhood, but he was considered a blowhard and not particularly well liked as a result.

---

5   Ibid., 5-7.

6   Michael Yockelson, *Grant: Savior of the Union* (Nashville: Thomas Nelson, 2012), 1-2.

7   Brooks D. Simpson, *Ulysses S. Grant: Triumph over Adversity, 1822–1865* (Boston: Houghton Mifflin Company, 2000), 2.

8   Ronald C. White, *American Ulysses, A Life of Ulysses S. Grant* (New York: Random House 2016), 19-20.

9   Yockelson, 2-3.

The Ulysses S. Grant Birthplace in Point Pleasant, Ohio, open seasonally, is operated by the Ohio History Connection. A small commemorative district and memorial bridge all overlook the Ohio River.

Chris Mackowski

Then what both Jesse and Hannah wanted, happened. Hannah had their first child on April 27, 1822, a large baby of some eleven pounds. The marriage of Jesse and Hannah was solidified with this birth and, although Jesse remained loud and Hannah stayed as quiet as ever, their lives changed fundamentally. Even the matter of Ulysses S. Grant's first name was not simple. The family met a month after the birth to decide what the new baby's first name should be. Hannah wanted to name him Albert, after Democratic-Republican politician and diplomat Albert Gallatin. Another relative suggested Theodore; a grandfather liked Hiram; and his step-grandmother chose Ulysses. To solve the disagreement, the family put all the names on slips of paper, tossed them into a hat, and finally the name "Hiram" was chosen with "Ulysses" next in line. And so, the firstborn came to be called Hiram Ulysses Grant.[10] This new child would be joined by five other children: Samuel Simpson, Clara Rachel, Virginia Paine, Orvil Lynch, and Mary Frances. Ulysses never grew close to any of these siblings, but they certainly filled the small two-story brick house, which Jesse added to as the children were born.[11] This, their second house in Georgetown, was where Grant lived during his early years.

It was in Georgetown, where Jesse moved his family one year after the arrival of his firstborn, that Ulysses grew up and developed his talent with horses. When he was only around two or three years old, he would sneak into the stables by himself and walk around the horses and through their legs. The neighbors saw what was happening and told his mother that she should stop such activity immediately because the boy might be trampled or kicked. Hannah listened politely and then

10   Boyd, 20.

11   William Conant Church, *Ulysses S. Grant and the Period of National Preservation and Reconstruction* (New York: G.P. Putnam's Sons, 1897), 9.

said softly: "Horses seem to understand Ulysses." By the time he was seventeen, he was doing a full man's work, and the neighbors seemed ready to allow him to share the stalls with the horses.[12]

A few years after Ulysses was born, Jesse took the youngster into town so he could see a parade. A resident of the town asked Jesse if he could put a gun near the two-year-old to see the effect of a shot on the toddler's ears. Jesse pointed out that his baby had never even seen a gun or a pistol before, but he agreed anyway to the firing of a weapon near the child's ear. The villager put the baby's fingers around the gun's trigger, and the child was told to pull. The gun went off with a huge bang, but Ulysses did not flinch. The villagers insisted, ever after, that this experience proved Ulysses was going to be a soldier.[13]

There was also another event that happened to the young man some years later that influenced him for the rest of his life. When he was no older than eight years old, his father sent him to purchase a horse that the father liked and Ulysses just had to have. The issue in debate proved to be the cost of the animal. The boy wanted to pay whatever it took, while Jesse insisted on a lower amount. Report of the cost varied depending on what people later said, but Jesse told his young son to offer the farm neighbor something like $20. If the neighbor refused that amount, then Ulysses should offer $22.50. If that was still not acceptable to the neighbor, Jesse told Ulysses to offer $25.

Ulysses hurried to the nearby farm and, always ready to tell the truth, he answered neighbor Ralston's inquiry about how much Ulysses should offer for the horse. Ulysses repeated what his father had told him: $20 dollars at first, but if that was not enough, he should raise it to $22.50. Finally, rather than not get the horse at all, he should offer $25. Needless to say, the neighbor smiled and insisted on $25. For the rest of his life, Ulysses had to live with the embarrassment of what a bad bargainer he was. Neighborhood boys never forgave him for his naivete.[14]

Most of the time, the young Grant kept to himself and his horses, a familiar figure around Georgetown who otherwise showed no particular talents. He was considered slow, yet people in the area seemed to like him. He had no bad habits that anyone knew about. He was loved by the young boys of the town because

12   Frank H. Jones, *An Address Delivered by Frank H. Jones Before the Chicago Historical Society at the Celebration of the 100th Anniversary of the Birth of General Ulysses S. Grant* (Chicago: R. R. Donnelly and Sons, 1922), 7-8.

13   J. B. McClure, *Stories, Sketches and Speeches of General Grant at Home and Abroad, in Peace and in War* (Chicago: Rhodes and McClure, 1879), 17-18.

14   *PMUSG-Annotated*, 14-15. The most detailed discussion of what life at West Point was like before the Civil War is James L. Morrison, Jr., *"The Best School in the World": West Point, the Pre-Civil War Years, 1833–1866* (Kent, Ohio: The Kent State University Press, 1986).

Grant's Boyhood Home is one of several Grant-related sites preserved in Georgetown, Ohio. The structure that served as Jesse Grant's tannery, across the street, also stands, as does Grant's Schoolhouse. The Boyhood Home and Schoolhouse are open seasonally, and the tannery is being developed for public visits. Georgetown also features two Grant statues.

Chris Mackowski

he went out of his way to protect them.[15] Whenever he was getting ready to say something funny, his eyes twinkled, and when he walked, his lack of rhythm and musical ability prevented him from walking smoothly. He slouched along rather than pushed forward.[16]

Jesse had great admiration for his firstborn son and hoped that Ulysses would follow in his footsteps in the tanning factory. The son hated tanning and would rather do anything except work at that trade. He told his father that he would stay at the tannery until he was 21 years old, but, after that, he would never step inside the building again. He hated grinding bark to produce the tannic acid it provided for the factory. The "beam room" was a particularly distasteful place for him because he hated to see the animal hides being stretched over the building's beams and the flesh scraped off the hide.[17] Instead of tanning, he took over all the horse-driven activities near his home and factory as soon as he could handle the plow. Soon after that, Jesse allowed his son to travel around the area and represent the family business. Grant remained more satisfied driving horses than working in the tannery.

Jesse remained proud of all that his son could do, but he still wished for more. Unlike him, his son was quiet and, other than manage the horses, he was not willing to reach out into the community. Jesse was a lenient father, though, and he saw Ulysses as close to perfect. Jesse could, for example, ensure the best education

---

15   Louis A. Coolidge, *Ulysses S. Grant* (Boston: Houghton Mifflin Company, 1917), 16.

16   Horace Porter, *Campaigning with Grant* (Lincoln: University of Nebraska Press, 2000), 14-16.

17   H.W. Brands, *The Man Who Saved the Union: Ulysses Grant in War and Peace* (New York: Doubleday, 2012), 7-8; Albert D. Richardson, *A Personal History of Ulysses S. Grant* (Washington, D.C.: The National Tribune, 1898), 51, 63.

his son might receive in that region, but Jesse had even bigger ambitions than that.[18]

The son of the town doctor and a friend of the Grant family, one G. Bartlett Bailey, received an appointment to the United States Military Academy at West Point in 1837 through the nomination of pro-slavery Congressman Thomas L. Hamer. Unfortunately, Bailey failed academically. He was then re-nominated by Hamer in July 1838, but he failed again in three months. Bailey's father and mother tried to keep the shame of the failure a secret, but Jesse, being the busybody that he was, found out immediately and tried to get the appointment for his son. He wrote to anti-slavery Senator Thomas Morris, but the only available opportunity for West Point was in the office of Jesse's longtime opponent congressman, Thomas Hamer. So Jesse swallowed his pride, wrote to Hamer, and luckily got the appointment for Ulysses, although there would yet be complications.[19]

And so, in 1838, Jesse sprang some news on his son. "I believe you are going to receive the [Bailey's] appointment," Jesse told Ulys. "What appointment?" the son responded. "To West Point," Jesse said. "I have applied for it." "But I won't go!" Ulysses said. But then, as the young man remembered it, Jesse "said he thought I would, *and I thought so too, if he did.*"[20]

And thus, the young Grant, thanks to his father's persistence and his willingness to humble himself before his old enemy Thomas Hamer, was able to get him into the United States Military Academy. But first, he had to travel there, and it was a long trip from Georgetown, his hometown, to West Point, New York. As it turned out, Grant saw the trip as a great opportunity. It gave him the chance to see places in the United States he had never seen before.

The day for his departure was set at May 15, 1839.[21] He found that he had nearly $100 in savings in his pocket, so he bought himself new clothes and shoes. Still looking like a hick, he first took the stagecoach, receiving a cold goodbye from his mother. When he had the coach stop at the Bailey house, Mrs. Bailey cried over his departure. Ulysses was taken aback and responded quizzically, "Why, Mrs. Bailey, my own mother didn't cry!"[22] Meanwhile, Hannah said nothing further. After all, she was carrying another baby, soon to be born.

---

18   William B. Hesseltine, *Ulysses S. Grant: Politician* (New York: Dodd, Mead & Company, 1935), 5-6, 9.

19   John Y. Simon, ed., *The Papers of Ulysses S. Grant*, 32 vols. (Carbondale, IL: Southern Illinois University Press, 1967–2012), 1:3n-4n, hereafter cited as *PUSG*.

20   Lloyd Lewis, *Captain Sam Grant* (Boston: Little, Brown and Company, 1950), 56.

21   Elbridge S. Brooks, *The True Story of U.S. Grant* (Boston: Lothrop Publishing Company, 1897), 40.

22   Hamlin Garland, *Ulysses S. Grant: His Life and Character* (Doubleday & McClure Co., 1898), 30.

From Ripley, Ohio, Ulysses took a boat on the Ohio River to Pittsburgh, Pennsylvania. There he moved to a canal boat and the railroad to visit his mother's relatives in Philadelphia, where he stayed for five days. After reaching New York, he floated up the Hudson River to West Point.[23] "I had always a great desire to travel," he exclaimed enthusiastically.[24]

Grant registered at Roe's Hotel near West Point as "U. H. Grant" and signed his name when reporting to Adjutant George Waggaman on May 29, 1839, as "Ulysses Hiram Grant."[25] He deposited what was left of his money—$48. An immediate problem arose. Waggaman or his clerk listed him on the official Army roll as U.S. Grant, even though he had signed in as Ulysses Hiram Grant. For the adjutant, seeing Grant's signature, there was no place at the Academy for an incoming cadet who went by a different name. Congressman Hamer had incorrectly assumed that his middle name was his mother's maiden name, Simpson. He could either take the full name as it was listed in the official book or go home and correct it all. He did not hesitate. He became Ulysses S. Grant, a title he carried for the rest of his life.[26] He easily passed the preliminary examination. He entered West Point on July 1, 1839. He was not impressive. He was a seventeen-year-old with small feet, small hands, and difficulty in marching.[27]

It did not take Grant long to fit into the Corps of Cadets. Upperclassmen yelled insulting names at him and the other newly arrived cadets. When he arrived at the Post headquarters, cadet corporals jumped all over him, telling him, for example, that he must always stand perfectly erect. Then someone asked him an innocent question. When he moved to answer it, he was insulted even more and told to keep looking forward no matter what. The insults just kept coming. What a shock!

Once he was repeatedly told precisely how he was to stand, he was sent to the quartermaster and issued all the supplies he would need for sleeping in his tent and keeping his surroundings clean. All this equipment was to be placed on his broom, and he was to carry it all through the West Point reservation to North Hall. After Grant was moved into barracks with other cadets in late August 1839, he was made to share a dim room with another cadet, Rufus Ingalls. It was an awful introduction to cadet life. He and all the new cadets were shaken.

---

23   Lewis, 59-61.

24   Garland, 31; Brands, 9.

25   Lawrence A. Frost, *U.S. Grant Album* (Seattle: Superior Publishing Company, 1966), 16; *PUSG*, 1:4*n*, 364.

26   Garland, 31-32.

27   Edward Howland, *Grant, as a Soldier and Statesman* (Hartford: J. B. Burr & Company, 1868), 20.

While all this was going on, cadets who had experienced just such belittlement only a short while ago continued to insult the new cadets. They then read names off the bulletin board, quickly thinking of nicknames to go with a cadet's initials. "U.S. Grant" was a particular butt of harassment. William Tecumseh Sherman, already in the first class and set to graduate in 1840, would note years later how he and other cadets had a field day with Grant's name. He must be "United States Grant," one cadet said, and another suggested a relationship to the famous American symbol, "Uncle Sam Grant." Or was he simply "Sam Grant?"[28] And so it was. For the rest of his life, Grant was "Sam" to his friend Sherman and all the other former cadets. Sherman later became one of Grant's favorite commanders and closest friends.[29]

One of the worst things about West Point, after Ulysses entered the cadets' barracks on August 28, was his discovery of just how awful the food was. Breakfast was usually hashed beef, while dinner was too often mutton, which the cadets met with loud "baa's" when it appeared on their plates. Forks had been washed so often that they actually smelled.[30] No matter the time of the week, the food was the subject of a variety of complaints from the cadets. One such individual said that his coffee the night before tasted like soapsuds, and he simply could not drink it. Ironically, despite their dislike of the food, the cadets complained that they just did not have enough time to finish their meals before they were rushed away from the mess hall.[31]

The way they were able to get some edible food was to sneak it from the mess hall at noon, mix it well, and create late-night hash over the open fire in their rooms. Hash gatherings took place regularly, and some of the cadets gained great reputations because of their cooking skills around the fireplace.

The amount of sleep the cadets received was also a cause for complaint. At 5 a.m. in the summer and 6 a.m. in the winter, drums would start banging away, tearing the cadets from their dreams and forcing them to march all over the military reservation, often on an empty stomach.[32] The first streaks of daylight forced the cadets to get up and do sadistic exercises, study in the dim light, and suffer chronic tiredness. Even on Sunday, they had to march to church, which

---

28   Garland, 42.

29   John F. Marszalek, *Sherman: A Soldier's Passion for Order* (New York: The Free Press, 1993).

30   Lovell Coombs, *Ulysses S. Grant* (New York: The Macmillan Company, 1916), 27-28.

31   Theodore J. Crackel, *West Point: A Bicentennial History* (Lawrence: University Press of Kansas, 2002), 122.

32   Henry C. Deming, *The Life of Ulysses S. Grant, General United States Army* (Hartford, CT: S.S. Scranton and Company, 1868), 31-32.

was Episcopal, not the Methodist denomination he had experienced at home. Grant had to sit erectly through a number of boring sermons.

There was, in fact, little time during the day for cadets to relax. After reveille had sounded at 5 a.m., the cadets had to pack in some study time and inspection of their rooms. At 7 a.m., the bugle sounded for breakfast, and during the summer, there was even a parade. Dinner call came at 1 p.m., after which there was a variety of class recitations, study, and drawing. Another parade, dinner, more study, and then at 10 p.m., it was time for bed. The next morning, it began all over again.[33] One time, Grant was talked into going to Benny Havens, the after-hours cadet drinking and gathering place. In fact, though, he did that only once during all the time he was at West Point.[34]

The little time Grant used to study meant he was never anywhere near the top of his class. He was good at math and engineering, but he was a terrible student in French. Yet he always seemed to hold his place in rank. The total number of cadets at the Point at that time was around 235, and Grant's place on the conduct roll over his four years was 147, 144, 157, and 156. One of his professors even said, "[T]he smartest man in the class is little Grant."[35] During his last six months at West Point, he developed a terrible cough, and his weight shrunk to one hundred seventeen pounds. He was not the same height as when he first entered the Point, either, growing some six inches. Several uncles had died from consumption (tuberculosis), so many people worried about him. But he survived.[36]

The one thing that helped break up the monotony at West Point, and it was not much, was the presence of cadets from all over the nation. Grant became friends with William Benjamin Franklin, who was the number-one graduate in the class of 1843. Others like Isaac F. Quimby, William F. Reynolds, James A. Hardie, Rufus Ingalls, and Grant's later brother-in-law, Frederick T. Dent, also became friends. In classes above and below Grant were William T. Sherman, James (Pete) Longstreet, and even George B. McClellan.[37] Grant also became friends with Simon Bolivar Buckner, Stonewall Jackson, and George E. Pickett.[38] A man whom Grant also came to know well was George Deshon, who later became a Catholic

---

33   Coombs, 26-27.

34   Thomas J. Fleming, *West Point: The Men and Times of the United States Military Academy* (New York: William Morrow & Company, 1969), 103.

35   Church, 15-16, 18.

36   Chernow, 26.

37   Herman Dieck, *The Most Complete and Authentic History of the Life and Public Services of General U.S. Grant, "The Napoleon of America"* (Philadelphia: Thayer, Merriam & Co., 1885), 59-60, 62, 105, 271-73, 627, 741-42.

38   Josiah Bunting III, *Ulysses S. Grant* (New York: Times Books, 2004), 15.

Grant was, by his own admission, an unenthusiastic cadet but nonetheless dutiful.

Library of Congress

priest.[39] Visits by Winfield Scott and Martin Van Buren were also welcomed.

Friendships aside, Grant still had to show the other cadets that, though small, he was tough. Early in his West Point career, while participating in a marching drill, Grant found himself face to face with a huge cadet named Jack Lindsay, the son of an army officer. The classman thought he had the right to push the diminutive Grant out of line. Taken aback, Grant told Lindsay not to do that again. Lindsay just laughed and once again pushed Grant. This time, Grant decked his tormentor. From that point on, Grant had no problems with Lindsay or any other cadet.[40] But the fact was he still had no sense of rhythm, so he always seemed out of step and was thus the butt of other cadets' harassment. As Grant himself told it: "I know two songs, one is 'Yankee Doodle' and the other is not!"[41]

Another difficulty for the West Point cadets was being called up to a blackboard during class and forced to explain a problem they were to master either the night before or that morning. Just before class one day, another cadet brought in a huge pocket watch, some four inches in diameter, to show to the other cadets. Just as the teacher, in this case Zealous B. Tower, walked in, Grant stuffed the watch out of sight in his uniform. Immediately Grant and several other cadets were called up to the blackboard. Then it happened: the watch started bonging. Grant, however, continued his recitation. Tower shut the door and searched the entire classroom for the noise. He never found the watch, while Grant simply kept talking until the watch stopped bonging. Grant and his nerves of steel became the talk of West Point.[42]

39   Frank A. Burr, *A New, Original and Authentic Record of the Life and Deeds of General U.S. Grant* (St. Paul, MN: Empyreal Publishing House, 1885), 80.

40   Fleming, 102.

41   Joan Waugh, *U.S. Grant: American Hero, American Myth* (Chapel Hill, NC: University of North Carolina Press, 2009), 22.

42   Fleming, 105-06.

Grant is pictured here with his West Point friend Alexander Hays. Hays, later known as "the Fighting Elleck," would be killed serving under Grant at the 1864 battle of the Wilderness.

Library of Congress

Having a particularly significant influence on Grant and the other cadets was Dennis Hart Mahan, a professor of engineering from 1830 to 1871. He was the only professor at the Point to ever include any study of strategy in his course. William H. C. Bartlett, philosophy, and Albert E. Church, mathematics, were other well-known faculty members.[43] Robert W. Weir was a professor of art and painter of the Hudson River School. Grant painted some pictures in Weir's class that have survived, in which he demonstrated his artistic ability.[44]

Grant loved Commandant Charles F. Smith and looked to him as a West Point leader and someone who fairly applied discipline on the cadets. When Grant served with Smith during the Civil War, he was thrilled.[45]

Grant spent most of his time at West Point reading novels, a fact he even admitted in his memoirs. In keeping with his West Point training, however, he indicated that most of the reading was "frivolous," the term the West Point faculty used for popular novels. He insisted, however, that he read good books, those written by writers like Edward Bulwer-Lytton, Sir Walter Scott, and James Fenimore Cooper. "In the midst of conflict, the hero wants to be a peacemaker," he drew from Scott. How foretelling that insight was for the young cadet.[46]

The rule at West Point was that no one could leave the reservation for the first two years that he was part of the corps. At that time, after getting ready for the third year, cadets were allowed to go home for a several-week furlough. During the time Grant was at West Point, his mother and father had moved to Bethel,

43   Crackel, 124-25.

44   White, 37-38.

45   Fleming, 103.

46   White, 34-37.

closer to Cincinnati than Georgetown was. When he arrived at the new home, his mother gave him a quick look and said to him: "Ulysses, you've grown much straighter!" "Yes," he responded with pride, "that was the first thing they taught me."[47] He had a wonderful time in his familiar haunts, visiting old friends and places from his youth. "This I enjoyed beyond any other period of my life," he later recalled.[48]

When he returned for his last two years, he kept his grades steady, and he enjoyed the fact that West Point now had twelve horses for the cadets to ride. Superintendent Richard Delafield had urged the secretary of war to send these animals to West Point, and in 1840, Delafield had brought in thirty more.[49] By this time, Grant was known as the best rider in the corps. In fact, he even set a record that no one matched for over a quarter century. It happened on one of the final days in June of 1843. Cadets and their guests and faculty had come together in the riding hall, one of the largest buildings on the campus. Superintendent Delafield, the academic board, and a number of visitors watched in awe. All the cadets formed a line in the middle of the hall, and Sergeant Henry Hershberger, the riding master, raised the bar so that it was higher than a man's head (no one knew how high it was for sure). He yelled out: "Cadet Grant." Suddenly, a slightly built rider thundered out on the academy's fiercest horse, a chestnut-sorrel named York, who was seventeen hands high. Grant sped to the end of the hall, turned around, and came galloping forward toward the high bar. The crowd gasped when Grant and York cleared the bar. The audience quickly realized no one else could make that high a jump, and those watching exploded in applause. "Very well done, sir!" Hershberger yelled out. Everyone realized Grant had just demonstrated to everyone there that he was the best horseman at West Point.[50]

Years later, just a couple of months before Grant's death in 1885, then-General James B. Fry, an observer of this great jump, asked the dying general if he had ever seen Hershberger again. "Oh yes, I have heard of him since the war," Grant replied. "He was at Carlisle, Pennsylvania, old and poor, and I sent him a check for fifty dollars."[51]

When the time came, Grant left West Point with more money in his pocket than he had arrived with. Proud of his new uniform, he was showing it off in

---

47   Ulysses S. Grant III, *Ulysses S. Grant: Warrior and Statesman* (New York: William Morrow Company, 1969), 27.

48   *PMUSG-Annotated*, 23.

49   Stephen E. Ambrose, *Duty, Honor, Country: A History of West Point* (Baltimore: The Johns Hopkins Press, 1966), 135; Fleming, 104.

50   Frost, 19; White, 43.

51   Nicholas Smith, *Grant, The Man of Mystery* (Milwaukee: The Young Churchman Co., 1909), 29.

Ulysses S. Grant, brevet second lieutenant, summer 1843, following his West Point graduation.

National Portrait Gallery

Cincinnati when a dirty street boy yelled out at him: "Soldier! will you work? No, sir—ree; I'll sell my shirt first!!" Then, at home in Bethel, a drunken stableman dressed up in pantaloons with white cotton sheeting along the seams that looked like Grant's new uniform. The stableman paraded in the street before Grant's house, trying to imitate the new soldier.[52] Grant was now a brevet second lieutenant making all of $779 a year.[53] But the fact was that he could not even celebrate his new uniform.

People remembered much about Ulysses S. Grant when he later became famous, and needless to say, most of the remembrances were favorable. Still, not even his classmates or best friends ever thought he would become the famous person he turned out to be, the great general and important president.[54]

In fact, said one later biographer, "The American masses seem to have felt that Grant was just like them; his triumphs could have been theirs, too, if the mantle of command had just happened to fall upon them."[55]

52   *PMUSG-Annotated*, 25.

53   Bruce Catton, *U.S. Grant and the American Military Tradition* (Boston: Little, Brown and Company, 1954), 21.

54   Henry Coppée, *Life and Services of Gen. U.S. Grant* (New York: Richardson and Company, 1868), 22.

55   Lloyd Lewis, *Letters from Lloyd Lewis* (Boston: Little, Brown and Company, 1950), 21.

Son of Methodism
Chapter Two | *Ronald C. White*

On March 1, 1873, President Ulysses S. Grant wrote his secretary of state, Hamilton Fish, inviting him, along with other members of the cabinet, to attend Sunday morning worship at the Metropolitan Methodist Episcopal Church two days before Grant's second inauguration on March 4. Grant concluded, "If you will attend I know you will hear a good sermon."[1]

Even as Grant has received a well-deserved upgrade in presidential rank in recent years—he has advanced thirteen places in the four C-SPAN Presidential Historians Surveys in the twenty-first century—a significant aspect of this new appreciation remains overlooked.[2] The story of his lifelong participation with Methodist churches and ministers is essential if we are to capture the whole Grant.

To begin to understand this influence, several questions need to be asked.

When, where, and how did he participate in Methodist churches? Did he have any Methodist ministers as mentors? In his eight years as president, what was his involvement in the new Metropolitan Methodist Church in Washington?

To put Grant's faith odyssey in context, it will be important to understand the ethos of nineteenth-century Methodism. In the beginning decades of the nineteenth century, as the nation began moving west, Methodists outpaced Congregationalists and Presbyterians, the largest Protestant denominations at the time of the American Revolution. By the Civil War, Methodism's growth had made it the largest Protestant denomination in America.

Starting in the early 1850s, the Methodist Church made plans to establish a national church in Washington—the first denomination to do so. By the time of Grant's election as president in 1868, the Methodists had become a middle-class denomination excited to erect a Gothic structure in the nation's capital at a cost

---

1   USG to Hamilton Fish, 1 March 1873, John Y. Simon, ed., *The Papers of Ulysses S. Grant*, 32 vols. (Carbondale, IL: Southern Illinois University Press, 1967–2012), 24:59, hereafter cited as *PUSG*.

2   "Presidential Historians Survey 2021, Total Scores/Overall Rankings," C-SPAN, accessed 21 May 2022, https://www.c-span.org/presidentsurvey2021/?page=overall.

The Metropolitan Methodist Episcopal Church, Washington, D.C.

Author's Collection

of $225,000. The press would call it "the Westminster Abby of Methodism."[3] The foundation stone for the National Cathedral of the Episcopal Church was not laid until 1907.

Those planning the new church rushed to complete construction, working with the president-elect to ensure the dedication took place in coordination with his inauguration. *The New York Times* reported that the dedication "has created more excitement in the religious community of Washington than anything that has occurred here for years."[4] *Harper's Weekly* wrote of Sunday, February 28: "General Grant and Mrs. Grant, accompanied by their family, and Mrs. Grant's father, arrived just as Bishop [Matthew] Simpson commenced his sermon."[5]

Grant's participation in Methodism began as a boy growing up in Georgetown, Ohio. His parents, Jesse and Hannah, helped establish the Georgetown Methodist Church in 1827, just as their first child turned five. The church met in a meeting house across from their home.

Methodism, barely forty years old in the new nation, grew rapidly due to circuit riders who rode through a geographic area or "circuit," both starting and supplying ministerial services to new congregations. Young Ulysses's parents invited these Methodist circuit riders to stay at their home. Under Pastor George W. Maley, the

---

3   Lillian Brooks Brown, *A Living Centennial Commemorating the One Hundredth Anniversary of Metropolitan Memorial United Methodist Church* (Washington, D.C.: Judd & Detweiler, 1969), 1-9. In 1845, largely over the contentious issue of slavery, the Methodist Church split, the southern branch taking the name of the Methodist Episcopal Church, South.

4   *New York Times*, 1 March 1869.

5   "The Memorial Methodist Episcopal Church, Washington," *Harper's Weekly*, 13 March 1869, No. 637, 13:173. For the dedication, see Brown, 7-14.

Georgetown congregation flourished. By 1834, within seven years of its founding, it grew to be recognized as the leading church on the circuit.[6]

Copying the style of early Methodism, begun in England in the eighteenth century as a renewal movement within the Church of England, Methodist churches in the United States kept their places of worship intentionally plain, meant to contrast with the more elaborate furnishings of neighboring Episcopal and Presbyterian churches.

Georgetown Methodists may have been plain, but they were not silent. A local church historian would write, "Believers were not tongue-tied, nor were converts still-born in pioneer days. Those old walls were accustomed to what would now be considered noise."[7]

Methodists were a singing people, drawing on the hymns of English Methodist founder Charles Wesley. But if Jesse and Hannah prayed for the life of their eldest child, they learned early that music would never bring him closer to God. He did not like hymn singing. He breathed a sigh of relief when each stanza was, in his words, "disposed of."[8]

Jesse and Hannah were not drawn to the emotional aspects prevalent in many early Methodist congregations. Chilton White, a boyhood friend of Ulysses's, noted later, "The Methodists shouted in those days but the Grant family never took a part in it."[9] Young Lyss, the name the boys and girls called him in Georgetown, also avoided revivals, not liking their emotion.[10]

Grant's parents taught their children respect for the Sabbath. Like most Methodists of that era, the family did not play cards. They did not dance, nor did they permit their children to dance. Ulysses was taught never to swear because this would take the Lord's name in vain. If young Lyss sometimes played hooky from Sunday worship, his parents hoped the values of Methodism would be ploughed deeply into the soil of his personality.[11]

Ulysses inherited his most enduring characteristics from his mother. Sometimes her quiet behavior has been depicted as unusual, if not strange. Boyhood friend

6   Nancy Purdy & Terry Cavanaugh, *The History of the Georgetown United Methodist Church* (Georgetown, OH: Georgetown United Methodist Church, 1997), 4.

7   Calvin W. Horn, *A Handbook of the Methodist Episcopal Church, Georgetown, Ohio* (Georgetown, OH: Press of The Georgetown Gazette, 1904), 10.

8   Ronald C. White, *American Ulysses: A Life of Ulysses S. Grant* (New York: Random House, 2016), 20, hereafter cited as *American Ulysses*; Lloyd Lewis, *Captain Sam Grant* (Boston: Little, Brown and Company, 1950), 49.

9   Chilton White interview, Hamlin Garland Papers, Doheny Memorial Library, University of Southern California.

10   Ibid.

11   *American Ulysses*, 20.

White, on the other hand, detected in Hannah Grant what many missed: that she was a woman of "[d]eep feeling but not demonstrative."[12] (Even as famed general and president, Grant too could be quiet, but that silence should not be misunderstood as a man who did not care deeply.) Hannah encouraged in her children an ethic of self-effacing Christian love. The Presbyterian tradition of her youth in Pennsylvania, and the Methodist piety of her adult life in Ohio, taught her to praise the Creator rather than the creature. Humility, or the nineteenth-century term "self-effacement," would come to characterize her son.

In May 1839, at barely seventeen, the shy boy, barely five feet tall, headed east to West Point. He went not from his own initiative, but because his father wanted him to attend a tuition-free academy known for its ability to turn out engineers.

Once arrived, Ulysses had no hesitation voicing his objection to one example of the academy's regimentation. West Point's "Regulations" stated, "Every member of the Academic Staff and Cadet shall attend divine service on Sunday."[13] Grant found the stone chapel, of Renaissance Revival design with a Roman Doric portico, erected two years before his arrival, so different from the Methodist meeting house he had experienced in Ohio.[14] He wrote home to a friend, "We are not only obliged to go to church but must *march* there by compan[ie]s."[15] Cadets then sat for two hours on backless benches listening to what they protested were dull sermons.[16]

The Episcopal Church served as the *de facto* established church of the academy. However, the cadets all knew that the chaplain, the Reverend Martin B. Parks, was in the midst of a journey from Episcopalianism to Roman Catholicism.[17] Ulysses, accustomed to worshipping in the Methodist church in Georgetown, decided he liked neither any establishment of religion nor the more formal worship of high church Episcopalianism. Used to hearing antislavery sermons in the Methodist churches of southwestern Ohio, he heard no such sermons from West Point's conservative Episcopal chaplain.

---

12   Chilton White interview.

13   *Regulations Established for the Organization and Government of the Military Academy, at West Point, New-York* (New York: Wiley & Putnam, 1839), 33.

14   Alan C. Aimone, "River Guide to the Hudson Highlands" (2009), accessed 23 May 2022, https://www.hudsonrivervalley.org/documents/401021/0/riverguidehudsonhighlands.pdf/cd37089f-88a8-44a8-905f-7d66588f2583, 11. Now called the Old Cadet Chapel, during Grant's time it was located on the site of the current Science Building. With the construction of a new chapel in 1910, the Old Chapel was moved stone by stone to the Post Cemetery in 1911.

15   USG to R. McKinstry Griffith, 22 September 1839, *PUSG*, 1:7.

16   Stephen E. Ambrose, *Duty, Honor, Country: A History of West Point* (Baltimore: The Johns Hopkins Press, 1966), 151.

17   *American Ulysses*, 41.

Some young adults, then and now, react against the faith tradition of their parents. Young Abraham Lincoln did. He rejected the emotional faith and worship of the Baptist churches he attended with his parents in Kentucky and southern Indiana. It would be some years later before Lincoln found a pattern of faith to his liking in the more rational sermons of the Reverend James Smith at the First Presbyterian Church in Springfield, Illinois, and even more so in the thoughtful sermons of the Princeton-educated Reverend Phineas Densmore Gurley at the New York Avenue Presbyterian Church in Washington. By contrast, Grant's exposure to high-church Episcopal worship at West Point only confirmed his allegiance to Methodism.

After graduation from West Point in 1843, Grant was posted to Jefferson Barracks, ten miles south of St. Louis. Upon hearing of Grant's assignment, Fred Dent, his fourth-year roommate, encouraged him to visit his parents, Frederick and Ellen Dent. They lived at White Haven, their country home located five miles from Jefferson Barracks. Upon meeting them, Lt. Grant learned that Mrs. Dent was the daughter of a Methodist minister.[18]

At White Haven, Ulysses met the Dents' oldest daughter, Julia. Falling in love, and enduring protestations from her father about his daughter marrying a nomadic soldier, the two wed in 1848 after Grant returned from participating in the war with Mexico.[19]

His initial peacetime postings were to Detroit and Sackets Harbor, New York. In Detroit in 1849, Grant was befriended by the Reverend George Taylor, the new pastor of the Congress Street Methodist Church, a congregation spun off three years earlier from the mother church of Detroit Methodism, Central Methodist. James E. Pittman, an army friend of Grant who also attended the Congress Street church, remembered Grant's close relationship with Taylor. Knowing he was subject to brief postings in a peacetime army, Grant nevertheless rented a pew in the Congress Street church.[20]

A significant encounter in Grant's faith journey occurred a decade later in Galena, Illinois. After resigning from the army following postings on the Pacific coast and struggling to make a living during six years in Missouri, he accepted a position in the small Illinois town in May 1860 to work under his younger brother, Simpson, in their father's leather goods store on Main Street.

18   Ibid., 45-48.

19   Ibid., 101-02.

20   James E. Pittman interview, William C. Church Papers, Library of Congress; Silas Farmer, *History of Detroit and Wayne County and Early Michigan,* 3rd ed. (Detroit: Silas Farmer & Co., 1890), 569.

Bench Street Methodist Church, Galena, Illinois
Author's Collection

It was not long before Ulysses, Julia, and their four children began attending the Methodist church on Bench Street. Galena Methodists had built a small frame church in 1832. As the congregation grew, they erected a larger brick and stone church in 1857.

The year before the Grants arrived, the church greeted a new, young pastor. John Heyl Vincent, twenty-seven-year-old, tall, and slender, was born in Alabama and grew up in Pennsylvania. At seventeen, he was licensed by the Methodist Church to become a circuit rider in the Keystone State, completing his circuit every four weeks. A winsome man with a resonant voice, Vincent delivered Methodist sermons that were, as his own son recalled, "simple, sensible, and practical."[21]

Grant had a first conversation with Vincent on a cold winter morning in the lobby at the Julien House across the Mississippi River in Dubuque, Iowa. The young minister remembered he met "a short, compactly built man in an army overcoat." Grant, in his old blue jacket, walked across the lobby and introduced himself. "I hear you preach every Sunday," he said. "My name is Grant." Vincent remembered that Grant's "animation and earnestness . . . surprised and interested me."[22] After that initial encounter, "I often watched, during the public services in my church at Galena, the calm, firm face of my interesting hearer."[23]

With the outbreak of the Civil War in April 1861, Grant, the only West Point graduate in Galena, set out to recruit volunteers in the region. On April 25, when the Jo Davies County Guards, along with Grant, prepared to entrain for

---

21   Leon H. Vincent, *John Heyl Vincent: A Biographical Sketch* (New York: The Macmillan Company, 1925), 29-31.

22   Ibid., 50; John H. Vincent, "The Inner Life of Ulysses S. Grant," *The Chautauquan*, (October 1899–March 1900), 30:634.

23   Ibid.

Springfield, Vincent, standing on top of a freight car, offered a farewell address and prayer.[24]

No one in Galena on that April morning in 1861 could know that Vincent would become one of the foremost national Methodist leaders in succeeding decades.[25] Nor could they know that the friendship begun between Grant and Vincent would deepen. In the years ahead, they would meet again and again at crucial moments as Grant's military and civilian leadership grew.

Grant did not leave his friendship with Vincent behind when he entered the Civil War. In 1862, after the battle at Shiloh, he received a letter from Vincent informing him that he was planning an educational trip to Europe, Egypt, and Palestine. Grant replied, "If you should make your expected trip to Palestine it would afford me the greatest pleasure to hear from you from that far off land and to reply punctually to all your letters." He told Vincent he could still recall "the pleasure of listening to your feeling discourses from the pulpit"—an intriguing choice of words for a man who had difficulty expressing his feelings.[26] Yet Grant's words captured sermons focused on the lived experience of the Christian faith that were the hallmark of nineteenth-century Methodism.

Grant and Vincent resumed their friendship two years later. In March 1864, when Grant welcomed President Lincoln to his City Point headquarters in Virginia, he also welcomed Vincent, whom he introduced to the president as the pastor in Galena whose sermons he never missed.[27] Vincent now represented the U.S. Christian Commission, an organization providing religious literature and medical services to Union troops. Grant invited Vincent to accompany him and the president on a Sunday trip up the James River, but he replied he could not because of prior commitments to preach and direct Sunday school for the troops.[28]

After Appomattox, while living in Washington, Grant accepted a variety of invitations to leave the nation's capital during the summer. He accepted an invitation to Chicago to attend a Sanitary Commission Fair, a volunteer citizen organization that had provided medical supplies and food to the troops. On a Saturday afternoon during the trip, hearing that Vincent was in Chicago, he sent Orville E. Babcock, one of his aides, to inquire about where his former Galena minister might be preaching. Babcock informed Grant that Vincent was preaching

---

24   Vincent, *John Heyl Vincent,* 51.

25   Russell E. Richey, Kenneth E. Rowe, and Jean Miller Schmidt, *The Methodist Experience in America: A History,* 2 vols. (Nashville, TN: Abingdon Press, 2010), 1:250, 266, 330.

26   USG to John H. Vincent, 25 May 1862, *PUSG,* 5:132; Vincent, *John Heyl Vincent,* 52-53.

27   Vincent, "The Inner Life of Ulysses S. Grant," 637.

28   Vincent, *John Heyl Vincent,* 98-99.

at the Trinity Methodist Church in the new southern suburbs. On Sunday morning, the general entered, unannounced, to listen once more to Vincent.[29]

Although still a pastor, by this time Vincent's interests had turned to education. In 1865, he founded the *Northwestern Sunday School Quarterly*, and in 1866, he started the *Sunday School Teacher*.[30]

At the end of the summer, Grant was excited to accept an invitation from Galena. He had known few people in the short twelve months he had lived there, but an astonishing number of people declared they remembered him.

Upon his arrival, Grant glimpsed a triumphal arch spanning Main Street, each side naming battles in which Grant had led his troops to victory. Congressman Elihu Washburne welcomed him. Grant, ever averse to speaking, responded briefly, "I am truly glad to meet you at this time, and I have requested Mr. Vincent, who came with me on the train, to return to you my very sincere thanks for this demonstration."[31]

Vincent, returning to the town where he had once served as Methodist minister, told the assembled crowd that though Grant's official business would mean he needed to remain mainly in Washington, he regarded Galena as his home.[32] Grant, the hero of the Civil War, had returned to his hometown and asked Vincent to speak for him.

In 1869, as president, Grant settled into regular participation in the Metropolitan Methodist Church. He accepted nomination to the first class of ten trustees.[33] The Reverend John Philip Newman served as the church's initial minister, helping to organize the new congregation. On March 8, 1869, Newman was also elected chaplain of the United States Senate.

Julia Grant became one of Newman's most supportive parishioners. She spent considerable time working for the Metropolitan church. She chaired the National Committee to liquidate the debt on the church. On November 25, 1869, she circulated a letter stating, "It is the wish of the Ladies in Washington, to celebrate the liquidation of our church debt in a suitable manner. We have therefore determined to hold our Jubilee in the Metropolitan church on Christmas Eve."

29   O. H. Tiffany, *Pulpit and Platform: Sermons and Addresses* (New York: Hunt & Eaton, 1893), 202-03.

30   Vincent, *John Heyl Vincent*, 86-88.

31   Ibid., 102; *American Ulysses*, 419.

32   Ibid.

33   Brown, 23.

In a ceremony at the service on December 24, President Grant, as a trustee of the church, received a check for $50,000 to pay off the outstanding indebtedness.[34]

Every Christmas, Julia made gifts on behalf of the church to Washington's hospitals, orphanages, and asylums. Sometimes her husband joined her in delivering fruit and candy. In the weeks leading up to Christmas, toy merchants in Washington came to expect Julia Grant as she led groups of children through their stores in her purchase of gifts.[35]

Newman retired from the Metropolitan church in the spring of 1872, but did not exit from Grant's life. Depending upon whom you listened to, in the years ahead, and especially as Grant lay dying, Newman would be either a nurturing presence—according to Julia—or an interfering busybody—according to Mark Twain.[36]

Newman was succeeded by the Reverend Otis H. Tiffany. Renowned as one of the outstanding preachers within Methodism, Tiffany corroborated Grant's initiative on the Sunday before his second inauguration. "He said he thought it would be appropriate to invite the members of his cabinet to attend service with him on that day," Tiffany recalled. "Accordingly, they were invited and came."[37]

President Grant became a fan of the new minister's sermons even as Tiffany became an admirer of Grant. "I found him one of the most regular of the congregation in attendance upon public worship." Tiffany was impressed that "[h]e seemed to be scrupulously careful on this matter, frequently explaining, when necessarily absent, the occasion of his non-attendance." Furthermore, "He enjoyed all of the religious services of the church, excepting the singing, having a constitutional inability to appreciate music."[38]

On May 21, 1874, Tiffany performed the wedding of Grant's only daughter, Nellie, not quite nineteen, to Englishman Algernon Sartoris in the East Room of the White House. In the wedding of the year, the president of the United States, the father of the bride, was overcome with tears.[39]

As the scandals in his second term began to add to Grant's stress, he looked forward each summer to getting away from Washington to his cottage at Long Branch on the Jersey shore. In the summer of 1875, he intended to stay in Long

---

34   An unaddressed circular letter, 25 November 1869, *PUSG*, 20:73n-74n.

35   Ishbel Ross, *The General's Wife: The Life of Mrs. Ulysses S. Grant* (New York: Dodd, Mead & Company, 1959), 217.

36   *American Ulysses*, 641-42.

37   Tiffany, 205.

38   Ibid., 203.

39   *American Ulysses*, 547-48.

John Philip Newman
Author's Collection

Branch for the entire summer, but in August, he accepted an invitation from an old friend. Vincent, now chief agent for the Methodist Sunday School Union, had founded in the summer of 1874 a two-week Sunday school teachers' educational event at Lake Chautauqua in southwestern New York. Methodists had convened camp meetings in that area for years, but Vincent, no supporter of the emotionalism of camp meetings, thought the time had come in American Methodism to move from experience to education to generate better-educated Christians.[40]

In this second summer, seeking a means to give his new endeavor national exposure, Vincent invited Grant to come to the new Chautauqua Assembly for a weekend in August. The President, busy all summer putting out political fires growing from the scandals in his second term, accepted the summons.

On Saturday afternoon, August 14, a crowd of nearly 20,000—many more than Vincent expected—greeted Grant. The president spoke briefly, quickly passing the baton "to Dr. Vincent, who is an old friend of mine, and a better talker than I, to tell you how happy I am to be with you."[41]

Grant stayed in a fully furnished tent. Over the tent's entrance was stitched the single word "REST."

The following day was by no means a day of rest. Early that morning, Grant attended Sunday school. At the 11 a.m. worship service, he took a seat on the platform in the large auditorium decorated with flags from many nations. At the end of the service, Vincent presented Grant two Bibles, "the symbol of our work"—a Bagster Bible, popular because of its parallel references, and a Bible from the American Tract Society. The day of rest ended with dinner at the home of Lewis

40   Jeffrey Simpson, *Chautauqua: An American Utopia* (New York: Harry N. Abrams, 1999), 37; Vincent, *John Heyl Vincent*, 116-21. The *Chautauqua Assembly Herald* was established in 1876, one year after Grant's visit, but several reminiscences of his visit were published in succeeding years. Vincent preserved many articles about these early years, which are in the Oliver Archives Center at the Chautauqua Institution.

41   *Chautauqua Assembly Herald*, 11 August 1905.

Miller, Ohio businessman and Vincent's partner in this educational undertaking that would one day be known as the world-famous Chautauqua Institution.[42] In one of the most vexing years of his presidency, forced to deal with multiple scandals in his administration, Grant accepted Vincent's invitation. He traveled to a remote destination, and once there, pointed beyond himself to the Methodist minister and educator.

President Grant had long championed the American Centennial Exposition set to open in Philadelphia on May 10, 1876. John Wanamaker, owner of Philadelphia's first department store, seeking a way to publicize the growing Sunday school movement at the Exposition, invited Grant to write a letter that would appear on the cover of a special edition of the *Sunday School Times* to be handed out to visitors to Philadelphia.[43] In his own hand, Grant wrote, "My advice to SUNDAY-SCHOOLS, no matter what their denominations, is: Hold fast to the Bible as the sheet-anchor of your liberties; write its precepts in your hearts, and PRACTISE THEM IN YOUR LIVES."[44] Wannamaker credited Grant's letter, looked at by millions of visitors to the Exposition, with boosting the *Sunday School Times* to new popularity.

Although Grant championed the use of the Bible, unlike Abraham Lincoln, he did not suffuse his speeches with biblical quotations. Unlike Lincoln, in Grant, there is not the sense of anguish over a God who acts in history, especially in the Civil War. However, the untold story of Grant's religious odyssey is not about eloquent words of faith that would make their way into his speeches or his *Personal Memoirs,* but rather about his lifelong participation in Methodist churches and appreciation of Methodist ministers.

The missing person in the biographies of Grant is the Reverend John Heyl Vincent. If Grant had a spiritual mentor, it was the winsome Vincent. When he invited Grant to come to a fledgling Chautauqua, in the middle of one of the worst summers of his presidency, Grant answered the summons.

Some years after Grant's death in 1885, Vincent offered an appraisal of his onetime parishioner, which he titled "The Inner Life of Ulysses S. Grant." Vincent wrote, "General Grant was a genuine Christian." Over long years, Vincent had observed Grant's "constant attendance upon public worship, his reverence for all the functions of the Christian church, his close and interested attention to the sermon, his reiterated expression of faith in the Holy Scriptures as God's Word."

42   Ibid.; *American Ulysses,* 561. For the Chautauqua Institution, see https://chq.org.

43   Herbert Adams Gibbons, *John Wanamaker,* 2 vols. (New York: Harper, 1926), 1:191-92.

44   USG to Editor, *Sunday School Times,* 6 June 1876, *PUSG,* 27:124.

The Rev. John Heyl Vincent (left) and the Rev. Otis Henry Tiffany (right)

Bridwell Library Special Collections, SMU; Author's Collection

Vincent believed, "His whole attitude toward the church was a positive confession of Christ before the world."[45]

In revisioning Grant in my biography, *American Ulysses,* I sought to understand not simply what Grant did—the general who won the Civil War, the two-term president whose presidency deserves an upgrade—but who he was: his character. In fresh research for writing this essay, I have become convinced that Grant was at heart a son of Methodism. At the root of the values that shaped his character—magnanimity, self-effacement, his continuing ability to give credit to others—was the nurture he received from his lifelong participation in American Methodism.

---

45   Vincent, "The Inner Life of Ulysses S. Grant," 637.

All in the Family: Ulysses and Julia Grant's Relationship with Their In-Laws
Chapter Three | *Nick Sacco*

W hen asked how they might describe Ulysses S. Grant's legacy in a few words, people visiting the many Grant-related historic sites around the country would probably mention his unbounded determination, his clarity of purpose, and his steady leadership under fire. It's worth remembering, however, that Grant's formative years sometimes appeared to portend the opposite. He was an indifferent student during his youth, openly admitting in his *Personal Memoirs* that he found his lessons boring and that he "was not studious in habit." When told by his father that he was to attend the U.S. Military Academy at West Point, Grant was an unwilling participant who resented his future plans being dictated and determined by someone else. Attending West Point against his own wishes, Grant was a successful but perhaps underwhelming cadet who was more interested in riding horses and reading literature than in military life. After graduation, he continued to feel uncertain about his future path in life and contemplated ways to get out of the army as soon as possible. "A military life had no charms for me, and I had not the faintest idea of staying in the army," Grant later remarked.[1] Other than his love for the lofty ideals of the Union he swore to defend, it seems that the only thing that sparked a sense of certainty and determination within Grant during his early adulthood was his deep and abiding love for Julia Dent of St. Louis, Missouri.

Anyone with experience in marriage will say that a marriage is between not just two people, but two families. The early love story and marriage of Ulysses and Julia Grant is well known among general audiences in large part because of the fascinating dynamic between the Dent and Grant families. Like the marriage of Abraham and Mary Todd Lincoln, the Grant marriage saw a convergence of Northern and Southern families with different lifestyles and political views uniting as one. It also saw a groom marry into a slaveholding family, whatever his own view of the institution may have been at the time. There is a certain uniqueness to

---

1   Ulysses S. Grant, *Personal Memoirs of U.S. Grant*, 2 vols. (New York: Charles L. Webster & Co., 1885–1886), 1:24-25, 32-34, 38, hereafter cited as *PMUSG*.

Col. Frederick F. Dent (1787-1873) was a boisterous man who was not afraid to share his views. Although he was originally skeptical of Ulysses S. Grant as a worthy suitor of his daughter Julia's hand, the two men grew to develop a sense of mutual respect for each other.

Library of Congress

this family union within the context of a national union that was already badly divided by the time the Grants married in 1848.

In looking at potential challenges that could have hampered Ulysses and Julia Grant's relationship, historians have focused much of their attention on the ways the Dent family applied pressure to the situation, particularly Julia's father, "Colonel" Frederick F. Dent. After all, Colonel Dent initially opposed his eldest (and favorite) daughter's marriage to an army officer, fearing that low pay and assignments to remote areas of the country would be too taxing for their relationship. Julia remarked in her *Personal Memoirs* that at one point, her father, not wanting to lose her presence at home, made the audacious suggestion that Ulysses get married to Julia's sister Nellie instead. And according to an 1890 article about their courtship, Colonel Dent reportedly said to Julia that "you are too young and the boy is too poor," concluding in a cold tone, "He hasn't anything to give you." These sources paint a portrait of Colonel Dent as a strong-willed and vocal father who did not fear sharing his opinions about his family, his political views, or any suitors for Julia's hand.[2] Simply put, the young man from an antislavery family in Ohio did not meet Colonel Dent's expectations. Biographer Ron Chernow's popular study of Grant goes the farthest in this interpretation by arguing that the Colonel "openly despised" Grant, "gloated over his misery," and later "wished to

2   Julia Dent Grant, *The Personal Memoirs of Julia Dent Grant*, John Y. Simon, ed. (New York: G.P. Putnam's Sons, 1975), 51, hereafter cited as *PMJDG*; Foster Coates, "The Courtship of General Grant," *Ladies' Home Journal* (October 1890), 4. For a small sampling of biographers' interpretations of the relationship between Ulysses S. Grant and Colonel Frederick F. Dent, see Lloyd Lewis, *Captain Sam Grant* (Boston: Little, Brown and Company, 1950), 112-13, 121-22; Brooks D. Simpson, *Ulysses S. Grant: Triumph Over Adversity, 1822–1865* (Boston: Houghton Mifflin Company, 2000), 18-23, 70-71, Jean Edward Smith, *Grant* (New York: Simon & Schuster, 2002), 38; Joan Waugh, *U.S. Grant: American Hero, American Myth* (Chapel Hill, NC: The University of North Carolina Press, 2009), 25-26, 42-45.

sabotage his marriage and steal away his children" in the 1850s while Grant was stationed with the army in the Pacific coast.[3]

To be sure, there was palpable tension in the relationship between Grant and his future father-in-law. Julia's fears that her father would reject their engagement were very real, and there were genuine political divides between the two men, particularly on the question of secession. For example, towards the beginning of the American civil war on May 10, 1861, Grant was tasked with mustering Illinois troops for service in the U.S. Army. Stationed for the day in Belleville, a small farming town just east of the Mississippi River, Grant decided to spend the night with his father-in-law on the other side of the river back in St. Louis. In a letter to Julia about the visit, Grant noted that he and Colonel Dent discussed politics during the night. Colonel Dent did not want to see the Union broken up, Grant noted, but he also did not want any states to be coerced to stay in the Union. This line of argument did not pass muster with Grant, who complained that his father-in-law "would have a secession force march where they please uninterrupted and is really what I would call a secessionist." Later in the war, Julia recalled that strong disagreements about secession were common during her own visits to see her father and that he believed the Constitution allowed for a state to legally secede from the Union.[4]

These tensions should be recognized by scholars and readers alike. However, the historical record presents an opportunity to question these typical stories told about Grant and his father-in-law and to examine other factors that may have influenced Ulysses and Julia Grant's relationship and marriage, both negatively and positively.

After graduating from the U.S. Military Academy in 1843, Grant was sent to St. Louis in September to begin his army career at Jefferson Barracks, at that time one of the largest military posts in the country. Invited by his former West Point roommate Frederick Tracy Dent (a son of Colonel Dent) to visit his family's home, White Haven, Grant traveled five miles from the barracks to meet members of the Dent family shortly after reporting for duty. It should be remembered, however, that Julia Dent was *not* at White Haven during this time. Away at boarding school in St. Louis city twelve miles away, she would not come back to White Haven and meet Grant for the first time until February 1844.[5] This chronology raises its own interesting questions. If Grant and the Dent family had such a difficult

---

3   Ron Chernow, *Grant* (New York: Penguin Press, 2017), 62-63, 78, 91, 104.

4   USG to Julia Dent Grant, 10 May 1861, John Y. Simon, ed., *The Papers of Ulysses S. Grant*, 32 vols. (Carbondale, IL: Southern Illinois University Press, 1967–2012), 2:26-27, hereafter cited as *PUSG*; *PMJDG*, 51, 113.

5   *PMJDG*, 48.

Colonel Frederick F. Dent purchased White Haven in 1820. Ulysses S. Grant lived at White Haven with his in-laws and his own family from 1854 to 1859; this picture of the home was taken in 1860.

National Park Service

relationship, why did Grant visit White Haven at least once or twice a week for dinner for upwards of five months before ever meeting Julia Dent? Why did the Dents enjoy having this young army officer as a regular visitor? While not the central focus of this chapter, one might also question why Grant—raised in a strongly antislavery household and educated at one point by the Reverend John Rankin, the famous abolitionist—felt comfortable regularly visiting an 850-acre plantation in which thirty African Americans were enslaved by the Dent family by 1850.[6]

One crucial answer lies in the relationship between Grant and his future mother-in-law, Ellen Wrenshall Dent. Little is known about Ellen's life beyond what is stated in Julia Dent Grant's memoirs, but the portrait painted by Julia conveys a sense of deep affection and compassion between Grant and his mother-in-law. For Grant, Ellen Dent was a generous homemaker who provided a fresh, home-cooked meal for a young soldier in a new city in which he faced plenty of uncertainties about his future. She provided comfort and stability to Grant during an important phase of his life as he entered into the world of military life full-time. After his marriage to Julia and subsequent move to White Haven to begin farming

6   For more information on Grant and his relationship with slavery, see Nicholas W. Sacco, "'I Never was an Abolitionist': Ulysses S. Grant and Slavery, 1854–1863," *The Journal of the Civil War Era* (September 2019), No. 3, 9:410-37.

in 1854, Ellen remained a steadfast supporter of Grant at a time when many people—perhaps even Grant himself—doubted his ability to provide for his own growing family. Conversely, Grant provided an important form of companionship for Ellen Dent. With four adult sons out of White Haven and pursuing their careers far from home, young Grant's presence in 1843 was undoubtedly a welcome sight for Ellen, who did not care for the St. Louis countryside and sometimes struggled with the loneliness that can accompany such a lifestyle.[7] In contrast to an image of anger and bitterness, one can easily imagine lively conversations at the dinner table between Grant and the Dent parents about military life, politics, and family matters. It is important to remember how different Grant's life could have been had he merely visited White Haven one time and never returned. In this sense, Ulysses and Julia Grant owe a debt of gratitude to Ellen Dent, whose stabilizing presence ensured that Grant would continue to feel welcomed as a regular visitor to White Haven.

Despite claims to the contrary, small moments of tenderness and affection between Grant and his father-in-law do occasionally show up in the historical record. While stationed in Corinth, Mississippi, in the summer of 1862, General Grant penned a letter to Julia, who was back at White Haven with their children and her father. "We all miss you and the children very much," Grant remarked, further asking, "How did you find your pa . . . and the rest of the folks at home? Give my love to all of them." Similar letters emerge during Grant's 1864 Overland Campaign, in which he asked Julia several times to "[r]emember me to your father" while wishing for happiness back in St. Louis. Upon hearing that Colonel Dent was dealing with poor health, Grant went even further and wrote to his father-in-law in September 1864, inviting him to join Julia and the children in their new eastern home in Burlington, New Jersey. While Colonel Dent decided to stay in St. Louis for the remainder of the Civil War, he did eventually move with the Grants to Washington, D.C., in 1867 after suffering a stroke. After Grant's election to the presidency, Colonel Dent joined the family at the White House and remained there until his death in December 1873.[8]

One of my favorite research discoveries regarding Colonel Dent occurred while going through the papers of Frederick Tracy Dent at the University of Southern Illinois-Carbondale Special Collections Research Center. Included in his modest collection of papers at the university is a small newspaper clipping without a title,

---

7   *PMJDG*, 33-35, 40-43, 91-92.

8   USG to Julia Dent Grant, 18 August 1862, 13 May, 11 September, 14 September, and 28 October 1864, *PUSG*, 5:308, 10:443-44, 12:150, 166, 362-63; Julia Dent Grant telegraph to USG, 5 September 1866, ibid., 16:308*n*; USG telegraph to Julia Dent Grant, 12 July 1867, ibid., 17:232*n*-33*n*; USG to Abel R. Corbin, 16 December 1873, ibid., 24:292-93.

date, or publication information. Frederick T. Dent himself probably cut out and stored away the article as a keepsake. In reading the article, I could see why it may have been special to him. The author—who was later determined to be journalist and politician John W. Forney—remarked that he had enjoyed a dinner with President Grant and Colonel Dent at the White House during the winter of 1869–70. In his early eighties by that point, "[Mr. Dent's] faculties were failing," Forney noted, "but he was so kind, humorous, and genteel that he won me over at once by his quaint remarks and curious candor. He was a rare specimen of the gentleman of the old school, showing . . . an independent spirit and a wonderfully retentive memory." Not one to pass up the chance to talk politics or to criticize his son-in-law's Republican Party, Colonel Dent remarked that "I am a Democrat, the same as ever, and don't believe in any other party . . . and you young fellows cannot bring me over to your new party," according to the reporter. In response, "the President's eyes twinkled more than once at his harmless and witty observations," seemingly unbothered by his father-in-law's views and perhaps finding them humorous.[9]

This short newspaper clipping nicely captures the spirit that defined the relationship between Grant and his father-in-law. The two men undoubtedly had their differences and did not always see eye-to-eye on politics or family matters, but there was also a unique dynamic marked by mutual respect, admiration, and perhaps even a bit of playfulness in their interactions. Contrary to Chernow's claims that Dent strongly disliked Grant, one could see a sense of concern and care from both men. Most importantly, we should remember that Grant lived in the same house as his father-in-law for nearly ten years of his life, in both St. Louis and Washington, D.C., the latter having been at his own invitation.

Conversely, historians ought to examine the ways Grant's parents, specifically his father Jesse, may themselves have applied negative pressure to Ulysses and Julia Grant's relationship. To start with, why did Grant's parents not attend Ulysses and Julia's wedding in St. Louis? The wedding took place at the Dent family's city home at the intersection of Fourth and Cerre Streets and was solemnized on August 22, 1848, in the presence of the Dent family and close friends such as Bernard Pratte and future Confederate generals Cadmus Wilcox and James Longstreet (who, contrary to popular myth, was *not* Grant's best man or a groomsman at

---

9   Untitled newspaper clipping, Frederick T. Dent Papers, University of Southern Illinois-Carbondale Special Collections Research Center. I thank Frank Scaturro for finding the original source of the newspaper article in John W. Forney, *Anecdotes of Public Men*, 2 vols. (New York: Harper & Brothers, 1873–1881), 2:200-01.

the wedding).[10] Some historians have speculated that the Grant family did not attend the wedding because of the "proslavery cast" that attended, with Jesse Grant allegedly saying at one point that the Dents were a "tribe of slaveholders." While the Grant family's true motivations are unknown—and the newly married couple *did* visit the Grant family in Bethel, Ohio, shortly after the wedding—one unexamined lens does give credence to the idea that slavery may have played a role in the family's absence at the wedding.[11]

The Dent and Grant families were both devout Methodists who regularly attended church services, but the politics of religion and slavery wreaked havoc on the church during the 1840s. The Methodist minister who officiated the Grant wedding, Reverend John H. Linn, played a small role in these national debates. Born in 1812 in Kentucky, Reverend Linn arrived in St. Louis in 1842 to help oversee the construction of Centenary Methodist Episcopal Church. Four years later, he transferred to the nearby Fourth Street Methodist Episcopal Church, located at Fourth and Washington Streets. This church became the religious home of the Dent family, who could take a short ride north from their city home to attend services during the 1840s. Reverend Linn was part of a group of Methodist ministers from Missouri who had attended a convention of Southern Methodists in Louisville, Kentucky, on May 1, 1845. Angered by the church's stance against slavery and anxious to form their own denomination friendly to the institution, the convention voted to form a breakaway sect, the Methodist Episcopal Church, South. The Missouri delegation originally opposed a split within the church; the state's leaders instead called for compromise and further discussion of the matter. Linn was considered a "liberal" on the issue of slavery with his support for colonization, a topic he had previously spoken on during a state Colonization Society meeting at Centenary Church in 1844. However, the Missouri delegation eventually agreed to join their fellow Southerners in breaking away from the Northern Methodists. Two months after the convention, the Dent family's church on Fourth Street voted to join the Southern Methodists and later accepted Reverend Linn as their leader the following year. The fact that the Grant wedding *was a Southern Methodist wedding* may have been a contributing factor to the Grant family's absence.[12]

10   *PMJDG*, 55-56. For an article that debunks the myth of Longstreet as Grant's Best Man, see Ulysses S. Grant National Historic Site, "Was James Longstreet the 'Best Man' at Ulysses and Julia Grant's Wedding?," National Park Service, 30 January 2020, accessed 15 June 2022, https://www.nps.gov/articles/was-james-longstreet-the-best-man-at-ulysses-and-julia-grant-s-wedding.htm.

11   Waugh, 33-34; Simpson, 64, 67.

12   William Hyde & Howard L. Conard, eds., *Encyclopedia of the History of St. Louis*, 4 vols. (St. Louis: The Southern History Company, 1899), 3:1290-1291, 1462-1463, 1472; J. Thomas Scharf, *History of Saint Louis City and County*, 2 vols. (Philadelphia: Louis H. Everts & Co., 1883), 2:1689-90, 1758.

Another piece of evidence can be found in two letters Grant sent to his father during his time as a St. Louis farmer at White Haven. While Jesse Grant had offered his son $1,000 to help start his farming operation in 1854, Grant struggled to support his family amid poor weather conditions; sickness among the Grants, Dents, and enslaved people at White Haven; and a weak economy. On December 28, 1856, Grant optimistically wrote to his father that "Ev[e]ry day I like farming better and I do not doubt but that money is to be made at it," going on to say that he had a vision for growing a wide range of fruit and vegetable crops for the 1857 planting season. To make this plan succeed, however, he needed more money from his father. "If I had an opportunity of get[t]ing about $500 00 for a year at 10 pr. cent [interest] I have no doubt but it would be of great advantage to me," wrote Grant. He then concluded the letter on a sad note. "[I] saw registered 'J.R. Grant, Ky.' on [a St. Louis hotel's] book [three weeks ago]. Making enquiry I found that J.R.G. had just [taken] the Pacific R. R. cars. I made [sure] it was you and that I should find you when I got home. Was it you?" The troubling thought of his father traveling to St. Louis and not seeing his son while in town undoubtedly pained Grant. Adding to the pain, the evidence suggests that Jesse Grant did not bother to respond to this letter, much less give Grant any money.[13]

Grant made a second appeal a month and a half later on February 7, 1857. "For two years I have been compelled to farm without either [tills or seeds], confining my attention therefore principally to oats and corn: two crops which can never pay . . ." he complained. "I want to vary the crop a little and also to have implements to cultivate with. To this end I am going to make the last appeal to you." While he recognized that his plans for farming had not yet worked out, Grant argued,

> It is always usual for parents to give their children assistance in beginning life (and I am only begin[n]ing, though thirty five years of age, nearly) and what I ask is not much. I do not ask you to give me anything. But what I do ask is that you lend, or borrow for, me Five hundred dollars, for two years, with interest at 10 pr. cent payable an[n]ually, or [semi-annually] if you choose, and with this if I do not go on prosperously I shall ask no more of you.

If the money wasn't forthcoming, Grant predicted that "without means, it is useless for me to go on farming, and I will have to do what Mr. Dent has given me permission to do; sell the [White Haven] farm and invest elsewhere." Once again, neither a response letter nor funds were forthcoming.[14] Amid continued

13   USG to Jesse R. Grant, 28 December 1856, *PUSG*, 1:334-35.

14   USG to Jesse Root Grant, 7 February 1857, ibid., 1:336-37.

Ulysses S. Grant used this desk to pen letters while living in St. Louis, including two painful letters asking his father for money. The desk was displayed at the 1904 World's Fair in St. Louis and is today housed in the Missouri Historical Society's collection.

Missouri Historical Society

struggles for his entire family, Grant ended his farming venture in the fall of 1858, and in the spring of 1860, the family left St. Louis for good and moved to Galena, Illinois. Grant accepted a job as a clerk for his father's leather goods store there, but the indignity of not being financially independent of his father as he approached his forties must have caused him stress and frustration.

Julia Dent Grant also bluntly stated in her memoirs that she struggled to maintain a good relationship with her husband's family. During their time in St. Louis, loose talk had emerged about the idea of the Grant family moving to Covington, Kentucky, rather than Galena. "I was bitterly opposed to this arrangement," Julia recalled, "and felt no chagrin when, through the interference of Captain Grant's sisters, the plan was not carried out." Expanding on her thoughts, she confessed that "the Captain's family, with the exception of his mother [Hannah Grant], did not like me." (Of Hannah Grant, Julia remarked that "she was the most self-sacrificing, the sweetest, kindest woman I ever met, except my own dear mother.") Julia was quick to suggest the conflict may have been her fault by too easily showing her feelings in conversations with the family, but she also remarked that "I always respected them and could have been fond of them, but we were brought up in different schools. They considered me unpardonably extravagant, and I considered them inexcusably the other way."[15]

Revealing letters from the war show that even General Grant got fed up with the way his family treated his wife. Even though their previous plans to move to Kentucky fell through, Grant did keep open the idea of his family moving there so the children could be closer to their grandparents and, if the opportunity arose, to see their father for a quick visit here and there. "It would be very pleasant living in

Covington," Grant remarked to Julia in a wishful tone, "but your prejudice against Clara, and her incorigible persiverance [sic] in practicing her rigid economy upon ev[e]rybody but herself would make it insupportable. I could not live there with her in peace," he admitted.[16] While Julia's original letters on the subject no longer exist, it appears that her husband was concerned about potential conflicts with his father and sisters, particularly with regard to his oldest sister Clara. The meaning of Grant's comments in the absence of his wife's original correspondence is somewhat ambiguous, but perhaps Clara's "rigid economy" referred to a condescending tone towards Julia or the possibility that she would try to discipline the children without Julia's advice or permission.

Julia and the four children nevertheless tried to live in Covington from February through June 1862. The plan failed miserably. As with earlier correspondence, Julia's specific complaints are unknown, but General Grant quickly received an earful and directed his wife to find an alternative living arrangement as soon as possible. "I see plainly from your letter that it will be impossible for you to stay in Covington," he acceded. As Grant had previously predicted, the root of the problem seems to have emerged from Grant's sisters Clara and Virginia (who went by Jennie), and possibly even Mary (who was fourteen years younger than Julia). "Such [unmitigated] meanness as is shown by the girls makes me ashamed of them," Grant remarked. "I am sorry you cannot stay in Covington pleasantly for it is such a good place for the children. But it is too mortifying to me to hear of my sisters complaining about the amount paid for the board of their brother['] s children. . . . You had better leave at one for some place. Tell them I direct it and the reason why."[17]

A few insights follow about the pressure Ulysses and Julia Grant faced from their families throughout their marriage. For one, it is clear that the marriage faced challenges from both directions of their family unit, not simply from the Dent family. Given the choice to work with his father or move in with the Dents after resigning from the army in 1854, Grant seems to have been very determined to be free of his father's influence and found Colonel Dent's offer to farm eighty acres of White Haven land a better path towards finding independence. When facing potential financial ruin during this time, Jesse Grant apparently chose to ignore his son's pleas for help. While Grant did continue to correspond with his father for the remainder of his life, there seems to be a coldness to this correspondence. While letters to Julia during the Civil War ask her to provide updates on how her father

16   USG to Julia Dent Grant, 29 September 1861, *PUSG*, 2:327-28. Julia did have kind things to say about Clara, at one point calling her "pleasant and kind," suggesting that their falling out may have taken place over time. See *PMJDG*, 57, 59.

17   USG to Julia Dent Grant, 23 March 1862, *PUSG*, 4:412-13.

was doing and to "remember me" to him, few inquiries about his own parents and siblings emerge in his letters during the war. The twinkle in Grant's eyes that sometimes emerged in conversations with his father-in-law is harder to find with his own parents, whom he rarely talked about publicly (although Grant did say that his mother "was the best woman he had ever known").[18] To a certain degree, Grant may have actually felt a closer relationship with his father-in-law than with his father, even if they did have genuine political differences. Grant's comfort at White Haven during his early visits in 1843 could be attributed, in part, to the intimacy and warmness he felt from the Dents as opposed to his own parents while growing up in Ohio. Finally, we can also see that while historians have stressed the challenges Ulysses S. Grant faced in transitioning to life with the Dent family, Julia Dent Grant had a more difficult time transitioning to life with the Grant family. After her short-lived experiment living with the Grants in 1862, she spent the rest of the war shuffling between White Haven (where she visited her father seven times during the war), her husband's headquarters, and, later in the war, her new family home in Burlington, New Jersey, never to return to Covington.[19]

The strength of Ulysses and Julia Grant's marriage was tested in many different ways throughout their thirty-seven years together, including frequent separations due to Ulysses's military service, the pressure of public scrutiny as Grant rose to fame, and financial struggles for much of their early relationship and marriage. The pressure applied by two families, both of whom were opinionated and anxious to assert their control over the Grants and their children, presented a consistent challenge within their marriage. That Ulysses and Julia Grant were able to withstand these outside pressures is a testament to their love and enduring commitment to each other, no matter how difficult the situation may have been for them.

18   Ben Kemp, "Like Mother, Like Son," Ulysses S. Grant Cottage National Historic Landmark, 11 May 2019, accessed 15 June 2022, https://www.grantcottage.org/blog/2019/5/11/like-mother-like-son.

19   For a chronology of Julia Dent Grant's movements during the American Civil War, see Ulysses S. Grant National Historic Site, "Julia Dent Grant Chronology," National Park Service, 7 January 2021, accessed 15 June 2022, https://www.nps.gov/articles/000/julia-dent-grant-chronology.htm.

Ulysses S. Grant and the Art of War
Chapter Four | *Timothy B. Smith*

Ulysses S. Grant took time out of his morning work on May 11, 1864, to write a quick synopsis of the fighting around Spotsylvania Court House, Virginia. His dispatch, headed 8:30 a.m. that day, spoke volumes not only about his current situation, but also about him as a general and his philosophy of war. "We have now ended the sixth day of very heavy fighting," he informed the Union's chief of staff in Washington, Maj. Gen. Henry W. Halleck. The casualties he described showed his humanity: "We have lost to this time 11 general officers killed, wounded, and missing, and probably 20,000 men." Sending back the wagons betrayed his worry over logistics: "I am now sending back to Belle Plain all my wagons for a fresh supply of provisions and ammunition." His desire for reinforcements revealed the need for a shot of morale for those who had been fighting those six long days: "The arrival of re-enforcements here will be very encouraging to the men, and I hope they will be sent as fast as possible." But no line in the short message gave more insight into Grant's theory of warfare than his declaration that amidst all the continuous fighting, massive casualties, and dwindling supplies, he was not giving up and would fight the enemy as long as it took: "I . . . propose to fight it out on this line if it takes all summer."[1]

Taking the fight to the enemy reflected many aspects of Grant's current situation, including the time of year, enemy position, and the political and military expectations surrounding him.

It also illustrated his own theory of war, one that emphasized continually fighting the enemy in search of a decisive victory that would end the conflict. Grant was going after Robert E. Lee's Army of Northern Virginia, knowing that if the Confederate army in the East ceased to exist, the rebellion would likewise. On the other hand Richmond, or other important points, could conceivably be taken

---

1   USG to Henry W. Halleck, 11 May 1864, *The War of the Rebellion: A Compilation of the Official Records of the Union and Confederate Armies*, 128 vols. (Washington, D.C.: U.S. Government Printing Office, 1880–1901), Series 1, Vol. 36, Part 1, 4, hereafter cited as *OR*.

This portrait of Grant comes from artist Thure de Thulstrup's 1885 lithograph titled *Grant from West Point to Appomattox*, which also included nine highlights from Grant's military career.

Library of Congress

yet the war could continue. The enemy army was the key.[2]

But where did Grant get this approach to warfare? Was it his training, or did he receive orders from higher-ups? Was it the result of failure, or was it common sense? Many military theorists of the day expounded on how to best fight a war, but the Civil War generation's examples mainly came from the previous major wars that had occurred long enough prior to enable them to be studied in depth: the Napoleonic Wars. The Crimean War was much too fresh, and despite the fact that the United States military had observers in Crimea in the 1850s, including George B. McClellan, the lessons of that war had not been properly distilled as yet in the early 1860s. Napoleon was thus the primary model both for Civil War commanders and the American military theorists who taught them in antebellum times.[3]

There were certainly many influential military theorists of the day, such as M. A. Thiers, Paul Thiébault, Carl von Decker, Henry Humphrey Evans Lloyd, and Adam Heinrich Dietrich von Bülow. Each took part in a growing and fascinating rivalry of European military theoretics, mostly based on the Napoleonic Wars. Yet, in terms of boiling down future theory, and certainly Civil War theory, there were two authorities of the day who were the most famous, Antoine-Henri Jomini and Carl von Clausewitz. While they agreed on much, these two nevertheless delineated an opposing art of war. While Grant admittedly knew little of either Jomini or Clausewitz, his training at the United States's top military school

2   Paul L. Schmelzer, "A Strong Mind: A Clausewitzian Biography of U.S. Grant" (Ph.D. diss: Texas Christian University, 2010), accessed 29 May 2022, https://repository.tcu.edu/bitstream/handle/116099117/4273/Schmelzer.pdf?sequence=1&isAllowed=y.

3   Carol Reardon, *With a Sword in One Hand & Jomini in the Other: The Problem of Military Thought in the Civil War North* (Chapel Hill, NC: University of North Carolina Press, 2012), 12.

certainly influenced him, although it was not the deciding factor in developing Grant's own theory of war.[4]

Swiss-born Jomini viewed the Napoleonic Wars from the French side, observing Napoleon and his art of war through the ups and downs of the early nineteenth century. Over the years, he wrote extensively on war, ultimately producing his iconic work in 1838, *The Art of War*. In that magnum opus, Jomini laid out a plan of warfare that was full of finesse, planning, and maneuver, which he hoped would yield the same results of victory without the bloodshed of huge battles that marked the Napoleonic years. Jomini described a perfect advance as being one with secure and guarded supply and communication lines, preferably with supporting columns that utilized interior lines of communication. These forces, Jomini argued, should advance on specific "decisive points" that were the objective. Rather than assaulting an enemy army defending these decisive points, a commander should instead turn the position, threatening the geographical point's own lines of communication and supply with his own army. Thus, by outflanking a position with maneuver, the place could be taken much less bloodily than with an outright frontal assault.[5]

The other major viewpoint came about in a collection of Clausewitz's writings together entitled *On War*, published originally in 1832, shortly after his death. Clausewitz emphasized a political/military mindset, arguing that everything done on the battlefield or in a war had political overtones, whether large or small. Accordingly, it was not enough to simply take geographic points. Rather, to win a real victory, the enemy's army itself had to be defeated, and Clausewitz, in detailing several choices of action, emphasized the need for an annihilating victory over the enemy army that likely encapsulated the whole of the enemy itself. If the army defending a geographic point fell, then that point would likewise fall.[6]

These two competing theories of war were certainly a known commodity by the time of the American Civil War, although not widely known in the United States. Jomini's French treatise was only published in English in 1854, but few future Civil War generals read it, Grant himself admitting that "I have never read it carefully." Clausewitz's German opus was not translated into English until 1873 and even later in America. But their influence was felt through back channels,

---

4   Reardon, 3, 9, 21.

5   Baron de Jomini, *Summary of the Art of War, or, A New Analytical Compend of the Principal Combinations of Strategy, of Grand Tactics and of Military Policy* (New York: G.P. Putnam & Co., 1854), 47, 61, 63, 69, 72, 78-82, 89, 93, 127, 131, 171, 181.

6   Carl Von Clausewitz, *On War* (London: N. Trübner and Co., 1873), 102, 271, 306, 414, 554, 585, 637, 640, 720. All references herein are to Carl Von Clausewitz, *On War*, Michael Howard & Peter Paret, eds. (New York: Knopf, 1993).

such as the West Point cadre of teachers who had, at a minimum, read Jomini and included it in their teaching of the European theories of war. Sylvanus Thayer and Dennis Hart Mahan taught the French model at West Point, and even America's early theorist, Henry W. Halleck, largely based his *Elements of Military Art and Science* (1846) on Jomini. One historian has noted Halleck's "slavish dedication to Jomini's ideas" even while he did not understand them fully. Historian Russell Weigley wrote that "Jomini, not Clausewitz, became the principal interpreter of Napoleonic strategy to Americans. . . . Jomini's interpretation of Napoleon became the foundation of the teaching of strategy at West Point." Others asserted that "West Point followed the French example. . . . Thayer sought to transplant French professional standards to the banks of the Hudson, using Mahan as his conveyor." Obviously, more Jomini than Clausewitz filtered down to the future Civil War commanders. Grant himself admitted of the fall of 1862: "Up to this time it had been regarded as an axiom in war that large bodies of troops must operate from a base of supplies which they always covered and guarded in all forward movements."[7]

Not only do Jomini and Clausewitz provide a stark dichotomy of the two prevailing schools of war-fighting theory during the Civil War, they also provide the stark difference between Grant (and a few other generals) and the vast majority of those conducting the Civil War. While there were numerous high-level commanders—generals such as Henry W. Halleck, George B. McClellan, and Joseph E. Johnston, among many more—who espoused, not surprisingly, Jominian theory, there were only a noted few who seemingly came to the opposite conclusions and increasingly fought the war based on more Clausewitzian principles. The Union's commander in chief himself, Abraham Lincoln, seemed to embrace the Clausewitzian ideals of neutralizing the enemy's fighting force rather than just taking cities. Robert E. Lee, in many ways, sought the decisive, annihilating victory, although often at the expense of reducing his own army much more than the enemy's. But Ulysses S. Grant espoused Clausewitzian

---

7   Donald Stoker, *The Grand Design: Strategy and the U.S. Civil War* (New York: Oxford University Press, 2010), 258, 412; John H. Brinton, *Personal Memoirs of John H. Brinton, Major and Surgeon U.S.V., 1861–1865* (New York: The Neale Publishing Company, 1914), 239; John F. Marszalek, *Commander of All Lincoln's Armies: A Life of General Henry W. Halleck* (Cambridge, MA: The Belknap Press of Harvard University Press, 2004), 43-46; Russell F. Weigley, *The American Way of War: A History of United States Military Strategy and Policy* (Bloomington, IN: Indiana University Press, 1973), 82-84; Allan R. Millett, Peter Maslowski, & William B. Feis, *For the Common Defense: A Military History of the United States from 1607 to 2012* (New York: Free Press, 2012), 119; Gene Allen Smith, David Coffey, & Kyle Longley, *In Harm's Way: A History of the American Military Experience* (New York: Oxford University Press, 2020), 208; Ulysses S. Grant, *The Personal Memoirs of Ulysses S. Grant: The Complete Annotated Edition*, John F. Marszalek with David F. Nolen & Louie P. Gallo, eds. (Cambridge, MA: The Belknap Press of Harvard University Press, 2017), 292, hereafter cited as *PMUSG-Annotated.*

principles far more readily than any other commander during the Civil War, and he was victorious.[8]

While numerous examples can be given, Grant proved how Clausewitzian principles dominated in at least four distinct areas. First, Grant firmly understood Clausewitz's theories on limited and absolute warfare, and he more and more implemented, following the political lead Clausewitz so emphasized, the absolute version as the war progressed. Yet early in the war, Grant embodied the restricted view of limited war aims. That was certainly what he had studied and viewed as a younger officer, particularly in Mexico under the tutelage of Winfield Scott. The American army had advanced only so far at a time into Mexico, hoping to bring the Mexicans to the negotiating table. Such tactics never worked, and Scott wound up taking Mexico City itself, which was a Jominian "decisive point." Certainly, there were also limited war advocates among major commanders early in the Civil War, including George B. McClellan.[9]

Despite claims in his memoirs that, after Shiloh, "I gave up all idea of saving the Union except by complete conquest," Grant actually did not reach that conclusion until later in the summer of 1862. Then, he realized that the war would need to be ratcheted up in terms of effect and harshness in order to succeed in reaching the full political goals of the United States to preserve the Union and eradicate slavery. Clausewitz's most famous statement, of course, was "war is merely the continuation of policy by other means." He also stated, in regard to the amount of effort put forth ultimately toward a total effort in a total war, that "in war too small an effort can result not just in failure but in positive harm." Grant's change in view during the Civil War encompassed everything from dealing with civilians to taking or damaging infrastructure, and most especially the contraband issue. Grant began even in the summer of 1862 to put former slaves to work and, throughout the fall, implemented contraband camps to employ escaped slaves rather than send them back to their owners. Soon, former slaves began to work for the Union war effort as well as fight in the Federal ranks.[10]

Second, concerning defensive operations, Clausewitz detailed how a commander retreating on the defensive should reel in the enemy, allowing them to overextend themselves to what Clausewitz described as the "culminating

8   Stoker, 79, 218.

9   Stoker, 90-92; Timothy D. Johnson, *A Gallant Little Army: The Mexico City Campaign* (Lawrence: University Press of Kansas, 2007).

10   Brooks D. Simpson, *Ulysses S. Grant: Triumph Over Adversity, 1822–1865* (Boston: Houghton Mifflin Company, 2000), 140, 145; USG to Henry W. Halleck, 3 July 1862, John Y. Simon, ed., *The Papers of Ulysses S. Grant*, 32 vols. (Carbondale, IL: Southern Illinois University Press, 1967–2012), 5:191, 191n-94n, 199; *PMUSG-Annotated*, 251; Clausewitz, 99, 707, 728-30, 738-40.

point." That was the point at which the aggressor became overextended, unable to sufficiently defend his rear lines of communication or supply lines, and the army up front—out of effective resupply range and diminished by garrisons left behind—was at its weakest. Clausewitz argued that the withdrawing defender was meanwhile growing stronger all the time and, at the "culminating point," should unleash a counterattack that would drive the enemy back and win the victory—a "flashing sword of vengeance." Clausewitz argued that this counterstroke was very much a part of the defense itself, "a tendency inherent in defense," and he stated further, "Every method of defense leads to a method of attack." Such a scenario took place in 1812 with Napoleon's advance into Russia, and more recently in the Peninsula Campaign in 1862 when George B. McClellan overextended himself and Robert E. Lee, utilizing Clausewitzian thought, hit McClellan hard in the Seven Days battles and drove him back.[11]

Grant employed these Clausewitzian defensive ideals on numerous occasions, mainly on the tactical level, as he rarely was on the defensive on the operational or strategic levels. But at Fort Donelson, Shiloh, Champion Hill, Chattanooga, and elsewhere in the Overland Campaign in Virginia, Grant was pushed back tactically only to unleash, once the enemy reached its point of overextension and exhaustion, a massive counterattack that in most cases won the battle. This is in direct opposition to more Jominian generals such as Don Carlos Buell, George B. McClellan, or William S. Rosecrans who, when they had the enemy tactically or at times even operationally overextended—such as at Corinth, Stones River, Perryville, or Antietam—did not follow up with the punishing counterattack and instead let the enemy slip away relatively intact.[12]

Grant also took care to guard against this being done to him when he was on the offensive on the operational level of war. Early in the conflict, he neared the culminating point in the expedition up the Cumberland River in February 1862, up the Tennessee River in April 1862, in the Mississippi Central campaign in December 1862, and in his inland campaign in Mississippi in May 1863. In the first two examples, the Confederates met him near his "culminating point," but he managed to parry their counterstroke. Significantly, along the Mississippi Central, there was no counterstroke but rather Jominian types of raids in the rear along Grant's lines of supply. When John C. Pemberton did stumble into something of a counterstroke at Champion Hill, Grant was able to parry that as well. But Grant was learning all the while, making sure in the operations around Chattanooga

11   Clausewitz, 443, 453, 633, 639, 684-93; Michael Howard, *Clausewitz: A Very Short Introduction* (New York: Oxford University Press, 2002), 57-58.

12   Howard, 57-58.

Lt. Gen. Ulysses S. Grant, Lt. Col. Theodore Bowers, and Brig. Gen. John Rawlins at Grant's headquarters, Cold Harbor, June 1864—a month into "fighting it out on this line if it takes all summer."

Library of Congress

and in Virginia that he never reached that "culminating point" that could successfully be used by the Confederate commander, who in Virginia was a like-minded Clausewitzian general, Robert E. Lee. Grant, the old quartermaster who understood logistics well, never gave Lee the chance to hit him at a "culminating point."[13]

Third, although on the defensive at times early in the war, for the most part tactically, Grant spent much more time on the offensive, both on the operational and tactical level. And he was in search of the annihilating victory that Clausewitz described in his writings as the best option. In developing his theory of a "center of gravity" (a far cry from Jomini's "decisive points" and most often the enemy's army itself), Clausewitz argued that "the defeat and destruction of his fighting

13   Clausewitz, 639.

force remains the best way to begin." Later, he added, "The fighting forces must be *destroyed*" and "the destruction of enemy forces must be regarded as the main objective." How to destroy the enemy's army was debatable. Clausewitz thought little of Jomini's maneuvering, stating, "Flanking operations . . . have always been more popular in books than in the field" and termed them "overrated" and "minor investments that can only yield minor dividends."[14]

Rather than merely aiming for geographical points and taking those methodically in a step-by-step formulated process of gaining territory and consolidating that gain—much as Halleck did at Corinth, thereby letting slip through his fingers a golden opportunity to speed up the war with a summer 1862 advance on Vicksburg—Grant continually sought to find and fight the enemy army. Clausewitz historian Michael Howard surmised that Clausewitz "laid down two principles of which his predecessors had lost sight. Military manœuvre was pointless unless it was designed to culminate in battle; and battle was pointless unless it was designed to serve the ultimate purpose of the war." Grant understood that taking geographic points was good, but defeating the enemy army was an even better, and quicker, path toward achieving the ultimate goal of winning the war. Accordingly, even in going after important places like Forts Henry and Donelson, Corinth, or Vicksburg, he always fought the opposing army to win the place. And in Virginia in 1864, Grant's primary target was Lee's army, not necessarily Richmond—although, as back in the West early in the war, the two objectives were often combined since the Confederates normally defended their cherished places with their cherished armies. Still, Grant's orders to George G. Meade, commanding the Army of the Potomac, were: "Lee's army will be your objective point. Wherever Lee goes, there you will go also." He also related to Meade that William T. Sherman in Georgia "will move at the same time you do, or two or three days in advance, Joe Johnston's army being his objective point." To Sherman himself, Grant wrote, "You I propose to move against Johnston's army, to break it up." He added likewise that the armies in Virginia will "operate directly against Lee's army wherever it may be found." In the end, significantly, the vast difference made by Grant was not so much in the capture of places that quickly became backwater areas of the war, but in the defeat and capture of the armies that defended them—most notably at the three great annihilating victories at Fort Donelson, Vicksburg, and Appomattox. In each, Grant obliterated the enemy army, and the places—and eventually the morale of the Confederacy and the government, as well—fell accordingly.[15]

14   Ibid., 102, 271, 306, 414, 554, 585, 637, 640, 720; Stoker, 8, 262.

15   USG to George G. Meade, 9 April 1864, *OR*, Series 1, 33:827-28; USG to William T. Sherman, 4 April 1864, ibid., Series 1, 32:3:246; Howard, 16.

Lastly, although still tied to the offensive, Grant certainly embodied Clausewitz's theories on momentum and continuing the fight until the political objective is achieved. Clausewitz dwelled at length on the positive attributes of momentum, writing that "frequent exertions of the army to the utmost limits of its strength" was one of the best ways to build spirit and morale and that "feeding the troops, though important, is a secondary matter" when it came to momentum. He also noted the dangers in pushing too far (the "culminating point"), outstripping supply lines, and overtaxing the health and morale of the army. But maintaining momentum was key for Clausewitz. And a significant means of doing so was the pursuit, with the "highest degree of pursuit" occurring when it was done with an entire army. Finally, Clausewitz asserted that the key to momentum and pursuit was speed: "[A]ct with the utmost speed. No halt or detour must be permitted without good cause."[16]

Implementing Clausewitz's view that "any kind of interruption, pause, or suspension of activity is inconsistent with the nature of offensive war," increasingly, Grant took the fight to the enemy offensively and, once he started, did not let up. Such actions as Grant's Vicksburg campaign, especially the overland portion from May 1 to 18 when he reached Vicksburg, were a lesson in Clausewitz's momentum argument. To a lesser degree, his efforts at Chattanooga were continuous and swift until the enemy army retreated to very defensible positions in north Georgia. But Grant's Overland Campaign in Virginia was certainly the height of momentum, with heavy and continuous fighting as he and Lee swept southward. Grant gave Lee little chance to turn the tide on him, to take advantage of any culminating point, because Grant did not reach any such point. Grant kept the pressure on continuously, and Lee's army dwindled as a result. In terms of pursuit, he had to learn his lessons as well—for instance, losing a golden opportunity to pursue after Shiloh when the enemy army was in shambles. But he learned his lesson well, and his pursuits became much more effective over the course of the war.[17]

Like only a few others during the Civil War, Grant was increasingly more Clausewitzian than Jominian. In essence, he began the war like the rest, in firm Jominian outlook, but over time gradually reached a new level of understanding more in line with Clausewitz's conception of "military genius," complete with the two fundamental ingredients, courage and determination. But how did Grant reach these conclusions? It was not at West Point. Grant asserted, "Every officer, from the highest to the lowest, was educated in his profession, not at West Point necessarily, but in the camp, in garrison, and many of them in Indian wars." He

---

16   Clausewitz, 221, 253-57, 312-21, 405, 725, 746.

17   Ibid., 312-21, 725.

admitted that at the military academy, "I did not take hold of my studies with avidity, in fact I rarely ever read over a lesson the second time during my entire cadetship." He added that he read more novels "than . . . books relating to the course of studies," but was careful to note they were "not those of a trashy sort." Furthermore, few of Clausewitz's principles had been taught at West Point, and accordingly, few Civil War commanders had his mentality.[18]

Rather, Grant, like Lee and Lincoln and only a handful of others, came to the same conclusions that Clausewitz had, and in the same manner: through experience and common sense. Grant noted that in the field, "[a] military education was acquired which no other school could have given." Although somewhat based on experience in the Napoleonic Wars, Clausewitz's theories depend on little else beyond common sense. And Grant, Lee, and a few others seem to have been able to likewise discern the dominant dynamics for winning the Civil War. Significantly, this was at a time when Clausewitz's theories were not well known, and certainly Clausewitz's name was not attached to them. In fact, much as Barbara Mandrell was "country when country wasn't cool," Grant was Clausewitzian when Clausewitz was not cool. Jomini stole the show and received what little limelight there was, but Clausewitz, as demonstrated by his later-generation soulmate Ulysses S. Grant, knew the winning formula for success in the American Civil War.[19]

---

18   Ibid., 115-31; *PMUSG-Annotated*, 21, 115; John F. Marszalek, ed., *The Best Writings of Ulysses S. Grant* (Carbondale, IL: Southern Illinois University Press, 2015), 3-4.

19   Clausewitz, 831; *PMUSG-Annotated*, 395.

Moments of Contingency and the Rise of Grant

Chapter Five | *Chris Mackowski*

We park in a small lot just off Plank Road. A narrow, rubberized path leads us through a strip of brush that hides the worn remains of a line of earthworks—one of three lines that the Federal II Corps built to protect this approach in May 1864. Here, Plank Road intersects with Brock Road, and the penultimate Confederate assault of the battle of the Wilderness came to a head. Along the Brock Road, the most visible of the three lines of works parallels the road, close enough that the grass-covered works are easily mistakable for a roadside embankment. A thin dusting of powder-blue forget-me-nots frosts the grass.

With me are Curt Fields and Thomas Jessee.[1] As living historians, they portray Ulysses S. Grant and Robert E. Lee, respectively, although they are off-duty today. Thomas once visited the Wilderness as a young boy, long before he ever knew he'd grow up to "be" Lee. Curt has never been here. To come here together, where their counterparts first clashed, proves powerful for both of them.

"This is it, right here," Curt says as we walk into a small roadside clearing on the southwest corner of the crossroads. "This is where Grant turns south." Thomas nods along.

Here in the Virginia Wilderness, their real-life counterparts met for their opening engagement on May 5. It was here at this intersection that Grant, on the night of May 7, steered his horse southward along the Brock Road. Unable to successfully get at Lee, Grant chose instead to just go around. It was first contact in a grapple that would continue for eleven months.

I help Curt and Thomas get their bearings. Confederates attacked from the west along the Plank Road. Grant, when he came to the intersection the next evening, rode in along the Brock Road from the north.

Cars coming from all four directions must stop at the intersection. Taking turns, they pass through in a steady pulse, one by one, mostly oblivious to the

---

1   With a tip of the hat, too, to Bill Miller of the Williamsburg Civil War Roundtable, who hosted Curt and Thomas and brought them up to the Wilderness to meet me on 14 April 2022.

"Grant" and "Lee" meet in the Wilderness: Curt Fields and Thomas Jessee at the Brock Road/Plank Road intersection.

Chris Mackowski

history that once took place here. Someone in a pickup truck, seeing a small group of people talking, plays true to stereotype and lays on the horn as he passes. "The High Water Mark at Pickett's Charge doesn't have to deal with that," I say.

History buffs love to talk "turning points." When asked, I always point to this place, to that evening of May 7 when Grant opted to continue southward.[2] Up to that point in the war, the armies would clash and then disengage, and they might take a couple weeks or even a couple months to resupply, reequip, and reinforce. Grant did not want Confederates to have that opportunity. He possessed a numerical advantage—in this campaign alone he started with 120,000 men compared to Lee's 66,000, and that's without factoring in all the other men in all the other armies in all the other theaters under Grant's overall command. Grant intended to use that advantage. With the election of 1864 coming in the fall, Grant needed to land a knock-out blow if possible; if not, attrition would work.[3]

Grant's move out of the Wilderness put that strategic vision into practice. "[T]here will be no turning back," he told a reporter when Federal forces crossed the Rapidan River on May 4.[4] Similarly, on May 11, he vowed in a message to Washington that he would "fight it out on this line if it takes all summer."[5] As my colleague, historian Ryan Longfellow, has explained, "Grant ended the cycle of attack and withdraw that had characterized the Army of the Potomac's efforts in Virginia."[6] In its place, the death grapple—the use of his overwhelming advantage in men, materiel, infrastructure,

2   The idea that Gettysburg was the turning point of the war is balderdash. Effective P.R. aimed at turning Gettysburg into a tourist destination is responsible for that well-loved myth.

3   For more on the strategic overview in the spring of 1864, see Chris Mackowski, *Hell Itself: The Battle of the Wilderness, May 5–7, 1864* (El Dorado Hills, CA: Savas Beatie, 2016).

4   Louis M. Starr, *Bohemian Brigade: Civil War Newsmen in Action* (New York: Alfred A. Knopf, 1954), 299.

5   USG to Henry W. Halleck, 11 May 1864, *The War of the Rebellion: A Compilation of the Official Records of the Union and Confederate Armies*, 128 vols. (Washington, D.C.: U.S. Government Printing Office, 1880–1901), Vol. 36, Part 1, 4, hereafter cited as *OR* (Series 1 unless otherwise noted).

6   Ryan Longfellow, "'Oh I am Heartily Tired of Hearing What Lee is Going to Do': Ulysses S. Grant in the Wilderness," *Turning Points of the American Civil War*, in Chris Mackowski & Kristopher D. White, eds. (Carbondale, IL: Southern Illinois University Press, 2018), 176-77.

and money to grab hold of the Confederates and not let go until he had worn them down—began.

For that reason, I've always believed that if there's "a" turning point of the war, it's here. As Ryan says, "Grant's decision to advance in the aftermath of the battle marked the Wilderness as the beginning of the end for the Army of Northern Virginia."[7] As I'm fond of telling people when I give battlefield tours of the Wilderness, "What begins here leads inexorably to the parlor of Wilmer McLean at Appomattox Court House eleven months later."

But as Curt and Thomas and I contemplate the import of the intersection, Curt contextualizes the moment a little differently. He places the Wilderness on a continuum with the November 1861 battle of Belmont and the February 1862 battle at Fort Donelson. "There are a number of other crucial moments for Grant, but I think these are the most significant for him and what he ultimately accomplished," Curt says.

Curt's observation reminds me of a story shared by Gordon Rhea, the dean of Overland Campaign scholars. Speaking at a symposium about turning points of the Civil War, Gordon honed in on Grant's decision to move south on May 7. "That showed he [Grant] was different than all the other generals," Gordon explained. "He was thinking in terms of campaigns. If he gets stymied, he immediately maneuvers in a positive way, and he doesn't simply retreat."

Sitting next to Rhea was Ed Bearss, former chief historian for the National Park Service. "He took a different position," Gordon recounted. "He said, 'Gordon, that's interesting, but I believe the turning point of the American Civil War was the battle of Belmont.'—the battle of Belmont was Grant's first battle—'It didn't really amount to much, but it began his climb up the chain of command and, ultimately, he became the chief commander."

"Well," Gordon replied, "that's an interesting idea. But if we follow your chain of logic, we'd have to say the real turning point of the American Civil War was when Grant's dad got a gleam in his eye."

The audience laughed as Gordon delivered his punchline, and he shrugged and smiled. "And so the debate goes on," he added.[8]

---

7   Ibid., 161.

8   Gordon shared this anecdote on 6 August 2022 at Emerging Civil War's 8th Annual Emerging Civil War Symposium at Stevenson Ridge, Spotsylvania, VA. The theme of the symposium was "The Great What Ifs of the Civil War," and Rhea was speaking on "The What Ifs of the Overland Campaign." The Symposium was part of a larger programming effort by ECW that included content on its blog, www.emergingcivilwar.com, and YouTube page, as well as the publication of a hardcover essay collection, *The Great "What Ifs" of the American Civil War* (Savas Beatie, 2022). The interpretive approach behind these counterfactual discussions was to look at what didn't happen as a way to better understand and appreciate what did. This larger framework has helped shaped my thinking for this essay.

Indeed, other historians have pointed at other moments in Grant's career as "the" turning point. Author Jack Hurst, for instance, sees Grant's victory at Fort Donelson as "the Campaign that Decided the Civil War." "[O]nce he got going— at Fort Donelson—Ulysses Grant was never beaten," Hurst points out.[9] My colleague Dan Davis, meanwhile, has identified Vicksburg as the crucial turning point. "[T]he city would fall, unlocking the door for Grant's final, meteoric rise. Vicksburg would alter the trajectory of his military life, which in turn would alter the complexion of the war itself," Dan argued. "While Vicksburg was not the apex of Grant's career, the Vicksburg Campaign firmly set the course for his ascension to the command of all Federal armies—the ultimate turning point for the Northern war effort."[10] Another colleague, Dave Powell, gives prominence to Grant's victory at Chattanooga. "Chattanooga made Grant in a way that Vicksburg's triumph had not," Dave says. "Within slightly more than a month of being given authority over the entire Western Theater, Grant erased the defeat of Chickamauga, saved the Army of the Cumberland, and routed [Braxton] Bragg."[11]

Our desire to hone in on a climactic moment for Grant springs from our very human tendency to creative narratives for ourselves that help us make sense of the world. One such narrative we Civil War historians talk about is something we call the "Rise of Grant," tracing Grant from a down-on-his-luck army washout to the most successful—and powerful—Union general of the war. From there, his rise transcends his military career and goes all the way to the White House. We talk about this "Rise of Grant" as a discrete *thing*, like "John Brown's Raid" or "the Gettysburg Campaign" or "the Emancipation Proclamation."

But Grant's rise was a discrete thing only in retrospect, tied together into an incredibly compelling narrative arc through the convenience of hindsight. We highlight key moments of that arc as though we are holders of special insights who can reveal lost secrets.

Yet within each moment, as each event in the larger sequence unfolded, Grant's rise seemed anything but inevitable (or inexorable, my own characterization as such notwithstanding). In fact, Grant spent a fair amount of time spinning his wheels, waiting, wondering, hoping. At least twice, it required events beyond his control to re-

---

9   Jack Hurst, *Men of Fire: Grant, Forrest, and the Campaign that Decided the Civil War* (New York: Basic Books, 2007), 379.

10   Daniel T. Davis, "Vicksburg: The Victory that Unleashed Ulysses S. Grant," in Chris Mackowski & Kristopher D. White, eds., *Turning Points of the American Civil War*, (Carbondale, IL: Southern Illinois University Press, 2018), 137, 152.

11   David A. Powell, *All Hell Can't Stop Them: The Battles for Chattanooga: Missionary Ridge and Ringgold, November 24–27, 1863* (El Dorado Hills, CA: Savas Beatie, 2018), 107.

jump-start his story. Victories were hardscrabble and ugly, and at times, Grant caught lucky breaks that saved him from disaster.

Curt's "three crucial moments" and Gordon's lighthearted "gleam in the eye" speak to a more constructive way of looking at Grant's military career. As my longtime collaborator Kris White and I have argued in *Turning Points of the American Civil War*, the war "unfolded as a continuum of events with several major turning points, one leading to the next leading to the next. . . . [T]he ripples from one 'turn' carry forward and create circumstances that lead to the next."[12] James M. McPherson, author of the Pulitzer Prize-winning *Battle Cry of Freedom*, has emphasized the "element of contingency" in those moments. "There were several major turning points, points of contingency when events moved in one direction but could well have moved in another," he says. "If they had done so, the course of the war might have been quite different."[13]

The Rise of Grant unfolded much the same way. There was never any smooth, inevitable upward arc. Nothing happened to unleash an unstoppable, meteoric rise. At best, one moment opened the path to the next—but that "next" moment always had complications and contingencies of its own. What we see today is that the Rise of Grant was, in reality, a series of "moments of contingency," where things in each moment might have easily gone another way.

*   *   *

Grant's November 1861 victory at Belmont, Missouri—if we can call it that—hardly triggered an ascension all the way to commander in chief, at least as Ed Bearss had apparently characterized it. I think historian Steven Woodworth articulated it rather more accurately: "Grant's day at Belmont was the first day's work in a very long task."[14] It was Grant's first step in the climb—and a bold first step at that.

I am reminded, of all things, of a quote by Scottish mountaineer William Hutchinson Murray, who thought he was quoting German writer Johann Wolfgang von Goethe: "Whatever you can do, or dream you can, begin it. Boldness has genius,

---

12   Mackowski & White, 4.

13   James M. McPherson, "Why Did the Confederacy Lose," *Drawn with the Sword: Reflections on the American Civil War* (New York: Oxford University Press, 1996), 134. "[W]e must turn from large generalizations that imply inevitability and study instead the contingency that hung over each military campaign, each battle, each election, each decision during the war," McPherson concludes (ibid., 136).

14   Steven E. Woodworth, *Nothing But Victory: The Army of the Tennessee, 1861–1865* (New York: Knopf, 2005), 58.

Grant, photographed in October 1861, dressed in flashier fashion than he would later in the war. As his trajectory rose, he would opt for plainer uniforms.

Library of Congress

power, and magic in it."[15] Belmont was Grant's beginning, and it demonstrated the genius, power, and I daresay magic that all resulted from the boldness that would become a defining Grant characteristic.

Grant's beginning in Belmont had a beginning of its own. Nathaniel Hughes, Jr., the first modern scholar of the battle, points out that Grant was in command in the first place not out of any genius or extraordinary skill but because of "minor displays of competence and energy" that made him stand out compared to his peers in the earliest days of the war. The Rise of Grant started somewhere in those small acts that got him noticed.[16]

When Confederates broke Kentucky's neutrality in September 1861, Grant looked for an opportunity to respond. Finally, on November 7, he led a 3,100-man force south from Cairo, Illinois, on an attack against a small Confederate outpost in Belmont, Missouri, across the river from a larger camp in Columbus, Kentucky. After a fight of about five and a half hours, Confederates fled across the river to Columbus. "At this point," Grant said, his men "became demoralized from their victory and failed to reap its full reward."[17] Exuberant at their first-ever victory, they began to pillage the abandoned camp, which Grant then torched. The distraction gave Confederates the chance to reinforce and counterattack, supported by heavy artillery from the Kentucky side of the river. "I announced that we had cut our way in and could cut our way out just as well," Grant later recalled, and

15   W. H Murray, *The Scottish Himalayan Expedition* (London: J.M. Dent & Sons Ltd., 1951), 7. For more on the misattribution, see Hyde Flippo, "A Well Known Quote Attributed to Goethe May Not Be Actually His," 24 June 2019, Thought Co.com, accessed 27 August 2022, https://www.thoughtco.com/goethe-quote-may-not-be-his-4070881. The quote and its variations has become ubiquitous.

16   Nathaniel Cheairs Hughes, Jr., *The Battle of Belmont: Grant Strikes South* (Chapel Hill, NC: The University of North Carolina Press, 1991), 3.

17   Ulysses S. Grant, *Personal Memoirs of U.S. Grant*, 2 vols. (New York: Charles L. Webster & Co., 1885–1886), 1:274, hereafter cited as *PMUSG*.

he proceeded to lead his men to the riverbank where transports awaited to carry the men to safety.[18]

If there was any magic, it came from the disappearance of 27th Illinois during the Federal escape. Grant was nearly left behind when he went to look for them, and he was nearly captured, too. He made it back to his transport just in time, and the missing regiment reappeared a little while later, marching up the west bank of the river in the direction of safety. The transports pulled over to take them on. At one point, Grant's boat came under fire and he got up from a couch he was resting on to watch the action. In doing so, he unknowingly evaded death: upon his return, he saw the couch had been hit by an enemy shell during the firefight.

Both sides claimed victory at Belmont. Confederates drove Federals off the battlefield—a criterion that would become a generally accepted definition of victory throughout the war—but Grant looked at Belmont as an important strategic, rather than tactical, achievement. "The two objects for which the battle of Belmont was fought were fully accomplished," he wrote in his memoirs. "The enemy gave up all idea of detaching troops from Columbus. His losses were very heavy for that period of the war."[19] Of the 5,000 Confederates engaged, they lost 641 killed, wounded, or missing, compared to Grant's 607.[20]

The northern public did not initially share Grant's interpretation of events, but as months passed, opinion swung in Grant's favor. It helped that his second-in-command, the relentlessly self-promoting political general John McClernand, continued to trumpet the battle as a success, which rang well in the ears of McClernand's friend, President Lincoln. Grant's prime political patron, Congressman Elihu Washburne, who also had Lincoln's ear, harmonized that same tune.[21]

Belmont gave Grant his first taste of independent command. It established him as an officer of bold action with an eye beyond tactics toward strategy. It gave his men their first taste of victory. And it gave President Lincoln a first—and positive—impression of Grant. "The discovery of an audacious general who would go looking for a fight downriver delighted Lincoln," observes Hughes in his study of the battle.[22]

18   Ibid., 1:274-77.

19   Ibid., 1:280.

20   "Belmont," American Battlefield Trust, accessed 27 August 2022, https://www. battlefields.org/learn/civil-war/battles/belmont.

21   Woodworth, 59, 60.

22   Hughes, 205.

Belmont was a near thing as it was, but Hughes identifies no fewer than thirteen major factors that could have gone even more wrong than already had. In the end, Hughes assesses, Grant "made mistakes and took risks and got away with it."[23] Had Grant's expeditionary force been wiped out or Grant himself captured or killed, none of these things would have happened, and the Rise of Grant would have been stillborn.

*   *   *

Grant's bold beginning at Belmont would have likewise led to nothing had he stumbled at his next major assignment, the capture of Forts Henry and Donelson in February 1862. The bold beginning also gives lie to author Jack Hurst's characterization of Grant as a "Union general whose tottering career was saved and transformed forever by this campaign."[24]

Grant initiated the plan that led to the fall of Fort Henry, although he had little to do with the fort's actual surrender. Flooded out, the garrison surrendered on February 6 to the Federal navy before Grant even arrived. Grant then turned his army east and marched twelve miles to force the capitulation of Henry's sister fort, Donelson. The navy proved less helpful there, blasted into inertness by Donelson's powerful river batteries.

Grant had tried to encourage the fleet to run the batteries and outflank the position. The naval commander, Flag Officer Andrew H. Foote had demurred, fearing the sort of bombardment he ended up suffering anyway. One of Grant's staff officers, William Hillyer, later identified this as an overlooked moment of contingency. "Now, had Foote had done this," he posited, "the rebels would have evacuated Fort Donelson, and the battle and capture there which made Grant historic would have never happened."[25]

Instead, Grant continued his operations without naval support. Between February 11–14, he squeezed the fort, finally forcing Confederates to attempt a break-out on February 15. Punching a hole in the Federal right flank, Confederates nearly succeeded in their escape. Grant wasn't on the scene when the Confederate attack began, but his timely arrival proved pivotal—one of those "three most significant moments of Grant's career" Curt Fields identified. "Grant ordered generals John McClernand and Lew Wallace to re-take the ground they lost during

23   Ibid., 205, 206.

24   Hurst, 2.

25   Edward Chauncey Marshall, *The Ancestry of General Grant, and Their Contemporaries* (New York: Sheldon & Company, 1869), 80.

The counterattack at Fort Donelson would secure victory for Grant—and a headline-grabbing nickname that would help ensure a place for "Unconditional Surrender" Grant in the public imagination.

Library of Congress

the Confederate break-out attempt," Curt said. "Then he told Gen. Charles Francis Smith to take the fort, which he promptly did."[26]

Confederate leadership slunk away in the night, forcing third-in-command Brig. Gen. Simon Bolivar Buckner to negotiate a surrender with his old prewar-army friend Grant. "No terms except an unconditional and immediate surrender can be accepted," Grant replied, in part. "I propose to move immediately upon your works."[27] The response made Grant a national celebrity and gave him a nickname to match his initials—"Unconditional Surrender" Grant—and his capture of 15,000 men again impressed Lincoln favorably. Grant earned promotion to major general.

However, this was not yet Lincoln's great moment of epiphany with Grant even though the president now clearly saw him as a valuable tool. By that point, Grant's success had earned him jealous ire, not praise, from his immediate commander, Maj. Gen. Henry Halleck, who seemed to lavish credit for the victory on everyone but Grant.[28] Halleck had also begun to secretly conspire with the army's general in chief, Maj. Gen. George McClellan, for Grant's removal. "Do not hesitate to arrest him at once if the good of the service requires it," McClellan authorized.[29] Halleck begged off his persecution, for the moment, when Lincoln ordered him to produce evidence for charges or else release Grant from administrative limbo.[30]

---

26   From our 14 April 2022, visit to the Wilderness.

27   USG to Simon B. Buckner, 16 February 1862, John Y. Simon, ed., *The Papers of Ulysses S. Grant*, 32 vols. (Carbondale, IL: Southern Illinois University Press, 1967–2012), 4:218, hereafter cited as *PUSG*.

28   *PMUSG*, 1:316-17.

29   George B. McClellan to Henry W. Halleck, 3 March 1862, *OR*, 7:680. See also Henry W. Halleck to George B. McClellan, 3 March and 4 March 1862, ibid., 7:679-80, 682-83.

30   Lorenzo Thomas to Henry W. Halleck, 10 March 1862, ibid., 7:683.

Round two of that conflict would come soon enough, but as it was, the Donelson victory earned Grant just enough presidential protection to clear the way for the "Rise of Grant" to continue its upward arc. Had Confederates successfully broken free of Donelson, had Grant not returned to the battlefield in time, had Grant's counterattacks not been carried out effectively, had Nashville not fallen, had Lincoln not intervened—any or all of these contingencies might have ended Grant's career on the banks of the Cumberland River.

*   *   *

Grant's success at Fort Donelson had a number of important ramifications: the capture of Nashville, the first Confederate state capital to fall; the collapse of the Confederate defensive line across Tennessee; and the opening of the Cumberland and Tennessee Rivers as routes of invasion deeper into the Confederate West. One of the most overlooked consequences of Grant's Donelson victory, though, is that it allowed him to survive the post-battle controversies of Shiloh.

The April 6–7, 1862, battle at Pittsburg Landing nearly ended in disaster for Grant's forces, which were caught completely off guard by an early morning assault on April 6. Grant was—once again—not on the scene when Confederates attacked. To his dying day, Grant denied he was surprised at Shiloh, but all evidence on the ground suggests otherwise. It took reinforcements from Maj. Gen. Lew Wallace's late-arriving division and from Maj. Gen. Don Carlos Buell's Army of the Ohio on the night of April 6 to turn a first-day rout into a second-day victory. "Lick 'em tomorrow" Grant had calmly vowed to his friend and subordinate, William T. Sherman, on the rainy night of the sixth, and on seventh, he fulfilled his own prediction.[31]

Shiloh's carnage was unlike anything America had ever known before: 13,047 Federals killed, wounded, and missing, and 10,669 Confederates. "The South never smiled again after Shiloh," one Confederate said. Another called the loss "the turning point of our fate."[32] Historian Larry J. Daniel recognized it as such, too, characterizing Shiloh as "The Battle that Changed the Civil War."[33]

Had Grant lost the battle, the duplicitous Halleck would surely have booted him; as the titular winner, though, Grant had the protection offered by victory,

---

31   Interview with Sherman in the *Washington Post*, quoted in the *Army and Navy Journal* for 30 December 1893, subsequently quoted in Bruce Catton, *Grant Moves South* (New York: Little Brown and Company, 1960), 242.

32   Novelist George Washington Cable quoted in Editors' introduction to "Shiloh" in Mackowski & White, 53; Jefferson Davis quoted in Stacy D. Allen, *Shiloh* (Columbus: Blue and Gray Enterprises, 2010), 39.

33   Larry J. Daniel, *Shiloh: The Battle that Changed the Civil War* (New York: Simon & Schuster, 1997).

even if the victory was widely seen as a disaster. Only because he also had the cleaner and more sensational victory at Donelson to his credit could Grant and his supporters credibly make the argument that Shiloh, although an ugly win, was still a win—and the latest in a string. "[T]hanks in great part to renown he already had achieved at Fort Donelson, Grant survived," author Jack Hurst has correctly contended.[34]

Grant's victory hinged on any number of contingencies: What if Confederates had attacked on April 5 as their commander, Albert Sidney Johnston, had originally planned? What if Johnston's battle plan had unfolded the way he had intended (it was instead bungled by his second in command, Gen. P.G.T. Beauregard)? What if Johnston had not been mortally wounded on the first day? What if Beauregard, taking over, had pressed a final attack at the end of the first day instead of prematurely wiring to Richmond that he had "gained a complete victory, driving the enemy from every position."[35]

"[C]ritics claim that Shiloh was won when Johnston fell, and that if he had not fallen the army under me would have been annihilated or captured," Grant scoffed in his memoirs. "*Ifs* defeated the Confederates at Shiloh. There is little doubt that we would have been disgracefully beaten *if* all the shells and bullets fired by us had passed harmlessly over the enemy and *if* all of theirs had taken effect."[36] Indeed, the "What ifs" of Shiloh sit at the center of Lost Cause wishful thinking in the Western theater. Timothy B. Smith, one of the foremost modern experts on Shiloh, dismisses them all. "[T]he most likely outcome for all is that none of the what-ifs would have made much difference," he writes. "Shiloh, a gamble as described by Albert Sidney Johnston himself, was from the beginning an extremely long shot for the Confederates, even if everything had gone perfectly for them." [37] But those What Ifs are central, too, to the Rise of Grant, for any one of them might have derailed Grant's ascension.

As it was, Shiloh nearly derailed Grant anyway.

*   *   *

Jealous of the success Grant was accumulating, Henry Halleck showed up at Pittsburg Landing on April 11 to take field command of the Army of the Tennessee

---

34   Hurst, 384.

35   P.G.T. Beauregard to Samuel Cooper, 6 April 1862, *OR*, 10:1:384.

36   *PMUSG*, 1:363.

37   Timothy B. Smith, "'Persistently Misunderstood': The What Ifs of Shiloh," in Chris Mackowski & Brian Matthew Jordan, eds., *The Great "What Ifs" of the American Civil War: Historians Tackle the Conflict's Most Intriguing Possibilities* (El Dorado Hills, CA: Savas Beatie, 2022), 17.

himself. He then took seven weeks to creep forward twenty-three miles in pursuit of the defeated Confederates, finally flushing them out of Corinth, Mississippi, on May 29. Throughout this time, historian Larry J. Daniel points out, "Grant was virtually ignored. . . ."[38] Halleck shuttled Grant into irrelevancy by promoting him to second-in-command of the department. The business of the army thus flowed around him, not through him. "Orders were sent direct to the right wing or reserve, ignoring me, and advances were made from one line of intrenchments to another without notifying me," Grant later explained. "My position was so embarrassing in fact that I made several applications during the siege to be relieved."[39]

Halleck, for his part, played coy. "I am very much surprised, general, that you should find any cause of complaint in the recent assignment of commands," he wrote.

> You have precisely the position to which your rank entitles you. . . .
> You certainly will not suspect me of any intention to injure your feelings
> or reputation or to do you any injustice. For the last three months, I
> have done everything in my power to ward off the attacks which were
> made upon you. If you believe me your friend you will not require
> explanations; if not, explanations on my part would be of little avail.[40]

Sherman counseled patience, optimistically predicting "some happy accident might restore him [Grant] to favor and his true place."[41]

That accident happened some 750 miles to the east, on May 31, 1862, outside the gates of Richmond. During the battle of Seven Pines, Confederate commander Joseph E. Johnston suffered a pair of wounds that knocked him out of action. His replacement, Robert E. Lee, regrouped the army and fortified the capital, and then in late June launched the bruising series of attacks that became known as the Seven Days battles, reversing all the spring successes of the Army of the Potomac and forcing its commander, George McClellan, into retreat. In March, at the beginning of the campaign, McClellan had been removed as the Federal Army's general in chief, and Lincoln had been trying to cover the post ad hoc ever since; events during and after the Seven Days reminded Lincoln how overwhelmed he really was, and he sought out a new general in chief. On July 23, Lincoln

---

38   Daniel, 309.

39   Ibid.; *PMUSG,* 1:377. Ironically, in the spring of 1864, Grant traveled with the Army of the Potomac, whose commander, Maj. Gen. George Gordon Meade, ended up feeling much the same way under Grant that Grant had felt under Halleck in the spring of 1862.

40   Henry W. Halleck to USG, 12 May 1862, *OR,* 10:2:182-83.

41   William T. Sherman, *Memoirs of General William T. Sherman,* 2 vols. (New York: D. Appleton and Company, 1875), 1:255.

summoned Halleck east to fill the role, leaving Grant, as second-in-command, in charge of the department.

This "happy accident" was completely beyond Grant's control—a moment of contingency in the Rise of Grant that was, itself, a moment of contingency in its own, other string of contingencies. Nonetheless, Halleck's departure cleared the way for Grant's rise to continue.[42]

*   *   *

For the rest of 1862 and into 1863, Grant's "rise" occurred on a flatter curve than most people realize. Halleck stripped troops from Grant and transferred them to Buell's army. Nonetheless, Grant oversaw fall victories at Iuka and Corinth. He also became entangled in various controversies with fellow Federal officers William S. Rosecrans and John McClernand—minor squabbles that nonetheless simmered into long-standing grudges—and issued a controversial December order to expel Jews from his department. In today's world, such an order would certainly spell the end of the Rise of Grant; instead, Lincoln immediately rescinded the order, Grant apologized, and he spent the rest of his life disavowing and trying to atone for it. "I have no prejudice against sect or race, but want each individual to be judged by his own merit," he wrote in 1868 to former Jewish Congressman Isaac N. Morris. "[General] Order[s] No. 11 does not sustain this statement, I admit, but then I do not sustain that order."[43]

Most importantly, Grant began his campaign to capture Vicksburg, Mississippi. Lincoln saw Vicksburg as "the key" and as such placed tremendous strategic value on it. "The war can never be brought to a close until that key is in our pocket," the president said.[44] Grant encountered setback after setback, but Lincoln's patience sustained him. On April 1, though, Halleck wrote to Grant that "the President . . . seems to be rather impatient about matters on the Mississippi," although Lincoln himself conveyed no such thing to Grant directly.[45] Whether a legitimate warning or more Halleck machinations, Grant sensed that time was running out. On April 29–30, 1863, he crossed his army to the east bank of the Mississippi

42   Historians frequently identify the battle of the Wilderness as the first meeting between Grant and Lee, but as this episode illustrates, their fates in fact became entwined beginning in the early summer of '62.

43   USG to Isaac N. Morris, 14 September 1868, *PUSG*, 19:37. See also Ulysses S. Grant National Historic Site, "Ulysses S. Grant and General Orders No. 11," National Park Service, accessed 22 September 2022, https://www.nps.gov/articles/000/ulysses-s-grant-and-general-orders-no-11.htm.

44   David Dixon Porter, *Incidents and Anecdotes of the Civil War* (New York: D. Appleton and Company, 1885), 95-96.

45   Henry W. Halleck to USG, 2 April 1863, *OR*, 24:1:25.

The statue of Grant at Vicksburg, designed by sculptor F.C. Hibbard and dedicated in 1918, reflects Grant's firmness of purpose in the campaign.

Chris Mackowski

River, struck out into the interior of the state, won a string of victories, captured the state capital, and eventually besieged Vicksburg. The so-called "Gibraltar of the West" fell on July 4, 1863.

On July 5, before Lincoln received the news of Vicksburg's fall, he affirmed his support for his general there. "[I]f Grant only does this thing down there—I don't care much how, so long as he does it right—why, Grant is my man and I am his the rest of the war!" the president promised.[46]

Lincoln would stay true to his word—but only after a puzzling two months passed. During that span, talk circulated in Washington about placing the victorious Grant at the head of the Army of the Potomac, which had won a victory at Gettysburg, Pennsylvania, but which had then been unable to follow it up. "There is . . . much dissatisfaction with the present state of things," Assistant Secretary of War Charles Dana confided to Grant.[47] Grant did not want the job, claiming "it would cause me more sadness than satisfaction to be ordered to the command . . . ." He predicted that "dissatisfaction would necessarily be produced by importing a General to command an Army already well supplied with those who have grown up, and been promoted, with it."[48] Nothing became of this speculation anyway.

Instead, Grant tried plotting a move against Mobile, Alabama, which he was "very anxious to take" and which he thought he could do "with comparative ease."[49] Halleck would have none of it, preferring to squander the momentum of the Vicksburg triumph rather than allow Grant the chance at another victory. Halleck began to detail portions of Grant's army away on various assignments, effectively dismantling it. "The General-in-chief having decided against me," Grant wrote, "the depletion of an army, which had won a succession of great victories, commenced."[50]

46   Brooks D. Simpson, *Ulysses S. Grant: Triumph Over Adversity, 1822–1865* (Boston: Houghton Mifflin Company, 2000), 215.

47   Charles A. Dana to USG, 18 August 1863, *PUSG*, 9:148*n*.

48   USG to Charles A. Dana, 5 August 1863, ibid., 9:145-46.

49   For the full exchange between Grant and Dana, including the text of the August 5 letter from Grant to Dana and the August 18 reply from Dana to Grant, see ibid., 9:145-47, 147*n*-48*n*.

50   *PMUSG*, 1:579.

Adding injury to insult, a horseback riding accident in New Orleans debilitated Grant for weeks.[51]

Lincoln, apparently preoccupied by other events, seems to have forgotten "his man" during this time period. I can envision Lincoln doing a proverbial double-take, suddenly wondering in mid-September why his star general was so quiet. He found Grant languishing with no army and no mission. That changed on October 16 when orders from the War Department elevated Grant to command of the entire Western theater. Lincoln's direct attention, plucking Grant out from beneath Halleck's jealous thumb, allowed Grant's rise to continue.

"By that time, Grant had honed his strategic skills and vision to such an extent that he was ready for the wider stage and, for him and for the nation, a new way of waging war," Dan Davis says.[52] That wider stage came in Chattanooga. Following its September loss at Chickamauga, a supply-strapped Army of the Cumberland had become bottled up in the city. "The administration as well as the General-in-chief was nearly frantic at the situation of affairs there," Grant wrote in his memoirs.[53] In late October, Grant lifted the semi-siege, and by late November, he scored victories that drove the Confederates into north Georgia for the winter.

But it wasn't necessarily Grant's own plans that led to Federal victory. Aggressive action by Maj. Gen. Joseph Hooker captured Lookout Mountain on November 24. The next day, a demonstration by Maj. Gen. George Thomas's Army of the Cumberland escalated into an impromptu sweep up the face of Missionary Ridge. Grant had instead intended Sherman to strike the ridge from the north and roll the Confederate line southward, but stubborn Confederate resistance prevented Sherman from doing much of anything. Grant nonetheless adapted to the circumstances—he won, after all, even if not at all in a manner he had envisioned.

Grant was rightfully proud of Chattanooga, even choosing to write about it for *Century Magazine* in 1884 instead of writing about Appomattox. Imagine the potential for disaster in that swirl of unexpected events, particularly if a less-elastic mind had been at the helm.

*   *   *

In the closing month of 1863, Abraham Lincoln began to make discreet inquiries about Grant. Did he, by chance, have his eye on higher office? After all,

---

51   Grant, by all accounts an outstanding horseman, had suffered a horseback riding accident prior to Shiloh, too. We tend to look at contingencies on the battlefield, but imagine if either of those horseback riding accidents had ended more severely.

52   Davis, 151.

53   *PMUSG*, 1:583.

voters loved a military hero, and Grant had certainly achieved an impressive string of victories. Might Grant be a contender for the presidential nomination in 1864? Lincoln had plans for Grant, but he did not want to elevate a potential political rival to a position that would then allow him to oust Lincoln for the Republican nomination. "I already have a pretty big job on my hands, and my only ambition is to see this rebellion suppressed," Grant told an intermediary, unaware of Lincoln's queries. "Nothing would induce me to think of being a presidential candidate, particularly so long as there is a possibility of having Mr. Lincoln re-elected."[54] Lincoln had expressed devotion to Grant as "his man" until the end of the war, and here Grant now reciprocated.

Reassured, Lincoln nominated Grant for promotion to lieutenant general, a position he assumed on March 9. The following day, he took over the job of general in chief of the United States Army. Lincoln had, by then, discovered just how ineffectual Henry Halleck was, privately describing him as "little more . . . than a first-rate clerk."[55] Secretary of the Navy Gideon Welles was more damning: "Halleck originates nothing, anticipates nothing . . . takes no responsibility, plans nothing, suggests nothing, is good for nothing."[56] Grant's new position made him Halleck's boss.[57]

Belmont, Forts Henry and Donelson, and Vicksburg each gave Grant the chance to coordinate ever-more-intricate army/navy partnerships. This, in turn, gave him the opportunity to expand his range of strategic thinking. Vicksburg expanded that further because of the sheer number of men he ended up commanding— more than 77,000 by campaign's end. Chattanooga widened his strategic thinking still more by giving him occasion to coordinate multiple armies. He applied this lesson to his grand strategy in March 1864. Knowing "[t]he resources of the enemy and his numerical strength were far inferior to ours," Grant determined

> first, to use the greatest number of troops practicable against the armed
> force of the enemy, preventing him from using the same force at
> different seasons against first one and then another of our armies, and

54   USG to J. Russell Jones, *PUSG*, 9:543. See ibid., 9:541, 542*n*-44*n* for the full exchange and related correspondence. See also John C. Waugh, *Reelecting Lincoln: The Battle for the 1864 Presidency* (New York: Crown Publishers, 1997), 122-25.

55   Michael Burlingame & John R. Turner Ettlinger, eds., *Inside Lincoln's White House: The Complete Civil War Diary of John Hay* (Carbondale, IL: Southern Illinois University Press, 1999), 191-92.

56   Gideon Welles, *The Diary of Gideon Welles*, 3 vols. (Boston: Houghton Mifflin Company, 1911), 1:384.

57   Hindsight allows us to see the delicious irony of this, but at the time, Grant still did not realize the extent of Halleck's machinations against him. Only when Adam Badeau began researching his three-volume *Military History of Ulysses S. Grant* did Halleck's paper trail surface. Adam Badeau, *Military History of Ulysses S. Grant*, 3 vols. (New York: D. Appleton and Company, 1868–1881), 1:65.

the possibility of repose for refitting and producing necessary supplies for carrying on resistance; second, to hammer continuously against the armed forces of the enemy and his resources, until by mere attrition, if in no other way, there should be nothing left to him. . . .[58]

Grant implemented this strategy all across the map, ordering Sherman—his anointed replacement in the Western theater—to move toward Atlanta, Nathaniel Banks to move on Shreveport with an eventual eye on Mobile, Franz Sigel to move up the Shenandoah Valley, Benjamin Butler to move on Richmond from the south, and George Gordon Meade to move on Richmond from the north. Grant accompanied Meade's army. It was a sweeping plan in its scope.

Grant's ascension to general in chief might really be the turning point of the war because Grant finally had the authority to implement a bold, deeply considered strategic vision—*except* that Grant's plans remained just that: plans. How would they hold up when they came into contact with the enemy? Only the crucible of battle could determine if Grant had the spine to execute the plan and stay committed to it— and not just with the Army of the Potomac under his direct gaze but also with other commanders of other armies far afield.

His old friend on the other side, Confederate Lt. Gen. James Longstreet, surely thought Grant would show the necessary staying power. "[T]hat man will fight us every day and every hour till the end of this war," Longstreet warned prophetically.[59] The battle of the Wilderness opened a six-week slugfest that went to Spotsylvania Court House, the North Anna River, Totopotomoy Creek, Cold Harbor, and across the James River to Petersburg. "We must destroy this army of Grant's before he gets to the James River," Robert E. Lee had warned along the way. "[I]f he gets there, it will become a siege, and then it will be a mere question of time."[60] Lee, too, proved prophetic. Unable to score his hoped-for knock out outside Petersburg, Grant settled in for a nine-month siege. The collapse of the Confederate line on April 2, 1865, sent both armies scrambling in a race that ended in Appomattox.

As "inexorable" as I always say the road to Appomattox was, plenty of moments of contingency cropped up along the way. We could do an entire essay on the "What Ifs" of the Overland Campaign alone. However, by far, the most important moment of contingency during that entire span occurred entirely beyond Grant's direct control: Lincoln's re-election in the fall of 1864. Grant derived his authority to prosecute the war from Lincoln. Had Lincoln lost the election, Grant would

---

58   General Report of USG, 22 July 1865, *OR*, 34:1:8:9.

59   Horace Porter, *Campaigning with Grant* (New York: The Century Co., 1897), 47.

60   Jubal Anderson Early, *The Campaigns of Gen. Robert E. Lee: An Address Before Washington and Lee University, January 19th, 1872* (Baltimore: John Murphy. & Co., 1872), 37.

Grant's decision to turn south in the Wilderness took
the war in a new direction.

Library of Congress

have had a hard deadline of March 4, 1865, to wrap up the war before the inauguration of a new president who would likely implement a new war policy.

Grant understood the stakes clearly. "I consider it as important for the cause that he should be elected as that the army should be successful in the field," he told a friend.[61] Those two factors were inextricably linked: Lincoln's fate rested almost entirely on events on the battlefield, and by the late summer of 1864, political and military prospects looked equally bleak: Lee had locked Grant in stalemate around Richmond; Sherman became bogged down outside of Atlanta; Jubal Early had driven Federal forces out of Virginia's Shenandoah Valley; and Mobile Bay had fallen but the city remained untouched. In a private note written August 23, Lincoln admitted, "it seems exceedingly probable that this Administration will not be elected."[62]

Ten days later, on September 2, Atlanta fell to Sherman, and Lincoln's fortunes began to shift. On September 19, Phil Sheridan's forces won at Third Winchester, beginning the process of driving Confederates from the Valley. Grant remained stymied, however, and so he had no direct role in affecting the military situation that Lincoln's (and, by extension, his own) fate rested on—except that it had been Grant's strategic vision that had put the necessary pieces in place and sustained them. His confidence in his overall plan allowed it to win out over time, even if he wasn't poised to strike a blow himself.

Lincoln's re-election, in turn, gave Grant the time he needed to continue on "until by mere attrition" there was nothing left of the enemy.

*   *   *

Belmont gave Grant his bold start. Donelson gave him the caché to survive Shiloh. Vicksburg developed his strategic thinking, and Chattanooga broadened it further. Promotion to lieutenant general gave him the authority to execute his

61   Waugh, 268.

62   Abraham Lincoln, Memorandum on Probable Failure of Re-election, 23 August 1864, Abraham Lincoln Papers, Series 3, General Correspondence, 1837–1897, Library of Congress.

vision. Laid out as such, the Rise of Grant looks a clear set of stepping stones, with each step along the way giving him the skills he needed to take the next step. "I think I should have failed in this position if I had come to it in the beginning, because I should not have had confidence enough," Grant later admitted.[63]

Indeed, "Grant developed wonderfully in the war," attested William Hillyer as the general prepared to make the shift from military to civilian command in 1868. However, Grant's steps were not always smooth, many obstacles confounded his progress, and he often needed outside help to keep on track. He also "attempt[ed] frequently to supersede his own good luck," according to Hillyer, which almost seemed to invite disaster.[64] Moments of contingency constantly threatened Grant's rise, and any one of them might have curdled against him.

Appreciating the contingencies Grant navigated helps us better appreciate just how remarkable his rise turned out to be and underscores the impressiveness of what he ultimately achieved. Those many moments of contingency could have unraveled, yet time and again they did not.

"The Grant who came to Virginia in 1864 had traveled a long, rocky road and survived," historian Michael Ballard observed.[65] That road eventually brought him to the intersection in the Wilderness where Curt and Thomas and I considered Grant's progress. The road from there to Appomattox would be long and rocky, too, but Grant would continue to survive, onward and upward.

---

63   Marshall, 76.

64   Ibid., 80.

65   Michael B. Ballard, *U.S. Grant: The Making of a General, 1861–1863* (New York: Rowman & Littlefield, 2005), 177.

U.S. Grant and the Surrender at Appomattox

Chapter Six | *Joan Waugh*

"**I** only knew what was in my mind," Ulysses S. Grant said, describing his feelings as he sat down to write out the terms of surrender at Appomattox Court House in Virginia on April 9, 1865.[1] Somehow that sentence makes it sound so simple. It was not. This essay looks at the meaning of the military surrender at Appomattox largely from the perspective of the top Union general, U.S. Grant, but also complicates and contextualizes Grant's famous remark. It briefly reviews the elements of the first two of his surrenders and looks at some of the political concerns that were raised regarding a military final surrender, turning to the story of Appomattox Court House.

Within the epic story of the Civil War, Appomattox attained mythic status as the ultimate symbol of reconciliation and, like many national myths, carries a potent mix of accurate information and exaggeration. Appomattox deserves its mythic status, even if the harsh reality of Reconstruction did not live up to the image of the harmonious reunion bestowed on the surrender. That early day in April was surely the height of Ulysses S. Grant's military career, cementing his reputation as a magnanimous warrior as well as foreshadowing his postwar role, including his two terms as president overseeing Reconstruction policy.

In early February 1862, Union strategy in the Western theater targeted two strategically important and strongly defended Confederate positions. The smaller one, Fort Henry, fell easily. The larger, Fort Donelson on the Tennessee state side of the Cumberland River, was more challenging. Sharp fighting gave the Rebels expectations of winning the battle, but disagreement between the fort's two senior Confederate commanders led them to abandon the scene of carnage and destruction, leaving the lesser-ranked officer, Brig. Gen. Simon Buckner, in charge.

---

1   Ulysses S. Grant, *The Personal Memoirs of U.S. Grant*, 2 vols. (New York: Charles L. Webster & Co., 1885–1886), 2:492, hereafter cited as *PMUSG*. Two recent biographies of Grant are Ronald C. White, *American Ulysses: A Life of Ulysses S. Grant* (New York: Random House, 2016) and Ron Chernow, *Grant* (New York: Penguin Press, 2017). This essay is a revised and shortened version of Joan Waugh, "'I Only Knew What Was in My Mind': Ulysses S. Grant and the Meaning of Appomattox," *The Journal of the Civil War Era* (September 2012), No. 3, 2:307-36. Copyright 2012 by the University of North Carolina Press. Used by permission of the publisher.

The meeting between Lee and Grant in Wilmer McLean's parlor has become the stuff of American legend.

Library of Congress

As Federal forces pressed their advantage, the overwhelmed Buckner sent General Grant a letter asking that the Union commander declare an armistice and hold a conference in which the two men would appoint representatives to discuss terms for Donelson's surrender. The result is famous. Grant's swift and terse reply: "No terms except an unconditional and immediate surrender can be accepted. I propose to move immediately upon your works." The statement electrified the northern public but was condemned by a helpless Buckner as "ungenerous and unchivalrous."[2] Buckner, whom Grant had known before the war, really had no choice but to accept. What made the military surrender at Donelson unconditional? An unconditional surrender is, most obviously, surrender without condition; it means that no guarantees are given to the losing army. When "Unconditional Surrender" Grant refused Buckner's initial request for a meeting to discuss terms, instead proposing "to move immediately upon your works," the surrender became unconditional. Riding to Buckner's headquarters through lines of Confederate soldiers, Grant and his staff dismounted at the Dover Hotel, a two-story wood building situated on the riverfront. There, after some preliminary pleasantries

2   USG to Simon B. Buckner, 16 February 1862, John Y. Simon, ed., *The Papers of Ulysses S. Grant*, 32 vols. (Carbondale, IL: Southern Illinois University Press, 1967–2012), 4:218, 218*n*, hereafter cited as *PUSG*.

shared by the two commanders, Grant got down to business and worked out the details. Notably, he dispensed with any notion of a formal surrender of the Confederate garrison of approximately 15,000 soldiers, the largest surrender in United States history up to that time.[3]

Grant believed that this formal ceremony—which would feature a lowering of the flag and Buckner handing over his ceremonial sword—served no purpose but to humiliate. He explained, "The surrender is now a fact. We have the fort, the men, the guns. Why should we go through vain forms and mortify and injure the spirit of brave men, who, after all, are our own countrymen."[4] Grant's last few words are worth a second look. "Our own countrymen" reflected his belief, shared by the majority of northerners, that southerners were engaged in a "rebellion," not a war between nations. Once the Rebellion ended, the eleven seceded states would be returned to their proper relationship within the United States.

In February of 1862, it was a still limited war that held out the distinct possibility that the two sections could be reconciled with "the Union as it was" (with slavery intact) and with a minimum of bitterness and destruction. Still, the seizure of Fort Donelson held profound consequences for the United States, where the news of the first major military victory for the Union was greeted with rapture. Grant's demand for an "unconditional surrender" meant the removal from the fighting theater of a corps-size number of enemy troops, making him the first great military hero of the Union. In the Western theater, the Rebel line of defense had been demolished: Kentucky and middle Tennessee had been secured for the Union, leading to the fall of Nashville, the state capital, and shortly thereafter, the capture of Memphis and New Orleans. As the Union forces moved to consolidate control of Confederate territory, they disrupted railroad lines, destroyed property, and liberated slaves, offering a preview of the larger devastation that would be in store for the Confederacy.[5]

Fort Donelson raised northern hopes for a quick end to the conflict, but Union setbacks in the Eastern theater, together with the introduction of emancipation in 1863, changed the nature of the war. Those hopes had long since faded by the date of Grant's second surrender agreement, signed at Vicksburg, Mississippi, on July 4, 1863. The Federal goal of securing the length of the Mississippi River was accomplished with U.S. Grant's 1862–63 campaign to take Vicksburg. The heavily fortified "Gibraltar of America" also contained a sizeable Confederate

3   Steven E. Woodworth, *Nothing But Victory: The Army of the Tennessee, 1861–1865* (New York: Alfred A. Knopf, 2005), 119.

4   Jean Edward Smith, *Grant* (New York: Simon & Schuster, 2001), 164.

5   See Timothy B. Smith, *Grant Invades Tennessee: The 1862 Battles for Forts Henry and Donelson* (Lawrence, KS: University Press of Kansas, 2016) for an excellent overview.

army, commanded by Lt. Gen. John C. Pemberton. Undaunted, Grant combined both naval and infantry forces to encircle and capture Vicksburg. After a series of smashing victories, Grant's forces besieged Vicksburg for forty-seven days from late May throughout the month of June. By July 1, Pemberton realized that he must capitulate, and he sent a letter out under a white flag of truce, reaching Grant on the morning of July 3. Like Buckner, General Pemberton requested a meeting to discuss terms. Grant refused, stating, "The useless effusion of blood you propose stopping by this course can be ended at any time you may choose, by an unconditional surrender of the city and garrison." He added, "Men who have shown so much endurance and courage as those now in Vicksburg, will always challenge the respect of an adversary, and I can assure you will be treated with all the respect due to prisoners of war."[6]

Despite his use of "unconditional surrender," Grant agreed to meet Pemberton at 3:00 p.m. that afternoon. Pemberton arrived dressed in full uniform, meeting Grant, in field dress, between the lines of the two armies. Grant repeated his terms of unconditional surrender, leading Pemberton to say angrily, "I can assure you, sir, you will bury many more of your men before you will enter Vicksburg."[7] Their conversation ended in failure, yet it established Grant's willingness to negotiate. Later, after consulting with his corps and division commanders, Grant reframed his surrender to conditional. His letter to Pemberton, delivered that night to Confederate headquarters, offered parole instead of incarceration; a few hours later, Pemberton accepted. The official surrender would take place on the morning of the fourth of July.

Why did Grant change his mind? First, he was reluctant to launch a wasteful assault on the city. Second, as Grant explained, "Had I insisted upon an unconditional surrender there would have been over thirty thousand men to transport to Cairo, very much to the inconvenience of the army on the Mississippi."[8] Instead, the whole Confederate garrison was paroled. This meant that the prisoners would go free if they promised not to re-enter the war until exchanged for Union prisoners. Thus it came to be that the general whose nickname was "Unconditional Surrender" did not insist on surrender without conditions at Vicksburg.

Grant received criticism for his decision. Would these soldiers, some asked, return to take up arms against the United States? Grant dismissed those worries, claiming that many, if not most, prisoners wished to avoid war altogether and that

---

6   USG to John Pemberton, 3 July 1863, *PUSG*, 8:455.

7   John C. Pemberton, "The Terms of Surrender" in Robert Underwood Johnson & Clarence Clough Buel, eds., *Battles and Leaders of the Civil War*, 4 vols. (New York: The Century Co., 1887–1888), 3:544.

8   *PMUSG*, 1:561. A bustling river port, Cairo, Illinois served as a major supply entrepôt and training base for the Union during the Civil War.

their possible escape was "precisely what I expected and hoped that they would do." Although many did return to the battlefield, a sizable number did not. Grant asserted, "I knew many of them were tired of the war and would get home just as soon as they could." He further elaborated the ideas behind his Vicksburg surrender policy: "The men had behaved so well that I did not want to humiliate them. I believed that consideration for their feelings would make them less dangerous foes during the continuance of hostilities, and better citizens after the war was over."[9] At both Fort Donelson and Vicksburg, Grant combined devastating military victories with sensible and even sensitive surrender policy pointing toward reunion of the two warring countries. His actions suggested that winning the peace would be as meaningful as winning the war.

Vicksburg's capture accomplished three important goals. It secured Union control of the Mississippi River, split the Confederacy in half, and delivered a blow to Southern morale. The great Union victories of the summer of 1863—at Gettysburg, Vicksburg, and Tullahoma—bolstered northern hopes for peace, but still, that peace seemed frustratingly distant as emancipation policy and the enrollment of black soldiers into the Union army added to the complications of reunion with the eleven rebellious states.[10]

Acting quickly after Vicksburg and another Grant victory secured in November at Chattanooga, Tennessee, President Lincoln brought the western man to Washington, D.C. On March 9, 1864, the newly appointed Lieutenant General Grant accepted command of all the Union armies. Grant and Lincoln, who had never met until then, would come to enjoy a close relationship. While Lincoln developed skills in military strategy that guided his ultimate national strategy of saving the Union, Grant developed the political skills that complemented his military abilities with the same ultimate goal in mind. By this time, he was the most important soldier-statesman of the conflict, developing a national perspective that anticipated reunion as the goal.

The six-week Overland Campaign pitted Grant and the Army of the Potomac against Confederate General Robert E. Lee, commander of the seemingly invincible Army of Northern Virginia. The two armies waged titanic battles in May and June across the Virginia countryside, only ending when Grant crossed the James River and pinned Lee's army inside Petersburg, the second-largest city in Virginia, just 25 miles south of Richmond. Grant conducted the Petersburg siege while his two principal lieutenants, Major Generals William T. Sherman and Philip H.

9   Ibid., 1:561, 569; USG to Marcus J. Wright, 30 November 1884, *PUSG*, 31:240.

10   Donald L. Miller, *Vicksburg: Grant's Campaign that Broke the Confederacy* (New York: Simon & Schuster, 2019), provides a sweeping assessment of Grant's generalship in the campaign.

Sheridan, took the war respectively to Georgia and Virginia's Shenandoah Valley, conquering territory, defeating Rebel armies, and destroying large swaths of the southern countryside. Their combined victories vindicated Grant's strategic vision and guaranteed Lincoln's re-election on November 8, 1864, bringing the Rebellion to its knees.[11]

As fall passed into winter, victory in early 1865 appeared more and more likely as Grant pressed Rebel forces on all fronts. During this tense period, Grant was alert to possibilities of the war ending through some form of a negotiated peace, bringing him into an even more complicated working relationship with President Lincoln and Secretary of War Edwin Stanton. Lincoln and Stanton worried that a military surrender handled wrongly might somehow usurp the president's political control over the goals and terms of reconstruction and reunion. The president desired a durable peace that *he* would dictate, not General Grant. The bottom line was this: momentous decisions had to be made, and soon, but so much was going to be determined by circumstances. Nevertheless, reconstruction of the former Confederate state governments was going to be determined by political concerns. Lincoln and Stanton made clear to Grant that his job was not to negotiate the conditions of peace. What Grant could do was to negotiate the surrender of Lee's army. Whenever and wherever that surrender was to take place, site unknown, it was going to be the surrender of one army to another. Lincoln said to Grant: "*I will deal with political questions and negotiate for peace. Your job is to fight.*"[12]

By late February 1865, Grant remarked on the many signs of "dissolution" that were appearing, including a wave of Confederate desertions. Doubtless, he was thinking constantly about the possibility of an impending surrender and the terms he would dictate. On March 20, 1865, General Grant invited President Lincoln to visit him at City Point for a few days, and in a meeting with Grant, Sherman, and Admiral David D. Porter aboard the *River Queen,* discussed at length and in some depth what the terms of a military surrender should entail, as well as articulating his own ideas about Reconstruction. Although the details of the meeting remain closed, Sherman's and Porter's later accounts stressed that Lincoln urged generous terms so that "they won't take up arms again."[13] Historians have assumed, quite reasonably, that Lincoln, while expressing his desire for a harmonious reunion, also insisted that two demands be made of the soon-to-be-former Confederates: they

---

11   A cogent overview of Lincoln's military leadership is found in James M. McPherson, *Tried by War: Abraham Lincoln as Commander in Chief* (New York: The Penguin Press, 2008). Still, the classic volume on Grant's Overland Campaign is Bruce Catton, *Grant Takes Command* (Boston: Little, Brown and Company, 1969).

12   Jay Winik, *April 1865: The Month That Saved America* (New York: Harper Collins, 2001), 181.

13   David Herbert Donald, *Lincoln* (New York: Simon & Schuster, 1995), 574.

swear a loyalty oath to the United States, and they accept emancipation. Together, these demands represented an unconditional surrender of the Confederacy to the United States.

The Appomattox Campaign, beginning on April 2, 1865, marked the end of the road for the Confederate nation. The Union's destruction of the Rebels' last supply line quickly resulted in the fall of Petersburg and Richmond. Grant's cavalry and infantry cut off Lee's remaining escape routes. On April 6, a further disaster was inflicted at Sayler's Creek. On the evening of April 7, Grant consulted with his commanders regarding what all agreed was a desperate situation for the Confederates. Grant remarked, "I have a great mind to summon Lee to surrender," sending this note to the Confederate commander: "The result of the last week must convince you of the hopelessness of further resistance on the part of the Army of Northern Va. in this struggle. I feel that it is so and regard it as my duty to shift from myself, the responsibility of any further effusion of blood by asking of you the surrender of . . . the Army of Northern Va."[14]

Lee replied, asking Grant to outline his proposed surrender, and received from the Union general this note on April 8: "I would say that *peace* being my great desire there is but one condition I insist upon, namely: that the men and officers surrendered shall be disqualified for taking up arms again, against the Government of the United States, until properly exchanged." Thinking he could break out and meet up with General Joseph Johnston's army in North Carolina, Lee answered that he was not ready to surrender but suggested a meeting to discuss possible peace negotiations. Grant's response to Lee was that he could not discuss peace but only accept surrender. A little while later, when Lee was advised by his closest aides that his army was completely surrounded, he said, "Then there is nothing left me but to go and see General Grant, and I would rather die a thousand deaths."[15]

A little after 1:30 p.m. on April 9, Grant and his staff rode into the tiny village of Appomattox Court House, where they were directed to a two-story brick house belonging to Wilmer McLean. Grant dismounted his beautiful dark horse "Cincinnati" and climbed the seven steps into the house. In the room to the left waited Robert E. Lee, seated, and his aide, Colonel Charles Marshall. Grant and Lee shook hands, marking the first time they met in the Civil War. Lee returned to his chair next to a pine table with a pedestal base and a square white marble top. Grant drew up a leatherback seat and also sat down, placing his gloves and hat on a nearby wooden trestle table with an oval top and two spool legs on each side.

14   Catton, *Grant Takes Command*, 456; USG to Robert E. Lee, 7 April 1865, *PUSG*, 14:361.

15   USG to Robert E. Lee, 8 April 1865, *PUSG*, 14:367; A.L. Long, *Memoirs of Robert E. Lee: His Military and Personal History* (New York, Philadelphia and Washington: J.M. Stoddart & Company, 1886), 421.

Tom Lovell's 1965 depiction of the surrender at Appomattox has become one of the most iconic.

National Geographic Magazine

He was approximately eight to ten feet from Lee. Outside, thousands of weary soldiers watched and waited for news.[16]

The two commanders engaged in an awkward exchange about their service in the Mexican War, with Lee bringing the conversation up short by asking for the terms of surrender. What would they be, he wondered? Grant responded that the terms were exactly the same as earlier indicated in his letter of April 8: Men and officers who surrendered were to be paroled and could not take up arms again until exchanged properly. The arms and supplies were to be turned over as captured property.[17] This was a military surrender.

Grant observed his counterpart's face during this conversation. "What General Lee's feelings were I do not know," Grant remembered. "As he was a man of much dignity, with an impassible face, it was impossible to say whether he felt inwardly glad that the end had finally come." Lee asked Grant to write out the terms of the surrender. Grant agreed and waited while his military secretary, Lieutenant Colonel Ely Parker, brought over a small table and his manifold order book, a tablet prepared with carbon paper for three copies. Puffing on a cigar, Grant prepared to write. "When I put my pen to the paper," he recalled of this moment, "I did not know the first word that I should make use of in writing the terms. I only knew what was in my mind, and I wished to express it clearly, so that there could be no mistaking it."[18]

And there was no mistaking "it." Acutely aware of Lincoln's desire for leniency—which was his desire, too—Grant rejected any fancy words for a straightforward, simple explanation of the process by which the officers and men of the Army of Northern Virginia would stack their arms and record their paroles. "As I wrote on," Grant explained, "the thought occurred to me that the officers had their own private horses and effects, which were important to them, but of no value to us;

---

16   Elizabeth R. Varon, *Appomattox: Victory, Defeat, and Freedom at the End of the Civil War* (New York: Oxford University Press, 2014), 53-54; Horace Porter, *Campaigning with Grant* (New York: Century, 1897), 472-74.

17   *PMUSG*, 2:489-92.

18   Ibid.

also that it would be an unnecessary humiliation to call upon them to deliver their side arms."[19] So then, these items were to be excluded from the weapons and property to be turned over to the Federal forces. Also excluded would be a request for Lee's ceremonial sword as a trophy of war. In the meeting, Grant did not ask for, nor did Lee offer, his sword. No need to inflict that humiliation.

And then, there was the final part of Grant's letter to Lee. The famous last sentence, which historian Bruce Catton described as "one of the great sentences in American history," is as follows: "[E]ach officer and man will be allowed to return to their homes not to be disturbed by United States Authority so long as they observe their parole and the laws in force where they may reside."[20] The sentence guaranteed a secure future for all Confederate soldiers, including the highest military officials, such as Robert E. Lee. It was profoundly important in ending the war and shaping the peace to follow. Parker at his side, Grant looked at his handiwork, made a few corrections, and then it was Lee's turn to review it. When Lee came to read the end, he looked up and remarked, "This will have a very happy effect upon my army."[21]

Lee had one more request. Would Grant consider letting the enlisted men keep their animals for spring farming? Grant agreed, prompting Lee to say, "It will be very gratifying, and will do much toward conciliating our people."[22] Around 3:30 p.m., Lee and Grant parted ways. They shook hands, and the ex-Confederate commander left the house and called for his horse, Traveller. When Lee mounted, Grant lifted his hat in salute, as did the other Union officers present. Lee did the same and then rode away.

News of the surrender spread quickly through the Union camps. Soon, thousands of soldiers were cheering and throwing their hats into the air. A 100-gun salute commenced, but Grant stopped it immediately, stating, "The war is over; the rebels are our countrymen again, and the best sign of rejoicing after the victory will be to abstain from all demonstrations in the field." No sustained celebration, no "victory dance," was allowed in Grant's presence. Winning the peace had now replaced winning the war as the main goal of the United States. Almost as an afterthought, Grant sent a telegram to Stanton tersely informing

19   Ibid., 2:492.

20   Bruce Catton, *U.S. Grant and the American Military Tradition* (Boston: Little, Brown and Company, 1954), 129; USG to Robert E. Lee, 9 April 1865, *PUSG*, 14:374.

21   Porter, 478-79. See also *PMUSG*, 2:492.

22   Porter, 479-80. See also *PMUSG*, 2:492-95.

him, "Gen. Lee surrendered the Army of Northern Va this afternoon on terms proposed by myself."[23]

Although several more armies would still surrender, the meeting between Grant and Lee at Appomattox Court House on April 9, 1865, Palm Sunday, is considered the virtual end of the Civil War. After meeting with Lee briefly the next morning, Grant traveled to Washington, D.C., deliberately missing the formal ceremony of the laying down of arms, which occurred on April 12. And when U.S. Grant did get to Washington City, Lincoln expressed his unqualified approval of the terms he had given Lee. The North celebrated—although approval of the Appomattox agreement was not as widespread as is usually portrayed in the history books. Grant's surrender agreement provoked controversy, stronger in force than Vicksburg's by far. From the perspective of those in April 1865 who were talking of traitors, treason trials, and hanging, the agreement seemed overly generous. These feelings, however, were checked by Lincoln's steadfast determination to stand behind Grant's surrender agreement. Indeed, despite misgivings, the overwhelming evidence suggests the majority of loyal citizens conflated the Appomattox terms with the securing of Union victory.[24]

Grant's terms at Appomattox arose out of his war experience, particularly at Fort Donelson and Vicksburg, and through his conversations and communications with Lincoln at City Point and elsewhere. The last part of the simple surrender document allowing "each officer and man . . . to return to their homes not to be disturbed by United States Authority so long as they observe their parole" represented something he had given a lot of thought to.[25] It revealed his view that, when the war was over, there should be no vindictive policy toward the enemy; revealed his agreement with Lincoln that favored clemency and generosity; revealed his belief that reconstruction would not, and should not, be simply acts of revenge. Grant's Appomattox surrender document, then, was not a product of a fleeting moment suggested by the statement, "I only knew what was in my mind," but reflected actions committed and policies formulated on the battlefield, as well as conversations held with the highest political authorities throughout the war. Grant's sentiment and his judgment joined him firmly with his president's vision of a reconstruction policy conducted with as little rancor as possible.

---

23   Adam Badeau, *Military History of Ulysses S. Grant*, 3 vols. (New York: D. Appleton and Company, 1868–1881), 3:608. USG to Edwin M. Stanton, 9 April 1865, *PUSG*, 14:375*n*.

24   For an illuminating Confederate perspective, see Porter Alexander, "Lee at Appomattox" in Peter Cozzens, ed., *Battles and Leaders of the Civil War*, vols. 5-6 (Urbana, IL: University of Illinois Press, 2002–2004), 5:636-52.

25   USG to Robert E. Lee, 9 April 1865, *PUSG*, 14:374.

Grant's words "Let us have peace" are inscribed outside his tomb—a theme reinforced inside by a mosaic of Lee and Grant.

Chris Mackowski

Here, Grant's final sentence made the military surrender into a peace agreement that would set the stage for true reconciliation, if not in the near future, then sometime within a few generations. In short, his terms offered peace and reconciliation to those who would embrace it. Because the final part packed so much punch, some have pointed out that Grant intruded into political reconstruction by fleshing out, by defining the conditions and consequences of the parole he was offering in these terms to the soldiers of the major Confederate army in the field. And they are right. Exceeding his instructions, Grant made a promise that rightfully belonged to another, but one that was rendered so perfectly that no complaint was lodged by his president. The Union commander who had accepted the cruelties of a hard war, who had waged that hard war without any illusion that victory could be achieved without fighting, who had borne the personal responsibility of bringing immense sacrifice on the part of both soldiers and civilians, also never forgot the ultimate goal of restoring a peaceful Union. Until his death, Grant believed that on April 9, 1865, he had produced a surrender document worthy of the sacrifices of his men in the war.

Simply put, the surrender reigns as one of the supremely perfect moments of our national history. After a bloody, bitter war, two brilliant but stunningly different commanders—one tall and perfectly attired in a new gray uniform, ceremonial sword by his side; the other, a plain, unpretentious figure born in humble circumstances and embodying the common man, his uniform sloppy and mud-splattered—met and forged the nation anew.[26]

This essay describes Grant's three surrenders, but it is equally about the nature of surrender during the American Civil War. A military or a political surrender is defined as giving up something valuable—a fortress, an army, a defined territory, a country, a set of demands—to an enemy. It can also mean something beautiful, tender, or forgiving. It can mean surrendering to a lover or surrendering a soul to God. It can mean a surrender of individual selfishness to a greater good. Surrender's

---

26   See Joan Waugh, *U.S. Grant: American Hero, American Myth* (Chapel Hill, NC: The University of North Carolina Press, 2009) for a work situating Grant in history and memory.

multiple meanings were present in full force in different ways at Donelson, at Vicksburg, and especially at Appomattox. All three places were at once sites of brutal warfare and conflict, sites of reunion, sites of reconciliation, and, almost immediately, sites of memory.[27]

On April 9, 2015, the 150th anniversary of the surrender by Confederate General Robert E. Lee to Union Lieutenant General Ulysses S. Grant was commemorated. At 3:00 p.m., bells rang out across the nation at schools, historic sites, churches, temples, and selected public buildings for four minutes—one for each year of the bloody conflict. The National Park Service coordinated the event with the following statement on their website: "Some communities may ring their bells in celebration of freedom or a restored Union, others as an expression of mourning and a moment of silence for the fallen. Sites may ring bells to mark the beginning of reconciliation and reconstruction, or as the next step in the continuing struggle for civil rights."[28] In many ways, that elastic interpretation exemplifies the traditional memorialization of the surrender at Appomattox.

On the same day, 10,000 people gathered at the national historical park just twenty miles south of Lynchburg, Virginia, to hear speeches from historians and national park officials, view battle reenactments and a restaging of the surrender, and listen to Civil War–era music. The ceremonies attending the commemoration, which actually spanned a full week, also offered some different perspectives from those of previous eras when reconciliation, not emancipation, would take center stage. In 2015, reflecting the changes in American culture and society over the past half-century, previously ignored or downplayed topics such as the role of slavery, the story of emancipation, the African American experience during and after the war, the extent of civilian suffering, and insights into the life of the common soldier were all highlighted in the museum exhibits, featured in books and pamphlets on

---

27   One of the primary definitions of the verb surrender is "[t]o give up (something) out of one's own possession or power into that of another who has or asserts a claim to it; to yield on demand or compulsion; esp. (*Mil.*) to give up the possession of (a fortress, town, territory, etc.) to an enemy or assailant." *The Compact Edition of the Oxford English Dictionary*, 2 vols. (New York: Oxford University Press, 1971): 2:244. Two scholarly works on surrenders and their aftermath are David Silkenat, *Raising the White Flag: How Surrender Defined the American Civil War* (Chapel Hill, NC: The University of North Carolina Press, 2019) and Caroline E. Janney, *Ends of War: The Unfinished Fight of Lee's Army After Appomattox* (Chapel Hill, NC: The University of North Carolina Press, 2021).

28   "Bells Across the Land," National Park Service press release, 10 March 2015, accessed 13   June   2022,   https://www.facebook.com/AppomattoxNPS/photos/a.216582371705786/ 928477217182961.

Living historians Curt Fields and Thomas Jessee, portraying Grant and Lee, cut through the fog of war during the Sesquicentennial commemoration of the surrender at Appomattox Court House.

National Park Service

sale in the store, and included in the reenactments.[29] That trend has continued in the tumultuous years following the Sesquicentennial.

Can Americans today still admire the generous spirit of reconciliation exhibited at Fort Donelson, Vicksburg, and Appomattox, even while allowing for the realities of a viciously fought war and the turbulent, tragic, difficult, and disappointing era that followed? My answer is yes, if we adopt the long perspective. The Union held, but the scars of the awful war were too deep to heal quickly or easily. The Union held, and that turned out to be the realized and recognized achievement for a majority of white northerners, while the promise of emancipation would remain "an unfinished revolution" for the freed people. Between the white people of North and South, there would be reconstruction and reunion, but precious little genuine harmony, accord, respect, or true reconciliation. What unity there was came out of the Appomattox surrender agreement, which secured the United States for all time and, with time, *just enough* reconciliation. The complex nature of surrender during the Civil War, encompassing hatred and love, despair and hope, bitterness and forgiveness, can somehow be summed up in one deceptively simple sentence, "I only knew what was in my mind."

29   Jim Burnett, "Bells to Ring on April 9 To Commemorate 150th Anniversary of Appomattox Surrender," 23 March 2015, accessed 13 June 2022, https/www.nationalparkstraveler.org/2015/03/bells-ring-april9-commemorate-150th-anniversary-appomattox-surrender26415; Katie Lawhorn & Mike Litterst, "National Park Commemorates the 150th Anniversary of the Surrender at Appomattox," U.S. Department of the Interior, 13 April 2015, accessed 13 June 2022, https://www.doi.gov/employees/news/national-park-service-commemorates-150th-anniversary-of-surrender-at-appomattox.

A Union Hero's Trajectory:
The Fall and Rise of U.S. Grant
Chapter Seven | *Gary W. Gallagher*

Ulysses S. Grant's standing in the American pantheon has undergone dramatic shifts. Contemporaries of Grant, at least those in the northern states where most Americans lived, would find it hard to believe that he has not occupied a lofty position all along. After all, it was Grant, more than anyone else but Lincoln, who ensured that the nation would crush the forces of rebellion and consequently stood as the most famous living American for the last period of his life. Yet, for many decades in the twentieth century, critics, both academic and nonacademic, cast him as an uncaring butcher with a predilection for strong drink and tolerance for corruption as president. The past twenty-five years have witnessed marked improvement in Grant's reputation, though he has yet to recover the position he held among the nation's loyal citizenry at the close of the Civil War.[1]

Grant's imposing stature between the end of the Civil War and the early years of the twentieth century cannot be disputed. The Union's greatest military hero, praised even by many former Confederates for his conciliatory demeanor at Appomattox, became the first four-star general in United States history before winning two terms as president. A courageous effort to complete his memoirs while dying of cancer further enhanced his reputation. More than a million people watched his funeral procession, which stretched for seven miles through the streets of New York City on August 8, 1885. On the seventy-fifth anniversary of his birth, April 27, 1897, the dedication of his tomb in Morningside Heights above the Hudson River also drew a million people, among them President William McKinley. Then and now the largest tomb in North America, it remained New York's leading tourist attraction until the Great Depression. The national capital dedicated its memorial to Grant on the centenary of his birth. Exceeded in size by only one equestrian statue in the world at the time, it took architect Edward Pearce Casey and sculptor Henry Shrady more than twenty years to complete. The monument occupies

1   This essay is a revised and expanded version of "The American Ulysses: Rehabilitating U.S. Grant," *Virginia Quarterly Review* (Summer 2005), No. 3, 81:234-41.

In early 1864, Congress debated a bill to revive the rank of lieutenant general with the general understanding that President Lincoln would appoint Grant to the position were it approved. Media outlets weighed in. "Thanks to Grant," declared *Harper's Weekly* on the front cover of its February 6 edition. Congress approved the rank in late February and, on the 29th, Lincoln signed it into law—and then sent forward Grant's nomination that same day. Lincoln presented Grant his commission at a White House ceremony on March 9.

Harper's Weekly

perhaps the most desirable site in the city—at the foot of Capitol Hill facing down the National Mall toward the Lincoln Memorial.[2]

By the time of the dedication in Washington, persistent characterizations of Grant as a butcher on the battlefield, a drunk, and a president surrounded by venality had clouded his reputation. Former Confederates writing in the Lost Cause tradition labored with great effect to diminish Grant's stature. They insisted that he defeated Lee only because of overwhelming advantages of men and material, presenting him as an officer who fed Union soldiers into a meat grinder until outnumbered Confederates capitulated. Jubal A. Early, a Confederate lieutenant general and leading Lost Cause controversialist, captured the dismissive attitude toward Grant in a widely circulated lecture delivered on the anniversary of Lee's birth in 1872: "Shall I compare Lee to his successful antagonist? As well compare the great pyramid which rears its majestic proportions in the valley of the Nile, to a pigmy perched on Mount Atlas." Winston Churchill, beguiled by Lost Cause writers and apparently unaware that Lee had incurred proportionately higher losses than his opponent,

---

2   On Grant's funeral and the dedication of his tomb in New York City, see Joan Waugh, *U.S. Grant: American Hero, American Myth* (Chapel Hill, NC: The University of North Carolina Press, 2009), chapters 5-6. On the statue in Washington, see Kathryn Allamong Jacob, *Testament to Union: Civil War Monuments in Washington, D.C.* (Baltimore: The Johns Hopkins University Press, 1998), 36-51; Kirk Savage, *Monument Wars: Washington, D.C., the National Mall, and the Transformation of the Memorial Landscape* (Berkeley and Los Angeles: University of California Press, 2009), 180-81, 201-03, 228-34. See also Louis L. Picone, *Grant's Tomb: The Epic Death of Ulysses S. Grant and the Making of an American Pantheon* (New York: Arcade Publishing, 2021).

wrote in *A History of the English-Speaking Peoples* of Grant's "unflinching butchery," insisting, "More is expected of the high command than determination in thrusting men to their doom." Overall, thought Churchill, Grant's performance against Lee "must be regarded as the negation of generalship."[3]

Critiques of Grant's presidency often focused on corruption, but the bitterness of Reconstruction undoubtedly played a major role. White southerners and many northern Democrats disapproved of his efforts to secure the fruits of victory for African Americans, and early academic historians who believed the United States government oppressed former Confederates during Reconstruction also found much to disparage. The idea that Grant had been a poor president persisted through the twentieth century, as evidenced by rankings overseen by prominent scholars starting with Arthur M. Schlesinger, Sr. For example, a survey of historians produced by the Siena College Research Institute in 1994 placed Grant 38th, ahead of only James Buchanan, Andrew Johnson, and Warren Harding; a similar canvass of scholars by the *Wall Street Journal* in 2000 located him 32nd, behind such marginal figures as Calvin Coolidge, Chester A. Arthur, and Benjamin Harrison.[4]

Despite the absence of credible evidence that Grant's drinking compromised his behavior on any Civil War battlefield, the image of a tippler who invites invidious comparison with the famously self-controlled Lee became ingrained in popular culture. Nothing better illustrates this phenomenon than celebrated humorist James Thurber's "If Grant Had Been Drinking at Appomattox," which appeared in *The New Yorker* on December 6, 1930. Thurber's Grant rises on the day of the surrender with a hangover from the previous night's imbibing. He first mistakes Lee for the poet Robert Browning and then, reminded that a solemn occasion beckons, takes another swig: "Slowly, sadly, he unbuckled his sword.

---

3   Jubal A. Early, *The Campaigns of Gen. Robert E. Lee. An Address by Lt. Gen. Jubal A. Early, before Washington and Lee University, January 19th, 1872* (Baltimore: John Murphy & Co., 1872), 50-51; Winston S. Churchill, *A History of the English-Speaking Peoples*, 4 vols. (New York: Dodd, Mead, & Company, 1956–1958), 4:253-54. Early's address is reprinted in Gary W. Gallagher, ed., *Lee the Soldier* (Lincoln, NE: University of Nebraska Press, 1996), 37-73.

4   For an example of a negative assessment of Grant's presidency by a leading scholar, see James G. Randall, *The Civil War and Reconstruction* (Boston: D.C. Heath and Company, 1937), chapters 36-37. See also William B. Hesseltine, *Ulysses S. Grant: Politician* (New York: Dodd, Mead & Company, 1935), viii, which found Grant "peculiarly ignorant of the Constitution and inept in handling men" as well as a "representative of the more reactionary economic interests of his day." For the presidential rankings, see "1994 President's Survey," Siena College Research Institute, accessed 11 June 2022, https://scri.siena.edu/wp-content/uploads/2018/08/1994-Presidents-rankings.pdf; James Taranto & Leonard Leo, eds., *Presidential Leadership: Rating the Best and the Worst in the White House* (New York: Free Press, 2004), 12; "Historical Rankings of Presidents of the United States," accessed 11 June 2022, https://en.wikipedia.org/wiki/Historical_rankings_of_presidents_of_the_United_States.

Then he handed it to the astonished Lee. 'There you are, General,' said Grant. 'We dam' near licked you. If I'd been feeling better we *would* of licked you.'"[5]

Thirty-seven years later, on November 27, 1967, an episode of the popular television series *The Beverly Hillbillies* reinforced the notion of Grant as a drunk. The Clampett family, transplanted from the South to one of California's wealthiest enclaves, mistakes a crew filming a Civil War movie for an actual Yankee invasion. Granny Clampett encounters the inebriated actor playing Grant, who is so drunk he has trouble staying on his horse. She takes a shot at Grant, who falls off his mount but quickly stands up. "I must have got him in the liver," she remarks: "That's what I done all right. It's gotta be cast iron after a hundred and fifty years of drinkin'.'" She subsequently produces some of her homemade "medicine," and the two pass the canteen containing her concoction back and forth.[6]

Publication of various presidential memoirs over the past thirty years prompted reviewers to discuss books by Grant and other ex-presidents. Many rightly noted that Grant's account ends at Appomattox and should not be considered a presidential memoir, and some took the occasion to deprecate Grant. In discussing Bill Clinton's *My Life* in *The New York Times Book Review*, novelist and screenwriter Larry McMurtry managed to trivialize Grant's struggle to finish his book before cancer claimed him, remarking, "Some people don't want slick Bill Clinton to have written a book that might be as good as dear, dying General Grant's." McMurtry then explained that one is a general's account and the other a politician's, adding a gratuitous Lost Cause flourish regarding Grant and Lee: "Grant's is an Iliad, with the gracious Robert E. Lee as Hector and Grant himself the murderous Achilles."[7]

In terms of scholarly treatments during the last quarter of the twentieth century, William S. McFeely's Pulitzer Prize–winning *Grant: A Biography*, published in 1981, served as the most notable benchmark. McFeely found military affairs distasteful, a fact that helps clarify why his handling of Grant's role in bringing Union victory struck far more false than true notes. Grant's actions during Reconstruction also failed to win McFeely's approbation. Most engaged with Grant as a man of "no organic, artistic, or intellectual specialness," McFeely wrote of his subject's "limited though by no means inconsequential talents" that allowed him to focus on certain tasks: "[H]e became general and president because he could find nothing better to do." McFeely's overriding purpose, one scarcely calculated to inspire a favorable

5   James Thurber, "If Grant Had Been Drinking at Appomattox," reprinted in *James Thurber: Writings & Drawings* (New York: The Library of America, 1996), 253-56.

6   *The Beverly Hillbillies*. 1967. Season 6, episode 13, "The South Rises Again." Directed by Joseph Depew. IMDb, accessed 11 June 2022, https://www.imdb.com/title/tt0522670/. Actor William Mims played Grant. The episode is available on YouTube at https://www.youtube.com/watch?v=l_2eHbbGV2s.

7   Larry McMurtry, "His True Love Is Politics," *New York Times Book Review*, 4 July 2004, 1, 8.

portrait, was to use Grant as a vehicle to explore the nation's failures to guarantee full African American rights during Reconstruction and to offer a "troubling picture of an America, often represented as in a period of boundless opportunity, that offered him and thousands of men like him no chance for fulfillment other than war."[8]

Filmmakers and artists apparently concurred with McFeely's conclusion that Grant lacked "specialness"—though few likely would have embraced the historian's unfortunate choice of phrasing. Lee appeared as a major character in two films over the past thirty years. In *Gettysburg*, a moderate financial success released in 1993, Martin Sheen played him as written in Michael Shaara's novel *The Killer Angels*. Ten years later, Robert Duvall rendered a Lost Cause version of Lee in *Gods and Generals*, a box office bomb based on Jeff Shaara's best-selling novel of the same name. Grant has not figured prominently in any mainline film, though Harry Morgan delivered a laconic reading, alongside John Wayne's William Tecumseh Sherman, in a brief sequence on the battle of Shiloh in the early-1960s epic *How the West Was Won*. Steven Spielberg's *Lincoln*, released in 2012, also allocated a few minutes to Grant. Paintings and sculptures marketed to Civil War enthusiasts between the 1980s and the early twenty-first century similarly revealed little interest in Grant. A survey of advertisements in popular magazines devoted to the conflict, all of which were published outside the former states of the Confederacy and reached national audiences, reveals that readers could choose from nearly ten items devoted to Lee for every one devoted to Grant.[9]

Much like consumers in the Civil War art market, tourists selecting Civil War–related destinations have exhibited relatively little interest in Grant's principal sites. Grant's Tomb reached its apogee as a tourist attraction in the early twentieth century and remained a significant magnet for visitation during the Civil War centennial years. By the early 1990s, the landmark had fallen on very hard times. Defaced by graffiti, extensively vandalized, and a gathering place for drug users, it registered annual visitation of only about 40,000. Descendants of the general deplored the National Park Service's stewardship of the tomb and threatened to remove his and Mrs. Grant's remains for reinterment elsewhere. Admirers created a new Grant Monument Association, which helped prod the National Park Service into making needed repairs. The tomb, partly refurbished, was rededicated on its

8   William S. McFeely, *Grant: A Biography* (New York: W.W. Norton & Company, 1981), xii-xiii.

9   On Grant in film and art, see Gary W. Gallagher, *Causes Won, Lost, and Forgotten: How Hollywood & Popular Art Shape What We Know about the Civil War* (Chapel Hill, NC: The University of North Carolina Press, 2008), especially chapters 3-4.

centennial in 1997, and visitation improved. Whether it will ever return to its past high level remains to be seen.[10]

Similarly, the imposing equestrian statue in Washington sits largely unknown and seldom viewed by anyone seeking out Grant. In her study of the city's Civil War monuments, Kathryn A. Jacob observed that designers intended that Grant and Lincoln would serve as crucial anchors at either end of the Mall. She wrote,

> Somehow things have not turned out as the planners hoped. . . . While the Lincoln Memorial remains one of the capital's most visited attractions, few visit the Grant Memorial. Its steps, designed as a reviewing stage for passing military parades, have instead been appropriated by commercial photographers, who pose and photograph there a perpetual parade of high school students.[11]

Change in popular perceptions of Grant will come only if sound scholarship dispels hoary misconceptions. Michael Korda's slim biography titled *Ulysses S. Grant: The Unlikely Hero* illuminated the problem by suggesting that most Americans, even in 2004, knew only two things about Grant—"his reputation as a drinker . . . and the fact that his portrait, with a glum, seedy, withdrawn, and slightly guilty expression, like that of a man with a bad hangover, is on the fifty-dollar bill." Korda thus managed to evoke a Grant who would coldly send men to their deaths, preside over a corrupt political regime, and drink too much (as well as describing a version of the fifty-dollar bill that must not have reached wide circulation). Korda readily conceded that he leaned most heavily on McFeely's *Grant* and W. E. Woodward's *Meet General Grant*, the latter a virtually worthless debunking effort from the late 1920s. He echoed McFeely in arguing that Grant served two terms as president because he did not know what else to do, as well as in finding his efforts on behalf of freedpeople insufficient. Korda closed with praise for Grant's *Personal Memoirs*, the pages of which, it must be said, reveal a man rarely glimpsed in Korda's own book.[12]

By the time Korda wrote, a significant reassessment of Grant had been underway for about a decade. Building on earlier favorable treatments by historians such as

10   Waugh, 263-67, 304-06.

11   Jacob, 36-37.

12   Michael Korda, *Ulysses S. Grant: The Unlikely Hero* (New York: HarperCollins, 2004), 2.

J.F.C. Fuller, Lloyd Lewis, Bruce Catton, and John Keegan,[13] four biographical studies published between 1997 and 2004, although differing in their assessments of various elements of Grant's life, contributed to an overall interpretation more positive and persuasive than William McFeely's. In *Ulysses S. Grant: Soldier & President*, military historian Geoffrey Perret lauded Grant's generalship, highlighting his adaptability in the face of enormous obstacles, his ability to coordinate the Union's gigantic war effort in 1864–65, and his success in teaching the Union army how to fight. Perret also found much to admire in Grant's efforts to suppress white violence against black people in the postwar South, most notably his targeting of the Ku Klux Klan in 1871, which he pronounced "Grant's biggest contribution to Reconstruction." Brooks D. Simpson's *Ulysses S. Grant: Triumph over Adversity, 1822–1865* dutifully noted shortcomings and failures but also identified in ample measure "bravery, integrity, determination, persistence, generosity, gentleness, and a self-confidence that if not as unshakable as is commonly portrayed was nevertheless astonishing. . . . Grant may not have carried himself as did Robert E. Lee . . . but generals are defined not by how they look or what they say but who they are and what they do." Jean Edward Smith's *Grant*, less rigorous as a piece of scholarship than Simpson's book, bestowed as much praise on Grant's presidency as on his years in a general's uniform. For Smith, most of Grant's failures grew out of his virtues, as when he trusted friends who betrayed him during a scandal-ridden second term as president.[14]

Josiah Bunting III's *Ulysses S. Grant* resembled Korda's book only in its brevity. Far more diligent in mining the rich lode of recent scholarship, Bunting delivered a balanced and convincing appraisal. Grant's postwar career impressed him as much as the years of Union command. "[B]equeathed heavier and less tractable burdens than any other president in our history" except Lincoln and Franklin D. Roosevelt, asserted Bunting, Grant dealt with the formidable task of reconstructing the nation, the final stage of conflict between the government and native peoples of the Great Plains, and a severe economic depression. "Of no president are biases in judgment

---

13   See J.F.C. Fuller, *The Generalship of Ulysses S. Grant* (New York: Dodd, Mead, and Company, 1929) and *Grant & Lee: A Study in Personality and Generalship* (New York: Charles Scribner's Sons, 1933); Lloyd Lewis, *Captain Sam Grant* (Boston: Little, Brown and Company, 1950); Bruce Catton, *U.S. Grant and the American Military Tradition* (Boston: Little, Brown and Company, 1954), *Grant Moves South* (Boston: Little, Brown and Company, 1960), and *Grant Takes Command* (Boston: Little, Brown and Company, 1969); John Keegan, *The Mask of Command* (New York: Penguin Books, 1987), chapter 3 titled "Grant and Unheroic Leadership." Catton finished the biography begun by Lewis.

14   Geoffrey Perret, *Ulysses S. Grant: Soldier and President* (New York: Random House, 1997), 414; Brooks D. Simpson, *Ulysses S. Grant: Triumph over Adversity, 1822–1865* (Boston: Houghton Mifflin Company, 2000), xviii; Jean Edward Smith, *Grant* (New York: Simon & Schuster, 2001). Simpson had examined Grant as a politician in *Let Us Have Peace: Ulysses S. Grant and the Politics of War and Reconstruction, 1861–1868* (Chapel Hill, NC: The University of North Carolina Press, 1991) and *The Reconstruction Presidents* (Lawrence, KS: University Pres of Kansas, 1998), chapters 5-6.

less well disguised," commented Bunting, "than in those that inform opinions about Ulysses Grant. There is much acidulous curling of the lip in depictions and opinions and judgments about him, an irremediable condescension stamped, it sometimes seems, on every page."[15]

Grant fared well in both the popular and academic arenas as the twenty-first century unfolded. Two expansive, annotated editions of Grant's memoirs joined the large number of earlier reprints, affording lay readers a chance to get the most out of the best reminiscence written by any military figure in U.S. history. A two-part PBS documentary in the American Experience series reached viewers on May 5–6, 2002. Titled "Warrior" and "President," the episodes featured prominent historians and portrayed Grant in a decidedly positive light. Eighteen years later, in May 2020, The History Channel served up a three-part miniseries based on Ron Chernow's biography titled *Grant*. The History Channel's site for the series averred that "today Ulysses S. Grant is largely forgotten, his rightful legacy tarnished by a fog of myth, rumor and falsehood." Presidential rankings reflected the changing interpretive landscape. A C-SPAN survey in 2021 placed Grant at number 20 overall and sixth in the category of "pursued equal justice for all"—behind only Lincoln, Lyndon Johnson, Barack Obama, Harry S. Truman, and Jimmy Carter—because of his pursuit of fuller equality for African Americans during Reconstruction.[16]

Four titles, including Chernow's biography, reveal the degree to which Grant's reputation has been ascending in the twenty-first century.[17] The earliest of the four, Joan Waugh's *U.S. Grant: American Hero, American Myth*, first explained why Americans of the Civil War generation celebrated the general as a great figure and then examined "Grant's illness and death, the writing of his memoirs, his funeral, and the building of Grant's Tomb in New York City." Waugh reminded modern

---

15   Josiah Bunting III, *Ulysses S. Grant* (New York: Times Books, 2004), 2-3.

16   For the *Memoirs*, see John F. Marszalek with David F. Nolen & Louie P. Gallo, eds., *The Personal Memoirs of Ulysses S. Grant: The Complete Annotated Edition* (Cambridge, MA: The Belknap Press of Harvard University Press, 2017); Elizabeth D. Samet, ed., *The Annotated Memoirs of Ulysses S. Grant* (New York: Liveright Publishing Corporation, 2019). For the PBS series, see *Ulysses S. Grant*. Directed by Adriana Bosch (part 1) & Elizabeth Deane (part 2). PBS, accessed 11 June 2022, https://www.pbs.org/wgbh/americanexperience/films/grant/. For the History Channel series, see *Grant*. Directed by Malcolm Venville. History, accessed 11 June 2022, https://www.history.com/shows/grant. The C-SPAN rankings are at "Presidential Historians Survey 2021, Total Scores/Overall Rankings," C-SPAN, accessed 11 June 2022, https://www.c-span.org/presidentsurvey2021/?page=overall.

17   Constraints of space prevent discussion of all recent books that offer positive portraits of Grant as a soldier or a politician. Three others that merit mention are H.W. Brands, *The Man Who Saved the Union: Ulysses Grant in War and Peace* (New York: Doubleday, 2012); Edward H. Bonekemper III, *A Victor, Not a Butcher: Ulysses S. Grant's Overlooked Military Genius* (Washington: Regnery Publishing, 2004); and Donald L. Miller, *Vicksburg: Grant's Campaign That Broke the Confederacy* (New York: Simon & Schuster, 2019).

readers that "Grant's bottom line was that the Civil War had to be fought, and won, by the United States"—an attitude that while "seldom expressed by Americans now about our wars past or present, reflected the most common memory of the Civil War generation." Only an appreciation of this foundational reality makes possible a true understanding of the mid–nineteenth century's massive upheaval. Waugh's deft connection of Grant's life and career to how he was later commemorated and remembered undergirds what she termed "a case study of the fascinating ways in which historical memory is shaped, and then reshaped, to suit current needs."[18]

Three thick volumes followed in the space of two years. Ronald C. White's *American Ulysses: A Life of Ulysses S. Grant* echoed Waugh in asserting that Grant's nineteenth-century contemporaries "offered him not simply admiration but affection. In their eyes he stood with Washington and Lincoln." Seeking to refocus his subject's image for a contemporary readership, White presented an introspective figure who possessed weaknesses but shone as a military commander and as an advocate for civil rights in the wake of emancipation. He quoted Frederick Douglass, who said that to Grant "more than any other man the Negro owes his enfranchisement and the Indian a humane policy." Douglass's observation illuminated the challenge "taken up by this biographer: the opportunity for the enigmatic, inspiring, and complex story of American Ulysses to become accessible to the wider audience he deserves."[19]

No book about Grant has reached a wider audience than Pulitzer Prize–winning biographer Ron Chernow's 1,000-page doorstopper. Like Waugh and White, Chernow directly countered popular misconceptions about Grant as a butcher, a drunkard, and a corrupt president and devoted considerable attention to the general's memoirs. Chernow summarized that "Grant was instrumental in helping the Union vanquish the Confederacy *and* in realizing the wartime ideals enshrined in the Thirteenth, Fourteenth, and Fifteenth Amendments." Indeed, continued Chernow in making a claim that some might challenge, Grant "was the single most important figure behind Reconstruction." As for Grant's drinking, Chernow devoted elaborate attention to alleged drunkenness and concluded: "As with so many problems in his life, Grant managed to attain mastery over alcohol in the long haul, a feat as impressive as any of his wartime victories."[20]

Charles W. Calhoun's *The Presidency of Ulysses S. Grant* set up its meticulous investigation with a clear statement of the historical interpretive arc. "Grant

---

18   Waugh, 5, 8.

19   Ronald C. White, *American Ulysses: A Life of Ulysses S. Grant* (New York: Random House, 2016), xxvii, 659.

20   Ron Chernow, *Grant* (New York: Penguin Press, 2017), xxii-xxiii.

had stout defenders and remained widely popular among his fellow citizens," Calhoun wrote, "but in retrospective accounts of his presidency, historians and others paid much more attention to the relentless execration by his enemies. Hence, for decades, most historical writing on Grant's presidency magnified its blemishes and slighted its achievements." Calhoun covered the volatile political environment, the challenges of Reconstruction, the economic disruptions, and other factors that affected Grant's two terms. A measured text that highlighted failures as well as successes awarded high marks for civil rights, for "genuine sympathy for Native Americans," and for some economic policies. But Calhoun raised doubts about the likelihood that new scholarship will vanquish the old: "The operation of confirmation bias exerts a powerful force against the overturning of ingrained understandings of the past. It is said that stereotypes are true until proved otherwise—and then they are still true."[21]

How Grant's reputation fares going forward will reveal a great deal about whether rigorous scholarship can affect popular conceptions of the American past. The Grant described in recent revisionist literature likely would be unrecognizable to most Americans who have any impressions at all of the general and president. Only if the revisionists prove as resilient and determined as their subject will there be any chance for Grant to resume his place among the most celebrated figures in United States history.

21   Charles W. Calhoun, *The Presidency of Ulysses S. Grant* (Lawrence, KS: University Press of Kansas, 2017), 5-7, 592-93.

Ulysses S. Grant: Politician
Chapter Eight | *Charles W. Calhoun*

As Union General Ulysses S. Grant racked up victory after victory during the Civil War, many Americans anticipated the day when he might transfer his proven qualities of leadership to the political arena. Some thought he should reach as high as the presidency. Grant himself, however, shuddered at the thought. "Nothing likely to happen would pain me so much as to see my name used in connection with a political office," he insisted while still fighting in the field. "I have always thought the most slavish life any man could lead was that of a politician."[1]

Nonetheless, he did indeed become a politician. Despite his initial diffidence, he accepted the presidency at the first election after the war, and he soon emerged as an adept politician and a civilian leader of great consequence. Inevitably, he also became a partisan, the pre-eminent leader of the Republican Party. For more than a decade, he dominated the American political landscape. Not for nothing did that period in the nation's political history come to be known as the Age of Grant.

Grant was not, however, a natural politician. In his early years in southern Ohio, he saw his glad-handing father achieve a modicum of prominence in local politics, but he harbored no such ambitions for himself. Yet he did absorb Jesse Grant's Whig political views as well as his opposition to the expansion of slavery. In the 1850s, the sectional conflict over that question grew so intense that Grant feared it would drive the South to secede. When the political crisis finally erupted in war in 1861, the West Point graduate and Mexican-American War veteran signed up to do his part in the struggle to preserve the Union.

---

1   USG to Barnabas Burns, 17 December 1863, John Y. Simon, ed., *The Papers of Ulysses S. Grant*, 32 vols. (Carbondale, IL: Southern Illinois University Press, 1967–2012), 9:541, hereafter cited as *PUSG*; USG to Daniel Ammen, 16 February 1864, ibid., 10:133. For a fuller treatment of the themes in this essay, see Charles W. Calhoun, *The Presidency of Ulysses S. Grant* (Lawrence, KS: University Press of Kansas, 2017).

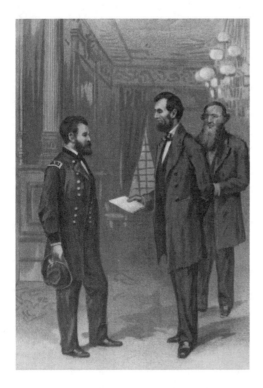

Before Lincoln would consider Grant a candidate for lieutenant general, he first made discreet inquiries as to any presidential ambitions Grant might have harbored. Assured Grant would not be a competitor for the presidency in 1864, Lincoln nominated him for promotion. Grant's association with Lincoln thereafter gave him important insights into politics at the highest level.

Library of Congress

As historian Brooks Simpson has shown, Grant's political acculturation began during the war.[2] While his command responsibilities grew larger, he learned to administer a large organization, adeptly managing those below him and propitiating those above, including President Abraham Lincoln. Moreover, he developed a keen understanding of the political nature of the conflict itself—a war to reunite the American Republic and, eventually, to end slavery. It was, however, during the immediate post-war years, while he served as general-in-chief in Washington, that Grant's political education began in earnest. While President Andrew Johnson and the Republican-dominated Congress clashed over Reconstruction, Grant found himself inevitably drawn into the strife. More and more, he aligned himself with the Republicans in that struggle, which culminated in the drive to establish the right to vote for African American males. When Johnson tried to undermine the program of military reconstruction mandated by Congress, Grant stood his ground, lecturing the president, "This is a republic where the will of the people is the law of the land."[3] Hoping yet to capitalize on the general's growing cachet, Johnson persuaded Grant to become interim secretary of war as part of his effort to drive Edwin Stanton out of the cabinet. But Grant resisted becoming Johnson's political pawn. When the Senate negated Stanton's dismissal, the general gladly relinquished the secretary's office. His five-month sojourn in the cabinet left Grant with bifurcated impressions; it reinforced his distaste for politics

2   Brooks D. Simpson, *Let Us Have Peace: Ulysses S. Grant and the Politics of Civil War and Reconstruction, 1861–1868* (Chapel Hill, NC: University of North Carolina Press, 1991).

3   USG to Andrew Johnson, 17 August 1867, *PUSG*, 17:278.

General U.S. Grant and Speaker of the House Schuyler Colfax headed the Republican ticket in 1868.

Library of Congress

and politicians, but it also confirmed his sense that the attacks on Reconstruction by Johnson and his allies posed a grave danger to the fruits of victory that the Union forces had won in battle.

By the election year 1868, Republicans had come to see Grant as their indispensable instrument to retain power and complete the work of Reconstruction. After witnessing four years of political warfare in Washington, Grant yielded to the party's call, driven by his sense of duty, not altogether unmixed with a trace of ambition. He accepted the nomination for president on the Republican ticket. To his friend General William T. Sherman, who bore an even deeper disdain for politics, Grant explained that he found himself in a position

> I would not occupy for any mere personal consideration, but, from the nature of the contest since the close of active hostilities, I have been forced into it in spite of myself. I could not back down without, as it seems to me, leaving the contest for power for the next four years between mere trading politicians, the elevation of whom, no matter which party won, would lose to us, largely, the results of the costly war which we have gone through.[4]

In a sense, Grant had come to see politics as war by other means.

In his first electoral campaign, which pitted him against the seasoned Democratic candidate Horatio Seymour, Grant's behavior did not differ markedly from that of many previous presidential nominees. He did no overt politicking. Aside from an ostensibly nonpolitical tour through the West with Sherman and General Philip H. Sheridan, he enjoyed a "quiet, pleasant time" during the summer and fall at his home in Galena, Illinois. But even though direction of the campaign lay with party leaders at Republican headquarters in New York, Grant maintained contact with them through his secretaries and especially his Galena neighbor and

4   USG to William T. Sherman, 21 June 1868, *PUSG*, 18:292.

long-time political mentor, Congressman Elihu Washburne. Candidate Grant took no active part, but over the months he drew on his vaunted ability to size up a situation and acquired a remarkable knowledge of the political condition of the diverse regions of the country. Days before the balloting, he handicapped the result, forecasting which candidate would carry each state and by what margin. On election night, observers monitoring the returns with Grant marveled that the first two states reporting "gave exactly the majorities he had predicted" and that "in nearly every case he proved a prophet." As one reporter wrote, Grant "seemed much more pleased at his political sagacity than at his success." Grant won with 52.7 percent of the popular vote and defeated Seymour in the Electoral College by the more comfortable margin of 214 to 80.[5]

Grant's deep understanding of the political complexion of the country surprised many people who thought they knew him well. But it was just one of many assets that equipped him for the job when he took up his duties as president on March 4, 1869. As his election prophesies showed, Grant was highly intelligent, in no sense the dullard his detractors portrayed. He was not an intellectual, but he possessed an excellent memory and grasped issues quickly. Here again, he caught some people unawares. During a conversation a few months into his term, *New York Times* editor John Bigelow was impressed that the new president "spoke at length of all the domestic questions of his administration and very well." Similarly, a talk with John Marshall Harlan convinced the future Supreme Court justice that Grant was "an honest, well-meaning man, with more intellect than I ever supposed he had. He has a clear well-balanced mind."[6]

Grant also arrived at the White House with substantial experience as an administrator. As an officer in the quartermaster's corps during the Mexican-American War, he first began to hone his organizational skills. During the Civil War, his responsibilities grew with each new promotion, and during the last year, he oversaw the entire Union Army. As a commander, he learned how to operate under pressure, see the big picture as well as the details of a situation, take the measure of his adversaries, frame a plan of action, delegate tasks, and manage subordinates to achieve his ends. As the *Chicago Tribune* argued during the 1868 campaign, performing "the executive duties of a vast army" had given Grant "an education and an experience in executive duty fully as ripe as any gentleman who

5   USG to William W. Smith, 25 September 1868, *PUSG*, 19:47; *New York Tribune*, 4 November 1868; *Presidential Elections, 1789–2000* (Washington, D.C.: CQ Press, 2002), 123, 194.

6   John Bigelow, Diary, 29 August 1869 [typescript], John Bigelow Papers, New York Public Library; John Marshall Harlan to Benjamin H. Bristow, 27 September 1871, Benjamin H. Bristow Papers, Library of Congress.

has spent his life in committee of the whole, or majestically presided over a court of last resort."[7]

Moreover, Grant's military experience had nourished in him a fierce determination to pursue his aims to a successful conclusion, a perseverance that President Lincoln had hailed as the general's "bull-dog gripe." Grant himself noted in his memoirs that a "superstition" had always compelled him when he "started to go any where, or to do anything, not to turn back, or stop until the thing intended was accomplished." In political life, he exhibited the same dogged tenacity, hailed by his friends as steadfastness and decried by his enemies as obstinacy.[8]

None of these character traits abandoned Grant when he made the transition from military to civilian service. Of course, his new field of operations required him to adjust to new kinds of issues—to execute new kinds of maneuvers to achieve his ends. But during the war, his ability to adapt had proven essential to his success, and the same would be true in the White House. Although his lack of civilian political experience may have heightened the difficulty of his new tasks, it also left him less hide-bound by tradition and more willing to challenge longstanding practices. Moreover, if he entered the presidency as a novice politician, he was not an ignorant one. His four-year sojourn in the nation's capital as general-in-chief had acquainted him with the major issues of the day—from Reconstruction to finance to foreign policy—and had offered him ample opportunity to size up the major players in the government and both political parties. In Washington's governing community, he had already cut a substantial figure. He was immensely popular in the nation at large, and entered the presidency with a wealth of good will. As one congressman wrote, "The loyal people of the country looked to Grant with an almost superstitious hope. They were prepared to expect almost any miracle from the great genius who had subdued the rebellion."[9]

Perhaps Grant's chief handicap as a politician was his aversion to public speaking. Innately modest, he disdained self-puffery in others and thought a person's deeds should speak for themselves. When he traveled as president and was presented to crowds, he would say almost nothing beyond a brief return of the greeting. He almost never gave anything like a formal speech. He thus missed the opportunity to use the public rostrum as a bully pulpit to tout his policies or inspire his fellow citizens. Moreover, his public taciturnity gave his detractors an opening to accuse him of lack of knowledge or even stupidity, or to portray him

---

7   *Chicago Tribune*, 14 December 1867.

8   *PUSG*, 11:425; Ulysses S. Grant, *Personal Memoirs of U.S. Grant*, 2 vols. (New York: Charles L. Webster & Co., 1885–1886), 1:49-50, hereafter cited as *PMUSG*.

9   George F. Hoar, *Autobiography of Seventy Years*, 2 vols. (New York: Charles Scribner's Sons, 1903), 1:246.

as simply a tool of party bosses, ready to do their bidding. His reluctance to speak made it more difficult to, in modern-day parlance, "control the political narrative."

Yet one should not make too much of Grant's public reserve. In Grant's day, the only people who saw or heard public figures give speeches were those physically present on such occasions. Vastly more people read them in the newspapers or in pamphlet form, and in the realm of the printed word Grant more than held his own. As his memoirs attest, he was a superb writer, and his presidential communications exhibited the same clear, straightforward prose. He composed compelling, sometimes eloquent, messages to Congress, which he aimed at citizens as well as legislators and which newspapers routinely printed in full.[10] He often arranged for the publication of letters or memoranda that outlined his positions or defended his actions. He gave interviews to reporters, and he and others in the administration engaged in the time-honored practice of leaking. Even though he shunned the speaker's rostrum, Grant found ways to articulate his message and to do so with lucidity and force.

During the transition period after his election and during the early days of his administration, Grant sought to present himself as being above the partisan fray. In the weeks before Inauguration Day, when Republicans pushed him to appoint dependable Republican partisans to his cabinet, they were surprised by reports that Grant had declared, "I am not the representative of a political party myself, although a party voted for me."[11] But it is not true, as some observers alleged then and later, that he did not consult with Republican leaders regarding his cabinet selections. From election day to Inauguration Day, Grant held almost constant conversations with countless party leaders and others. During trips to attend receptions and dinners in Boston, New York, Chicago, Philadelphia, and elsewhere, he always found time for private conversations with party representatives. In Washington, he met a steady stream of visitors at Army headquarters and occasionally journeyed to Capitol Hill for private sessions with congressional leaders. As one of his aides noted, Grant "is willing to be informed of the various views" and "gives all respect to those especially whose positions in the party which elected him entitle them to be considered." What he did not do was reveal his cabinet selections in advance, primarily to avoid criticism from those who favored other individuals.

---

10   In a special message on southern affairs in 1875, for instance, Grant wrote, "I have repeatedly and earnestly entreated the people of the South to live together in peace, and obey the laws; and nothing would give me greater pleasure than to see reconciliation and tranquillity everywhere prevail, and thereby remove all necessity for the presence of troops among them. I regret, however, to say that this state of things does not exist . . . [N]either Ku-Klux-Klans, White Leagues, nor any other association using arms and violence to execute their unlawful purposes, can be permitted in that way to govern any part of this country." USG to Senate, 13 January 1875, *PUSG*, 26:13-14.

11   *New York Times*, 26 February 1869. This quotation varies slightly in different reports.

He announced his choices after the inauguration. The critics who complained the loudest about his method of vetting were those whose recommendations he heard but did not accept. Although a bit of reshuffling of the cabinet occurred in the first days of the term, the considerations that motivated Grant's selections included appointees' talents and experience, geographic balance among the secretaries, personal acquaintance, and an aim to allay party factionalism in some states. He tapped no party grandees or presidential aspirants. Ohio Governor Rutherford B. Hayes hailed the new cabinet as "organized for harmony. No man being conspicuous, Grant's leadership and rule is beyond question. It seems to mean business and not political scheming."[12]

In his First Inaugural Address, Grant strove to underscore the impression that he entered upon his duties free of political obligations. "The office has come to me unsought," he declared. "I commence its duties untrammeled." Similarly, he called upon his fellow citizens to embrace reconciliation over political, racial, and sectional rancor. He called for a "patient forbearance one toward another throughout the land, and a determined effort on the part of every citizen to do his share toward cementing a happy union." In the spirit of healing, he proposed to conduct his office in a manner in marked contrast to that of the imperious, solipsistic Andrew Johnson. In his letter accepting the Republican nomination, Grant had spoken of a president as "a purely Administrative officer" who should "execute the will of the people." "I shall on all subjects have a policy to recommend," he said in the Inaugural, "but none to enforce against the will of the people."[13]

And yet, unfortunately, despite his wide popularity and the goodwill that surrounded his accession to office, Grant soon found that his appeal for governance marked by forbearance and conciliation won scant acceptance by political opponents who showed little inclination to adopt his notions of a new nonpartisan dispensation. From the beginning, partisan enemies denigrated his capacity for civilian leadership and actively worked for his failure. Andrew Johnson and his cabinet refused to attend the inaugural ceremonies and offered no assistance to their successors preparing to take up their duties. Johnson thought "Grant represented all the worst principles" of the Republican Party and considered him "a liar, . . . false to his duty and his trust." One of Johnson's cabinet secretaries labeled the new president "a man of low instincts, . . . wanting in truthfulness and sincerity, and . . .

---

12   Adam Badeau to John Russell Young, 20 February 1869, John Russell Young Papers, Library of Congress; Charles Richard Williams, ed., *Diary and Letters of Rutherford Birchard Hayes*, 5 vols. (Columbus, OH: Ohio State Archaeological and Historical Society, 1922–1926), 3:59.

13   James D. Richardson, ed., *A Compilation of the Messages and Papers of the Presidents*, 20 vols. (New York: Bureau of National Literature, 1897–1916), 9:3960, 3962; USG to Joseph R. Hawley, 29 May 1868, *PUSG*, 18:264.

Grant's first presidential inauguration took place on March 4, 1869.

National Archives

grossly, shamefully ignorant of the Constitution and of the structure of the government."[14]

This sort of contempt for Grant permeated the Democratic Party and lay at the heart of that party's approach to the new administration. Democratic newspapers were unrelenting in their criticism, and the party's leaders invoked the congressional power of investigation to blacken Grant and his administration. As one prominent Democratic House member explained to a party editor when Grant's first Congress convened, "There is only one way for a Dem in opposition,— that is, to *charge the other side*. I charge them with making all the mischief & failing in any remedy." One week after the inauguration, famed Democratic lobbyist Sam Ward told a southern senator that Grant "is simply damned; before two years, probably much sooner, he will be impeached & removed."[15]

Entering upon his duties in this noxious milieu, Grant had no choice but to become a politician and a partisan. In short order, he realized that there would be no adjournment of politics-as-usual, no cooperative handshakes across the aisle. Willy nilly he was going to have to deal with "mere trading politicians" on their own terms. He soon saw that his success as president hinged on his accepting responsibility as the leader of the Republican Party. To that end, he recognized the importance of cultivating good relations with Republicans in Congress. After witnessing how Johnson's pitched battles with the legislature had taken the American government to the brink of dysfunction, Grant understood that for him to achieve his agenda, he must win acceptance from party allies on Capitol Hill. "A government machine must run, and an Executive depends on Congress," he later

14   Theodore Calvin Pease & James G. Randall, eds., *The Diary of Orville Hickman Browning*, 2 vols. (Springfield, IL: Illinois State Historical Library, 1925–1933), 2:211; Howard K. Beale, ed., *Diary of Gideon Welles*, 3 vols. (New York: W.W. Norton & Company, 1960), 3:363, 500.

15   S. S. Cox to Manton Marble, 17 December 1869, Manton Marble Papers, Library of Congress; Samuel Ward to Thomas F. Bayard, 11 March 1869, Thomas F. Bayard Papers, Library of Congress.

observed. "If he wants to get along with Congress, have the government go smoothly, and secure wholesome legislation, he must be in sympathy with Congress."[16]

As a pragmatist, Grant realized that the politically-minded members of Congress saw patronage—exercising influence over the appointment of federal officials—as the coin of the realm. As he later put it, "In a government where there are senators and members, where senators and members depend upon politics for success, there will be applications for patronage. You cannot call it corruption—it is a condition of our representative form of government." At the outset of the administration, the new president confronted the Tenure of Office Act, which Republicans had passed to curtail what they considered Johnson's abuse of the patronage power. Potentially barred from making a wholesale replacement of officeholders, Grant insisted that just "[b]ecause one horse needs a curb-bit you should not crowd a curb-bit into another horse's mouth." Within a month, he persuaded Congress to revise the law, and the appointment of Republicans proceeded apace. But not just any Republicans, for Grant quickly grasped the policy leverage that the patronage power afforded him. As Secretary of State Hamilton Fish observed, it became the president's practice "to withhold political patronage from those recommended by Senators & others in opposition to the policy or attitude of the Administration."[17]

Of course, no president could satisfy all who sought patronage, and inevitably many suffered disappointment. The most vocal among the supplicants who failed to win either office or influence included members of an intellectual elite based largely in the Northeast. These men believed that their education, elevated principles, and theoretical understanding of government ideally equipped them for public service, which they hoped to enter without soiling themselves in the odious practices of quotidian politics. Some of these "best men" had scant respect for Grant, and they imagined that without their help his administration would become, as Henry Adams put it, "a reign of western mediocrity." Although Grant appointed some such men to office, he left many others out. In reaction, some became severe critics of the administration and embraced civil service reform as a way to assuage their disappointment. As historian Ari Hoogenboom has noted, many of these so-called reformers "recognized the evils of the spoils system only after it thwarted their ambitions."[18]

16   John Russell Young, *Around the World with General Grant*, 2 vols. (New York: The American News Company, 1879), 2:265.

17   Ibid., 2:264; *Washington National Republican*, 19 February 1869; Hamilton Fish, Diary, 7 January 1870, Hamilton Fish Papers, Library of Congress.

18   J. C. Levinson et al., eds., *The Letters of Henry Adams*, 6 vols. (Cambridge, MA: Harvard University Press, 1982), 2:20; Ari Hoogenboom, "Civil Service Reform and Public Morality," in H. Wayne Morgan, ed., *The Gilded Age* (Syracuse, NY: Syracuse University Press, 1970), 81.

In 1869, Ulysses S. Grant, aged 46, was the youngest person who had ever been sworn in as president of the United States.

Library of Congress

Yet Grant was hardly blind to the irksome nature of the spoils system. He found that "no duty . . . so much embarrasses the Executive" as spending hours on end dealing with appointments.[19] He established a commission to devise a program of civil service reform and used a series of executive orders to launch a new merit-based method for federal hiring. But Congress showed little enthusiasm for relinquishing the patronage influence that members had long exerted to nourish party organizations. They refused to pass legislation to make Grant's hiring reform permanent and eventually denied funds to the civil service board. Although the great experiment thus came to an end, Grant deserved credit as the first president to make a serious attempt at civil service reform.

But "reformers"—many in his own party—gainsaid Grant's sincerity and refused to give him credit for what he had done. Moreover, many of these same detractors denounced Grant's vigorous approach to Reconstruction, especially his sometimes forceful intervention in the South to uphold the rights of African Americans. They increasingly acquiesced in rule by the white southern elite, and assailed Grant's interventionist policies as militaristic and liable to concentrate undue power in the federal government. Such aspersions by persons whom Grant considered apostates from the Republican Party's true faith served only to strengthen his identification with the party as an organization. Gone was his pre-inaugural insistence, "I am not the representative of a political party." After two years in office, he wrote to an aide, "I do feel a deep interest in the republican party keeping controll of affairs until the results of the war are acquiesced in by all political parties." If that be partisanship, he regarded it as a partisanship with a larger purpose. Embracing the party's essential principles, he grew ever more

19   Richardson, 9:4063.

willing and determined to work with Republican Party regulars to further his and the party's goals.[20]

Thus, gone too was Grant's initial conception of the chief executive as a purely administrative officer, for he soon stepped forward as an energetic legislative president. To that end, patronage proved a useful tool, but he had other means at hand as well. Each year in December, he used his annual message to Congress not only to report on the previous year's achievements but also to set a course for the future, putting the weight of his office behind policies he favored. As specific issues or events occasioned, he submitted special messages, sometimes directly intervening in ongoing legislative debates. In these communications, Grant's robust prose served him well.

Moreover, despite his abjuring public speaking, the president felt quite at ease counseling senators and representatives who conferred with him at the White House. In these friendly sessions he not only gauged congressional opinion, he also shaped it. Sometimes he entertained a whole committee to push for a particular measure. On some occasions, the White House provided drafts of bills. Perhaps most remarkable, Grant himself often journeyed up Capitol Hill to lobby in person for measures he favored. In one notable episode, when reports of racial violence in the South reached a crescendo, Grant gathered legislators together for a strategy session in the President's Room in the Capitol. On the spot, he wrote a message urging them to pass legislation granting him enhanced powers to meet the crisis. As one reporter noted, the "palpable effect" was "promptly to unite the Republicans who have been wrangling over this question." The result was passage of the Ku Klux Klan Act, one of the most significant enforcement laws to emerge during Reconstruction. In another instance, in the last hours of a congressional session, the Senate voted 30 to 29 to kill a controversial tax bill. Upon hearing the news, Grant immediately adjourned a Cabinet meeting in progress and headed up the Hill to push for the bill. After his intervention, the Senate voted once more and passed the measure, 30 to 29. "The President saved us again," one Republican senator wrote. "There never was such a President in the White House. One so absolutely fearless."[21]

Over the years, Grant formed strong alliances with leaders of the Republican Party, especially in Congress. Once again, the former general found himself at the head of a fighting force. In one observer's estimate, Grant aimed "to introduce the discipline of a regular army into this free militia organization of the republican

20   *New York Times*, 26 February 1869; USG to Adam Badeau, 19 November 1871, *PUSG*, 22:239.

21   *New York Tribune*, 24 March 1871; Timothy O. Howe to Grace Howe, 8 March 1875, Timothy O. Howe Papers, Wisconsin Historical Society.

party."[22] Forming an administration party in Congress, leaders such as Roscoe Conkling, Oliver Morton, and Simon Cameron came to serve as Grant's comrades in arms in the political wars—his new Shermans and Sheridans. These men worked closely together, and whether or not Grant gave them direct orders, they often could sense his aims and acted accordingly.

A prime example was their defense of the president's interests against assaults by one of his bitterest enemies, Senator Charles Sumner of Massachusetts, a member of the disaffected New England elite. Disappointed in his apparent desire to become secretary of state, and loath to concede party leadership to a mere military man, Sumner opposed Grant's initiatives at nearly every turn. Most notably, he moved heaven and earth to block Grant's attempt to acquire Santo Domingo. The president envisioned the Caribbean island nation as an ideal location for a naval base and a potential haven where formerly enslaved Americans could seek refuge or threaten to do so in order to leverage better treatment at home. Grant was deeply disappointed by the defeat of his annexation proposal, but he also worried that Sumner would use his position as chairman of the Senate Foreign Relations Committee to undermine another initiative, delicate negotiations with Great Britain aimed at settling the *Alabama* claims. This contentious dispute grew out of Britain's unneutral behavior during the Civil War, and Grant feared it could lead to war. Just as the talks began, the Republican Party leaders reorganizing committees in the Senate removed Sumner not only from his chairmanship of Foreign Relations but from his membership on the committee altogether. Although Grant denied dictating the make-up of congressional committees, no one could mistake the import of Sumner's overthrow. "In bold relief," said the *New York Herald*, "it brings out General Grant in a new character—as the recognized head of the republican party."[23] With Sumner's capacity for mischief curtailed, the negotiations resulted in the Treaty of Washington, which called for arbitration of the claims by an international tribunal, where the United States won a substantial monetary settlement from Britain.

Grant's hold on the Republican Party was such that he coasted to renomination in 1872. But he had never developed a politician's thick skin, and he deeply resented what he considered unfair animadversions of his character by opponents. He later said that 1872 was the only time he really desired to run for president, to give the people a chance to decide between himself and his critics. Dissenters within the party, professing "reform" and styling themselves Liberal Republicans, broke away to make a separate nomination, but in an odd twist, they wound

22   *New York Herald*, 13 March 1871.

23   Ibid.

up with Horace Greeley, editor of the *New York Tribune*, who had meager reform credentials. Out of desperation, the Democrats also backed Greeley, despite his having trashed their party for decades in his paper. Besides the Liberals' personal attacks, what disturbed Grant most was their abandonment of the central tenets of the Republican Party relating to Reconstruction. He had long warned that their willingness to enter into an unholy alliance with the Democrats would yield "nothing more nor less than the overthrow of the party which saved the country from disruption, and the transfer of controll to the men who strove for disruption."[24]

Greeley's campaign, pushing for universal Confederate amnesty and tinged with racism, seemed to validate Grant's warning. Greeley told one audience that "the first of all questions is the emancipation of all the White men of the country, so that they shall enjoy equal rights with the Black men." For his part, Grant renewed his call for "a speedy healing of all bitterness of feeling between sections, parties or races." But he rejected a racial hierarchy and insisted that "the title of citizen" should carry "with it all the protection and privileges to the humblest that it does to the most exalted." Grant easily prevailed, defeating Greeley with 55.6 percent of the popular vote, the largest margin of victory in a presidential election between 1828 and 1904, and by more than four-to-one in the Electoral College. The Liberal movement collapsed, and Grant retained his position at the head of the Republican Party. In his Second Inaugural Address, he told his fellow citizens that having been "the subject of

---

24   USG to Charles W. Ford, 20 October 1870, *PUSG*, 20:314.

abuse and slander scarcely ever equaled in political history," he regarded their election verdict as "my vindication."[25]

The anti-Reconstruction animus fueling the opposing coalition in the 1872 campaign left Grant more than ever convinced of the indispensability of the Republican Party to the country's well-being. He continued to foster the party's commitment to securing the rights of African Americans. But persistent white supremacist violence in the South, coupled with Supreme Court decisions limiting federal power to respond, plus growing disapproval of government action by Northerners, all made the promise of racial justice increasingly more difficult to fulfill. Moreover, a financial panic in 1873 and subsequent lengthy depression accelerated the decline in Americans' attention and support for the Reconstruction project and moved economic issues more toward center stage. In dealing with these financial questions, Grant again attached himself to Republican doctrine.

Over the years, Grant had secured legislation to lower taxes and refinance and reduce the national debt. In the contention over the so-called currency question, which roiled politics for decades, he placed himself squarely behind sound money. As early as his First Inaugural, he insisted on the payment of every dollar of the postwar government debt in gold "[t]o protect the national honor," and he called for an expeditious return to specie payments for the greenback paper currency emitted during the war. After the panic triggered a general contraction, inflationists aiming to relieve debtors and stimulate the economy urged Congress to expand the money supply by authorizing a re-issue of greenbacks. But in the spring of 1874, Grant blocked the Inflation Bill with a ringing veto, denouncing the proposal as "a departure from true principles of finance, national interest, national obligations to creditors, Congressional promises, [and] party pledges." Supporters hailed the president's interdiction as "Jackson-like," and his allies in Congress defeated an override attempt. Grant threatened further vetoes of any similar legislation and redoubled his push for a return to the gold standard, which Congress enacted a few months later with the Specie Resumption Act.[26]

In confronting the national economic crisis, Grant emphasized stability in the monetary system in order to animate business confidence, which he considered the key to rebuilding the economy. Although inflationists, including some in his

---

25   *New York Tribune*, 14 October 1872; *New York Times*, 11 June 1872; *Presidential Elections*, 113, 124, 132, 195; Richardson, 9:4177. Grant won 286 electoral votes. Greeley died before the electors convened to vote; his 66 electors scattered their votes: 42 for Thomas Hendricks, 18 for B. Gratz Brown, 2 for Charles Jenkins, 1 for David Davis, and 3 for Greeley (not counted). William G. Shade and Ballard C. Campbell, eds., *American Presidential Campaigns and Elections*, 3 vols. (Armonk, NY: Sharpe Reference, 2003), 2:458.

26   Richardson, 9:3961, 10:4223; Joseph Medill to Elihu Washburne, 1 May 1874, Elihu Washburne Papers, Library of Congress.

own party, disagreed, Grant's policies contributed much to the Republican Party's embrace of financial orthodoxy. In this he won praise from former Liberals as well as regular Republicans. "Grant never exhibited more courage and good sense than he has shown in regard to these late financial measures," one party leader wrote. "It looks to me as tho he had saved our party and commands the situation."[27]

Indeed, despite some disagreements over the veto, Grant's position among Republicans was such that, around the middle of his second term, press critics began to allege that he was angling for a third-term nomination in 1876. Grant did nothing to encourage these assertions, which revealed less about Grant's ambition than about his detractors' recognition of his pre-eminence in the party. One journalist wrote, "I am astonished to find how strong is the feeling in favor of continuing Grant in power, and how many are ready to elect our President for life."[28] But after the Republicans had held sway for nearly fifteen years, economic hardship, continued troubles in the South, and allegations of scandal eroded the party's following. In the South, Democrats were determined to retake power by whatever means necessary, violent or otherwise, and their revived strength there contributed to their party's winning a majority in the national House in Grant's second mid-term elections in 1874. Once in power, they did not hesitate to put the president in the investigative crosshairs. The next year, after more than a decade of extraordinary public service, Grant took himself out of the running for the Republican nomination in 1876.

Grant naturally favored a Republican victory that year as tacit endorsement of his administration's achievements, and he lent what discreet support he could to nominee Rutherford Hayes. He made no speeches but allowed a member of his cabinet to become Republican national chairman. Moreover, a weak law recently passed to impose minor limits on the assessment of campaign contributions from federal employees did little to curtail such fundraising. During the electoral crisis after the balloting, Grant correctly embraced nonpartisanship, favoring the creation of the Electoral Commission to resolve the dispute and laboring to keep the peace until the issue was settled, as it turned out, in Hayes's favor. At Grant's departure, James A. Garfield observed, "No American has carried greater fame out of the White House."[29]

Grant soon set off on a world tour, happy to escape after years of political wrangling. But he did not abandon his commitment to the Republican Party's

27   Marshall Jewell to Benjamin H. Bristow, 23 June 1874, Bristow Papers.

28   John Bigelow, Diary, 3 November 1874 [typescript], Bigelow Papers.

29   Harry James Brown & Frederick D. Williams, eds., *The Diary of James A. Garfield*, 4 vols. (East Lansing, MI: Michigan State University Press, 1967–1981), 3:454.

success. Even from a distance of thousands of miles overseas, he kept tabs on events at home. He soon found fault with Hayes's management, particularly his seeming abandonment of the party's commitment to protect African Americans' rights in the South and his apparent reluctance to use the levers of executive power to advance the party's agenda. After a year, Grant had concluded that Hayes "exercises but little influence with the legislation," a failing largely due "to the Utopian ideas he got, *from reformers*, of running a government without a party."[30]

Even before his election, Hayes had sworn off a second term, and many in the party disenchanted with what they considered his lukewarm Republicanism favored bringing Grant back as the party's presidential nominee in 1880. Some of Grant's most fervent past supporters managed the drive. While not openly avowing his candidacy, Grant did not stop his advocates' work. Moreover, in the spring, he gave a series of ostensibly nonpartisan speeches that kept him in the public eye. During his world tour, circumstances had left the distinguished visitor no choice but to address enthusiastic crowds, and even though he never lost his distaste for public speaking, he had gained facility at it. Grant entered the Republican national convention with the largest contingent of delegates in the field of candidates, and he led the voting on thirty-five successive ballots. But his managers could not quite assemble a majority, and the delegates finally chose dark horse James A. Garfield.

Though disappointed, Grant vowed to pull his weight in the general election campaign. Garfield's Democratic opponent, Winfield Scott Hancock, had served as one of Grant's ablest subordinates during the Overland Campaign in 1864, but during the Johnson years, the two men had strongly disagreed over Reconstruction policy, and Hancock had sought the Democratic nomination to run against Grant in 1868. After the 1880 convention, Grant assured Garfield of his "very deep interest in the success of the republican ticket." The former president presided at a large campaign rally in the nominee's home state of Ohio, declaring, "I am a Republican as the two great political parties are now divided, because the Republican Party is a national party seeking the greatest good for the greatest number of citizens." He went on to give a series of speeches across New York state. Thanks in part to Grant's efforts, Garfield narrowly carried that key swing state and, with it, the election. "[B]y the defeat of the democratic party," Grant told the victor, "the nation has escaped a calamity."[31]

It thus came as a shock to the party wheelhorse Grant to discover how little success he had in recommending appointments in the new administration. Grant

30   USG to Daniel Ammen, 25 March 1878, *PUSG*, 28:367.

31   USG to James A. Garfield, 5 August 1880, ibid., 29:440; Speech, 28 September 1880, ibid., 29:478, USG to James A. Garfield, 11 November 1880, ibid., 30:74.

was convinced that Garfield had fallen under the sway of his secretary of state, James G. Blaine, Grant's arch-rival, whose candidacy had thwarted the former president's nomination in 1880. After Garfield's assassination, Grant man Chester A. Arthur ascended to the presidency, but Grant was surprised once again to see how little clout he wielded. He thought that Arthur was "more afraid of his enemies" than guided by his friends and that he waffled on issues central to the Republican Party's identity. "The republican party to be saved must have a decisive declared policy," he wrote after two years of Arthur. "It has now no observable policy except to peddle out patronage to soreheads in order to bring them back into the fold, and avoid any positive declaration upon all leading questions."[32]

The leading question that still stood uppermost in Grant's mind was the one that had drawn him into politics to begin with: securing the results of the Civil War. In late 1883, he told a would-be supporter that he declined to be considered as a presidential candidate in 1884, but the condition of the country left him no choice but to renew his commitment to the Republican Party. "Nothing is so important, in my view, as the breaking down of sectional lines," he wrote, but the Democrats remained incorrigible.

"[T]he only principle actuat[ing] the so called democratic party in the South is 'Controll,'" and "[i]n the North the party has been equally inconsistent." In his memoirs, he renewed his call for sectional reconciliation, but he also warned that a failure to improve "[t]he condition of the colored man within our borders" could lead to dire consequences. Hence, he wrote privately a few months before his death, "I have been a republican ever since the war began, and shall continue so as long as the states in rebellion continue to cast a solid vote for the party that supported rebellion, whether they have the numerical strength to do so, with a free ballot and fair count, or not."[33]

Grant, the reluctant politician, never abandoned his belief that politics must not be the exclusive preserve of "mere trading politicians" but instead the vehicle to fulfill some higher purpose. The bedrock American principle, he believed, was popular participation in a representative government, where the right to vote was the right preservative of all others. "It is my firm conviction," he said in his Second Inaugural Address, "that the civilized world is tending toward republicanism, or government by the people through their chosen representatives, and that our own great Republic is destined to be the guiding star to all others." In that pursuit, he embraced the Republican Party as the true champion of republicanism. "The

---

32   USG to Adam Badeau, 28 February 1885, ibid., 31:22; Adam Badeau, *Grant in Peace* (Hartford, CT: S.S. Scranton & Co., 1887), 552.

33   USG to Patrick H. Winston, Jr., 24 December 1883, PUSG, 31:98-99; PMUSG, 2:550; USG to Alonzo V. Richards, 30 September 1884, PUSG, 31:209.

Republican Party," he declared after leaving office, "is a party of progress." It aimed to secure the "entire equality before the law of every citizen, no matter what his race, nationality, or previous condition. It tolerates no privileged class."[34]

But at the time of Grant's death in 1885, that aim remained far from fulfillment. Two years earlier, the Supreme Court had nullified the Civil Rights Act that Grant had signed in 1875. In 1894, a Democratic Congress and president, Grover Cleveland, repealed much of the voting rights legislation Grant and the Republicans had enacted in the 1870s. States in the South moved swiftly to adopt measures that placed severe restrictions on the right to vote and otherwise relegated formerly enslaved African Americans and their descendants to second-class citizenship. The civil rights struggles of the twentieth century succeeded in undoing many of those repressive measures, but recent events tell us that the right to vote for all is still fiercely contested. In 1865, Grant the soldier secured the preservation of the American Union. But the fight that Grant the politician waged to secure what he saw as the essential corollary to Union victory—a fair and just polity open to participation by all—is not yet finished.

---

34   Richardson, 9:4175; Speech, 28 September 1880, *PUSG*, 29:478.

Ulysses S. Grant and Civil Rights
Chapter Nine | *Alvin S. Felzenberg*

U lysses S. Grant entered the presidency with two major goals: securing the "results" of the Civil War and staying true to words he wrote in accepting the Republican presidential nomination in 1868, "Let us have peace." For Grant, the "results" of the war were a reunited nation, bereft of slavery, with the four million freed slaves enjoying the full rights of citizenship. "Let us have peace" was consistent with the spirit of Lincoln's Second Inaugural Address, in which the sixteenth president urged the binding up of the nation's wounds "with malice toward none" and "charity for all." As his presidency advanced, many observers recognized the tension between the goals of justice and sectional reconciliation. Grant could not advance one without slowing the other.

On his watch, Grant made good on his promise to secure the results of the war. He vigorously enforced the newly enacted Fourteenth Amendment, which bestowed citizenship to the recently emancipated slaves; pushed for and obtained ratification of the Fifteenth Amendment, which banned using race as a disqualification for voting; pressed for passage of legislation to use force against those who committed organized violence against southern blacks and their white allies. Grant destroyed the first Ku Klux Klan (founded in late 1865); established the Department of Justice to try cases in federal courts and before federal juries; appointed hundreds, if not thousands, of newly established non-white citizens to federal posts; attempted to annex new territory in the Caribbean to enable recently emancipated slaves to exert leverage over their former owners for better treatment and higher wages; repeatedly sent federal troops to protect freedmen exercising their newly obtained rights under the Constitution; and secured passage of what would become the last-enacted civil rights bill in what would be 82 years.

By any measure, this was an extraordinary legacy usually associated with "transformational" presidents. But many of Grant's achievements did not endure for more than a generation after he left office. Gradually, a determined opposition diminished and undid Grant's accomplishments by using all means at its disposal—legal and otherwise. Changes in party fortunes, the erosion of public support in

Grant signed the Ku Klux Klan Act as a way to enforce the Fourteenth
Amendment—one of his most significant, and long-overlooked, actions
as president.

Frank Leslie's Illustrated

Northern states, the coming to the fore of what were deemed more immediate
and more pressing issues (*i.e.*, the Panic of 1873), Supreme Court decisions that
appeared to re-write the intentions of the architects of constitutional amendments
and enabling legislation, and a series of presidents who either lacked Grant's
political prestige or personal concern for African Americans assisted this rollback.

The template for Southern white resistance and obstruction that eventually
prevailed had been struck during Andrew Johnson's presidency. It remained an
obstacle to Grant throughout his time in office. After he departed, the South
began a slow descent into the abyss of Jim Crow. In the 1890s, the 11 states that
had been part of the Confederacy began enacting laws mandating various forms
of racial segregation. In 1883, the U.S. Supreme Court declared the 1875 Civil
Rights Act, a major Grant initiative, unconstitutional. In 1896, it upheld legally
mandated racial segregation in *Plessy v. Ferguson*. Between 1890 and 1910, 10 of
the states that had seceded from the Union ratified state constitutions that had
provisions effectively disenfranchising black males through poll taxes, literacy
tests, and residency and record-keeping requirements. By 1915, legally mandated
segregation had spread beyond the reconstructed states to Kentucky, Missouri,
Maryland, Oklahoma, West Virginia, and to the District of Columbia.

To those who explore the history of racial justice in the United States, Grant's record appears all the more aspirational and visionary. Grant serves as a reminder that there can be times when a president with the highest character, best intentions, deepest commitment, and overwhelming political support cannot overcome deeply entrenched forces beyond his immediate control.[1] It would be almost a century before legal segregation would end.

In his final annual message as president, Grant summarized the situation that had awaited him eight years earlier. He described the interval between Lincoln's assassination and his own inauguration as a time of incessant "wranglings" between Congress and the Executive as to "whether the control of the Government should be thrown immediately into the hands of those who had so recently and persistently tried to destroy it, or whether the victors should continue to have an equal voice with them in this control."[2] He included among those victors four million former slaves who were now U.S. citizens. Grant sensed a special bond with the recently freed men and women. Grant was certain that slavery caused the war. But for slavery, there never would have been secession. "[S]lavery fired on the flag," Grant said, in a reference to Fort Sumter. He used the word "slavery" to convey all the Confederacy represented.[3]

Grant's parents were abolitionists. Yet some of his closest friends at West Point were from slave-holding families. Grant married into one. Over time, however, he came to share his parents' view that slavery should be eradicated. While working a small farm, Grant hired several African American male slaves and came into possession of one of his father-in-law's slaves. Eschewing the role of overseer, Grant worked beside his laborers in the field. At soon as he was able, Grant manumitted the only slave he ever owned on March 29, 1859.[4] Not being wealthy, Grant would have benefited financially had he sold the 35-year-old slave. However, selling the slave would have sentenced any children the man sired to a life in slavery. Grant would be no party to that.

During the Civil War, Grant was the leading force in bringing African Americans into the ranks of the Union army, making them a cornerstone in what became a "war of attrition" against the Confederacy. "Every slave," he explained,

---

1   Sean Wilentz, "President Ulysses S. Grant and the Battle for Equality," in Walter Isaacson, ed., *Profiles in Leadership: Historians on the Elusive Quality of Greatness* (New York: W.W. Norton & Company, 2010), 73-74. See also Josiah Bunting III, *Ulysses S. Grant* (New York: Times Books, 2004), 107-11.

2   James D. Richardson, ed., *A Compilation of the Messages and Papers of the Presidents*, 20 vols. (New York: Bureau of National Literature, 1897–1916), 10:4354.

3   Wilentz, 57-58.

4   Ron Chernow, *Grant* (New York: Penguin Press, 2017), 101, 106.

"withdrawn from the enemy is the equivalent of a white man put *hors de combat*."[5] As Lincoln recognized when issuing the Emancipation Proclamation, in times of war or insurrection, the Constitution empowers the president to seize enemy property to weaken the enemy's ability to inflict hardship on the U.S.—and, legally, slaves were, in fact, "property." Many did not need to be "confiscated" as "contraband." As Union troops marched southward, thousands of enslaved people ran toward Union lines, and once under the army's protection, many of them enlisted.

By the war's end, 179,000 African Americans had served in the Union army, constituting 10 percent of the total. An additional 19,000 served in the Navy.[6] At first, these new recruits worked as paid cooks, hospital attendants, and teamsters. In his memoirs, Grant traced the origins of what became the Freedman's Bureau to his treatment of African Americans that had come under his protection at military encampments. Grant retained clergyman John Eaton to supervise the contrabands.[7] Of Grant's dedication to the well-being of his new guests of all genders and ages, Eaton recalled, "Never before . . . had I heard the problem of the future of the Negro attacked so vigorously and with such humanity and combined with practical good sense."[8]

Impressed at their performance as civilians, Grant ordered that African Americans be allowed to serve in the Union army. His action breathed life into Frederick Douglass's vision that "Once let the black man get upon his person the brass letters U.S.; . . . an eagle on his button, and a musket on his shoulder, and bullets in his pocket, and there is no power . . . which can deny that he has earned the right of citizenship in the United States."[9] Although Grant had not yet publicly advocated extending the franchise to former slaves, he came to believe that the service of the freedmen entitled them to the full benefits of citizenship.

African Americans responded positively to the respect and generosity Grant had shown them during and after the war and repeatedly rewarded him with their loyalty. In his first presidential campaign, Grant received 52.7 percent of the popular vote. Over 450,000 votes he received were cast by African Americans in the states

5   Ibid., 228.

6   "Black Soldiers in the Military During the Civil War," National Archives, accessed 12 February 2022, https://www.archives.gov/education/lessons/blacks-civil-war.

7   Ulysses S. Grant, *Personal Memoirs of U.S. Grant*, 2 vols. (New York: Charles L. Webster & Co., 1885–1886), 1:424-25.

8   Chernow, 229-30.

9   W.E. Burghardt Du Bois, *Black Reconstruction* (New York: Harcourt, Brace and Company, 1935), 102.

Columbia presents a wounded black veteran willing to fulfill
the civic responsibilities his military service had made possible.

Library of Congress

that comprised the former Confederacy.[10] These votes inflated the size of Grant's winning margin, not only in the popular vote, but also in the Electoral College, which he carried 214 to 80. In 1868, African Americans comprised a majority of the population in Mississippi, South Carolina, and Louisiana and majorities in several counties elsewhere. With most Southern whites voting Democratic, African American voters often tipped the elections in Southern states to the Republicans.

Four years later, African American voters—their ranks inflated with the passage of the Fifteenth Amendment, which enfranchised black males throughout the country—helped Grant win the presidency by an even wider margin. "To [Grant]

10   William Gillette, *The Right to Vote: Politics and the Passage of the Fifteenth Amendment* (Baltimore: Johns Hopkins University Press, 1969), 40.

more than to any other man the negro owes his enfranchisement," Frederick Douglass proclaimed in 1872.[11] Douglass listed the number of blacks Grant had named ambassadors, customs collectors, internal revenue agents, postmasters, and clerks.[12] African Americans, along with northern and midwestern political machines, Union veterans, and southern Republicans constituted the core of Grant's political base.

Before Grant could empower those he had helped set free, the nation first had to endure the nearly four-year administration of Andrew Johnson. In June 1864, with a Union victory still uncertain, Lincoln made a move calculated to help his re-election. Convinced that his path to victory ran through the slaveholding "border states," Lincoln sought to replace Vice President Hannibal Hamlin with a pro-Union—but not necessarily anti-slavery—Democrat. Lincoln settled on Andrew Johnson, military governor of Tennessee. Weeks after the two were officially nominated, Admiral David G. Farragut's forces took control of Mobile Bay (on August 5), and General William T. Sherman's advancing army captured Atlanta (on September 2). These victories assured Lincoln's re-election. Johnson's selection proved unnecessary. Replacing Hamlin with Johnson proved among the most consequential and the most tragic decisions Lincoln ever made.

Throughout the war, Johnson proved a pro-Union man. As military governor, he had shut down anti-Union newspapers, dismissed anti-Union officeholders, and abolished slavery within Tennessee. While Lincoln and Johnson were similar in background, they differed greatly in outlook, especially in the empathy they exhibited toward African Americans and in what responsibilities the federal government had toward the former slaves. Lincoln always abhorred slavery, but recognized that the Constitution, prior to 1865, did not allow Congress to abolish slavery within states where it already existed. As a presidential candidate in 1860, Lincoln opposed allowing slavery into the territories. He also recognized the humanity of the enslaved and argued that the rights guaranteed by the Declaration of Independence applied to them, even if he was uncertain as to whether they should enjoy standing with whites as citizens.

While Johnson had abolished slavery in Tennessee as a useful war measure to weaken the power of secessionists, he showed no concern for freed slaves after the war had ended. Born in North Carolina, Johnson opened his own tailor shop in Greeneville, Tennessee, and made his way in local politics. In rapid succession, he served as mayor of Greeneville, state representative, congressman, and governor

---

11   John W. Blassingame et al., ed., *The Frederick Douglass Papers*, 5 vols. (New Haven: Yale University Press, 1979–1992), 5:202. Douglass referred to both the results of the war and passage of the Fifteenth Amendment.

12   Chernow, 642.

before the state legislature named him to the U.S. Senate. Like his hero, Andrew Jackson, Johnson professed to champion the "common (white) people" against elites. Also, like Jackson, he favored a strong executive, the preservation of the Union, and states' rights. As governor, Johnson ruled as a populist. He favored public schools, a public library system, and other measures that primarily benefited poor whites.[13] While in Congress, Johnson was an avid enthusiast for homesteading. "Pass the bill," he said, "and you will make many a poor man's heart rejoice."[14] He could have inserted the word "white" before "poor man's," as he did not want to allow blacks to acquire public lands.

Prior to his death, Lincoln had not articulated a comprehensive plan for postwar Reconstruction. He preferred a rapid readmission of the rebellious states to the Union after 10 percent of eligible voters in the 1860 election had sworn allegiance to the United States. While he had been largely silent as to how the newly emancipated slaves might participate in American governance, Lincoln suggested in a letter to the military governor of Louisiana that the vote be given to African Americans who had some education and served in the armed forces. Lincoln voiced support for a new state constitution that would provide for the education of both white and black children.

In the eight months between Lincoln's death in April 1865 and the convening of Congress in December, Johnson enjoyed a free hand over Reconstruction. The new president began to implement the "10 percent plan." For readmission, he insisted that rebellious states renounce slavery and secession and repudiate debts they had incurred during the war. On May 29, Johnson issued proclamations recognizing a provisional government in Virginia and granting amnesty to former Confederates with property valued at less than $20,000 (with others eligible for presidential pardons). He named a temporary acting governor in North Carolina and instructed the remaining states to draft new constitutions, hold ratifying conventions, and organize state governments.

In the readmitted states, Johnson did not envision substantial changes to their plantation-based agricultural economies other than that African Americans were no longer slaves. He showered pardons on wealthy planters. He supported state efforts to limit the mobility of blacks and restore as much of the pre-war plantation system as possible. Johnson tacitly supported Black Codes. These codes required black workers to hold one-year employment contracts, sometimes at the very plantations where they once lived, with the threat of forfeiting their earnings

---

13   Eric Foner, "Andrew Johnson," in Alan Brinkley & Davis Dyer, ed., *The American Presidency* (New York: Houghton Mifflin Co., 2004), 189-90.

14   Annette Gordon-Reed, *Andrew Johnson* (New York: Times Books, 2010), 48.

if they left early. These codes included vagrancy laws, through which blacks lacking proof of employment were compelled to work wherever local authorities decreed. As groups of night marauders began harassing, terrorizing, and even killing former slaves, Johnson maintained that the federal government lacked the power to protect them. Insisting that only states could determine the franchise, Johnson opposed extending citizenship and the right to vote to the four million former slaves.

Johnson's early actions encouraged past, present, and future tormentors of former slaves. While Republicans voiced surprise and disappointment at his actions, Southern white Democrats saw Johnson as the means through which they could regain much of what they had lost on the battlefield. Johnson set down this path when the South was at its lowest point—with Union forces omnipresent and the southern economy in tatters. If there ever was a time since the American founding to build a biracial republic throughout the United States based on equal rights for all and a transformed southern economy not dependent on the plantation system, the beginning of Reconstruction was the occasion. Johnson's disastrous presidency prevented this from happening.

After Johnson had left office, Christopher Memminger, the former Confederate secretary of the treasury, said that at the war's end, the South was so devastated and demoralized that it would have accepted almost any terms the Union handed down.[15] Johnson, however, gave hope to ex-Confederates of re-instituting a "white man's government" that would "set aside negro suffrage." Not long after the surrender at Appomattox, Robert E. Lee suggested that southerners had expected that the franchise would be extended to the freedmen as a result of the war.[16]

Hoping to run for president in 1868, Johnson tried to forge a coalition among white southern Democrats, northern Democrats, and moderate Republicans against African Americans and their Republican allies (demeaned as "carpetbaggers" and "scalawags" in the South). Johnson railed against Radical Republicans that wanted to treat the South as conquered territory. He showed special disdain for Sen. Charles Sumner of Massachusetts and Rep. Thaddeus Stevens of Pennsylvania, who advocated making land that Union forces had seized from Confederate landowners available to Union loyalists, regardless of race. Johnson blocked the Freedmen's Bureau from proceeding with its much-publicized plans to divide these lands into 40-acre plots to be used for this purpose.[17]

---

15   Ibid., 118-19.

16   Brooks D. Simpson, *The Reconstruction Presidents* (Lawrence, KS: University Press of Kansas, 1998), 140.

17   Gordon-Reed, 115-16.

Johnson correctly surmised that the Radicals never constituted a majority of Republicans in or out of Congress. However, Johnson drove moderate Republicans into the Radicals' camp. He might well have forged a new governing majority had he restrained his new southern allies. Their mistreatment of the recently emancipated, more than former slaves' inability to vote, alienated the northern moderates. (Prior to passage of the Fifteenth Amendment, African Americans had been granted the right to vote in few places in the North outside New England.) Recalcitrant, defiant, and making no pretense at moderation, southern voters and state legislatures filled their congressional delegations with former Confederate military officers and political leaders. Congress refused to seat them.

When Congress reconvened in December 1865, moderate Senate Judiciary Chairman Lyman Trumbull, an Illinois Republican, introduced the first federal civil rights bill in U.S. history, which extended the rights of citizenship to former slaves, and another bill extending the life of the Freedman's Bureau. Johnson vetoed both, arguing that they violated states' rights and discriminated in favor of blacks at the expense of whites.[18] Congress overrode Johnson's veto of the civil rights bill and, on a second try, overrode his veto of the Freedman's Bureau's extension.

Johnson strenuously opposed the Fourteenth Amendment, which Congress passed on June 18, 1866, and which was ratified on July 9, 1868. The Fourteenth Amendment extended citizenship to all persons born under the jurisdiction of the United States. The amendment indirectly encouraged the enfranchisement of black males by providing for the reduction of representation for states that denied law-abiding male citizens who were 21 or older the franchise.

Thus began a three-year tug of war, which Grant referred to as "wranglings," between Congress and the Executive. Moderate and Radical Republicans enacted Reconstruction measures, and Johnson promptly vetoed them. If overridden, Johnson failed to enforce them. Eventually, Congress divided 10 of the 11 former Confederate states into five military districts, each headed by a military commander, who would organize provisional governments to draft new state constitutions.

As military commanders sought to extend legal protections and the franchise to former slaves, Johnson undermined their authority. Congress responded by bolstering the commanders' authority with language aiming to prevent presidential subversion. Grant, in his capacity as senior military officer of the government, was given enhanced responsibilities that included full appointment and removal power

18   Ibid., 122-24, 128.

in the military districts.[19] As Johnson's term advanced, Grant, concerned for the welfare of those his armies had set free, increasingly came to side with the Radicals.

Congress also enacted—over Johnson's veto—the Tenure of Office Act, which forbade the president from dismissing cabinet officers without the acquiescence of the Senate. When Johnson dismissed Grant's superior, Secretary of War Edwin Stanton, the House impeached the president. The Senate, in a vote of 35 to 19, fell one vote short of the two-thirds necessary to convict Johnson.[20]

On May 21, the Republican National Convention nominated Grant for president.[21] "Let us have peace"—the concluding sentence of his letter accepting the Republican presidential nomination in 1868—effectively became his campaign slogan. Compressed into those four words were two promises: one of sectional reconciliation; another of racial harmony and shared citizenship.

As a candidate and as president-elect, Grant threw his prestige behind passage of the Fifteenth Amendment, which forbade the disenfranchisement of citizens based on race, color, or previous condition of servitude across the country. Congress approved the amendment days before Grant's inauguration. Throughout his first year as president, Grant took personal charge of the campaign for state ratification. He advised Nebraska on strategy, twisted legislative arms in Nevada, and considered speeding up readmission of seceded states so black males in Connecticut could vote in a forthcoming election.[22] The Fifteenth Amendment was ratified on February 3, 1870.

After ratification, Grant issued a proclamation celebrating what he called "the most important event that has occurred, since the nation came into life."[23] He called upon whites to "withhold no legal privilege of advancement to the new citizen [the African American]."[24] Grant also called upon Congress not to disband the Bureau of Education. "With millions of ex-slaves to be educated, now is not the time to suppress an office for facilitating education," he insisted.[25]

Given the pushback he received as he strove to enforce the Fourteenth and Fifteenth Amendments, Grant contemplated ways the federal government might

19   Mark L. Bradley, *The Army and Reconstruction, 1865–1877* (Washington, D.C.: Center of Military History, United States Army, 2015), 38-40; 15 Stat. 14–16.

20   Over several days, three separate votes were taken on three different articles. The results were identical on each.

21   Simpson, *Reconstruction Presidents*, 126-28; Gordon-Reed, 135-39.

22   Simpson, *Reconstruction Presidents*, 143-44.

23   Ibid., 144.

24   John Y. Simon, ed., *The Papers of Ulysses S. Grant*, 32 vols. (Carbondale, IL: Southern Illinois University Press, 1967–2012), 20:131, hereafter cited as *PUSG*.

25   Simpson, *Reconstruction Presidents*, 144.

In this commemorative print celebrating the ratification of the Fifteenth Amendment, Grant is surrounded by his political and military allies (including Lincoln) while a portrait of John Brown hovers above them. Small scenes depict "Justice for All" and "A Freeman's Right."

Library of Congress

enable the freedmen to exert economic leverage over their former masters, who remained powerful in their respective states and sought to keep former slaves in a subordinate status not all that different from slavery. He thought he had found a means of doing so when he learned that the president of Santo Domingo (today's Dominican Republic) wanted to sell the country to the United States.

Obtaining territories through purchase had been an instrument of American foreign policy since Jefferson's acquisition of the Louisiana Territory in 1803. Johnson's Secretary of State William Seward had tried and failed to secure the annexation of two small republics that shared the island of Hispaniola, Santo Domingo and Haiti. Grant saw the economic and security advantages that an American outpost in the Caribbean would bring the United States. A coaling station, already there, and a possible U.S. naval base would augment an American presence in the region and guard the entrance to the canal that so many expected to be constructed in Central America.

"What I desired above all," Grant recalled, "was to secure a retreat for that portion of the laboring classes of our former slave States, who might find themselves under unbelievable pressure."[26] He had hoped that the mere option of freed people relocating from Southern states to Santo Domingo might encourage Southern whites, who depended on African American labor, if only out of self-interest, to raise their wages and respect their constitutional rights. The annexation issue consumed much of Grant's time and attention in 1870 and beyond. Grant biographers Ron Chernow and Josiah Bunting likened Grant's interest in Santo Domingo to an obsession.[27]

Whatever the merits of Grant's proposal, the way he pursued it may have contributed to its doom. The Santo Domingo annexation was the only significant policy defeat that Grant suffered during his presidency. Grant had done little to build public or congressional support for his proposal before he submitted two treaties to the Senate for ratification. Concerned that other nations might have an interest in the territory, his penchant for secrecy was understandable. Whether his failure to see them ratified resulted from an honest misunderstanding, duplicity on the part of a tacit administration ally-turned-bitter-foe, or Grant's failure to pick up on a cue, Grant's proposal ran into difficulty at the outset.

For decades Charles Sumner, chairman of the Senate Foreign Relations Committee, had been a towering public figure. A strident abolitionist, Sumner took on martyr status before the Civil War, when South Carolina Congressman Preston Brooks violently assaulted him with a cane as the senator was delivering a speech, nearly beating him to death. An ardent champion of equal rights for African Americans after the war, Sumner had been a strong advocate for removing Johnson from office. Known for his vanity, social snobbery, and enormous ego (Grant referred to him as all "puffed-up"), Sumner believed that he was more qualified than Grant to run the nation.[28]

After taking office, Grant had been exceedingly deferential to the senator. He appointed allies of Sumner to attorney general, secretary of the treasury, and minister to the United Kingdom, as well as to scores of lower-level posts. Nevertheless, Sumner delayed confirmation of Grant's choices for other positions and intervened in the Grant administration's negotiations with the British government over the resolution of the so-called *Alabama* claims. (The dispute between the two nations

---

26   Ibid., 145.

27   Chernow, 660; Bunting, 105.

28   Charles W. Calhoun, *The Presidency of Ulysses S. Grant* (Lawrence, KS: University Press of Kansas, 2017), 255.

arose after Confederate ships, which had been assembled in the United Kingdom during the recent war, fired upon and damaged several American vessels.)

After a draft treaty to annex Santo Domingo was written, Grant took the unusual step of calling upon Sumner at his home one evening to brief him on the treaty that the president planned to submit to the Senate.[29] Grant departed from the meeting with the impression that Sumner would be supportive. Friends of Sumner and a member of the cabinet, who sat in on Sumner's meeting with Grant, concluded likewise. However, Grant may have ascribed too little importance to a matter the senator had twice broached during their discussion.

At the very time the president was seeking Sumner's support for the Santo Domingo initiative, Grant was in the process of removing Sumner's friend, James M. Ashley, who may have made insulting comments about Grant, as governor of the Montana Territory. When Sumner asked Grant whether Ashley might retain his post or be named to another, Grant referred to Ashley, a former Radical Republican congressman from Ohio, as "a mischief-maker and a worthless fellow." Grant expressed the hope that Sumner would not oppose the nomination of Ashley's successor. When Sumner brought up the matter a second time that evening, the President kept his silence.[30]

Looking back on the Santo Domingo episode later on, Secretary of State Hamilton Fish recalled that Sumner mentioned his interest in Ashley whenever the topic of Santo Domingo was raised.[31] Senator Timothy O. Howe, a Wisconsin Republican, reported that Sumner became particularly venomous in his criticisms of the treaty and upped his personal attacks upon Grant and Fish after Grant submitted the name of Ashley's replacement to the Senate for consideration.[32]

Had Sumner presented the president with a *quid pro quo?* Grant thought not. Sumner, he told a colleague, "could never have been bribed but in one way. . . . by flattery."[33] Despite this recognition, Grant did not appear to have flattered Sumner very much after his initial visit to the senator's home. Sumner, as Ron Chernow noted, "wanted his vanity stroked, but Grant, pure in his sense of rectitude, refused to appease him . . . ."[34] If Sumner's version was accurate, he had certainly allowed himself some room to maneuver. He recalled saying, "I am an Administration

29   Ibid., 230-31.

30   Chernow, 691-92; David Donald, *Charles Sumner and the Rights of Man* (New York: Alfred A. Knopf, 1970), 434-36.

31   Calhoun, 234.

32   Chernow, 692.

33   Donald, 436.

34   Chernow, 694.

man, and whatever you do will always find in me the most careful and candid consideration."[35] Sumner, in his subsequent opposition to Grant's proposal, may also have been acting out of a sense of wounded pride. Sumner told Fish that Grant sought the chairman's vote, but never sought his "advice & counsel."[36]

Given the high priority that Grant awarded to improving the lives of African Americans, was finding a spot for Ashley, if it would solidify Sumner's support for the treaty, too high a price to pay? Over his eight years as president, Grant regularly appointed and replaced people at the request of persons outside his inner circle whom he sensed a need to please.[37] Sumner biographer David Herbert Donald noted that Sen. Simon Cameron of Pennsylvania had changed his position on the treaty—from "against" in committee to "for" on the floor—after Grant had, in the interval between the two votes, named Cameron's son-in-law minister to Turkey.[38]

After Grant formally presented the document to the Senate, Sumner delayed holding hearings, perhaps in the hope the Ashley matter might be resolved. He remained non-committal until after his committee colleagues had voiced their opinions. His subsequent behavior underscores the view that his eventual opposition had been rooted in factors other than the treaty's merits. In his attempts to defeat it, Sumner voiced contradictory arguments, on the one hand arguing that a greater American presence in the Caribbean would dwarf efforts by black-led republics to govern themselves, while at the same time questioning whether non-whites in the region were capable of self-rule.[39]

On March 15, the Foreign Relations Committee voted 5 to 2 against the treaty. As the full Senate began to debate its merits, Grant mounted an intensive

---

35   Donald, 436.

36   Chernow, 720.

37   After Sumner came out against the treaty, a group of Southern congressional Republicans, seeking to cement their ties with Grant, complained that they were under pressure from African American constituents, who regarded Sumner as much of a hero as they did Grant, not to break with the New Englander. The emerging bloc suggested they would have an easier time doing so if Grant named a southerner to the cabinet. Grant complied, replacing his first attorney general, Ebenezer R. Hoar, a Sumner ally, with Amos T. Akerman, a transplanted Georgian, who went on to be a relentless pursuer of the paramilitary Ku Klux Klan. A year later, Grant, now under pressure to remove Akerman, who had opposed granting subsidies in land grants and bonds to railroad interests, replaced Akerman with former Oregon senator George H. Williams, who followed Akerman's tough pursuit of the Klan.
   In 1875, Grant, alerted to an allegation that Williams' wife had extorted $30,000 from a corporation in exchange for a promise that she would have her husband drop the government's case against it, Grant replaced Williams with Edwards Pierrepont. While this furthered Grant's objective of bringing the corrupt within his administration to justice, Pierrepont awarded less of a priority to using federal troops to protect former slaves than had his two predecessors. In his final year in office, Grant replaced Pierrepont with Alphonso Taft, who enthusiastically supported Grant's interventions in South Carolina and Louisiana to uphold the right of African Americans to vote.

38   Donald, 452.

39   Chernow, 715; Calhoun, chapters 9–10.

lobbying campaign of the kind he would repeat on behalf of a groundbreaking Ku Klux Klan bill. Grant went to the Capitol and made his case directly to senators, one by one. He hosted skeptics at the White House and tried to persuade them. As the vote neared, Sumner argued that the best way to assist southern blacks was to increase federal pressure on southern whites. Grant predicted that the free markets he expected to emerge on Santo Domingo would sound the death knell to slavery in Puerto Rico and Cuba, as slaves on these islands escaped to the new American territory.[40]

The battle for ratification disrupted longstanding allies and produced some unanticipated coalitions. The rift between Sumner and Grant embarrassed the administration and delighted white supremacists. Siding with Sumner were all Democrats, Republican "reformers" such as Senator Carl Schurz of Missouri, and luminaries such as Henry Adams, angry that they had been excluded from Grant's administration.[41] Reformers denounced the "spoils system" and the patronage associated with it as corrupt and argued instead for a professional civil service. Frederick Douglass and other advocates for former slaves defended the spoils system Grant practiced as the vehicle that would enable African Americans to rise at a more accelerated pace.

The debate over the treaty occasioned some of the most racist, nativist, and religiously prejudicial language ever heard on the floor of the U.S. Senate. E. L. Godkin, editor of the *Nation,* voiced concern that a high number of Santo Domingo's 120,000 residents were Roman Catholics.[42] Charles Francis Adams, Jr., predicted that universal male suffrage, which Grant advocated, would produce "the government of ignorance and vice . . . [with] a European, and especially Celtic, proletariat on the Atlantic coast, an African proletariat on the shores of the Gulf; and a Chinese proletariat on the Pacific."[43] Standing with Grant were party wheelhorses such as Roscoe Conkling of New York, Oliver P. Morton of Indiana, and others, whose organizations depended upon the political largesse Grant sent

40   Chernow, 695.

41   Henry Adams, *The Education of Henry Adams* (Boston: Houghton Mifflin Company, 1918), 280-81. "I have always considered that Grant wrecked my own life, and the last hope or chance of lifting society back to a reasonably high plane," Adams told his brother. Adams's comment that the progress of evolution from President Washington to President Grant "was alone evidence enough to upset Darwin" remains the most famous insult Grant ever suffered. Adams, 266.

42   Eric Foner, *Reconstruction: America's Unfinished Revolution, 1863–1877* (New York: Harper & Row, 1988), 496.

43   Ibid., 497.

their way. Undergirding them were those David Herbert Donald described as "the New Radicals."[44]

After the treaty was defeated in a tie vote of 28 to 28, short of the two-thirds vote required for ratification, Grant continued to pursue this policy. He persuaded Congress to authorize a commission to visit Santo Domingo and recommend other options of making it part of the United States.[45] In his next annual message, Grant suggested annexation by joint resolution and cited the precedent of Texas, which had joined the Union in 1845 after being an independent republic.[46]

But the moment had passed. As the commission worked on its report, opposition to the idea had crystalized, and public interest and support waned. Given Grant's initial motivation in advancing the Santo Domingo annexation—providing freed slaves with options through which they might leverage improved economic opportunities, living conditions, and security, either in the American South or elsewhere—one wonders why the eighteenth president did not seek to bring this about through other means. One approach might have been to authorize the Freedmen's Bureau to assist the relocation of former slaves to the vast, and largely unsettled, American West. (Historians estimate that one in four cowboys who migrated westward after the Civil War were African American.[47])

While the Santo Domingo affair constituted an early setback for the president, Grant learned valuable lessons from the experience. Historians David Herbert Donald and Brooks D. Simpson suggest that because the break between Grant and Sumner came early in the administration, Grant was able to build a formidable and reliable base of support by solidifying his support among other Republican members of Congress, especially from Southern states.

Grant also emerged from the episode more willing and able to communicate his goals to the public and the press through messages, public appearances, and letters to colleagues that were leaked. In the aftermath of the treaty's defeat, Grant

---

44   Donald, 446.

45   The commissioners were former Radical Republican senator Ben Wade; founding president of Cornell University Andrew D. White; and Samuel G. Howe, husband of Julia Ward Howe. Frederick Douglass served as its assistant secretary. Calhoun, 298-99. All, save White, had been close allies of Sumner in the battles to abolish slavery.

46   Draft Annual Message, 5 December 1870, *PUSG*, 21:39.

47   Katie Nodjimbadem, "The Lesser-Known History of African-American Cowboys," *Smithsonian*, February 13, 2017, accessed 12 February 2022, https://www.smithsonianmag.com/history/lesser-known-history-african-american-cowboys-180962144/. See also Paul W. Stewart & Wallace Yvonne Ponce, *Black Cowboys* (Broomfield, CO: Phillips Publishing, 1986); Monroe Lee Billington & Roger D. Hardaway, eds., *African Americans on the Western Frontier* (Niwot, CO: University Press of Colorado, 1998); Philip Durham & Everett L. Jones, *The Negro Cowboys* (Lincoln, NE: University of Nebraska Press, 1983); Tricia Martineau Wagner, *Black Cowboys of the Old West: True, Sensational, and Little-Known Stories from History* (Guilford, CT: Twodot, 2011).

acted swiftly to assure the success of another high priority of his, resolving the *Alabama* claims. He dismissed Sumner's friend as minister to the U.K. Meanwhile, his allies in the Senate stripped Sumner of his committee chairmanship and removed him from the Foreign Relations Committee. Grant's team may have had little choice, given that the *Alabama* claims negotiations were proceeding apace, and their resolution would entail a treaty between the U.S. and the U.K. Historians consider Grant's securing a permanent peace between the U.S. and the U.K. through arbitration his greatest achievement in foreign affairs.[48]

In the first two years of the Grant administration, the sporadic eruptions of violence against and intimidation of former slaves evolved into an organized resistance through "guerilla warfare." One historian compared the strategy and tactics of the former Confederates to those North Vietnam later employed against the United States in the 1960s and 1970s. The strategy entailed a weaker power exhausting the patience of the stronger, relying on its capacity to inflict high costs upon its more powerful adversary. This, in turn, reduced public support for the stronger side to the point that it was ready to yield.[49] All over the South, the Ku Klux Klan, founded in 1865 by former Confederate officers, and other terrorist groups engaged in intimidation, violence, kidnappings, murders, and anything else they could think of to keep freedmen and southern Republicans from voting or from taking office if elected.

These terrorist groups were the military arm of the Democratic Party in southern states. With the guerillas taking the initiative, the administration had to decide whether and when to intervene militarily. Always factoring into its decision were what effects its actions would have on northern public opinion, how the Republican Party would fare in northern state elections, and whether Republican state governments in the South were strong enough to sustain themselves without an overwhelming federal presence.

Grant varied his tactics accordingly, depending upon Republican strength in Congress and the internal politics in the various states. In response to a series of successful military interventions to maintain order and assure fair elections during Grant's early years in office, Democrats modified their overall tactics. Under the label of the "New Departure," they tailored their approach and timing of their actions in ways to maximize their influence with northern public opinion. Their established leaders professed allegiance to the Constitution and to recently enacted constitutional amendments and federal statutes and promised to treat blacks and whites equally, all in exchange for a return to "home rule." While they spoke to

48   Calhoun, 7.

49   Bunting, 108-09.

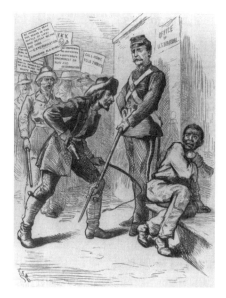

While white Southern men openly threatened violence against newly enfranchised freedmen, Grant used the power of the army to intervene. The strategy had only limited success.

Library of Congress

outsiders of compromise and conciliation, they and their minions often conspired, surreptitiously or through emissaries, with paramilitary organizations in their region, who continued to terrorize black voters and their Republican allies.

With Grant's strong support, Congress enacted several Enforcement Acts between 1870 and 1872 that enabled the president to use military force, among other means, to curb violence against the former slaves and guaranteed them their rights under the Constitution. The first of these, passed in May 1870, protected voting rights and prohibited people from banding together in groups, traveling in disguise along public highways, and trespassing on the property of another with the intention of violating citizens' constitutional rights. Senator Oliver P. Morton introduced a resolution in December of that year requiring the president to communicate information about threatened resistance to the laws of the United States. A select Senate committee was formed to investigate evidence Grant submitted.[50]

Also in 1870, Grant and his congressional allies established the Department of Justice, headed by the attorney general, who had been functioning primarily as the government's lawyer. The new department brought federal prosecutors operating throughout the country into a network of United States attorneys (then known as "district attorneys"). The new department aggressively prosecuted violations of the post–Civil War constitutional amendments and recently enacted statutes. Within the department, Congress established the Office of Solicitor General and charged it with bringing cases on behalf of the U.S. government to the Supreme Court.

The following year, Congress created a joint committee of both houses to expand its investigation and passed two additional acts to enforce the Fourteenth and Fifteenth Amendments. The first of these, which became law in February 1871, "federalized" national elections and empowered federal judges and U.S.

---

50   "The Enforcement Acts of 1870 and 1871," U.S. Senate, accessed 12 February 2022, https://www.senate.gov/artandhistory/history/common/generic/EnforcementActs.htm.

marshals to supervise local polling places. The second, passed in April 1871 and known as the "Ku Klux Klan Act," empowered the president to use the armed forces to combat those who conspired to deny equal protection of the laws and to suspend *habeas corpus*, if necessary, to enforce the act. Grant, though wary of being portrayed as a "military dictator," pressed for the legislation to enable the federal government to maintain order, quell violence, and secure citizens their rights. Although he acted within established republican institutions, those who opposed his Reconstruction policy derided him as "Kaiser Grant."[51]

In April Grant, accompanied by key figures of his administration, appeared at the Capitol to lobby in person on behalf of the Ku Klux Klan bill.[52] It passed the House 93 to 74 and the Senate 36 to 13. Under this legislation, for the first time, the president received the power to act directly against individuals and organized entities that violated the rights of citizens.[53] Grant made ample use of his newly acquired powers to police elections and maintain order at the request of elected southern governors.

Acting at the behest of the governors preserved the principle of federalism, providing both the appearance and reality of republicanism, as opposed to military rule. Grant found the newly enacted statute authorizing him to suspend *habeas corpus* in response to acts of violence a particularly effective mechanism. One of its purposes was to reduce witness tampering in the interval between the arrest of accused violators and their subsequent indictments and trials. Grant's second attorney general, Amos T. Akerman, though a native northerner, had spent much of his life in the South and had served as a Confederate military officer. He and the new Solicitor General, Benjamin H. Bristow, proved vigorous enforcers of the new statute.[54]

Upon the request of the governor of South Carolina, Grant ordered troops in to assist federal agents in breaking up bands of nightriders. In October, he suspended *habeas corpus* in nine South Carolina counties. With Akerman taking personal charge of the federal operation, hundreds were arrested, and order was restored. Throughout the South, federal grand juries brought 3,384 indictments and obtained 1,143 convictions. Akerman was most effective in persuading ringleaders to provide information about the worst offenders in exchange for their release from custody.

51   Ibid.; Chernow, 705; Simpson, *Reconstruction Presidents*, 155.

52   Chernow, 705.

53   *Congressional Globe* 19 April 1871, 42nd Congress, 1st Session, 808, 831.

54   Calhoun, 321.

The years Akerman had spent in the South, living and working with many of his future adversaries, served him and Grant well. He wrote a friend that he was up against nothing less than "a community, nominally civilized, [which] has been so fully under the domination of systematic and organized depravity."[55] Akerman advised his superior not to be taken in by either sweet-talk or promises of peace and conciliation in exchange for leniency: "They [the extremists] take all kindness on the part of the Government as evidence of timidity, and, hence are emboldened to lawlessness by it."[56] Having been predisposed to be more accommodating in the expectation of building goodwill in the southern states, Grant came to appreciate the soundness of Akerman's advice.

From the outset of his presidency, Grant recognized that the ultimate endurance of his civil rights and Reconstruction policies rested upon Republicans retaining control of Congress and of northern state governments. Those who worked to thwart him, attuned to this, made sure that the violence they provoked was most intense whenever Republican grasp over its northern base was most tenuous. They regarded northern impatience with Reconstruction and the public's desire to move on to other matters, like the downturn of the economy in 1873, as resources they could use to their advantage and planned their moves accordingly.

Grant's power to shape the course of Reconstruction, if not his resolve, began to weaken after Republicans lost control of the House of Representatives in the 1874 election and saw their hold on the Senate reduced by nine seats. Still, Grant was of no mind to abandon his goals. To those who said that he concerned himself too much with the plight of African Americans, he had a simple response: "Treat the negro as a citizen and a voter, as he is and must remain, and soon parties will be divided, not on the color line, but on principle. Then we shall have no complaint of sectional interference."[57] Contemptuous of southern assertions that in enforcing newly enacted constitutional amendments and statutes, Grant was infringing upon southern liberties, the president proclaimed to a colleague that what these critics really sought was "the right to kill negroes and Republicans without fear of punishment and without loss of caste or reputation."[58]

In the final months of the lame duck Congress, Grant pressed vigorously for the Civil Rights Act of 1875. It was to be the last such law until Dwight D. Eisenhower signed the 1957 Civil Rights Act into law on September 9 of that

---

55   Chernow, 709.

56   Ibid., 706; Simpson, *Reconstruction Presidents,* 155.

57   Simpson, *Reconstruction Presidents*, 175.

58   Ibid., 190-91.

year.[59] Again, Grant journeyed to the Capitol in person to lobby on behalf of the bill. The battle to enact it briefly reunited two former allies-turned-personal-enemies, Grant and Sumner. Sumner died prior to the bill's passage. On his coffin appeared a shield bearing the words: "Don't Let the Civil Rights Bill Fail."[60]

The new civil rights measure outlawed segregation in public accommodations and travel facilities—which Grant had called for in his Second Inaugural Address—and forbade the exclusion of African Americans from juries. Congress struck from the bill provisions that would have banned segregation in public schools and cemeteries. It reasoned that the schools measure would receive considerable opposition and possibly threaten the continuation of education of African American children.

By the fall of 1875, intimidation, violence, and disruption had become routine in statewide elections in the Deep South. In 1872, the year Grant was re-elected, both sides claimed victory in the hotly contested Louisiana gubernatorial election. After a federal judge proclaimed the Republican the victor, Grant put aside his reservations about the competence of the state administration and sent federal troops to uphold the judge's ruling. In response, a mob that included many former Confederate soldiers mounted an open rebellion. In the town of Colfax, over 100 blacks affiliated with the local militia and the Republican organization took refuge in a makeshift courthouse with a band of about 140 whites in pursuit, under the command of a Democratic candidate for sheriff. The attackers mowed down those who had fled and went on to murder those who had surrendered or had been taken prisoner. Grant's administration brought indictments against ninety-eight alleged perpetrators, tried nine, and secured convictions of three.[61]

Angered when congressional critics, including Democrats and reform Republicans, denounced federal intervention as "tyranny, despotism, and jack-boot domination," Grant declared in a message to the Senate that "every one of the Colfax miscreants goes unwhipped of justice, and no way can be found in this boasted land of civilization and Christianity to punish the perpetrators of this bloody and monstrous crime."[62] Grant vowed to do all within his power to maintain order in Louisiana. Under the command of General Philip H. Sheridan, federal troops prevented the Democrats, backed by mobs, from organizing the state legislature by force.

59   Later that month, Ike became the first president since Grant to use the full powers of the federal government to protect the rights and persons of African Americans when he sent the 101st Airborne to Little Rock, Arkansas.

60   Donald, 8.

61   Calhoun, 407.

62   Simpson, *Reconstruction Presidents*, 178.

With a similarly disputed election underway in Mississippi in 1875, Grant summarized to his new attorney general, Edwards Pierrepont, the situation he faced: "The whole public are tired out with these annual, autumnal outbreaks in the South, and there is so much unwholesome lying done by the press and people in regard to the cause and extent of these breaches of the peace that the great majority are ready now to condemn any interference on the part of the Government."[63] He had taken care to add that he did not see how he could evade a governor's call for help if it were made within the Constitution.[64]

The president instructed Pierrepont to draw up a proclamation, but not to issue it until Gov. Adelbert Ames demonstrated that he had used all the resources at his command to preserve order. Pierrepont, not enthusiastic about federal Reconstruction efforts, may have put more hurdles in Ames's way than Grant intended. With Grant away from Washington, D.C. Pierrepont, in constant touch with Republican operatives in Ohio, delayed taking action until the results of the gubernatorial election in Ohio were known.

Meanwhile, Mississippi Democrats marched under a mantra telegraphing their intentions: "Carry the election peaceably if we can, forcefully if we must." In the local idiom, "peaceably" did not necessarily convey an orderly election or an honest tally. Caught in a vise between satisfying Pierrepont's demands and not wanting to appear "incendiary," Ames entered into negotiations with local Democrats. He agreed to disband the primarily black state militia in exchange for promises that, if returned to office, Democrats would respect civil and political rights of both whites and blacks. After Rutherford B. Hayes was declared the winner in Ohio, federal troops were ordered to Mississippi, but arrived too late to do much good. The Democrats' strategy of intimidation by means that entailed little actual violence had been sufficient to hold down black turnout. Democrats seized control of the state's governorship, Mississippi proclaimed itself "Redeemed," and Ames was allowed to resign as an alternative to impeachment.[65]

Afterwards, Grant confided to an African American Mississippi congressman, John Roy Lynch, that he had tried as President to balance "duty on one side, and party obligation on the other." Grant termed his error in hesitating "one of the

---

63   Ibid., 186.

64   Chernow, 814.

65   Ibid.; Blanche Ames Ames, *Adelbert Ames, 1835–1933: General, Senator, Governor* (New York: Argosy-Antiquarian Ltd., 1964), 446; Simpson, *Reconstruction Presidents*, 185-88. For more on Ames, see Richard Nelson Current, *Three Carpetbag Governors* (Baton Rouge, LA: Louisiana State University Press, 1967); Richard Nelson Current, *Those Terrible Carpetbaggers* (New York: Oxford University Press, 1988); and George Plimpton, "A Clean Well-Lighted Place," *New York Review of Books*, 18 December 1980, accessed 12 February 2022, https://www.nybooks.com/articles/1980/12/18/a-clean-well-lighted-place/.

head and not of the heart."[66] Reflecting upon all this later, Grant lamented that the Southern states had not remained in conquered territorial status for a longer period of time so that their residents would have had more time to rise above "the madness of their leaders."[67]

Grant's capacity for self-reflection and capacity to admit mistakes were among his strengths as a leader. No place does this quality of his shine through more brightly than in the last annual message. "Mistakes have been made . . ." he admitted, "claiming only that I have acted in every instance from a conscientious desire to do what was right, constitutional, within the law, and for the very best interests of the whole people. Failures have been errors of judgment, not of intent."[68]

From the dawn of his administration until its twilight, Grant continually pressed to secure the results of the war he had won. He stayed true to these ends regardless of the pressures of immediate situations, the naivete with which he approached politics as a novice, fluctuations in political fortunes, and steady reshuffles in administrative personnel. While the slow unraveling of Reconstruction began its course with Supreme Court decisions handed down late in Grant's second term and the loss of congressional will after the elections of 1874, Grant courageously held the line.

When students, scholars, and political practitioners think of "transformational leaders," they conjure up images of achievements that endured well beyond the times of their initiator. In several areas, including the establishment of a permanent peace between the United States and Great Britain; the establishment of international arbitration as an all but universally accepted part of international diplomacy; the undergirding of the American economy on sound fiscal principles, first established by Alexander Hamilton; and the precedent of setting aside natural treasures as preserves for posterity to enjoy, Grant was certainly a transformational leader.[69]

Yet, in the establishing of equality before the law and in the use of republican institutions to safeguard citizens' constitutional rights, Grant's example may be cause for some pause before rendering such a judgment. To be sure, Grant had the character and courage to stand true to what he considered the actual cause of the Civil War and fought until his last day as president to preserve what he

66   Simpson, 188.

67   Brooks D. Simpson, "Mission Impossible: Reconstruction Policy Reconsidered," *Journal of the Civil War Era* (March 2016), No. 1, 6:100; John Russell Young, *Around the World with General Grant*, 2 vols. (New York: The American News Company, 1879), 2:362-63.

68   Richardson, 10:4354.

69   Theodore Roosevelt was in his teens when Grant signed legislation designating Yellowstone and the first national park.

regarded as the fruits of the war. Yet, as has been noted above, within a generation of his leaving office, many of his achievements were either allowed to erode or were dismantled through a combination of southern recalcitrance, northern apathy, and a succession of presidents and congresses who were less committed than Grant was to these important principles.

But not everything he achieved fell away or was pushed asunder. Although it would for many years go unenforced in the formerly seceded states and other areas, the Fifteenth Amendment permanently granted the franchise to African Americans in large portions of the nation where it had not existed prior to the Civil War. Likewise, legal and other precedents of Grant and his administration, while allowed to atrophy, had not all been entirely erased. In assessing Grant's record in securing equal rights for all Americans, the tools of the poet may offer better guidance than those of historians and political scientists. In "A Psalm of Life," first published in 1838, Henry Wadsworth Longfellow spoke of "Footprints on the sands of time," left by the departed, from which

> A forlorn and shipwrecked brother,
> Seeing, shall take heart again.[70]

During the second half of the last century, in the aftermath of yet another devastating war, also waged to preserve and fulfill the nation's founding principles and secure the survival of democratic institutions, bands of forlorn brothers and sisters took up a long-dormant cause. Bolstered by substantial shifts in public opinion, some of which they helped change, through a series of court cases, protests, marches, executive orders, enacted legislation, and a string of presidents from Harry Truman to Lyndon Johnson, they led the United States into what historians regard as its "Second Reconstruction."

With revisionism one of the few constants in the study and writing of history, historians are at last doing justice to the old soldier who, as a general and as a president, tried to make the promise inherent in the American founding a reality for the four million persons he helped free from bondage. History has at last caught up with Ulysses S. Grant, and the vision, courage, and grace he displayed in office are at last being appreciated.

---

70   Henry Wadsworth Longfellow, *The Works of Henry Wadsworth Longfellow*, 8 vols. (Boston: Houghton, Mifflin & Co., 1910), 1:21-22.

The United States on the World Stage: Foreign Policy During the Grant Administration

Chapter Ten | *Ryan P. Semmes*

Ulysses S. Grant entered the Executive Mansion with the weight of the nation on his shoulders. The top priority for the millions of recently freed black Americans was the ratification of the Fifteenth Amendment and the federal government's promise to support the rights of liberty and equality for these new citizens. Grant supported the Reconstruction Amendments, and he saw the bestowing of equal rights and citizenship on African Americans as an important step in the strengthening of the American Union. By supporting equality, Grant hoped that the violence in the South toward African Americans would subside and that those who were newly freedmen would prosper through their free labor. Along with these serious domestic issues, the Johnson administration handed Grant several foreign policy issues that, when combined with the domestic, represented an opportunity for the new administration to craft a single policy for achieving success in both arenas. Foreign and domestic policy during the Grant administration revolved around a set of principles that defined Reconstruction: protecting the rights of American citizens both at home and abroad, expansion in the Caribbean and the West, and maintaining a peaceful coexistence with Europe.

Americans did not agree on the policies of Reconstruction. Nor did they agree on the policies of foreign relations. But most Americans shared a sense of nationalism and exceptionalism about the United States's place in the world. Grant and his secretary of state, Hamilton Fish, believed that the United States was the arbiter of peace and liberty in the Western Hemisphere—the purveyor of civilization and democracy. They set out to establish a foreign policy that centered the United States as the beacon of freedom and as an antidote to European monarchy and uncivilized culture. To Grant, African Americans, European immigrants, and those from the Caribbean were all civilized men. In contrast, Native Americans, Mormons, unreconstructed Confederates, and immigrants from the Far East were uncivilized. Of these groups, though, Grant believed that Native Americans were best equipped to embrace republicanism and Western

Prior to his presidency, Ulysses S. Grant served together with Hamilton Fish on the board of the Peabody Education Fund. Standing, left to right: Admiral David Farragut, Fish, Grant, Bishop Charles P. McIlvaine, Samuel Wetmore. Seated, left to right: George Peabody, Robert C. Winthrop, William C. Rives.

Ulysses S. Grant Presidential Library

civilization; they were on a pathway to assimilation into the American body politic and, eventually, full citizenship. Mormons, through the practice of polygamy, were either unwilling or unable to accept traditional western morality and, by extension, republicanism. "That polygamy should exist in a free, enlightened, and Christian country, without the power to punish so flagrant a crime against decency and morality, seems preposterous," Grant wrote in his 1875 Annual Message. "But, as an institution, polygamy should be banished from the land. While this is being done, I invite the attention of Congress to another, though perhaps no less an evil, the importation of Chinese women, but few of whom are brought to our shores to pursue honorable or useful occupations." Chinese immigrants were hard workers, in Grant's eyes, but they were brought to the United States through a system that was essentially slavery, and Chinese women, he believed, were often brought as prostitutes. "I advise such legislation as will forever preclude the enslavement of [Chinese] people, upon our soil, under the name of Coolies," Grant wrote in his 1869 Annual Message to Congress. Grant viewed Chinese immigrants, both male and female, as victims of an unrepublican system. As for unreconstructed Confederates, Grant used the full force of the federal government to stamp out their violent reactions to equality. Grant's foreign policy, then, is best viewed as an extension of the Reconstruction arguments over who was best equipped to join the republican experiment. The Fifteenth Amendment provided voting rights for all male citizens, black and white, and all who embraced republicanism and civilization were, in Grant's eyes, welcome to the blessings of liberty. Such a policy, though, was constantly tested by international events that forced Grant to put expediency over republican principles.[1]

In 1862, Confederate naval Capt. Raphael Semmes, along with two young officers, boarded ship number 290 as it took its maiden voyage from the shipyards of Liverpool, England. Soon after, Semmes raised a Confederate flag on his newly christened *C.S.S. Alabama*. The *Alabama* proved to be one of a handful of British-made ships the Confederate Navy utilized to decimate American shipping. The powerful man-of-war easily destroyed American merchant ships that crossed its path, and the owners of these ships filed claims for lost goods and materials. After the United States achieved victory in the Civil War, these merchants looked to Great Britain to pay the claims, arguing that the British allowed the Confederate ships out of the port of Liverpool. Great Britain countered that the nation was not responsible for the misdeeds of a privately owned shipbuilding company and that they had remained neutral during the war. Then-Secretary of State William H. Seward tasked Maryland Senator Reverdy Johnson with resolving the issues between the United States and Great Britain, which included not only the *Alabama* claims, but also border disputes in the American Northwest, disputes due to fishing rights, and the problem of British subjects claiming American citizenship. Johnson and the British secretary of state for foreign affairs, the Earl of Clarendon, agreed to a convention that sent the claims to arbitration. However, the United States Senate summarily rejected the convention, with the chairman of the Senate Foreign Relations Committee, Charles Sumner, arguing that the British refused to take responsibility for the *Alabama*. With this refusal, Sumner boasted that they owed the United States for not only the direct claims that merchants filed for lost ships and goods, but also indirect claims arising from all Confederate victories after the summer of 1863. Sumner estimated the cost was upwards of $2.5 billion. Instead of payment, he argued, the United States would accept Canada.[2]

---

1   Annual Message, 7 December 1875, John Y. Simon, ed., *The Papers of Ulysses S. Grant*, 32 vols. (Carbondale, IL: Southern Illinois University Press, 1967–2012), 26:415, hereafter cited as *PUSG*; Annual Message, 6 December 1869, *PUSG*, 20:36; Andrew F. Lang, *A Contest of Civilizations: Exposing the Crisis of American Exceptionalism in the Civil War Era* (Chapel Hill, NC: University of North Carolina Press, 2021).

2   Benjamin Moran Journal, 1 September 1862, Sarah Agnes Wallace & Frances Elma Gillespie, eds., *The Journal of Benjamin Moran, 1857–1865*, 2 vols. (Chicago: University of Chicago Press, 1948–1949), 2:1063-64; Phillip E. Myers, *Dissolving Tensions: Rapprochement and Resolution in British-American-Canadian Relations in the Treaty of Washington Era, 1865–1914* (Kent, OH: Kent State University Press, 2015), 80-85. See also Frank J. Merli, *The Alabama, British Neutrality, and the American Civil War*, David M. Fahey, ed. (Bloomington, IN: Indiana University Press, 2004), 129-40.

The Johnson-Clarendon Convention landed on Grant's desk in early 1869, and the president was as unhappy about it as the Senate. He understood that a conflict with Britain would be detrimental to the economic growth of the United States. Grant wanted Secretary of State Fish to find a solution to the *Alabama* claims so he could implement his plan to expand the reach of the United States across the Western Hemisphere. Another concern for the Grant administration was the development of treaties with other nations regarding naturalized American citizens. Thousands of immigrants arrived in the United States from Europe, Asia, and the Caribbean, and with the changes in citizenship effected by the Fourteenth Amendment, the administration sought to renegotiate naturalization treaties with other countries. George Bancroft, minister to Prussia, negotiated the first in a series of treaties that allowed individuals to switch citizenship loyalty. These treaties, known as the Bancroft Treaties, came with several caveats that allowed each nation to revoke or reinstitute citizenship for their former citizens. European immigrants were desirable citizens as they had embraced the republican values of the United States. As for immigrants from Asia, diplomat Anson Burlingame negotiated a treaty that allowed trade between the United States and China, lifting previous restrictions on trade and on Chinese immigration for the purposes of labor; however, the treaty forbade naturalization. Grant supported the Burlingame treaty because he wanted to expand the reach of American economic trade in the East. He supported the lack of naturalization for Chinese immigrants because he did not believe that Chinese immigrants were civilized enough to embrace republicanism, an important caveat in his views on citizenship. He was willing to send Americans to China to educate the Chinese in what he believed was civilized and modern culture, but he was not ready to regard them as assimilable.[3]

Immigrants who traveled to the United States and became naturalized citizens did not always remain in the United States. Many of these naturalized citizens returned to their homelands for work, for family reasons, or to spread liberty to their former country. In Ireland, British authorities arrested Irish American nationalists—members of the Fenian Brotherhood—for seditious activities against the Crown. Spanish authorities arrested Cuban Americans living in Cuba and working with the rebellion against Spain. Many of these immigrants asserted their rights as American citizens and sought the authority of the United States for assistance. Accordingly, the Grant administration sought to codify in treaties exactly how these nations were to treat naturalized Americans. The negotiation of a Bancroft Treaty with Great Britain and the national call for the Grant administration

---

3   Ronald C. White, *American Ulysses: A Life of Ulysses S. Grant* (New York: Random House, 2016), 502-03; Adam Badeau to Anson Burlingame, 28 December 1868, *PUSG*, 19:326.

to intercede on behalf of Irish and Cuban Americans made up a great deal of the work of Grant's secretary of state. Therefore, a primary objective of Grant's foreign policy was the settlement of citizenship claims for naturalized Americans so similar problems could be avoided in the future. Reconstruction changed citizenship rights in the United States, and naturalized citizens were just as affected by these changes. Grant addressed this issue by first issuing a proclamation outlawing American citizens, both natural-born and naturalized, from interfering in political strife in other nations. This was a direct result of the political interference of both the Fenian Brotherhood and the Cuban Junta.[4]

The ideas of equal rights, free labor, and liberty that Grant espoused and that the United States Constitution instilled following the Civil War had a profound effect on naturalized Americans. These new citizens embraced American republicanism and wanted to bring the blessings of liberty back to the oppressed in their homelands. The Fenian Brotherhood sought independence for Ireland and the end of British rule on the Emerald Isle. To strike a blow against the British, the Fenians began conducting raids from the United States into Canada. One group even purchased a ship and sailed to Ireland in the hopes of fomenting rebellion there. In all cases, the Irish nationalists were arrested, after which they claimed American citizenship. At the same time, exiled Cubans and naturalized Cuban Americans began to organize expeditions to Cuba to supply the rebellion there with material needs and manpower. Whereas the membership of the Fenian Brotherhood consisted almost entirely of members of the Democratic Party, the Cuban Junta had widespread support within Grant's Republican Party. As such, arguments within his own cabinet over recognizing the belligerent rights of the Cuban rebels versus offering only limited support to the Fenians threatened to fracture his administration. No one supported the Cuban belligerents more than Grant's trusted friend and secretary of war, Gen. John A. Rawlins. Rawlins was a devoted supporter of the independence movement in Cuba and the emancipation of slaves throughout the Western Hemisphere. As one of Grant's most trusted advisers during the American Civil War, the president placed stock in Rawlins's opinion. Secretary Fish, on the other hand, understood that the recognition of the Cuban rebels would undermine the tenuous relations between the United States and Great Britain over the *Alabama* claims.[5]

Late in the first year of his first term, prominent Republicans such as John Sherman, Henry Highland Garnet, and Frederick Douglass all hoped the

---

4   Lucy E. Salyer, *Under the Starry Flag: How a Band of Irish Americans Joined the Fenian Revolt and Sparked a Crisis over Citizenship* (Cambridge, MA: The Belknap Press, 2018), 189-94.

5   White, 506-07.

president would supply material support to the independence movement in Cuba. In early autumn of 1869, Rawlins seemingly had convinced the president that supporting the cause of liberty in Cuba was the right thing to do. As Republicans, the end of slavery in the Western Hemisphere was a central tenet of their political philosophy. Grant agreed; however, in September 1869, Rawlins, who had been sick for months, succumbed to tuberculosis. At the same time, Hamilton Fish was pushing Grant in the opposite direction. Fish argued that the Cubans were not an equal belligerent against Spain but were Spanish subjects in open rebellion. The Cubans held no territory, Fish argued; they had no organized government, and they were incapable of defeating the Spanish volunteer forces. The United States could end slavery there with diplomacy rather than support of the rebellion. More pragmatically, Fish argued that to recognize the Cubans would undermine the American argument against Great Britain. According to that argument, the British violated neutrality in the American Civil War by providing material support for the Confederates, who were not a separate government but were American citizens in open rebellion against the United States government. Therefore, Britain was not a neutral party in the Civil War but was openly supporting a rebellion against the United States. The Spanish made the same argument about the Cubans: They were Spanish subjects in rebellion against the central authority in Spain.[6]

American citizens found guilty of supporting rebellions in other nations were violating national sovereignty. Fish convinced Grant to issue a proclamation stating that the United States would not allow its citizens to undermine the authority of either the United States or of sovereign nations. "[I] hereby declare and proclaim that all persons hereafter found within the territory or jurisdiction of the United States committing any . . . violations of the sovereignty of the United States for which punishment is provided by law, will be rigorously prosecuted," Grant proclaimed. "[U]pon conviction and sentence to punishment, [these citizens] will not be entitled to expect or receive the clemency of the Executive to save them from the consequences of their guilt." This proclamation led to the arrest of hundreds of Irish and Cuban nationalists who were supporting the rebellion against their European oppressors. With this proclamation, though, Grant bowed to diplomatic expediency over his own republican beliefs.[7]

Along with the troubles with Great Britain and Spain, the Grant administration received an offer the president could not refuse. On April 5, 1869, Secretary Fish was finishing a long day of meetings at both the White House and his office

---

6   Hamilton Fish, Diary, 13 December 1869, Hamilton Fish papers, Library of Congress, hereafter cited as HF Papers.

7   Proclamation, 12 October 1870, *PUSG*, 20:307-09.

when a stranger asked to see him. The man, Joseph W. Fabens, claimed he was the authorized representative of the Dominican Republic in Washington, sent to offer the Dominican Republic as a territory to the United States. Fish informed Fabens that the United States was not interested in the scheme; however, he was duty-bound to report the meeting to President Grant. Upon doing so, he found the president interested in the idea. Grant believed that the economic and national security of the United States relied upon a presence in the Caribbean, and the Dominican Republic was perfectly situated for such a purpose. Grant argued that the United States should be the arbiter of freedom in the Western Hemisphere and, to support liberty and emancipation in the region, the United States must have a military outpost in the Caribbean.[8]

Grant's beliefs stemmed from his concern that war was a real possibility between the United States and Great Britain over the *Alabama* claims. The president worried that the British, as well as the Spanish, held control over too many territories in the Caribbean. In the event of a war with either European power, the powerful navies of both nations would cut off shipping from the southern United States to the Atlantic Coast. At the same time, Grant saw the Dominican Republic as an answer to the economic issues of the United States, as well as the violent racist terrorism in the American South. Grant was hoping to build a biracial society that allowed for equality for all civilized republican men, regardless of race. To Grant, the racial makeup of the Dominican Republic was hardly an issue; rather, he was more interested in the political and economic strength of the nation. Grant understood that the Dominican Republic contained tens of thousands of acres of uncultivated land. As a United States territory, American citizens could work the land and grow the staple crops that flourished in the Caribbean—such as coffee, sugar, and tropical fruits—instead of importing crops produced by enslaved labor in Cuba, fulfilling the promise of freedom inherent in Reconstruction. The Dominicans, as new American citizens, would profit from the development of this land and the growing American market. Grant's political foe, Carl Schurz, and others calling themselves "Liberal Republicans" believed the racial makeup of the Dominican Republic was a detriment to the United States' Reconstruction efforts, as they did not want to see more than one hundred thousand nonwhite Dominicans becoming American citizens. Grant, in contrast, saw these people as worthy of inclusion in the American experiment. In short, the annexation of the Dominican Republic as a territory of the United States was the first step in Grant's

8   Hamilton Fish, Diary, 5 April 1869, HF Papers.

plan to rid the Western Hemisphere of the sin of slavery and his plan to export the principles of Reconstruction throughout the region.[9]

When Grant's private secretary, Orville E. Babcock, returned from the Dominican Republic with a treaty of annexation in late 1869, the president assumed the Republican Party would support him. However, Charles Sumner immediately accused the Grant administration of corruption in the dealings, due in part to his anger at not having been informed of the treaty negotiations months earlier. As such, Sumner refused a vote on the treaty in the Senate Foreign Relations Committee. His comrades in Congress then appointed a Select Committee to investigate the treaty negotiations under the guise of an investigation into the treatment of an American named Davis Hatch, who was imprisoned by the Dominicans. Hostile members sought to cast Babcock as a corrupt conspirator who undermined Hatch's rights to hasten the acceptance of the treaty in the Dominican Republic. The committee found Babcock had acted with integrity and honor. Sumner, though, used the investigation as an opportunity to excoriate Grant in a lengthy closed-session speech in which he charged the president with corruption, claiming that the Dominican annexation was a scheme to steal Haiti. Grant's allies were indignant at Sumner's speech and vociferously defended him during debate on the treaty. However, after debate ended, the president was unable to acquire the necessary two-thirds majority vote in the Senate needed to ratify the treaty. The failure to secure annexation was one of Grant's greatest regrets as president, a subject he often returned to in his speeches and writings.[10]

9   Memorandum, [1869–1870], *PUSG,* 20:74-76; Brooks D. Simpson, *The Reconstruction Presidents* (Lawrence, KS: University Press of Kansas, 1998), 145-148; Stephen McCullough, *The Caribbean Policy of the Ulysses S. Grant Administration: Foreshadowing an Informal Empire* (Lanham, MD: Lexington Books, 2018), 53-56.

10   Grant worked with members of the Senate to appoint a special commission to investigate the political and financial situation in the Dominican Republic as well as the desire of the Dominicans to join the United States. Grant appointed political and academic leaders to the commission, but he angered many African American supporters when he named Frederick Douglass not as a commissioner, but as assistant secretary to the commission. In Santo Domingo, Douglass witnessed the poverty throughout the nation and the desire of the Dominicans to join the United States. He became a full supporter of annexation. Douglass's support for annexation caused a rift between him and Sumner, but it strengthened his support for President Grant. The commission returned to the United States reporting to Congress its full support of annexation. But the Senate again failed to take up the treaty proposal, and annexation was finished. Jean Edward Smith, *Grant* (New York: Simon & Schuster, 2001), 499-506; White, 507-11; Ron Chernow, *Grant* (New York: Penguin Press, 2017), 693-96; Charles W. Calhoun, *The Presidency of Ulysses S. Grant* (Lawrence, KS: University Press of Kansas, 2017), 240-53; H.W. Brands, *The Man Who Saved the Union: Ulysses S. Grant in War and Peace* (New York: Doubleday, 2012), 460-62; David W. Blight, *Frederick Douglass: Prophet of Freedom* (New York: Simon & Schuster, 2018), 536-45; Ulysses S. Grant, *The Personal Memoirs of Ulysses S. Grant, The Complete Annotated Edition,* John F. Marszalek, David S. Nolen, & Louie P. Gallo, eds. (Cambridge, MA: The Belknap Press of Harvard University Press, 2017), 760-61; Joan Waugh, *U.S. Grant: American Hero, American Myth* (Chapel Hill, NC: University of North Carolina Press, 2009), 137.

As the administration was attempting to annex the Dominican Republic, a crisis was taking shape in Europe. Ulysses S. Grant's longtime political mentor and friend, Elihu B. Washburne, had settled easily into his role as minister to France. The position was a reward for Washburne's help to Grant, not only during the American Civil War, but also in his bid for the presidency. When, during the summer of 1870, France declared war on Prussia, Washburne found himself in the middle of a significant European conflict, with many American and German citizens living in France looking to him and the United States for protection after the French government labeled them enemies of the nation. Grant himself was more sympathetic to the Prussian side of the war, writing to Washburne that "The war has developed the fact here that every unreconstructed rebel simpathyses [sic] with France, without exception, while the loyal element is almost as universally the other way."[11] Grant issued a proclamation of neutrality in the European conflict, noting that "great numbers of the citizens of the United States reside within the territories or dominions of each of the said belligerents and carry on commerce, trade, or other business, or pursuits, therein protected by the faith of treaties." The United States, Grant proclaimed, would remain neutral in the conflict, and American citizens were barred from joining either the French or Prussian militaries and, most importantly, from providing arms "or attempting to fit out and arm . . . any ship or vessel with intent that such ship or vessel shall be employed in the service of either of the said belligerents."[12]

While Grant and Washburne were supporting the German people in Paris and preventing American citizens from joining the fight, the Grant administration was selling off arms and ammunition to private American contractors, notably Remington and Sons, who in turn sold the materiel to the French. Grant's political opponents in the Republican Party seized on these transactions as evidence that the administration was in league with the French and not a supporter of the German people or German American citizens. German Americans made up a large voting bloc in the Republican Party, and Grant's enemies jumped at the chance to sever their support of the president. After the war ended, Charles Sumner proposed a Senate investigation into the issue, with support from Liberal Republican and German immigrant Senator Carl Schurz, claiming the arms sales were a direct

11   Alison Clark Efford, "The Arms Scandal of 1870–1872: Immigrant Liberal Republicans and America's Place in the World," in David Prior, ed., *Reconstruction in a Globalizing World* (New York: Fordham University Press, 2018), 94-120; David Paull Nickles, "Telegraph Diplomats: The United States' Relations with France in 1848 and 1870," *Technology and Culture* (January 1999), No. 1, 40:1-25; USG to Elihu B. Washburne, 22 August 1870, *PUSG*, 20:254.

12   Proclamation, 22 August 1870, *PUSG*, 20:235-37; Daniela L. Caglioti, "Waging War in Civilians: The Expulsion of Aliens in the Franco-Prussian War," *Past & Present* (November 2013), No. 221, 168-75; Calhoun, 173-75.

violation of United States neutrality. Sumner and Schurz cited the sales as one example in a long line of corruption emanating from the Grant administration. This corruption, they charged, revolved around the doling out of government offices and, more importantly, the management of Reconstruction. To Schurz, and to a lesser extent Sumner, the Grant administration was a dictatorship that utilized "ignorant" and unprepared African American voters as a means of keeping Grant's Republicans in political power. Once in power, Schurz charged, Grant and his cronies fleeced the treasury and positioned the executive to take more power from the people. Schurz's charges stoked a base made up of German Americans who were no friends to African Americans or the concept of racial equality. They compared Grant to the oligarchs of Europe and the American South, casting him as an American Napoleon. As such, Schurz and his Liberal Republican allies represented a significant challenge to the Grant administration in Congress. Though Schurz was successful in rallying numerous German Americans to call upon the Senate to create a special committee to investigate arms sales, ultimately, the committee found that the Grant administration had not violated any laws by selling arms to third parties who in turn sold the arms to France.[13]

Amidst the annexation controversy and war in Europe came the settlement of the *Alabama* claims. Having successfully maneuvered all parties into negotiations in Washington, D.C., Secretary Fish set out to settle the most important foreign policy issue on the Grant administration's agenda. Grant appointed a commission, with Fish as its chair, and the British sent a commission of their own (which included representatives from Canada) to Washington in early 1871. Grant wanted to make sure all diplomatic issues between the United States and Great Britain were on the table, and Fish and Sir John Rose of Canada negotiated that the northwest border disputes—disagreements over the San Juan Islands—as well as Canadian and American fishing rights, and other issues were included along with the *Alabama* claims. In the spring of 1871, the two commissions met and began the work of negotiating a compromise. The Americans were willing to send many of the disputes to an international arbitrator, as Grant viewed this method of settling concerns between two nations as a civilized alternative to war. Speaking to a crowd in Glasgow, Scotland, after he left office, Grant noted, "I was always a man of peace, and I shall always continue of that mind. Though I may not live to see the general settlement of national disputes by arbitration, it will not be very many years before that system of settlement will be adopted."[14]

13   *Congressional Globe*, 42nd Cong., 2nd Sess., 953, 1040-48 (1872); Efford, "The Arms Scandal," 109-11; Alison Clark Efford, *German Immigrants, Race, and Citizenship in the Civil War Era* (New York: Cambridge University Press, 2013), 186-88; Calhoun, 370.

14   Speech, Glasgow, 13 September 1877, *PUSG*, 28:271-72; Calhoun, 329-41.

The Joint High Commission that convened in Washington worked to arrange an agreement amenable not only to the Grant administration, but also to the United States Senate and the British Parliament. Unfortunately, the chair of the Senate Foreign Relations Committee, Charles Sumner, refused to support Grant unless the British agreed to withdraw entirely from North America. Such an act would give Canada full independence and, Sumner hoped, open the door to American annexation of Canada. To remove this obstacle, Grant and Fish orchestrated Sumner's removal as chair of Foreign Relations. Fish conferred with Republican senators, explaining the problems Sumner had created for Republican politics and administration foreign policy, and party leaders voted to strip Sumner of his chairmanship. With Sumner out of the way, Fish was able to steer foreign policy on his own by negotiating a treaty with Britain without the Senate as an obstacle. With the Treaty of Washington, the United States and Great Britain agreed to send all disputes to international arbitration, with a commitment to abide by the rulings. The terms sent the northwest boundary dispute to Wilhelm I, King of Prussia, whose commission decided that the San Juan Islands were the property of the United States. The fisheries question was sent to arbitration that was not settled until 1877, with another commission ruling that the United States owed Canada and Great Britain $5.5 million. The debt was paid in 1878, but the two North American countries continued to squabble over territory until they reached a final settlement in 1888, three years after Grant's death.[15]

Finally, the treaty sent the arbitration of the *Alabama* claims to a tribunal in Geneva, Switzerland, where the United States was awarded $15.5 million for the direct claims against the *Alabama* and her sister ships. Grant and Fish supported the inclusion of the indirect claims—the cost of extending the war due to the destruction of American commerce—in the arbitration because they wanted an unbiased international body to rule on their inadmissibility. Fish believed that no nation should be able to charge another with indirect claims, and the ruling in Geneva set international precedent for just that. Grant was pleased with the outcome of the treaty and the arbitration, especially since the two nations peacefully avoided war, noting that the treaty was "the best settlement possible of the outstanding differences between us and Great Britain. . . . The point aimed at was . . . the settlement of an irritating and disturbing question likely any day to bring the two nations into armed conflict. My aim was by this treaty to secure peace through justice, and I believe I have succeeded."[16]

While the administration was managing the conflict in Europe and negotiating the Treaty of Washington, they were also attempting to open new markets and

15   Myers, 161-68; 223-38.

16   *New York Herald*, 3 June 1871; Chernow, 721-27.

President Grant appointed his secretary of state, Hamilton Fish (seated, center), as chairman of the American commissioners of the American-British Joint High Commission that negotiated the Treaty of Washington. As a result, the British agreed to international arbitration of several disputes between the United States and Great Britain.

Ulysses S. Grant Presidential Library

diplomatic relations in Asia. In the summer of 1871, American diplomats and naval forces in Asia sailed to the Korean coastline to not only map the coastal terrain but also begin diplomatic negotiations with the Koreans. American shipmen had complained to United States officials that members of their crews who had shipwrecked on the coast of Korea were killed by locals. American diplomats were appalled by such treatment of stranded American sailors; therefore, the Grant administration sought to negotiate a treaty of mutual understanding with the Koreans to avoid further distress. Yet the Koreans were uninterested in any diplomatic relations with the United States or any Western nation. This flummoxed the Americans because diplomatic and economic relations were considered key components for including a nation as part of the civilized world. The fact that the Koreans not only avoided contact with the Western world but actively sought to deter Westerners from approaching their shoreline led Americans to label them uncivilized and barbaric. Thus, the Americans were further appalled when the Koreans stated that they were unwilling and uninterested in speaking to any representatives from Western nations. The Koreans themselves believed westerners to be barbaric and uncivilized and, as such, wanted nothing to do with them. The irony that both nations believed the other to be barbaric and uncivilized was lost on them all. Angered by the Koreans' lack of diplomacy,

American Minister Frederick Low and Admiral John Rodgers of the United States Navy then sailed headfirst into an international debacle.[17]

The first official United States engagement in East Asia, the expedition to Korea in 1871, marked the Grant administration's foray into an international conflict. The American fleet arrived off the Taeyong Islands on May 19, 1871, eventually heading toward Inch'on. By May 30, the fleet reached the mouth of the Yomha River, heading up the Han River—a straight shot to the capitol in Seoul. From this spot, the Americans began what they believed were careful negotiations with the Koreans to not only map the region but to enter into diplomatic trade agreements. The Koreans, however, saw the American expedition as an invasion of their homeland, and no amount of diplomacy was going to change its practice of isolating itself from the Western world. Therefore, Korean forces viewed the American ships sailing up the Han River as a threat. Admiral Rodgers, though, viewed the expedition as a legitimate diplomatic mission to engage the Koreans in treaty negotiations. This difference of opinion led to conflict. On the outskirts of Seoul, Korean fortifications fired upon the American ships, hoping they would turn back. Admiral Rodgers ordered his men to return fire, decimating the Korean fortifications. The Admiral believed the firefight had the proper effect, and the American ships turned back and returned to the fleet. Rodgers demanded an apology for what he deemed a cowardly attack on a peaceful diplomatic mission, but the Koreans countered that the American ships were armed with cannon and soldiers, so their intent must have been hostile. Rodgers and Low gave the Koreans five days to apologize and to conduct friendly negotiations before they would return upriver and answer the Koreans with violence. The Koreans, bent on remaining isolated from the Western world, declined to apologize or to meet with the Americans. Five days later, Rodgers sent a detachment of Marines and numerous armed vessels up the Han River, where the Americans destroyed fortifications, killed over 200 Korean soldiers, and burned several villages (many of which were empty because the Korean citizens had fled in the previous days). The American expedition stopped short of Seoul, satisfied that the teenaged Korean king, Kojong, and his father, Taewon'gun, understood their overture. The Americans then continued to map the Korean coastline before returning to Japan.[18]

News of the Battle of Ganghwa, as it was known, reached Washington within a fortnight. President Grant and Secretary Fish decried what they saw as a cowardly

---

17   Gordon H. Chang, "Whose 'Barbarism'? Whose 'Treachery'? Race and Civilization in the Unknown United States-Korea War of 1871," *The Journal of American History* (March 2003), No. 4: 89:1331-65.

18   Chang, 1342-44. See also "H-063-5: The Battle of Ganghwa, Korea, 1871," H-Grams, Naval History and Heritage Command, accessed 16 January 2022, https://www.history.navy.mil/about-us/leadership/director/directors-corner/h-grams/h-gram-063/h-063-5.html.

attack on American forces. Diplomatic dispatches reveal that Minister Low and Admiral Rodgers were anticipating a fight before they even reached the Korean coastline. Prior to the battle, Low wrote to Secretary Fish: he hoped "that the object sought for may be accomplished peacefully; but if it becomes necessary to use force, I shall endeavor to confine it to repelling unprovoked attacks, and redressing actual wrongs and insults." Low prepared for a clash between two nations who each believed their civilization was superior to the other. Grant viewed his role as president as a champion of Western civilization, and he desired to place the United States at the forefront of the world stage, entering new markets and enveloping peoples who welcomed republicanism into the American orbit.[19]

In the autumn of 1873, amidst the financial panic gripping not only the United States but also Europe, the rebellion in Cuba continued to vex the Grant administration. While the financial markets were in turmoil, American citizens, including many naturalized Cubans, fitted out a ship with guns and ammunition to aid the Cuban rebels against Spain. This ship, known as the *Virginius*, was captured by the Spanish near the Bahamas and brought to Cuba under suspicion of rebellion. The Spanish Volunteers proceeded to execute 53 sailors and passengers, including American citizens and British subjects. News of the capture and executions reached Washington in early November, and President Grant and Secretary Fish were bombarded by angry political leaders, newspaper editorials, and citizens clamoring for a declaration of war against Spain. As Grant had spent his first term avoiding a war with European powers, he had no interest in entering a war with Spain in his second term. However, he was also bound to answer the horrific treatment of American citizens at the hands of the Spanish. Grant empowered Fish and Minister to Spain Daniel Sickles to negotiate a peaceful settlement to the *Virginius* affair—and to do so as quickly as possible. Sickles responded by publicly shaming the Spanish for such a barbaric act—echoing Fish's instructions that the executions were barbaric and unlawful—but exceeded any authority he had to negotiate a peace. In his frustration with the Spanish government, Sickles overtly supported war. As such, Grant informed Sickles he was to close the legation in Madrid and to confer with Fish, who took over negotiations from Washington, D.C. Fish understood that he was posing an important argument. "We owe it to ourselves and the World to be right," he implored, "before resorting to the extreme

---

19   Frederick F. Low to Hamilton Fish, 13 May 1871, Department of State, *Papers Relating to the Foreign Relations of the United States Transmitted to Congress with the Annual Message of the President, December 4, 1871* (Washington, D.C.: Government Printing Office, 1871), 115; Chang, 1344. Chang notes that the Korean king and his father declared victory over of the United States when the American Navy stopped short of Seoul and returned to Japan, even though Korean losses heavily outweighed American losses. See also Paul Kahan, *The Presidency of Ulysses S. Grant: Preserving the Civil War's Legacy* (Yardley, PA: Westholme, 2018), 139.

measures of war." With Spanish Minister to the United States Admiral José Polo de Bernabé, Fish set about to determine the legal status of the *Virginius* and to negotiate reparations to the families of those executed by the Spanish Volunteers.[20]

Fish and Polo worked hard to negotiate a peace while politicians in the United States and Sickles in Madrid clamored for war. In late November 1873, Polo proffered a solution to Fish: that the United States accept the *Virginius* and its surviving crew without an official salute of the American flag (a gesture of respect) until Spain could prove whether the ship was falsely flying the American banner. If the Spanish could prove the ship was not American, they would not have to salute the flag, and the United States would prosecute the crew members for violating international law and the laws of the United States. Fish took the compromise to Grant, who readily approved the diplomatic gesture. After settling a sticking point over when the American flag was hoisted over the *Virginius*, Fish and Polo set about to determine who was the owner of the ship and whether it was legally allowed to register as an American vessel. Testimony revealed that the purported owner of the ship, John F. Patterson, was not, in fact, the owner and that it was owned by a group of Cuban Americans. The man listed in the logbooks, Ramon Quesada, claimed that the vessel was purchased by the Cuban Junta. Thus, Grant informed Fish and Polo that the salute of the American flag was unnecessary. In mid-December, the Spanish authorities in Cuba handed the *Virginius* over to American officials. The ship was in terrible condition, and its engines failed soon thereafter. On the day after Christmas, 1873, off the coast of Cape Fear, North Carolina, the *Virginius* sank to the bottom of the Atlantic Ocean, an appropriate ending for a troublesome vessel. The other issue of the *Virginius* affair, the execution of crew members and passengers, remained a sticking point into 1875. Grant had replaced Sickles with Caleb Cushing, a former attorney general who assisted the administration at the Geneva arbitration, and Fish authorized him to negotiate reparations for the loss of life. After months of negotiations, Fish told Cushing to accept an indemnity of $2,500 for each American killed. In the end, Fish accepted a total reparation of $80,000 for the families of Americans killed onboard the *Virginius*. With this resolution, the crisis between the United States and Spain ended.[21]

The influx of immigrants from Europe into the eastern United States upended labor dynamics that sent many of these immigrants—Irish and German—westward. When they arrived in the West, they competed for new labor opportunities in mines and on railroads with African Americans and with Chinese immigrants.

20   Richard H. Bradford, *The Virginius Affair* (Boulder, CO: Colorado Associated University Press, 1980), 57-73, 87-91; Calhoun, 426-30; Hamilton Fish, Diary, 18 November 1873, HF papers.

21   Bradford, 97-102, 109-14, 123-27; Calhoun, 430-31.

White laborers looked upon all their competition with distrust and sought to create alliances and legal frameworks that would keep labor in their own hands. American infrastructure development relied on cheap Chinese labor to build railroads and to dig mines. Alongside this development of industry in the West grew a suspicion of the "heathen chine"—the uncivilized Asian whom Americans could not trust. White laborers in the West argued that Asians could not be trusted and that they were unwelcome as immigrants to a republican nation such as the United States. While Grant agreed with political and labor leaders that Chinese immigrants were victims of an unsavory system, particularly women brought to the United States as prostitutes, he did not agree that they were unwelcome as laborers. In fact, Grant initially supported increasing Chinese immigration to the United States because he believed that many Chinese laborers were enslaved by unscrupulous industrial leaders and plantation owners, a decidedly unrepublican practice. Chinese laborers, known colloquially as "coolie" laborers, lived a life of slavery on the plantations in Cuba, in the shipyards of San Francisco, and on the railroads crossing the West.[22]

Grant's faith in republicanism motivated him to issue numerous statements against such a practice of slavery. Influential political leaders in the West regaled Grant with stories of Chinese women brought to the United States as prostitutes to serve laborers in the mines and on the railway. Rather than being prostitutes, Grant surmised, these women were victims of sex enslavement, and it was the federal government's responsibility to protect them. Accordingly, Grant signed the Page Act of 1875, which outlawed the entrance of Chinese men and women to the United States "for lewd and immoral purposes" and any importation of women "for the purposes of prostitution." To Grant, this act protected Chinese women from the horrors of slavery and prostitution, and it kept criminals out of the United States. The reality, though, was that most Chinese women immigrating to the United States were wives, daughters, or mothers of laborers already working in the West, not sex slaves or prostitutes. In Grant's effort to protect Chinese men and women from enslavement by unscrupulous brokers, he authorized a law that authorities used for the exclusion of a population of immigrants who desired to come to the United States in search of honest labor. As such, many Chinese women who were not prostitutes were excluded from immigrating to the United States because they were assumed to be prostitutes. While the number of Chinese men immigrating to

---

22   This was not the first time the Grant administration condemned the importation of Chinese workers as a form of slavery. Hamilton Fish accused the British of supporting the "coolie" or Chinese immigrant trade, arguing that it was just another form of slavery. Hamilton Fish, Diary, 7 November 1873, HF papers.

the United States either remained the same or increased, the number of Chinese women dropped significantly in the years after the authorization of the Page Act.[23]

Ulysses S. Grant's foreign policy, largely implemented by Hamilton Fish, was bold in its desire to bring the blessings of Reconstruction to all who sought the embrace of republicanism. Unfortunately, roadblocks and international concerns prevented the president from exporting republicanism to all whom he believed wanted to join. Personality clashes between Grant and Charles Sumner prevented any chance of the president's success in exporting Reconstruction to the Dominican Republic. His Republican allies implored him to intercede on behalf of the Cuban rebels—freedom fighters attempting to throw off the yoke of monarchy on behalf of liberty—yet his secretary of state wisely steered him to neutrality so as not to undercut their argument in the *Alabama* claims and their desire to stay out of European conflict altogether. Even when provided the opportunity to declare war with Spain over the killing of American citizens, Grant looked for a peaceful solution, which Fish ably provided. Finally, Grant's own beliefs in Western civilization led to a clash with the supposedly barbaric Koreans and to being influenced by public opinion on Chinese laborers in the West. Grant's foreign policy was marked by successful resolutions to problems between the United States and the European nations of Great Britain and Spain. At the same time, though, his efforts to export republicanism into new territories—welcoming people outside the United States who previously would have been excluded from the American experiment—were defeated by his political foes. The idealism that underscored domestic Reconstruction remained a part of the American political system, even when political and legal forces in the United States embraced white supremacy over equality. While the Grant administration's foreign policy opened new markets and negotiated immigration treaties, for many immigrants of color, the blessings of liberty, much to Grant's chagrin, remained out of their reach until the twentieth century.

---

23   Andrew Gyory, *Closing the Gate: Race, Politics, and the Chinese Exclusion Act* (Chapel Hill, NC: The University of North Carolina Press, 1998), 54-59; George Anthony Peffer, "Forbidden Families: Emigration Experiences of Chinese Women under the Page Law, 1875–1882," *Journal of American Ethnic History* (Fall 1986), No. 1, 6:29; Yong Chen, *Chinese San Francisco, 1850–1943: A Trans-Pacific Community* (Stanford, CA: Stanford University Press, 2000), 47. For a brief discussion on Horace Page's opposition to Chinese immigration, see George Anthony Peffer, *If They Don't Bring Their Women Here: Chinese Female Immigration before Exclusion* (Urbana, IL: University of Illinois Press, 1999), 33-36; Hidetaka Hirota, *Expelling the Poor: Atlantic Seaboard States and the Nineteenth-Century Origins of American Immigration Policy* (New York: Oxford University Press, 2017), 181.

President Grant Belongs in the Pantheon

Chapter Eleven | *Frank J. Scaturro*

The president had earned his fame as a professional soldier commanding armies in a major American war before serving two terms as his country's chief executive. He was a famously taciturn man whose intellect was questioned by a number of contemporaries.[1] He could be thin-skinned in the face of attacks lobbed at him in the acrimonious political environment of his time. Several subordinates in whom he had placed his trust had engaged in scandalous behavior.[2] In his Farewell Address, he acknowledged "the inferiority of my qualifications" and "experience" upon taking office, but noted his "good intentions" and "the best exertions of which a very fallible judgment was capable." Despite being "unconscious of intentional error," he said he was "too sensible of my defects not to think it probable that I may have committed many errors," but he carried with him "the hope that my country will never cease to view them with indulgence."[3]

That president was George Washington. But this description sounds more like historians' depiction of Ulysses S. Grant. And other than his being a general-turned-two-term-president, that is not what Americans think of when they think of the first president of the United States. They think first of the pathbreaking example he set for his successors and firmly hold him near the very top of the pantheon of presidents, alongside Abraham Lincoln in the first rank of American leaders. The eighteenth president occupied that same top echelon in the public mind during the nineteenth century.

But during the twentieth century, Grant's reputation was battered by historians, with different facets of his career suffering to differing degrees. His

1   Ron Chernow, *Washington: A Life* (New York: The Penguin Press, 2010), 605; David O. Stewart, *George Washington: The Political Rise of America's Founding Father* (New York: Dutton, 2021), 215.

2   Lindsay M. Chervinsky, *The Cabinet: George Washington and the Creation of an American Institution* (Cambridge, MA: The Belknap Press of Harvard University Press, 2020), 68, 185-88, 223-25, 230-31, 271-301.

3   James D. Richardson, ed., *A Compilation of the Messages and Papers of the Presidents*, 20 vols. (New York: Bureau of National Literature, 1897–1916), 1:205, 216.

These illustrations reflect the change in Grant's reputation over time: pictured with Lincoln and Washington as "Our Three Great Presidents" in an 1872 litograph and with Harding, Nixon, and Reagan in a 1987 *American Heritage* cartoon.

Library of Congress; American Heritage

military reputation fell precipitously after his death but, by our own time, has substantially recovered. The collective historical memory of Grant that emerged would accord him the nation's gratitude for his heroic leadership during the Civil War and for the memoirs he penned about his military service—and nothing else. That has been changing with the scholarship of recent decades, but to what degree is still unclear for a president whose reputation has, perhaps more than that of any other president, been in flux.

The bicentennial of Grant's birth is a fitting occasion to take stock of his presidential standing, from its fall to its more recent recovery, and to ponder whether the eighteenth president's reputation is on a trajectory that should continue.

Polemic-infused history and Grant's changing historical standing

In his autobiography *The Education of Henry Adams* (1918), Adams dedicated a chapter to President Grant. It included a notorious diatribe that concluded, "The progress of evolution from President Washington to President Grant, was alone evidence enough to upset Darwin."[4] Adams, along with a good number of prolific contemporary critics of Grant, had an ax to grind after realizing that neither they nor

---

4   Henry Adams, *The Education of Henry Adams* (Boston: Houghton Mifflin Company, 1918), 266.

their friends would gain position or influence in the administration, at least not to the degree to which they felt entitled.[5]

The only two comprehensive narratives dedicated to the Grant presidency to be published in the twentieth century—William B. Hesseltine's *Ulysses S. Grant: Politician* (1935) and Allan Nevins's study of Grant's secretary of state, *Hamilton Fish: The Inner History of the Grant Administration* (1936)—helped embed into historical memory the polemic-infused criticism of the Grant administration. A major theme of Nevins's book was to assign credit for foreign policy achievements to "one of our ablest Secretaries of State" while denying it to the president he served, whose administration but for Fish courted "total disgrace."[6] Historians readily give other presidents credit for achievements made possible by cabinet members on whom they relied at least as much as Grant relied on Fish, as illustrated by the examples of George Washington and Alexander Hamilton, James Monroe and John Quincy Adams, and Harry S. Truman and George C. Marshall. Or, looking at subordinates beyond cabinet members, as illustrated by Abraham Lincoln's reliance on General Grant. This is just one of many double standards that permeated literature on Grant's presidency.

Hesseltine, for his part, acknowledged that "many of the more persistent charges of Grant's stupidity and corruption were born in partisan politics and derive their validity from the political stump," but he concluded that President Grant was "peculiarly ignorant of the Constitution and inept in handling men," possessed a "mental endowment" that "was not great," "filled his state papers with platitudes rather than thoughts," and "became the 'safe' representative of the more reactionary interests of his day."[7] C. Vann Woodward piled on in 1957 with an article entitled "The Lowest Ebb" that called the Grant administration "the all-time low point in statesmanship and political morality in our history."[8]

Polls of historians to rate the presidents reflected similar hostility. They were pioneered by Arthur M. Schlesinger Sr. with surveys of 55 experts in 1948 and 75 experts in 1962. Subject to classification by the participants as great, near great,

---

5   Prominent examples included Charles Eliot Norton, Charles A. Dana, James H. Wilson, Horace White, and Grant's opponent for re-election in 1872, Horace Greeley. Frank J. Scaturro, *President Grant Reconsidered* (Lanham, MD: University Press of America, 1998), 19; Charles W. Calhoun, *The Presidency of Ulysses S. Grant* (Lawrence, KS: University Press of Kansas, 2017), 89, 114-15, 149-50, 188; Mark Wahlgren Summers, *The Era of Good Stealings* (New York: Oxford University Press, 1993), 78, 81.

6   Allan Nevins, *Hamilton Fish: The Inner History of the Grant Administration* (New York: Dodd, Mead & Company, 1936), vii.

7   William B. Hesseltine, *Ulysses S. Grant: Politician* (New York: Dodd, Mead & Company, 1935), vii-viii.

8   C. Vann Woodward, "The Lowest Ebb," *American Heritage* (April 1957), No. 3, 8:53.

average, below average, or failure, Grant fared second only to rockbottom Warren G. Harding both times, with those two presidents the only ones rated failures.[9]

Over the years, other presidential polls would periodically follow. Despite a wide range in the number and nature of their participants, Grant's place showed little upward movement in the most notable polls conducted through the rest of the twentieth century, despite the increase in the number of presidents being considered over time. A 1982 survey of some 846 Ph.D.-holding members of college history departments by Robert K. Murray and Tim H. Blessing placed Grant again second to Harding at the bottom.[10] Grant was ranked among the bottom five presidents in other noteworthy polls published by David L. Porter in 1981; the *Chicago Tribune* in 1982; the Siena College Research Institute (SCRI) in 1982, 1990, and 1994; and William J. Ridings Jr. and Stuart B. McIver in 1997.[11] A 1996 poll by Arthur M. Schlesinger Jr., reprising his father's work, placed Grant sixth from last.[12]

Polls taken during the early 2000s initially continued with substandard assessments of Grant, but he would later rise to the middle tier. In 2000, a Federalist Society–*Wall Street Journal* poll ranked him number 32 out of 39, and C-SPAN, in its first of a series of polls, similarly placed him at 33 out of 41. He then rose in later C-SPAN polls to 23 in 2009, 22 in 2017, and 20 in 2021—the most dramatic rise of any president both in C-SPAN's shorter history of polling and in the broader history of such surveys.[13] SCRI's periodic surveys during the twenty-first century similarly lifted Grant from 35 in 2002 to 26 in 2010, 24 in 2018, and 21 in 2022.[14]

9   Arthur M. Schlesinger, "Historians Rate U.S. Presidents," *Life*, 1 November 1948, 65; Arthur M. Schlesinger, "Our Presidents: A Rating by 75 Historians," *New York Times Magazine*, 29 July 1962, 12.

10   Murray, Robert K. & Tim H. Blessing, *Greatness in the White House* (University Park, PA: The Pennsylvania State University Press, 1994), 11, 14, 16.

11   Ibid., 16-17; "American Presidents: Greatest and Worst," Siena College Research Institute, 22 June 2022, accessed 31 August 2022, https://scri.siena.edu/2022/06/22/american-presidents-greatest-and-worst; William J. Ridings, Jr. & Stuart B. McIver, *Rating the Presidents: A Ranking of U.S. Leaders, From the Great and Honorable to the Dishonest and Incompetent* (Secaucus, NJ: Citadel Press, 1997), xi.

12   Arthur M. Schlesinger, Jr., "Rating the Presidents: Washington to Clinton," *Political Science Quarterly* (Summer 1997), No. 2, 112:189.

13   The number of presidents considered by the two polls in 2000 varied because the Federalist Society–*Wall Street Journal* poll excluded William H. Harrison and James A. Garfield due to the brevity of their terms. James Taranto & Leonard Leo, eds., *Presidential Leadership: Rating the Best and the Worst in the White House* (New York: Free Press, 2004), 12; Presidential Historians Survey 2021, Total Scores/Overall Rankings, C-SPAN, accessed 31 August 2022, https://www.c-span.org/presidentsurvey2021/?page=overall.

14   US Presidents Study Historical Rankings, Siena College Research Institute, accessed 31 August 2022, https://scri.siena.edu/us-presidents-study-historical-rankings.

These polls are more useful as a measure of the historical profession than as an objective measure of the presidents themselves. There is something odd in the assumption that everyone who becomes president is automatically entered into a contest against all predecessors and successors. Different presidencies have among them such differences in the challenges before them and in the institutional and other political factors distinctive to their times that they resist numerical ranking in the sense embodied in historians' polls. This is not to be too deconstructionist on the topic of assessing presidents or making comparisons. It seems a straightforward, even obvious judgment that Abraham Lincoln was a great president and that he was a better president than, say, Millard Fillmore. The two men's records on slavery and Union and their respective contributions to American government make that clear. Similar factors should also make it obvious that Grant was a better president than Fillmore, whose principal legacy was a compromise designed to avoid civil war that stoked national strife over slavery. Yet in all the historians' polls cited above before the 2000s, Fillmore was rated more highly than Grant. Is that not a reflection on historians more than on Grant?

To make sense of historical memory in the context of U.S. presidents, it helps to ponder the role of collective emotion even more than that of collective intelligence. In *Presidential Greatness* (1966), Thomas A. Bailey discussed the collective judgment embodied in the Schlesinger polls and "reluctantly conclude[d] that historical judgments are sometimes as much visceral as cerebral."[15] "Sometimes" includes Grant's presidency. Indeed, Bailey unwittingly demonstrated the power of inherited distortion. He found room in his book to heap upon Grant dozens of insults parroting his rabidly partisan critics, including "bewildered," "subordinary," "pathetic," "gullible," "politically obtuse," the "dupe[] of thieves," "ignorant," having "no grasp of politics," and "not interested in the boring details of his job;" and referencing his supposed "fumblings and bumblings" during "eight scandal-seared years."[16] To the substance of policy, however, he allocated two dismissive paragraphs, one asserting, Nevins-style, that Hamilton Fish deserved credit for the *Alabama* claims resolution and the other downplaying national progress during that period as coming "without much help or hindrance from Grant."[17] He covered Reconstruction with a fleeting reference to "the South" being "reconstructed by bayonet."[18]

---

15   Thomas A. Bailey, *Presidential Greatness* (New York: Appleton-Century, 1966), 34, 61.

16   Ibid., 31, 35, 47, 78, 101, 108, 138, 147, 164, 171, 217, 229, 232, 295-96, 326, 335.

17   Ibid., 42, 296.

18   Ibid., 296.

Consider that Bailey published this one year after the Voting Rights Act of 1965, arguably the apogee of the twentieth century's Civil Rights Movement. That movement, sometimes called the nation's "Second Reconstruction," might have been expected to produce a rapid turnaround in the reputation of a man who had presided over the first Reconstruction, but it did not. When a major biography of Grant did come along in 1981, its author, William S. McFeely, did little to conceal the skepticism toward the military typical of the post-Vietnam era toward a soldier of a different period. Seemingly oblivious to Grant's ethic of duty to country, the author found his subject's story, forged as it was by war, a "troubling" one—the rise of a man of "limited talents" who "became general and president because he could find nothing better to do" and who failed to "make his administration a credit to American politics."[19] The book won the Pulitzer Prize for biography.

Over the past quarter century, President Grant's low standing began to change with a succession of new studies. Brooks D. Simpson, an early critic of McFeely, encouraged much of this scholarship with commentaries that included two books, *The Political Education of Henry Adams* (1996) and *The Reconstruction Presidents* (1998), the latter devoted to the issue at the heart of Grant's presidency.[20] Another 1998 publication was my own *President Grant Reconsidered*, which emphasized the Reconstruction issue but argued for a sweeping reassessment of Grant's presidency. While they varied in length and in their treatment of some of the particulars about the age of Grant, biographies by Geoffrey Perret (1997) and to a greater extent by Jean Edward Smith (2001), Josiah Bunting III (2004), H.W. Brands (2012), Ronald C. White (2016), and Ron Chernow (2017) depicted his presidency in a distinctly more favorable light than the consensus that had emerged during the twentieth century.[21] So did Joan Waugh's study of Grant historiography in 2009, (more tepidly) Paul Kahan's on Grant's presidency in 2018, and Bret Baier's 2021

19   William S. McFeely, *Grant: A Biography* (New York: W.W. Norton & Company, 1981), xii-xiii, 522.

20   Simpson's earlier commentary included "Another Look at the Grant Presidency," in Peter Becker, ed., *The Proceedings of the South Carolina Historical Association* (Columbia, SC: The South Carolina Historical Association, 1990), 7-16, and "Historians and Political Scientists: Observations on Presidential Studies," *Congress & the Presidency* (Autumn 1993), No. 2, 20:87-91. His *Let Us Have Peace: Ulysses S. Grant and the Politics of War and Reconstruction, 1861-1868* (Chapel Hill, NC: The University of North Carolina Press, 1991) includes an exploration of Grant's motivations in accepting the presidency.

21   Geoffrey Perret, *Ulysses S. Grant: Soldier & President* (New York: Random House, 1997); Jean Edward Smith, *Grant* (New York: Simon & Schuster, 2001); Josiah Bunting III, *Ulysses S. Grant* (New York: Times Books, 2004); H.W. Brands, *The Man Who Saved the Union: Ulysses Grant in War and Peace* (New York: Doubleday, 2012); Ronald C. White, *American Ulysses: A Life of Ulysses S. Grant* (New York: Random House, 2016); Ron Chernow, *Grant* (New York: Penguin Press, 2017).

account that emphasized Grant's role surrounding the election of 1876.[22] Charles W. Calhoun's *The Presidency of Ulysses S. Grant* (2017), the first comprehensive narrative devoted to Grant's presidential years in the more than eight decades since Hesseltine and Nevins, provided the most definitive account for this new generation of scholarship. A short biography by Michael Korda (2004) and a shoddy, polemical attack on Grant's presidency by Philip Leigh (2019) in the mold of earlier Grant critiques were outliers that failed to catch on.[23]

The recent reassessments shared to one degree or another an emphasis on Grant's handling of Reconstruction, particularly his commitment to equal rights, for their sympathetic depictions of his presidency. Corruption was no longer the defining component of the administration, though the various studies differed in the extent to which they deemphasized the issue or challenged the very premise of the long-dominant corruption narrative. Calhoun's study noted, regarding perceptions of President Grant, "The operation of confirmation bias exerts a powerful force against the overturning of ingrained understandings of the past."[24]

Corrections to the hard-to-shake inherited wisdom have been making their way to non-Grant-specific works of history, but it has been a slow process. Grant was still among the subjects of books dedicated to the worst presidents by Nathan

---

22   Joan Waugh, *U.S. Grant: American Hero, American Myth* (Chapel Hill, NC: The University of North Carolina Press, 2009); Paul Kahan, *The Presidency of Ulysses S. Grant* (Yardley, PA: Westholme, 2018); Bret Baier, *To Rescue the Republic: Ulysses S. Grant, the Fragile Union, and the Crisis of 1876* (New York: Custom House, 2021).

23   Michael Korda, *Ulysses S. Grant: The Unlikely Hero* (New York: HarperCollins, 2004); Philip Leigh, *U.S. Grant's Failed Presidency* (Columbia, SC: Shotwell Publishing, 2019).

24   Calhoun, *Presidency*, 593.

Miller in 1998 and Philip Abbott in 2013.[25] In his 2017 tome exploring the Gilded Age, Richard White's depiction of Grant largely repeated the outdated scholarship between Henry Adams and William McFeely.[26] On the other hand, Alvin S. Felzenberg's 2008 book on presidential ratings was the first study of its kind to give Grant high marks, tying him with several other presidents for seventh place based on overall score applying six criteria.[27] In 2010, Sean Wilentz predicted that Grant would be vindicated "as one of the great presidents of his era, and possibly one of the greatest in all American history."[28] Max J. Skidmore's *Maligned Presidents* (2014) called Grant "routinely the most underrated, misinterpreted, and misrepresented of all American presidents."[29]

Pillar of a multiracial republic

Grant's dramatic rise from near bottom to roughly the middle in presidential polls poses the question of whether he is destined to be viewed as a middling president or whether he will in fact crawl or even soar toward the top. To understand why President Grant belongs in the pantheon of best-regarded presidents, first consider Reconstruction. While the Constitution does not assign presidents a direct role in the ratification of constitutional amendments, presidents can still use the power they do have to secure them. The most foundational constitutional developments in which presidents played a significant role were those of the founding and of the Civil War–Reconstruction era. Three presidents in particular played such a role: Washington, Lincoln, and Grant.[30] As the first president, George Washington provided form to the office that the Constitution created. The Civil War–Reconstruction era saw the ratification of three new sweeping

25   Nathan Miller, *Star-Spangled Men: America's Ten Worst Presidents* (New York: Scribner, 1998); Philip Abbott, *Bad Presidents: Failure in the White House* (New York: Palgrave Macmillan, 2013).

26   Richard White, *The Republic for Which It Stands: The United States during Reconstruction and the Gilded Age, 1865–1896* (New York: Oxford University Press, 2017), 206-07, 287, 378-79; Joan Waugh, review of *The Republic for Which It Stands: The United States during Reconstruction and the Gilded Age, 1865–1896*, by Richard White, *Journal of the Civil War Era* (September 2018), No. 3, 8:551.

27   Alvin S. Felzenberg, *The Leaders We Deserved (and a Few We Didn't): Rethinking the Presidential Rating Game* (New York: Basic Books, 2008), 378.

28   Sean Wilentz, "Who's Buried in the History Books?," *New York Times*, 14 March 2010, WK9.

29   Max J. Skidmore, *Maligned Presidents: The Late 19th Century* (New York: Palgrave Macmillan, 2014), 26. See also Max J. Skidmore, "The Presidency of Ulysses S. Grant: A Reconsideration," in Robert W. Watson et al., eds., *White House Studies Compendium*, 12 vols. (New York: Nova Science Publishers, 2007–2014), 5:221-36.

30   Another transformation in constitutional understandings certainly occurred during Franklin D. Roosevelt's New Deal, but that is a separate discussion as it did not arise from the adoption or amendment of the Constitution.

amendments to the Constitution, the first and last of which came about with significant presidential intervention.

The Thirteenth Amendment, which Lincoln helped move through Congress before its ratification by the states was consummated in December 1865, prohibited slavery and involuntary servitude. The Fourteenth Amendment, among other things, established both national and state citizenship for people "born or naturalized in the United States" and guaranteed "the equal protection of the laws." That was ratified in 1868 without any help from Lincoln's successor, Andrew Johnson, who opposed measure after measure to protect former slaves advanced by Radical Republicans in Congress, including the temporary military rule enacted over the president's veto and overseen by Grant as the army's commanding general.

A Fifteenth Amendment providing a constitutional guarantee against racial discrimination in voting was proposed by the House and Senate in the week prior to Grant's inauguration on March 4, 1869. Grant played a decisive role in securing the amendment's ratification, a process that would take nearly a year.[31] He urged ratification in his First Inaugural Address. By a statute he signed into law just over a month into his presidency, the three southern states still under military rule— Virginia, Mississippi, and Texas—were required to ratify the proposed amendment. In December, Grant requested Georgia's temporary return to military rule until the state ratified the Fifteenth Amendment—the previous year its legislature had expelled its black members—and Congress followed by passing the requested legislation.[32] These and other arm-twisting measures succeeded. By ensuring for former slaves the full political equality inherent in the right to vote, the Fifteenth Amendment was in some respects the apex of the most profound changes to the Constitution since the founding period. During Reconstruction, around 2,000 African Americans were elected or appointed to public office.[33]

In a role that corresponded to Washington's at the republic's inception, Grant would play a major role in shaping a new paradigm of government under the Fourteenth and Fifteenth Amendments. The fifth section of the Fourteenth Amendment and second section of the Fifteenth Amendment made explicit the power of Congress to enforce the respective amendments "by appropriate legislation." Grant called for legislation to enforce both amendments and, in fact,

31   George S. Boutwell, *Reminiscences of Sixty Years in Public Affairs*, 2 vols. (New York: McClure, Phillips & Co., 1902), 2:229-30.

32   Scaturro, *President Grant*, 67; Calhoun, *Presidency*, 99-100.

33   Eric Foner, "'The Tocsin of Freedom': The Black Leadership of Radical Reconstruction," in Gabor Boritt & Scott Hancock, eds., *Slavery, Resistance, Freedom* (New York: Oxford University Press, 2007), 118-19.

was responsible for the only enacted laws enforcing their equal rights guarantees until the Civil Rights Movement of the next century.

In his first term alone, he secured laws creating a new Department of Justice along with five Enforcement Acts between 1870 and 1872. The most sweeping of these acts was the Ku Klux Klan Act of April 20, 1871. Pursuant to these statutes, Grant employed federal troops to protect former slaves, most dramatically by suspending *habeas corpus* in nine South Carolina counties in October 1871. The prosecution that followed through 1872 crushed the nineteenth-century Klan.[34] Throughout his presidency, Grant would repeatedly make public statements embracing equality, including when he advocated in his 1875 speech at an Army of the Tennessee reunion in Des Moines "Equal Right & Privileges to all men irrespective of Nationality, Color or Religion."[35] No president before him had ever endorsed a full accommodation of such a wide range of people into the scheme of American democracy.

Beyond the most prominent example of South Carolina, Grant deployed federal troops to southern states to enforce Reconstruction in a number of troubled jurisdictions throughout his presidency. White southerners, who with few exceptions had regained their own right to vote by the time the Amnesty Act of 1872 became law, were opposed to black political power in great enough numbers that a racial party line defined much of the divide between the Democratic and Republican parties in the South. That fueled much of the drive by southern whites to "redeem" African American–supported Republican governments with Democratic governments, a goal that tended to be pursued with the most abusive behavior by whites where black citizens were most numerous. Even after the Klan's demise, white southern resistance would continue in forms that combined Klan tactics with social ostracism and economic pressure as more subtle methods of intimidation.[36] African American voter turnout for Republicans increased in some southern states, but during the mid-1870s, more white voters who had abstained from voting came to the polls than blacks who had not previously voted, expediting a number of Democratic state takeovers.[37]

Grant's interventions evoked recurring condemnations throughout his presidency from both political adversaries and the press. They accused him of monarchical and militaristic repression, often captured in the charge of

34   Scaturro, *President Grant*, 70-72.

35   Speech, Des Moines, 29 September 1875, John Y. Simon, ed., *The Papers of Ulysses S. Grant*, 32 vols. (Carbondale, IL: Southern Illinois University Press, 1967–2012), 26:344, hereafter cited as *PUSG*.

36   Scaturro, *President Grant*, 78, 90.

37   Michael F. Holt, *By One Vote: The Disputed Presidential Election of 1876* (Lawrence, KS: University Press of Kansas, 2008), 13.

Grant as president—an office he did not initially seek but which he accepted as his duty to better secure the fruits of victory his armies had won on the battlefield.

Bultema-Williams Collection

"Caesarism."[38] During his second term, Grant had to grapple with the intensifying opposition to southern intervention among white northerners, among whom racial prejudice fed a double standard that disparaged southern blacks as backward where they did not assert their rights and obnoxious where they did. While he was cognizant that overuse of troops where they were not necessary could cause the collapse of the Republican coalition he depended on for success, he stood ahead of an increasing number of fellow Republicans who were ready to abandon enforcement. This was particularly evident by 1875, when denunciations of his intervention to sustain the Republican government in Louisiana reached a fever pitch.[39] This remained true even in the case of Mississippi, where Grant was ready to send troops for the state's 1875 election if necessary despite intense political pressure, but was not persuaded. A number of factors were in play, including communications with the governor, who sent mixed messages about his ability to manage the situation, and white liners in the state calibrating their activity to avoid military intervention, even to the point of inducing an illusory truce with the governor. After the Democrats won the election, Grant denounced Mississippi's "fraud and violence such as would scarcely be accredited to savages, much less to a civilized and Christian people."[40]

That denunciation was one of numerous statements Grant made defending the principles of Reconstruction throughout his presidency, including—indeed, most stridently—when it was most unpopular. In fact, in early 1875, Grant delivered

38   Calhoun, *Presidency*, 5, 315, 364-65, 381, 416; William Hepworth Dixon, *White Conquest*, 2 vols. (London: Chatto and Windus, Piccadilly, 1876), 2:71-72.

39   Scaturro, *President Grant*, 79, 85-87, 90-91.

40   Ibid., 88-91, 106; John R. Lynch, *The Facts of Reconstruction* (New York: The Neale Publishing Company, 1913), 153; Brooks D. Simpson, "Mission Impossible: Reconstruction Policy Reconsidered," *Journal of the Civil War Era* (March 2016), No. 1, 6:94.

one of the most impassioned messages ever made by a president on any subject, detailing racial violence in Louisiana and justifying his widely denounced military intervention on behalf of African Americans and white Republicans against whom "the spirit of hatred and violence is stronger than law."[41] Soon afterwards, fulfilling an appeal he made in his Second Inaugural Address, he signed into law the Civil Rights Act of 1875, which prohibited segregation in various modes of public accommodations and transportation. During the 1876 election, the last to occur during his tenure, Grant used both troops and federal marshals to protect the polls in the jurisdictions where they were most vulnerable.[42]

The withdrawal of troops from their posts in South Carolina and Louisiana by Rutherford B. Hayes soon after he took office in 1877 was followed by Democratic takeovers in both states. It has entered the national lore that this decision was the product of an eleventh-hour compromise brokered to end a protracted presidential electoral crisis in exchange for a Hayes victory, but Hayes had already held the widespread view against the use of troops in the South as early as 1875, and any efforts by southern Democrats to extort from him a commitment to such a policy in 1877 occurred when they had little leverage to do so.[43] In any event, the troop withdrawal would be remembered as a repudiation of Grant's policy and as the end of Reconstruction.

What is telling is how Reconstruction came to be remembered by history and the relationship between its falling and rising reputation and that of Grant. The Dunning School, which was an academic offshoot of the broader Myth of the Lost Cause that came to define the Civil War–Reconstruction era for much of the last century, rose as the era of Jim Crow segregation and disfranchisement emerged in the South. William A. Dunning himself condemned Reconstruction for its rejection of what he called the "fact of racial inequality."[44] Grant was simultaneously condemned for clinging to Reconstruction.[45] Allan Nevins, who

---

41   Richardson, 10:4259-68.

42   Richard M. Valelly, *The Two Reconstructions: The Struggle for Black Enfranchisement* (Chicago: The University of Chicago Press, 2004), 120; Pamela Brandwein, *Rethinking the Judicial Settlement of Reconstruction* (Cambridge: Cambridge University Press, 2011), 16, 88; Holt, 150-51, 158-59.

43   Calhoun, *Presidency*, 506, 561-62; Charles W. Calhoun, *Conceiving a New Republic: The Republican Party and the Southern Question, 1869–1900* (Lawrence, KS: University Press of Kansas, 2006), 122-23, 131-32; Michael Les Benedict, "Southern Democrats in the Crisis of 1876-1877: A Reconsideration of Reunion and Reaction," *Journal of Southern History* (November 1980), No. 4, 46:518-20.

44   William Archibald Dunning, *Essays on the Civil War and Reconstruction and Related Topics* (New York: The Macmillan Company, 1904), 384.

45   William Archibald Dunning, *Reconstruction, Political and Economic, 1865-1877* (New York: Harper & Brothers, 1907), 341; Edwin C. Woolley, "Grant's Southern Policy," in *Studies in Southern History and Politics*, inscribed to William Archibald Dunning (New York: Columbia University Press, 1914), 199.

came of age during the era of Dunning's dominance, not only considered "the weakest portion of Grant's record" to be his southern policy, but also added that Grant was "far more worthy of impeachment than Andrew Johnson" in part due to "his arbitrary acts in the South."[46]

The Dunning School pervaded the perception of Reconstruction all the way to the U.S. Supreme Court. In 1945, three justices—Owen J. Roberts, Felix Frankfurter, and Robert H. Jackson—blithely asserted in a dissenting opinion regarding Reconstruction laws drafted to enforce the Fourteenth Amendment, "It is familiar history that much of this legislation was born of that vengeful spirit which to no small degree envenomed the Reconstruction era."[47] Seven years after the Court's landmark desegregation ruling in *Brown v. Board of Education* (1954), Frankfurter, who along with Jackson had joined the Court's unanimous opinion in *Brown*, echoed a law review article in a dissent in a case involving a statute derived from the Ku Klux Klan Act: "It is very queer to try to protect human rights in the middle of the Twentieth Century by a left-over from the days of General Grant."[48] The visceral contempt that had been baked into the memory of Reconstruction in general and Grant's presidency in particular closed some of the nation's most distinguished legal minds to the historical import of the laws in front of them, even as they advanced civil rights in their own time.

For many years after the Civil Rights Movement discredited the Dunning School, the contempt that attached to Grant persisted.[49] It was as if the visceral reaction to him needed another rationale. Perhaps it was tempting for some historians with a living memory of Jim Crow to question Grant's commitment to Reconstruction—it had collapsed, after all—without looking carefully at his record, employing historical perspective, or considering how other presidents fared with the population of the late nineteenth century. While a number of works, including Eric Foner's acclaimed 1988 narrative synthesizing Reconstruction revisionism, took notice of Grant's battle against the Klan, in-depth studies of Grant's policy by William Gillette in 1979 and McFeely in his biography two years

---

46   Nevins, 601, 641.

47   Screws v. United States, 325 U.S. 91, 140 (1945).

48   Monroe v. Pape, 365 U.S. 167, 244 (1961) (quoting Zechariah Chafee, Jr., "Safeguarding Fundamental Human Rights: The Tasks of States and Nation," *George Washington Law Review* (April 1959), No. 4, 27:529).

49   Richard N. Current, "President Grant and the Continuing Civil War," in David L. Wilson and John Y. Simon, eds., *Ulysses S. Grant: Essays and Documents* (Carbondale, IL: Southern Illinois University Press, 1981), 8.

later focused on whatever part of the glass seemed empty. [50] In Gillette's case, that meant indiscriminately criticizing Reconstruction's leaders for doing either too little or too much and operating from crass political motives, no matter how many of the sources he cited painted a different picture.[51] McFeely drew from fewer sources and jumped to conclusions about Grant's indifference to racial issues that drew more from cynicism than from evidence, making him vulnerable to a future generation of historical correctives.[52] Earlier historians had already recognized Reconstruction to be Grant's highest priority when it was unpopular, and no, that basic fact did not change once Reconstruction earned historians' respect.

C. Vann Woodward, author of the classic *The Strange Career of Jim Crow*, was no friend of segregation, but the native southerner had a penchant for attacking what he perceived as Yankee arrogance.[53] In 1957, he depicted Grant as the tool of Radical Republicans, whom he called "extremists," and charged that "Grant fell under the influence of the extremists and went over completely to their southern policy," disillusioning moderates.[54] Yet in 1981, he pulled an about-face, attacking Grant for his supposed "hostility toward the more radical war aim of the few for black franchise and racial equality" and blaming him for the abandonment of Reconstruction.[55] Eight years later, writing more generally, Woodward threw up his hands and confessed his "failure to find a satisfactory explanation for the failure of Reconstruction," inviting other historians to seek the answer.[56]

These authors did not represent the views of African Americans of Grant's time. No less than Frederick Douglass held that Grant belonged in the pantheon. Days after joining the eighteenth president to dedicate the emancipation monument honoring Lincoln in Washington's Lincoln Park in April 1876, Douglass implied that Grant deserved a monument, asserting, "The mere act of breaking the negro's chains was the act of Abraham Lincoln . . . . But the act by which the negro was made a citizen of the United States and invested with the elective franchise was

50   Eric Foner, *Reconstruction: America's Unfinished Revolution, 1863–1877* (New York: Harper & Row, 1988), 458-59.

51   Scaturro, *President Grant*, 93-110; J. Morgan Kousser, review of *Retreat from Reconstruction, 1869–1879*, by William Gillette, *Register of the Kentucky Historical Society* (Spring 1981), No. 2, 79:191-94.

52   Brooks D. Simpson, "Butcher? Racist? An Examination of William S. McFeely's *Grant: A Biography*," *Civil War History* (March 1987), No. 1, 78-83; Scaturro, *President Grant*, 3, 66, 69, 72-73, 88-89, 96-98, 105-06, 112-14.

53   Simpson, "Mission Impossible," 87.

54   Woodward, "Lowest Ebb," 57.

55   C. Vann Woodward, "The Enigma of U.S. Grant," *The New York Review of Books*, 19 March 1981, 3-6.

56   C. Vann Woodward, *The Future of the Past* (New York: Oxford University Press, 1989), 198-99.

pre-eminently the act of President U.S. Grant."[57] An oblivious McFeely would write a century later, "By the summer of 1876 there was no one around the White House who gave a damn about the black people."[58] But as that summer drew to a close, the *Hartford Courant* editorialized that the president "seized hold of the meaning of the revolution—equal civil rights for all" and that "[h]e has never wavered, not for a moment, in securing" to African Americans "the rights given by the late amendments. . . . Not a man in the party has been more faithful to the idea that formed the party than Gen. Grant. Whoever has wavered, he has not."[59]

That Grant distinguished himself on this score among presidents should be obvious from what followed him. His four Republican successors who served during the sixteen-year period between Hayes and Benjamin Harrison repeatedly expressed the importance of the recent amendments and pursued a variety of different, sometimes indirect strategies toward that end.[60] None of these efforts brought meaningful success in stemming white southern resistance, and the demise in the Senate in 1891 of the Harrison-supported federal elections bill that would step up voting-rights enforcement—which partially invoked an enforcement tactic of the Grant years—marked the last gasp of Republican legislative efforts on the federal level to enforce the Fifteenth Amendment.[61] The same sixteen-year period between Hayes and Harrison saw more than 1,200 voting-rights prosecutions in the former Confederacy—under statutes signed into law by Grant.[62]

But for all their overlooked efforts to address the southern question, Grant's immediate successors appear anemic by comparison. During the first federal election cycle of the conciliation-driven Hayes administration, in 1878, African American voter turnout plummeted from 1876, with fewer than half as many black-majority counties going Republican as two years earlier. Through the 1880s, voting trends in more heavily African American areas did not return to 1876 levels, and by the end of the decade, the Republican Party had fewer white

57   *National Republican*, 19 April 1876.

58   McFeely, 439.

59   *Middlebury Register*, 23 September 1876 (running the *Courant*'s commentary).

60   Vincent P. De Santis, *Republicans Face the Southern Question: The New Departure Years, 1877–1897* (Baltimore: The Johns Hopkins Press, 1959), 67, 93, 138-39, 152, 166-69, 179, 196; Stanley P. Hirshson, *Farewell to the Bloody Shirt: Northern Republicans & the Southern Negro, 1877–1893* (Bloomington, IN: Indiana University Press, 1962), 90, 107, 116, 253; Calhoun, *Conceiving*, 188-91.

61   De Santis, 67, 179-80, 210-12, 262; Hirshson, 44, 120, 254; Xi Wang, *The Trial of Democracy: Black Suffrage and Northern Republicans, 1860–1910* (Athens: The University of Georgia Press, 1997), 263. During his brief presidency, Garfield had little opportunity to develop his program.

62   Robert M. Goldman, *"A Free Ballot and a Fair Count:" The Department of Justice and the Enforcement of Voting Rights in the South, 1877–1893* (New York: Fordham University Press, 2001), xxix.

supporters in the South than it did during Grant's presidency.[63] Yet even that period immediately after Grant was far from the low point for African Americans. It took a disfranchisement movement during the 1890s to attain that.[64] Earlier extralegal tactics that diminished the black vote such as violence, intimidation, and fraud increased, and southern states advanced measures to disfranchise blacks, including literacy tests, poll taxes, and grandfather clauses. Those factors led to the freefall in African American turnout that marked the disfranchisement that culminated in the early twentieth century.[65] In 1894, during the second Grover Cleveland administration, forty sections of the Enforcement Acts of the 1870s were partially or entirely repealed, effectively ensuring the end of enforcement.[66]

Of course, the story of the Reconstruction amendments does not end there. Those same provisions of the Constitution provided the basis for federal action during the Civil Rights Movement. A surviving section of the Ku Klux Klan Act, for which Grant had personally lobbied with a visit to the Capitol, was taken out of its dormancy and invoked by Dwight D. Eisenhower when he federalized the national guard to enforce a desegregation order in Little Rock. The same authority was invoked to utilize the national guard and the army by John F. Kennedy to enforce court-ordered desegregation in Mississippi and by Lyndon B. Johnson to protect civil rights marchers from Selma to Montgomery, Alabama.[67] Another surviving provision of the Ku Klux Klan Act now codified as 42 U.S.C. § 1983, which among other things protects those who are deprived of constitutional rights "under color of" state law, is widely litigated and arguably the most important civil rights law apart from the Constitution itself.

For years, those more recent presidents received more recognition for achievements in civil rights than Grant did. When C-SPAN conducted its historians' surveys, the category in which Grant consistently fared best was "pursued equal justice for all," with ranks at 18 (2000), 9 (2009), 10 (2017), and 6 (2021).[68] Those attuned to recent Grant scholarship often place Grant after Lincoln and Lyndon

---

63   De Santis, 100-02, 178-80, 190-93.

64   Hirshson, 251-52.

65   Valelly, 128; Brandwein, 185; J. Morgan Kousser, *The Shaping of Southern Politics: Suffrage Restriction and the Establishment of the One-Party South, 1880–1910* (New Haven: Yale University Press, 1974), 211-12, 240-44.

66   Wang, 258-59, 263, 294-99.

67   U.S. Library of Congress, Congressional Research Service, *The Posse Comitatus Act and Related Matters: The Use of the Military to Execute Civilian Law*, by Jennifer K. Elsea, R42659 (2018), 17, 41-42.

68   Presidential Historians Survey 2021, Pursued Equal Justice for All, C-SPAN, accessed 31 August 2022, https://www.c-span.org/presidentsurvey2021/?category=9.

Critics condemned Grant's sweeping Reconstruction measures—including his intervention in Louisiana and elsewhere—as radical, but Grant saw them as a natural extension of the freedoms secured during and after the Civil War.

Library of Congress

Johnson for his efforts in the realm of equal rights.[69] If only three chief executives could occupy a pantheon of great civil rights presidents, it would be those three.

Numerical ranking from there, even as a matter of a single category of achievement, might be an exercise in folly. The argument for putting Lincoln on top would rest on emancipation. A persuasive argument can be made that the emancipation of slaves was the single greatest step toward equality for any group of Americans and that it was a prerequisite for the progress on race that followed. But does that surpass the cumulative total of measures in the other two administrations that actually amounted to civil and political equality? Johnson's civil rights achievements can be said to extend beyond race to other categories of discrimination, including sex and age, not substantially covered during the nineteenth century. But racial caste was so distinctive as to pose a uniquely grave impediment to America's ability to achieve its ideals of liberty and equality. In that area, Johnson could point primarily to three legislative achievements: the Civil Rights Act of 1964, Voting Rights Act of 1965, and Fair Housing Act of 1968. But the constitutional foundations for these achievements were already in place, thanks in part to his predecessor ninety years earlier—and other groundwork had been laid by the Supreme Court's repudiation of segregation, plus new civil rights acts in 1957 and 1960, during the decade before Johnson's ascension to the presidency. Grant secured the addition to the Constitution of voting rights, the true culmination of political equality regardless of race, and added to that five Enforcement Acts covering all the Reconstruction amendments, a Department of Justice, and even an anti-segregation law. The 1964 and 1965 acts under Johnson addressed Jim Crow measures that arose after Grant's

69   Sean Wilentz, "President Ulysses S. Grant and the Battle for Equality," in Walter Isaacson, ed., *Profiles in Leadership: Historians on the Elusive Quality of Greatness* (New York: W.W. Norton & Company, 2010), 80.

time, and the former act carried the desegregation principle farther than the 1875 Civil Rights Act, which the Supreme Court struck down in 1883. But Grant started with less of a foundation in place for equal rights when he was inaugurated and had to traverse more territory—executive as well as legislative—than Johnson did. For example, as violent as white southern resistance to civil rights was during the 1960s, it was an order of magnitude greater during Reconstruction, with Grant repeatedly intervening in a South plagued by a scale of recalcitrance far beyond that which faced Johnson.

In short, on the issue of racial equality, it is difficult to rank any president's efforts above Grant's. From his starting point, his measures were more sweeping, and the barrage of obstacles he confronted greater, than those of any president during the Civil Rights Movement. As twentieth-century civil rights leaders have assumed something like the status of founding fathers for a modern age, it is incongruous to denigrate those who established a strikingly similar paradigm of equality during America's second founding. Historians who have run circles in search of an explanation faulting Reconstruction's leaders for the lack of a sustained biracial democracy in the South appear less credible as the broad trajectory of American history affirms how intractable the race issue would be. To fail to recognize some of America's most accomplished leaders because they were later repudiated—a repudiation that would not last—appears even more senseless as Jim Crow recedes into the past and the Fourteenth and Fifteenth Amendments are an operative reality for a growing span of U.S. history.

While judicial greatness is not entirely analogous to presidential greatness, the example of a Supreme Court justice who came to be widely regarded as great—John Marshall Harlan—is instructive. Harlan's often lone dissents stood against the Supreme Court's retreat from Reconstruction and earned him a special place in history even though his voice was loudest in protest.[70] During the next century, Justice Thurgood Marshall admired Harlan's courage more than that of any other Supreme Court justice. Marshall was even more moved by Harlan's dissent from the Court's segregation-validating decision in *Plessy v. Ferguson* than he was by Chief Justice Earl Warren's desegregation decision in *Brown v. Board of Education*, a case the future justice had argued as an advocate. While Warren wrote for a unanimous Court, Harlan kept fighting after his contemporaries had abandoned the cause, "a solitary and lonely figure writing for posterity."[71] So where should posterity hold Grant, who built much of what Harlan defended on the Court

70   Frank J. Scaturro, *The Supreme Court's Retreat from Reconstruction: A Distortion of Constitutional Jurisprudence* (Westport, CT: Greenwood Press, 2000), 56, 72-76, 133-36, 152-53.

71   Constance Baker Motley, "Thurgood Marshall," *New York University Law Review* (May 1993), No. 2, 68:210-11.

and outlasted so many of his fellow elected officials in his dedication to equality? To value America as a multiracial republic should be to reject any conception of presidential greatness that is too narrow to include Grant's example.

Achievements out of hiding

Grant's presidency was rich in both domestic and foreign policy achievements. In his First Inaugural Address, Grant committed himself to stabilizing fiscal and monetary policy, a strong foreign policy, reform of Indian policy, and the ratification of the Fifteenth Amendment.[72] He would follow through on all fronts during his presidency. The Fifteenth Amendment has already been noted. On the economic policy front, he successfully took on the most serious fiscal problems the government had ever faced and, in the process, substantially raised the nation's credit.[73] The demands of fighting the Civil War had fueled an unprecedented national debt of more than $2 billion when Grant was inaugurated and had given rise to new kinds of currency unbacked by specie (gold or silver), which left contentious questions of monetary policy after the war.[74] Through a combination of legislation the president secured and measures taken by his Treasury Department, especially under his secretary of the treasury during his first term, George S. Boutwell, the national debt was refinanced and reduced by about one-fifth—$435 million—while taxes were reduced by $300 million.[75] The federal government ran at a surplus throughout Grant's eight years in office, and appropriations declined by 25%.[76]

One significant first-term achievement rarely recognized until recently was Grant's putting a stop to the attempt by Jay Gould and Jim Fisk to corner the gold market in 1869, averting what could have been a financial catastrophe of national proportions.[77] During his second term, when the nation was hit with a severe depression following the Panic of 1873, Grant set the course on monetary policy, vetoing an 1874 inflation bill and fulfilling a pledge from his First Inaugural by securing legislation that provided for the resumption of specie payments.[78] The Resumption Act of 1875 restored the country to the gold standard by requiring

---

72   Richardson, 9:3961-62.

73   Scaturro, *President Grant*, 49-50; Calhoun, *Presidency*, 6; Boutwell, 2:228.

74   Calhoun, *Presidency*, 10-11, 110.

75   Ibid., 109-10, 113-16, 567; Boutwell, 2:228.

76   Calhoun, *Presidency*, 119.

77   Scaturro, *President Grant*, 31-32; Smith, 18, 490; White, *American Ulysses*, 485.

78   Scaturro, *President Grant*, 50.

the redemption of greenbacks in specie on demand starting January 1, 1879. After several years of working toward that goal, Grant preferred resumption to occur earlier, but the legislation was a significant achievement in the eyes of most contemporaries.[79] This was for good reason. Resumption in 1879 was accompanied by a surge in business confidence and demand for labor and an abrupt end to the depression.[80]

When the studies by Hesseltine and Nevins came out, it was the height of the New Deal, and neither author showed much compunction about viewing with partisan hostility the contrasting economic policy of what then had been the only Republican administration of two full terms. The studies were less an objective analysis of those years and more a foil by which to validate the later Progressive and New Deal eras, and historians made few distinctions between the early and late Gilded Age, let alone did they consider whether their methodology was ahistorical. Those who continue to sweep the Grant administration into blanket condemnations of supposed Gilded Age economic oppression overlook that the period between 1870 and 1940 witnessed a more dramatic improvement in Americans' standard of living than any other period in history, conditions that encouraged massive waves of immigration of those who sought a better future in America.[81]

Grant's foreign policy achievements made his presidency a benchmark for peace. On three occasions, he resisted the public clamor for war while enhancing the nation's standing. The Cuban rebellion against Spain, which began in 1868, garnered much sympathy among Americans and pressure from Congress for military intervention on behalf of the rebels. Grant put an end to that possibility with a message to Congress in June 1870 asserting that the Cuban insurgents had no valid claim to be recognized as belligerents.[82]

The resolution of the *Alabama* claims controversy with Great Britain was just one component of a much broader foreign policy achievement. The *C.S.S. Alabama* was the most famous of several Confederate ships that were constructed in and set sail from British ports during the Civil War. Although they were built in private shipyards, the British government allowed these ships to escape and inflict a great

---

79   Calhoun, 482-84; Michael Les Benedict, "Ulysses S. Grant," in Frank N. Magill, ed., *The American Presidents: The Office and the Men*, 3 vols. (Pasadena, CA: Salem Press, 1986), 2:376.

80   Scaturro, *President Grant*, 51-53.

81   Robert J. Gordon, *The Rise and Fall of American Growth: The U.S. Standard of Living Since the Civil War* (Princeton: Princeton University Press, 2016).

82   Nevins, 359-60; Calhoun, *Presidency*, 194-96.

deal of destruction upon Union merchant shipping.[83] After the war, Americans demanded reparations, and the quarrel between the two countries presented the most menacing situation between them since the War of 1812.[84] The terms of settlement of the dispute were provided by the Treaty of Washington, which was signed in 1871 by members of the Joint High Commission appointed by Grant and by the British government. The *Alabama* claims would be resolved through arbitration by a tribunal that convened in Geneva and in 1872 awarded the United States $15.5 million in damages.[85] The treaty also provided for the settlement of a number of other disputes between the United States and Great Britain, including controversies over Americans' privileges to use Canadian fisheries, the water boundary in the vicinity of the San Juan Islands in the northwest, claims of both American citizens and British subjects growing out of the Civil War apart from the *Alabama* claims, and numerous navigation and trade issues between the United States and Canada.[86]

In 1936, John Bassett Moore, a leading authority on international law, called the Treaty of Washington "the greatest treaty of actual and immediate arbitration the world had ever seen; and it still holds that preeminence."[87] Besides marking a turning point in Anglo-American relations, and well beyond the immediate importance of the award to the United States, the settlement of the *Alabama* claims established the principle of international arbitration for the resolution of disputes between nations involving questions of paramount importance. The peaceful submission of this major controversy to arbitration demonstrated to other nations an alternative to war that would provide an unprecedented impetus toward world peace.[88] Grant's diplomatic triumph led to several organized efforts that promoted

83   Adrian Cook, *The Alabama Claims: American Politics and Anglo-American Relations, 1865–1872* (Ithaca, NY: Cornell University Press, 1975), 15-16.

84   John Bassett Moore, *History and Digest of the International Arbitrations to Which the United States Has Been a Party*, 6 vols. (Washington, D.C.: Government Printing Office, 1898), 1:495.

85   Scaturro, *President Grant*, 52.

86   Treaty Between Great Britain and the United States for the Amicable Settlement of All Causes of Difference Between the Two Countries, 8 May 1871, U.S.-Gr. Brit., art. 12-42, 143 Consol. T.S. 145, 152-62.

87   Nevins, xv.

88   John Russell Young, *Around the World with General Grant*, 2 vols. (New York: The American News Company, 1879), 1:50, 83, 120; 2 Cong. Rec. 5114, 5407 (1874) (resolutions promoting international arbitration); Nevins, 494; George F. Hoar, *Autobiography of Seventy Years*, 2 vols. (New York: Charles Scribner's Sons, 1903), 2:127; C. Peter Magrath, *Morrison R. Waite: The Triumph of Character* (New York: The Macmillan Company, 1963), 79; David Dudley Field, "American Contributions to International Law," *Albany Law Journal*, 14 October 1876, 14:260; John Russell Young, *Men and Memories: Personal Reminiscences*, 2 vols. (New York: F. Tennyson Neely, 1901), 2:465.

alternatives to war, including the Hague Conventions of 1899 and 1907 and, years later, the League of Nations and the United Nations.[89]

Yet another episode in which the Grant administration averted war—once again with Spain—was the *Virginius* affair. In 1873, the *Virginius*, a steamer flying the American flag and commanded by Captain Joseph Fry, a U.S. citizen, was captured by the Spanish gunboat *Tornado*. Claiming that the vessel was aiding Cuban rebels, Spanish military authorities executed 53 prisoners, including Fry and many other Americans.[90] Resisting pressure to declare war on Spain, Grant and Fish secured a peaceful resolution of the crisis, including the release of surviving captives and ultimately an $80,000 indemnity from the Spanish government.[91] An investigation into the matter had revealed that the *Virginius* was illegally registered and had no right to fly the American flag.[92] War with Spain would come 25 years later, but the Grant presidency, free of international war, contributed more than any other to the 33-year period between the Civil War and the Spanish-American War—the longest in American history—in which the United States went without the affliction of a major war.

Grant had one conspicuous foreign policy failure: his inability to win ratification of the treaty for the annexation of Santo Domingo in 1870. That stood out not because it was unusual for nineteenth-century presidents to fall short on their goals for territorial expansion—indeed, Andrew Johnson had called for the acquisition of both the Dominican Republic and Haiti near the end of his presidency—but because Grant raised the issue's profile and, unaccustomed to losing, repeatedly returned to note the merits of his case until the end of his life.[93] The president's fundamental objectives were simultaneously grounded in the country's strategic and economic value and a vision for America's political and social fabric.[94] Grant pursued annexation peacefully, with a view toward statehood and conditioned on the people's assent.[95]

Unappreciated for many years was the extent to which Grant pursued the venture to help fulfill the post-Civil War paradigm set by the Reconstruction

89   Scaturro, *President Grant*, 54; Louis A. Coolidge, *Ulysses S. Grant* (Boston: Houghton Mifflin Company, 1917), 311; A.C.F. Beales, *The History of Peace: A Short Account of the Organised Movements for International Peace* (London: G. Bell & Sons Ltd., 1931), 140-41.

90   Richard H. Bradford, *The Virginius Affair* (Boulder, CO: Colorado Associated University Press, 1980), 35, 39-42, 47, 52-53, 62; Nevins, 669-70.

91   Nevins, 673-88; Bradford, 107, 123-26.

92   Bradford, 102; Nevins, 689.

93   Calhoun, *Presidency*, 201, 295, 567, 585.

94   Ibid., 226-27.

95   Ibid., 223, 227; Scaturro, *President Grant*, 69-70.

amendments. He hoped Santo Domingo, with the opportunity it presented to those who emigrated there, would offer African Americans economic leverage to enable them to "demand" their "rights at home on pain of finding them elsewhere."[96] It would also have the effect of doing away with slavery in Cuba and Brazil, where the institution persisted, by "mak[ing] slave labor unprofitable;" the United States was slavery's "largest supporter" by way of the high percentage of exports from those countries to the United States.[97] His aspiration to make Santo Domingo into several states while recognizing that their "citizens would be almost wholly colored" reflected the extent of his commitment to America as a multiracial republic.[98] In the end, Grant would not succeed in his principal goal for territorial expansion—the Senate vote on the annexation treaty split 28 to 28, far below the two-thirds margin required for approval—although on another front, he would secure a commercial reciprocity treaty with Hawaii that paved the way for its eventual annexation.[99]

Grant's humanitarian impulse spurred what became known as his Indian peace policy. The eighteenth president elevated the reform of the government's policy toward Native Americans to a new level of urgency in the face of their impending extermination under the status quo. The nominal reservation system in place offered little protection in the face of the string of broken treaties, the repeated removal of tribes, the stampede of settlers and explorers to the West in unprecedented numbers, the disappearance of the Indian frontier, the periodic battles and massacres, and the corrupt and exploitative Indian service that could not be trusted to protect Indian welfare.[100] Grant made the "proper treatment of the original occupants of this land" and "any course toward them which tends to their civilization and ultimate citizenship" a priority in his First Inaugural Address.[101] Over the course of numerous messages that followed, he appealed to the nation's conscience and refused to mince words about the wickedness of extermination, which he recognized as the likely future if the nation did not change its course.[102]

---

96   Scaturro, *President Grant*, 69-70; Memorandum, [1869–1870], *PUSG*, 20:74; Draft Annual Message, 5 December 1876, ibid., 28:69.

97   Memorandum, [1869–1870], *PUSG*, 20:75-76.

98   Ulysses S. Grant, *Personal Memoirs of U.S. Grant*, 2 vols. (New York: Charles L. Webster & Co., 1885–1886), 2:550.

99   Calhoun, *Presidency*, 257, 485; Scaturro, *President Grant*, 55.

100   Elsie Mitchell Rushmore, *The Indian Policy During Grant's Administrations* (Jamaica, NY: The Marion Press, 1914), 13-14; R. Pierce Beaver, *Church, State, and the American Indians: Two and a Half Centuries of Partnership in Missions Between Protestant Churches and Government* (St. Louis: Concordia Publishing House, 1966), 123-24.

101   Richardson, 9:3962.

102   Scaturro, *President Grant*, 55.

The peace policy emphasized fair dealing and humane treatment and made the federal government directly responsible for the welfare of Native Americans as individuals, departing from a treaty paradigm that too often treated tribes like foreign adversaries.[103] The policy entailed the replacement of Indian agents, first with army officers, but after Congress barred army officers from playing that role, Grant, refusing to cater to Congress' patronage preferences, gave that role to various Christian denominations.[104] On reservations, Native Americans were to be taught agricultural methods and provided sufficient means at reasonable costs to pursue them. A number of medical and educational programs were established for their relief. Over the course of Grant's presidency, housing, schools, teachers, cultivated land, and livestock for Native Americans would multiply. Tons of food, clothing, and books were donated by churches and Indian aid organizations.[105] Grant held Native Americans to be "entitled to all the rights of citizens" and wished them to "cease to be nations and become States."[106]

At the time Grant took office, Indian–white relations were too deeply ingrained to expect a sudden cessation of past problems he inherited—problems that for years had resulted in the succession of armed conflicts known collectively as the Indian wars.[107] Conspicuous among the Indian wars of the 1870s were the Modoc War, the Red River War, and the Great Sioux War.

Indian policy was not a major electoral issue in Grant's time and was not a focus of the ire of most of his twentieth-century biographers. As a topic of scholarship, it tended to occupy its own niche, with generally positive commentary on Grant's reform efforts from authors including Lawrie Tatum (1899), Elsie Mitchell Rushmore (1914), and R. Pierce Beaver (1966).[108] In recent decades, much scholarship tends not only to condemn the forced dislocation, exploitation, and death inflicted upon Native Americans—which has justifiably been a fixture in public discussion for well over a century—but also to denounce proponents

---

103   Ibid.; Calhoun, *Presidency*, 263, 273-74.

104   Mary Stockwell, *Interrupted Odyssey: Ulysses S. Grant and the American Indians* (Carbondale, IL: Southern Illinois University Press, 2018), 87-91.

105   *Eighth Annual Report of the Board of Indian Commissioners for the Year 1876* (Washington, D.C.: Government Printing Office, 1877), 7; Robert H. Keller, Jr., *American Protestantism and United States Indian Policy, 1869–82* (Lincoln, NE: University of Nebraska Press), 210.

106   *New York Times*, 26 January 1870. See also Speech, 12 October 1874, *PUSG*, 25:253, 257.

107   Keller, 210.

108   Lawrie Tatum, *Our Red Brothers and the Peace Policy of President Ulysses S. Grant* (Philadelphia: John C. Winston & Co., 1899); Elsie Mitchell Rushmore, *The Indian Policy During Grant's Administrations* (Jamaica, NY: The Marion Press, 1914); R. Pierce Beaver, *Church, State, and the American Indians: Two and a Half Centuries of Partnership in Missions Between Protestant Churches and Government* (St. Louis: Concordia Publishing House, 1966).

The June 18, 1870, edition of *Harper's Weekly*, reporting on Grant's
efforts on behalf of Native Americans, captioned its cover image
with one of Grant's most famous lines: "Let us have peace."

Library of Congress

of assimilation, painting all of them, including Grant, with a broad brush as
destroyers of culture who had little to nothing of value to show for their efforts.[109]
Other scholars have looked to the vision of Grant and Ely S. Parker, the Seneca
Indian who was Grant's commissioner of Indian Affairs until 1871, which entailed
a more limited and gradual assimilation, as a desirable alternative to the more
sweeping process that occurred during the late nineteenth century.[110] The peace
policy's contemporary critics tended to accuse Grant of being too lenient and
protective toward Native Americans.[111]

Grant embraced the most humanitarian views on the political spectrum of his
time. His course was another component of the broader paradigm of inclusive national

109   Akim D. Reinhardt, *Ruling Pine Ridge: Oglala Lakota Politics from the IRA to Wounded Knee*
(Lubbock, TX: Texas Tech University Press, 2007), 22-23.

110   C. Joseph Genetin-Pilawa, *Crooked Paths to Allotment: The Fight over Federal Indian Policy after the
Civil War* (Chapel Hill, NC: The University of North Carolina Press, 2012), 2-12, 73-94; Stockwell, 67,
93-95, 186, 189.

111   Stockwell, 111, 117, 141, 143, 158.

citizenship that defined Reconstruction. Through at least the first century and a half of American history, no other president had done as much in a humanitarian direction as Grant. During the 1930s, Franklin Roosevelt implemented his Indian New Deal, further changing the paradigm to bolster tribal sovereignty.[112] Days before Grant retired from the White House, a delegation of Choctaws, Chickasaws, Cherokees, and Creeks thanked him for his "just and humane" course.[113] Quanah Parker, the Comanche chief who had led warriors from several tribes in the Red River War, became an advocate of Grant's peace policy among his people.[114] Chief Joseph, who had led warriors in the Nez Percé War months after Grant's retirement, went to New York City to help lead the procession dedicating Grant's Tomb in 1897, riding with the grand marshal, Gen. Grenville Dodge.[115] Perhaps these living witnesses of Grant's peace policy saw more clearly what today's reflexive critics miss—that the eighteenth president was the best friend Native Americans could have realistically hoped for in the White House. Too many historians overlook that, on the eve of what could have been a very different fate, Grant helped save Native Americans from extinction.[116]

Twentieth-century historians valued assertive and expansive exercises of presidential power, but they failed to recognize such traits in Grant's presidency.[117] This supposedly pliant president vetoed 93 bills, more than all his predecessors combined, with only four of the vetoes overturned. During his second term, he became the first president to call for the power to exercise the line-item veto and set the chief precedent—and the argument for—the presidential impoundment of funds.[118] More broadly, Grant emerged after an initial period of conflict with Congress as an unusually effective legislative president who was able to advance his agenda in every major area of domestic policy from Reconstruction to economic matters and in most areas of foreign policy.

As presidential historians emerged during the twentieth century whose writings elevated assertive presidents, the traits that had roiled Grant's contemporaries were largely forgotten, and historians conjured a passive and ineffective president. It

---

112 Ibid., 2-3.

113 Peter P. Pitchlynn, Choctaw delegate, and eight other Chickasaws, Cherokees, and Creeks to USG, 26 February 1877, *PUSG*, 28:168*n*.

114 Stockwell, 146, 151.

115 Louis L. Picone, *Grant's Tomb: The Epic Death of Ulysses S. Grant and the Making of an American Pantheon* (New York: Arcade Publishing, 2021), 179; *New York Times*, 28 April 1897.

116 Scaturro, *President Grant*, 55-56; Smith, 541.

117 Simpson, "Another Look," 12.

118 Scaturro, *President Grant*, 60-61; Richardson, 10:4196, 4331.

was as if the inherited animus against Grant overrode a sense of obligation to do their homework. Great presidents are assertive, poor presidents passive; Grant was a poor president; therefore, he must have been passive.

Grant would close his presidency by addressing the electoral crisis of 1876–77. Threats to the orderly and peaceful inauguration of a new president were more pronounced then than at any time in American history other than 1860–61. Grant adeptly navigated the crisis by garnering support for the creation of an electoral commission, remaining impartial throughout the process, quietly strengthening forces around Washington, and making clear that disrespect for the law would not be tolerated.[119] It was a significant accomplishment—one made possible by public recognition of Grant's character, firmness, and respect for the law, all of which bely the smear that would be used to define the Grant presidency.[120]

What about corruption?

The earlier historical consensus buried the Grant administration beneath the sordid corruption narrative—the notion that corruption served primarily to discredit Grant's presidency and bears primacy over policy issues. That flawed premise has been dissipating with recent scholarship, but to what degree is unclear. Recent studies place less emphasis on the corruption issue, basically suggesting that Reconstruction was more important, but they differ in how much they challenge the rest of the underlying narrative. Too many current students of history still have the impression that the two most fundamental features of Grant's presidency were Reconstruction and corruption. But such a narrative itself cannot stand on its merits. It is permeated with distortions that were often linked to the very misunderstandings about policy—especially but not exclusively Reconstruction— that have called for historical correction.

Presidential culpability for corruption should track the same standards applied to personal culpability in the law—and for that matter in human interactions generally. A president who engaged in intentional misconduct—acting with corrupt intent, whether being part of the underlying corrupt activity or covering up the misdeeds of others—deserves the harshest condemnation from history. Those who have knowledge of corrupt activity that they refuse to address merit censure as well, though their cases are distinguishable from those who act with corrupt intent. Presidents who are negligent—who fail to exercise due diligence in addressing corruption—are accordingly subject to criticism as well, albeit less

---

119   Scaturro, *President Grant*, 56; Calhoun, *Presidency*, 553-57, 562-64; White, *American Ulysses*, 581-83; Chernow, *Grant*, 849-50; Baier, 273-78, 284.

120   Scaturro, *President Grant*, 43.

than those who act with knowledge or intent.[121] Due diligence is a broad concept that can be difficult to discern in particular cases, and perhaps all presidents who had greater longevity in office than William H. Harrison, who served only one month, face reasonable questions about whether their approach to corruption at times fell short of that standard. Grant is not among the presidents whose record distinguishes him for the greater culpability of knowledge or intent. Yet the association of his presidency with corruption, even by historians who recognized his innocence, was so pronounced that his standing could hardly have been worse if he had personally dispensed bribes.

Note the exceedingly broad, sometimes haphazard way Grant's enemies defined corruption. It was hardly limited to the widely accepted definition of corruption: acts of malfeasance, culpable conduct that violates the law for personal or political gain. Much of their definition encompassed the very practice of the spoils system, the use of partisan criteria in the distribution of appointments, or government extravagance, defined as spending beyond the bare minimum needed to advance expenditures the critics deemed essential.[122] Yet the spoils system had been in place for generations and was used extensively by Grant's immediate predecessors—and while Grant would use the patronage power to secure his goals, he would also take pioneering steps to rein in the system. Contrast Jackson, who pioneered the spoils system that would expand as government grew, and Lincoln, who unhesitatingly employed it to meet his objectives. Those two presidents were long deemed master politicians in their approach to the system while Grant was incongruously subjected to a different standard. In the same vein, historians derided Grant for his alliances with spoilsmen like Roscoe Conkling and Zachariah Chandler (to take two examples) even when those same men had earlier been Lincoln allies, with no similar discredit to the sixteenth president.[123] Neither should Grant be singled out for extravagance when he championed economy in public expenditures and attained a significant reduction in both debt and spending as the government ran consistent surpluses.

As legitimate concerns about government perfidy went, Mark Wahlgren Summers, who wrote books exploring the subject of corruption both during the dozen years after the Civil War and the dozen years preceding it, concluded that "the postwar years were *not* unusually corrupt. They were no worse than the 1850s," and he found the lamentations of graft and fraud in newspapers during the earlier

---

121 Ibid., 28.

122 Calhoun, *Presidency*, 12, 118-19; Scaturro, *President Grant*, 21-24.

123 Simpson, "Another Look," 8; Scaturro, *President Grant*, 23-24.

period to be "more strident than the postwar ones."[124] Many historians view the Civil War itself as a source of corruption, and those "who drew the dividing line between the days of honesty and those of depravity at the war's beginning certainly come closer to the truth than those who place it between the administrations of Andrew Johnson and Ulysses S. Grant. . . . Yet . . . scholars would have been wiser to draw no line at all."[125]

To take a few examples, when Grant was first inaugurated, the Treasury Department already had a sordid reputation, including from the tax evasion and bribery scheme known as the Whiskey Ring and customhouse abuses, as did various branches of the Interior Department, perhaps most prominently the Indian service. Grant's critics did not hesitate to misattribute Johnson-era trends to the Grant years, from customhouse revenue lost to appointments originally made by Johnson.[126] But Grant's appointees actually introduced reforms to the largest and the most troubled realms of government early on, including among other measures new testing standards in the Treasury and Interior Departments, improving the Indian service, breaking (temporarily) the Whiskey Ring, and significant improvements to the operation of the Post Office Department.[127]

After years of civil service reform measures failing to make it through Congress, Grant secured the creation of the nation's first civil service commission in 1871.[128] It promulgated ambitious standards that classified most positions, required competitive examinations for entrance, and barred the levying of "any assessment of money for political purposes" by government officials upon their subordinates. Grant made clear he retained the authority to alter the rules, including the power to appoint and remove officers.[129] The commission lasted for several years, but

124 Summers, *Stealings*, x; Mark W. Summers, *The Plundering Generation: Corruption and the Crisis of the Union, 1849–1861* (New York: Oxford University Press, 1987), xi-xii.

125 Summers, *Stealings*, 16.

126 Ibid., 32, 44, 91-92; Chernow, *Grant*, 628-29; *Official Proceedings of the National Republican Conventions of 1868, 1872, 1876 and 1880* (Minneapolis: Charles W. Johnson, 1903), 67; Genetin-Pilawa, 76-78; Beaver, 123-24; Stockwell, 80-81; Scaturro, *President Grant*, 23, 45; 9 Cong. Rec. 2327 (1879) (statement of Sen. Conkling).

127 Ari Hoogenboom, "Civil Service and Public Morality," in H. Wayne Morgan, ed., *The Gilded Age* (Syracuse, NY: Syracuse University Press, 1970), 89; Scaturro, *President Grant*, 18, 22-23; Calhoun, *Presidency*, 277, 281-82, 368-70; Summers, *Stealings*, 96, 100, 188; Smith, 541; U.S. Library of Congress, Congressional Research Service, *Franking Privilege: Historical Development and Options for Change*, by Matthew E. Glassman, RL34274 (2016), 3.

128 U.S. Office of Personnel Management, *Biography of an Ideal: A History of the Federal Civil Service* (Washington, D.C.: Government Printing Office, 2003), 30; Ari Hoogenboom, "Thomas A. Jenckes and Civil Service Reform," *Mississippi Valley Historical Review* (March 1961), No. 4, 47:637-56; Calhoun, *Presidency*, 292-93.

129 Richardson, 9:4111-13; U.S. Office of Personnel Management, 35-36.

Congress in 1874 refused to fund it, and after Grant's request for legislative support went unheeded, he disbanded it in 1875. Individual examinations would still be implemented under existing law, but a broader requirement for competitive examinations would be abandoned. As for political assessments, in 1876, Grant signed into law the Anti-Assessment Act, which barred non-Senate-confirmed executive officers or employees from soliciting or giving to other government officers or employees.[130]

Popular fervor for civil service reform—at least of the kind sought by Gilded Age reformers—did not arise until after Garfield's assassination in 1881 at the hands of an insane office seeker, which was cynically exploited by advocates to advance the cause. The result was the Pendleton Civil Service Act of 1883, signed by Chester Arthur, which established a merit system that would last and be expanded substantially through the twentieth century.[131] And thanks to the merit system, waste, inefficiency, and corruption in the federal government would become a thing of the past. That, of course, would be an absurd statement to make, but it is not far from the impression created by the triumphalist history of the merit system. That reflexive embrace of the emerging paradigm for the civil service fed its largely unquestioned expansion during the twentieth century, and it did not seem to matter how insulated most of the executive branch became from the influence of elected officials.[132] Once again the Grant administration was treated like a foil— the dark years that necessitated the redemptive Pendleton Act—regardless of how little that squared with the record.

A more nuanced view of the issue would recognize that with the expansion of the size of the executive branch during the nineteenth century, it made sense to impart structure to a chaotic civil service and to set standards of proficiency that corresponded to the demands of different government jobs. With the expansion of the role members of Congress played in demanding patronage, it was imperative that the presidency reclaim its prerogative in making appointments and removing appointees. Grant's commission advanced both of those aims. In fact, the 1871 provision Grant signed into law authorizing him to prescribe civil service rules and ascertain each candidate's fitness for government positions remained on the books and would provide an even stronger basis for presidential control over the civil service

130   19 Stat. 169.

131   Scaturro, *President Grant*, 25-26.

132   Jay M. Shafritz et al., *Personnel Management in Government: Politics and Process*, 5th ed. (New York: Marcel Dekker, 2001), 14.

than the 1883 act.[133] But over time, the civil service did become more insulated from presidential control. That presented a tension with constitutional structure as it undermined accountability to the one official to whom the first sentence of Article II of the Constitution vests executive power.[134]

The corruption narrative at its inception was actually not about Grant's principal subordinates meeting the widely accepted definition of corruption as culpable misconduct. It was about the other ways politics as practiced—including the new order of Reconstruction—could be cast as a violation of the republican ideal, rendering reform imperative and the administration hostile.[135] The reformers' most persistent charge not surprisingly involved Grant's appointments. Their worldview was what Ari Hoogenboom described as "an 'out' versus 'in' pattern. Reformers invariably wished to curtail the appointing power after they thought it had been abused, and to them abuse occurred when men of their own social station or political faction were not appointed to office."[136] As recent studies have highlighted, the reformers' perspective was tainted not only by racial prejudice, but also by class-based prejudice, expressed by elite critics anticipating "a reign of western mediocrity" from the start and calling Grant "vulgar-minded" and "ill bred."[137] The reformers held Republican regimes in the South to be an embodiment of the corruption they condemned, an affront to their aspirations for government by the "best men."[138]

To employ historical perspective about the executive branch the cabinet inherited is to recognize that its members were, for the most part, serious about reform and lacking the reformers' anti-Reconstruction agenda. Not only did cabinet appointees Hamilton Fish, George Boutwell, and Postmaster General John A. J. Creswell distinguish themselves during Grant's first term and beyond (in Fish's case through the end of the administration), but so did several second-term appointments, including Secretary of the Treasury Benjamin H. Bristow, Postmaster General Marshall Jewell, Attorney General Edwards Pierrepont, and

133   16 Stat. 514; Lionel V. Murphy, "The First Federal Civil Service Commission: 1871–75 (Part I)," *Public Personnel Review* (January 1942), No. 1, 3:29; Lionel V. Murphy, "The First Federal Civil Service Commission: 1871–75 (Part III)," *Public Personnel Review* (October 1942), No. 4, 3:322-23.

134   Scaturro, *President Grant*, 25.

135   Brooks D. Simpson, *The Political Education of Henry Adams* (Columbia, SC: University of South Carolina, 1996), xiv.

136   Ari A. Hoogenboom, "An Analysis of Civil Service Reformers," *The Historian* (November 1960), No. 1, 23:64.

137   Calhoun, *Presidency*, 62, 364; Chernow, *Grant*, 740, 854.

138   Scaturro, *President Grant*, 75-77; Summers, *Stealings*, 162; White, *Republic*, 202; Simpson, *Henry Adams*, 27, 100-01.

Secretary of the Interior Zachariah Chandler.[139] Mark Summers concluded, "The Age of Corruption had been the Age of Reform all along," even if it did not go as far as the reformers wished.[140]

Operating in a hyperpartisan environment, Grant's critics strained to find corruption even where particular charges were oversimplifications or outright fabrications.[141] Many traditional accounts of the administration would reduce it to another term: scandal. That word has many legitimate applications, but in its ambiguity, it can also be a weasel word to obfuscate the differences between cases of malfeasance and those that turned out to involve extravagance or negligence— or were all scandal and no offense.[142]

Start with Jay Gould and Jim Fisk's scheme to corner the gold market—the one Grant foiled. To succeed, the two hoped to influence administration policy on the monthly sale of government gold with the help of Grant's brother-in-law, but they failed after Grant directed Boutwell to sell $4 million in government gold. A House committee investigating the episode was able to conclude without overstatement that "the testimony has not elicited a word or act of the President inconsistent with that patriotism and integrity which befit the Chief Executive of the nation."[143] But for generations of historians working with hostile and unreliable sources, the takeaway was not a presidential accomplishment, but an item to log as a scandal.

A host of other events would be crammed into this narrative. The attempt to annex Santo Domingo was spun into a sordid scheme for government officials and cronies to exploit the territory through real estate deals for their own profit, not an unusual criticism where territorial expansion is concerned, but here a red herring that did not gain much traction. Grant made clear that the U.S. government would treat as null and void any land grants made by the Dominican government after the annexation treaty was signed, rendering many questions about self-interest moot. The most that can be said is that Grant's private secretary, Orville E. Babcock, was accused of having Santo Domingo land interests with an advocate of annexation. But the allegation fell flat, and an investigating Senate committee concluded Babcock had conducted himself "with perfect honesty and sincerity"—

---

139   Summers, *Stealings*, 187-90, 258, 269; White, *American Ulysses*, 556-57, 560; Stockwell, 170.

140   Summers, *Stealings*, 301.

141   Ibid., 15, 29.

142   Ibid., x.

143   Scaturro, *President Grant*, 31-32; Calhoun, *Presidency*, 129-49, 620-21.

though unknown to anyone, a diary entry obliquely admitted an expectation of getting land on the island's southern coast.[144]

The corruption narrative was already in place by the start of the 1872 election season as the breakaway Liberal Republican Party included denunciations in its May convention of supposedly corrupt appointees and tyrannical behavior.[145] At that time, not a single major appointee of Grant had been demonstrated to have engaged in wrongdoing.[146] But such details were unimportant. The term "Grantism" had also already emerged by that time, reflecting the fusion of the corruption narrative with criticism of Reconstruction.[147]

Before the election season was over, the Credit Mobilier would be added to the catalog of Grant scandals. This involved the unseemly sale of shares of stock of the company that had financed the construction of the Union Pacific Railroad to several members of Congress at bargain prices. It did not matter that the underlying conduct had occurred in a different branch of government and even prior to Grant's inauguration.[148] Then there was the so-called "Salary Grab," a provision in the government's general appropriations bill that made a congressional salary raise retroactive for the prior two years. Once again, the primary issue was congressional greed, and while it was part of legislation Grant signed, it was passed during the last hours of the Forty-Second Congress. A veto would have left the federal government unfunded and necessitated a special session in the next Congress to start the appropriations process all over again.[149]

The corruption narrative was cued up to make the most of whatever allegations arose in connection with Grant's cabinet or other principal appointees, but it was not until his second term that opponents could find such targets—and they nearly always fell short of demonstrating the official's malfeasance. It was revealed in December 1873 that Attorney General George H. Williams, at his wife's urging, had bought an expensive landaulet carriage and horses and employed servants out of the Justice Department contingent fund, and he rode in the vehicle for personal

144   Calhoun, *Presidency*, 201, 210, 215, 221-22, 224, 239-40, 247, 250-51; U.S. Congress, Senate, *Report of the Select Committee Appointed to Investigate the Memorial of Davis Hatch*, 41st Cong., 2d Sess., 25 June 1870, S. Rep. 234, xxi-xxii, xxx, xlvi, 43, 49, 104, 111, 176, 194, 207, 258, 264.

145   *Proceedings of the Liberal Republican Convention, in Cincinnati, May 1st, 2d and 3d, 1872* (New York: Baker & Godwin, 1872), 18-19; Calhoun, *Presidency*, 372.

146   Scaturro, *President Grant*, 26.

147   Summers, *Stealings*, 256-57; Chernow, *Grant*, 740-42.

148   Summers, *Stealings*, 50-54, 231, 234-35.

149   Ibid., 238-41; Calhoun, *Presidency*, 402-03; Ari Hoogenboom, *Outlawing the Spoils: A History of the Civil Service Reform Movement, 1865-1883* (Urbana, IL: University of Illinois Press, 1968), 126; Scaturro, *President Grant*, 30.

and social visits (albeit with judges and members of Congress among others).[150] Other government officials, including cabinet members in prior administrations, had made some social use of official carriages.[151] Williams also put the Justice Department's chief clerk in charge of his personal funds, which invited the mingling of personal and department accounts—of which the attorney general said he was unaware—and the occurrence of temporary deficiencies that were soon made up for between the accounts. Those effectively were improper advances in pay, notwithstanding that a number of other public officials did the same, but there was no evidence to suggest Williams ever profited from these transactions.[152] His avaricious and vindictive wife, however, would be a recurring problem, and Grant would replace his attorney general in 1875 after an alarming but unconfirmed account that she had extracted a $30,000 bribe from the firm of Pratt and Boyd in exchange for getting the Justice Department to drop a lawsuit against it.[153]

The mistakes of George Williams (as opposed to his wife) were deeds of negligence and far from unique. Comparisons extend well beyond other cabinet members; household extravagance allegations and connected issues of advancing government funds plagued presidents themselves, including the most esteemed among them. George Washington was embarrassed by revelations that he had repeatedly overdrawn his salary during both of his terms.[154] James Monroe obtained interest-free advances from the treasury on the French furniture from his personal collection he had brought to the White House and faced two congressional

150 Hamilton Fish, Diary, 30 December 1873 and 7 January 1874, *PUSG*, 24:286n-87n; Calhoun, *Presidency*, 433-34; Sidney Teiser, "Life of George H. Williams: Almost Chief-Justice, Part Two," *Oregon Historical Quarterly* (December 1946), No. 4, 47:427-31; A.J. Falls testimony, 16 December 1873, 4, 11-18, 26-33, 35, 128-32, George H. Williams to George F. Edmunds, 3 January 1874, George H. Williams to George F. Edmunds, 17 January 1874, U.S. Congress, Senate, Nomination of George H. Williams to Be Chief Justice, Supreme Court, Senate Judiciary Committee, hereafter cited as Williams Report.

151 George H. Williams to George F. Edmunds, 3 January 1874, George H. Williams to George F. Edmunds, 7 January 1874, George H. Williams to George F. Edmunds, 17 January 1874, A.J. Falls testimony, 16 December 1873, 3, Williams Report; John P. Frank, "The Appointment of Supreme Court Justices: Prestige, Principles and Politics," *Wisconsin Law Review* (March 1941), No. 2, 1941:199-200; Summers, *Stealings*, 124; *Chicago Tribune*, 1 January 1874; *New York Tribune*, 20 May 1874; *Morning Oregonian*, 12 August 1903.

152 Committee report, 26-30, A.J. Falls testimony, 16 December 1873, 4-5, 7-9, 34, 113-17, George H. Williams to George F. Edmunds, 3 January 1874, A.J. Falls to George H. Williams, 15 January 1874, George H. Williams to George F. Edmunds, 17 January 1874, Williams Report; Frank, 198-201.

153 Calhoun, *Presidency*, 488-90; USG to George H. Williams, 28 April 1875; *PUSG*, 26:105; Hamilton Fish, Diary, 12 April 1875; ibid., 26:107n-08n.

154 Chervinsky, 231; John Alexander Carroll & Mary Wells Ashworth, *George Washington: First in Peace* (New York: Charles Scribner's Sons, 1957), completing Douglas Southall Freeman, *George Washington*, 7 vols., 7:320; James Tagg, *Benjamin Franklin Bache and the Philadelphia* Aurora (Philadelphia: University of Pennsylvania Press, 1991), 278-80.

investigations.[155] Mary Todd Lincoln made so many exorbitant purchases of White House furnishings that she exceeded the congressional appropriation for it by $6,700 and tried to get the government to cover the expenses.[156]

As it turned out, Mary Lincoln's White House extravagance paled next to her outright corruption. Among other things, she procured falsified bills in order to extract money from the public treasury and accepted bribes for a range of influence-peddling activity that included leaking parts of Lincoln's 1861 annual message before it was issued.[157] It is unnecessary to speculate how differently historians would have approached anything like the same fact pattern if it had existed in the case of Ulysses and Julia Grant, because even in the absence of such circumstances, history's condemnation was unsparing.

The hostile standard toward the Grant administration manifested itself in the balance of cases selectively recounted as little more than scandals that discredited the president. Secretary of the Treasury William A. Richardson came under fire in 1874 for contracts he signed under which John Sanborn was authorized to seek out delinquent taxes and collect a moiety of 50%. The underlying arrangement was legal, but Sanborn operated with enough deception that he was able to claim a commission of $213,500 on $427,000 in taxes collected, most or all of which would have been collected anyway by internal revenue officials without losing so much in a commission payment.[158] Richardson had acted negligently, not corruptly. He assumed the inefficacy of moiety contracts from past experience and did not read Sanborn's contracts.[159] Usually omitted from summaries of the episode is the broader context: Moiety contracts were nothing new for the federal government. The Grant administration and Congress had been in the process of phasing out the practice, first enacting legislation that reduced the allowance for such contracts to three, and then, after the Sanborn revelations, abolishing them completely.[160]

155   James M. Banner, Jr., ed., *Presidential Misconduct: From George Washington to Today* (New York: The New Press, 2019), xxxii, 45-46.

156   Michael Burlingame, *An American Marriage: The Untold Story of Abraham Lincoln and Mary Todd* (New York: Pegasus Books, 2021), 187-91.

157   Michael Burlingame, ed., *At Lincoln's Side: John Hay's Civil War Correspondence and Selected Writings* (Carbondale, IL: Southern Illinois University Press, 2000), 185-203; Burlingame, *Marriage*, 42, 113-14, 120-25, 131-37, 150-58, 166-68, 181-87, 271.

158   Scaturro, *President Grant*, 34; U.S. Congress, House, *Discovery and Collection of Monies Withheld from the Government*, 43rd Cong., 1st Sess., 4 May 1874, H. Rep. 559, 2-7, hereafter cited as *Sanborn Contracts Report*.

159   *Sanborn Contracts Report*, 87-91.

160   Ibid., 1; 17 Stat. 256; 17 Stat. 69; 18 Stat. 192; Calhoun, *Presidency*, 446; Hoogenboom, *Outlawing*, 131.

Another account of supposed cabinet corruption involved Secretary of the Interior Columbus Delano. In a department that had long been rife with public land schemes designed to fleece the government, Delano's adversaries in government and the press tried to pin on him a transaction involving his son, who had been a silent partner on surveying contracts from which he profited without doing work. The secretary was not implicated in and apparently did not know the relevant details about the underlying contracts. He did thank the Wyoming Territory surveyor general through whom the contracts were made in broad terms for his kindness toward his son but coupled that with a warning to avoid anything that would appear wrong.[161] While his overall record would pale next to that of his successor, Chandler, Delano was an honest man, overwhelmed by the Interior Department's chronic problems, but not corrupt.[162]

The Whiskey Ring provided a genuine example of nefarious corruption in the executive branch, but not at the cabinet level. In fact, the Ring, which had reconstituted itself after earlier prosecutions in several locations with often new combinations of government officials and whiskey distillers intent on profiting off tax evasion, was broken through the zealous efforts of a cabinet member, Bristow, and prosecuted by Pierrepont's Justice Department. Given the long history of tax dodges, even specifically with respect to the tax on spirits, Grant biographer H.W. Brands asserted, "The surprise of the whiskey scandal wasn't that the underpayment occurred but that it suddenly was prosecuted."[163] More than 350 indictments resulted as the Ring was broken up in Chicago, Milwaukee, St. Louis, and elsewhere.[164]

The traditional corruption narrative reduces the episode to another Grant scandal and focuses on the president's defense of his private secretary, Orville Babcock, who was charged with conspiracy to defraud the revenue in connection with the Whiskey Ring. Supposedly that illustrated the president's haplessness or worse in blindly defending guilty subordinates under fire. When Grant received a letter during the summer of 1875 intimating among other things that Babcock

---

161 Arthur M. Schlesinger, Jr., *The Age of Roosevelt*, vol. 2, *The Coming of the New Deal* (Boston: Houghton Mifflin Company, 1958), 286; Chernow, *Grant*, 628-29; Calhoun, *Presidency*, 492-93; U.S. Congress, House, *Surveys in the Territory of Wyoming*, 44th Cong., 1st Sess., 2 August 1876, H. Rep. 794, i-ii, v, 1-2, 7, 11-12.

162 Summers, *Stealings*, 105, 268-69; The Detroit Post and Tribune, *Zachariah Chandler: An Outline Sketch of His Life and Public Services* (Detroit: The Post and Tribune Company, 1880), 340; Mrs. John A. Logan, *Reminiscences of a Soldier's Wife: An Autobiography* (New York: Charles Scribner's Sons, 1913), 273; Calhoun, *Presidency*, 493; USG to Columbus Delano, 26 August 1875 and 22 September 1875, *PUSG*, 26:274, 329; Columbus Delano to USG, 27 September 1875, ibid., 26:330n-31n.

163 Brands, 556.

164 Scaturro, *President Grant*, 36; Calhoun, *Presidency*, 497-98.

was involved with the St. Louis branch of the Whiskey Ring, he did the opposite of trying to cover it up. He sent it to Bristow with the endorsement, "Let no guilty man escape if it can be avoided—Be specially vigilant . . . agains[t] all who insinuate that they have high influence to protect, or to protect them. No personal consideration should stand in the way of performing a public duty."[165] This was not mere bluster. Grant would repeatedly communicate to subordinates that if Babcock was guilty, he wanted him punished, calling such a scenario "the greatest piece of traitorism to me that a man could possibly practice."[166] "Let no guilty man escape" became the general watchword among prosecutors.[167] But it was also clear that Bristow and several attorneys working closely with him were ambitious for the secretary of the treasury to succeed Grant in the White House. A number of observers, including the president himself, were increasingly put off by the perception that Bristow's team was being overzealous in pursuit of targets that would generate sensational headlines without sufficient evidence.[168]

The case against Babcock, presented at his February 1876 trial, was circumstantial. It was primarily based on his correspondence with an internal revenue supervisor and an agent who coordinated the Whiskey Ring in St. Louis, and with whom he was well acquainted, prior to their exposure and indictment. Prosecutors relied on four telegraph messages sent by Babcock (three of which were admitted into evidence) that were so ambiguous as to be susceptible to innocent interpretations.[169] The prosecution argued that Babcock was acting as an informant seeking to prevent revenue agents from surprising distilleries with a raid and discovering the whiskey frauds before they could get their houses in order. But evidence suggested Babcock had other reasons to be responsive to the internal revenue supervisor and the agent without thinking he was advancing a fraud, that he did not bring about the abandonment of the planned raid, and that the ringleaders had another official acting as their informant.[170] No witnesses testified that Babcock was ever informed about, admitted, or otherwise knew about the

---

165   Endorsement, 29 July 1875, *PUSG*, 26:232.

166   U.S. Congress, House, *Whisky Frauds*, 44th Cong., 1st Sess., 25 July 1876, H. Misc. Doc. 186, 11, 116, 124, 360; Calhoun, *Presidency*, 515.

167   *Whisky Frauds*, 62.

168   Ibid., 35, 73-75, 77, 139, 375, 378; Smith, 591; James Pickett Jones, *John A. Logan: Stalwart Republican from Illinois* (Tallahassee, FL: University Presses of Florida, 1982), 87-88; Scaturro, *President Grant*, 37-41.

169   *St. Louis Globe-Democrat*, 18 February, 23 February, and 24 February 1876; *Whisky Frauds*, 66.

170   *Whisky Frauds*, 56, 93, 541, 544-45; *St. Louis Globe-Democrat*, 9 February, 12 February, 13 February, 15 February, 16 February, 17 February, 18 February, 19 February, 22 February, and 23 February 1876; Deposition, 12 February 1876, *PUSG*, 27:41; Smith, 591; Coolidge, 480.

conspiracy.[171] Prosecutors also fell short of establishing what they maintained was his motive to participate in the conspiracy—pecuniary gain—with an attempt to establish a single instance of payment sent to Babcock that had a number of holes in it.[172] Because the prosecution had to prove Babcock's guilt beyond a reasonable doubt, the jury's verdict was amply justified by the evidence. Grant submitted a deposition for the trial conveying that Babcock had never tried to influence him to stop the investigation, that he had consistently undertaken his duties for him with integrity, and that he never observed him taking an interest in the charges against his St. Louis correspondents.[173] While the deposition naturally helped the defense, historians often erroneously conclude it saved Babcock from conviction when the evidence already pointed to acquittal with or without it. Still, Babcock came out of the trial appearing at a minimum too indiscreet for Grant to trust him. He was not permitted to remain a private secretary in the White House after the trial, and he ended up an inspector of a lighthouse district shortly before Grant's retirement.[174]

Accounts of Grant's belief in Babcock's innocence usually omit the many others who felt the same way, which facilitates criticism of his judgment as uniquely deficient. Yet his conclusion was the dominant one. General Sherman testified in person vouching for Babcock's reputation, as did numerous other distinguished character witnesses.[175] Army colleagues and people who knew both Babcock and the Ring's coordinators, including enemies as well as friends in St. Louis, overwhelmingly believed the secretary lacked criminal intent.[176] Babcock recorded in his diary that President Hayes told him "he had observed the lying about" him and would stay on the federal payroll during the three presidencies that followed Grant's. He was nominated for a military promotion by Arthur before drowning while on duty in Florida in 1884.[177]

Shortly after Babcock's trial, Grant was hit with allegations that his secretary of war, William W. Belknap, had taken bribes in connection with an Indian post tradership. In 1870, Belknap's wife Carrie had approached a friend, Caleb P. Marsh,

171 *St. Louis Globe-Democrat*, 17 February 1876.

172 United States v. Babcock, case file 4180, National Archives at Kansas City, jury instructions, 11-15; *St. Louis Globe-Democrat*, 11 February, 18 February, 19 February, 22 February, 23 February, and 25 February 1876; *Whisky Frauds*, 90-91, 108-10.

173 Deposition, 12 February 1876, *PUSG*, 27:28-41, 43-45.

174 Calhoun, *Presidency*, 526; Chernow, *Grant*, 807.

175 *St. Louis Globe-Democrat*, 18 February 1876.

176 *Whisky Frauds*, 548; Summers, *Stealings*, 184; Nathaniel P. Banks to Annie Babcock, 1876 (undated), Orville E. Babcock Papers, Newberry Library.

177 Orville E. Babcock, Diary, vol. 2, 8 March 1877, Orville E. Babcock Papers, Newberry Library; Hoogenboom, *Outlawing*, 164; *Boston Globe*, 9 April 1884.

about arranging his appointment to the position at Fort Sill in the Indian Territory when it was about to open up. The post's incumbent, John S. Evans, wanted to keep the lucrative position, so he entered an agreement with Marsh in which he would remain in his position while he would pay Marsh $12,000 annually. Marsh in turn arranged with Carrie Belknap to pay her half that sum. Soon after this arrangement commenced, Carrie died, after which Belknap received payments directly. Three years after his wife's death, he would marry her sister Amanda. Both sisters were accustomed to a lavish lifestyle, which the money helped fund.[178]

A congressional committee had taken testimony from Marsh in secret and was planning to move quickly toward impeachment. On the morning of March 2, 1876, an emotional and incoherent Belknap tendered his resignation to Grant, who promptly accepted it. At the time, Bristow had spoken to the president in vague terms about troubling congressional findings, but he had not been informed about specifics.[179] Despite Belknap's resignation, the House voted to impeach him later that day.[180] A divided Senate decided that it could proceed against an officer who had already resigned, but its ultimate verdict on the charges against Belknap at his impeachment trial was an acquittal. Tellingly, the vast majority of senators who voted for acquittal explained their votes by their view that the Senate lacked jurisdiction over a former officer.[181]

The customary attack on Grant was that he adhered too long to supposedly corrupt subordinates. Yet when he quickly accepted the resignation of the cabinet member who actually presented a strong case for malfeasance, he was criticized for trying to save his subordinate from being held accountable for his actions in an impeachment trial. The general public approved of Grant's acceptance of Belknap's resignation.[182] But the attack would echo over the years, including in Allan Nevins's conclusion that it was a reason Grant himself was worthy of impeachment![183] Under the full weight of the rest of American history, the premise of this criticism is demonstrably false. In no other instance has a cabinet member or any other executive branch appointee been impeached. Allegations of misconduct by such officials before and after Belknap invariably were resolved with resignation or the

---

178   Scaturro, *President Grant*, 41; Calhoun, *Presidency*, 528-29. *Proceedings of the Senate Sitting for the Trial of William W. Belknap* (Washington, D.C.: Government Printing Office, 1876), 567-68, 742, hereafter cited as *Belknap Trial*.

179   Scaturro, *President Grant*, 41; Calhoun, *Presidency*, 528-29, 531.

180   *Belknap Trial*, 1.

181   Calhoun, *Presidency*, 532. See generally *Belknap Trial*.

182   Calhoun, *Presidency*, 531; Scaturro, *President Grant*, 42.

183   Nevins, 641.

expiration of the appointment without impeachment following. In no other case has history held a president delinquent for not keeping potentially impeachment-worthy subordinates in office in order to subject them to the impeachment process (even assuming a negative answer to the disputed question of whether a departed official can be impeached).

Grant notably directed Attorney General Pierrepont to proceed with a prosecution of Belknap. Ultimately, however, there was insufficient evidence to convict. Near the end of his term, Grant accepted the appraisal of the case by the district attorney in charge, who opined that "a long, expensive and laborious trial" would likely result in a hung jury, and ordered the case dismissed.[184] Belknap's impeachment proceedings had illustrated why there was reasonable doubt as to the war secretary's criminal intent. Marsh asserted that he made the arrangement with Evans without Belknap's knowledge and that he and the secretary never had an agreement to pay the latter in consideration for retaining Evans.[185] He added that when he made the financial arrangement with Carrie, she warned him in reference to her husband to "be careful to say nothing to him about presents, for a man once offered him $10,000 for a tradership of this kind, and he told him that if he did not leave the office he would kick him down stairs."[186] A preponderance of the evidence suggested at a minimum a willful blindness to the connection between the recurring payments and his official duties. But a criminal conviction required a higher level of proof.

The year 1876 found the Democratic House of Representatives in overdrive to effect maximum damage to the Republican Party as the presidential election approached. Some 33 House committees investigated every executive department, from the cabinet level on down, in search of corruption to expose. This herculean effort reaped paltry rewards, Belknap notwithstanding, and the ill-fated fishing expeditions discredited congressional investigators.[187] The Democratic majority of the Committee on Naval Affairs issued a report finding waste, favoritism, and political activity in the Navy Department, but they overplayed their hand, transparently inflating their conclusions well beyond the evidence and trying to establish by innuendo Secretary of the Navy George M. Robeson's misconduct.

184 Scaturro, *President Grant*, 41; Calhoun, *Presidency*, 533.

185 U.S. Congress, House, *Malfeasance of W. W. Belknap, Late Secretary of War*, 44th Cong., 1st Sess., 2 March 1876, H. Rep. 186, 8-9, hereafter cited as *Belknap Report*; *Belknap Trial*, 729, 779, 997.

186 *Belknap Report*, 3.

187 9 Cong. Rec. 2320, 2324-25 (1879) (statements of Sen. Windom); Summers, *Stealings*, 266; Calhoun, *Presidency*, 538-39.

Robeson had personally prospered, but the notion that he had displayed malfeasance or committed crimes was unfounded.[188]

Interestingly, at the height of the 1876 attacks by administration opponents, the Treasury Department released a comparative breakdown by presidential administration of defalcations (misappropriations) in office over the nation's history through the most recent numbers from mid-1875. Losses per $1,000 of the federal government's receipts and disbursements were less under the Grant administration than under any previous administration.[189] Obviously such figures are methodologically limited—they would not reflect metrics like tax evasion or bribery—but this rarely cited report is a reminder of the stark absence of quantitative analysis behind the Grant administration's reputation for corruption.

"I leave comparisons to history"

As an illustration of historians' inconsistency, compare their treatment of various cases of delinquency close to the top of the administrations of other presidents that are not primarily remembered for corruption or "scandal." While serving under George Washington, Secretary of the Treasury Alexander Hamilton chose as assistant secretary a notorious speculator who sought private gain from inside information and, after leaving office, triggered a financial panic fueled by money he owed the government.[190] Secretary of State Thomas Jefferson handed out what appeared to be a political sinecure, a part-time position as a translator in the State Department, to someone who proceeded to launch an anti-administration newspaper.[191] Secretary of State (and former Attorney General) Edmund Randolph, who succeeded Jefferson, resigned after casting the government he served into disrepute amid highly sensitive domestic and diplomatic challenges, though fellow cabinet members likely went too far accusing him of treasonously soliciting a bribe from the French government to instigate civil strife.[192]

---

188 Summers, *Stealings*, 128-29, 265-66; Scaturro, *President Grant*, 35; U.S. Congress, House, *Investigations of the Navy Department*, 44th Cong., 1st Sess., 25 July 1876, H. Rep. 784, 172-98.

189 "Credit of the Nation in 1860 and 1876; The Democratic Platform and Tilden's Letter Answered; By an Official Letter from the Treasury Department" (n.p. 1876), 4; 4 Cong. Rec. 5414, app. 282 (1876).

190 Ron Chernow, *Alexander Hamilton* (New York: Penguin Books, 2004), 292-94, 360, 381-88; Banner, 9.

191 Editorial Note, "Jefferson, Freneau, and the Founding of the *National Gazette*," in Julian P. Boyd et al., eds., *The Papers of Thomas Jefferson*, 45 vols. to date (Princeton, NJ: Princeton University Press, 1950–2021), 20:718-53; Banner, 5-6; Chervinsky, 185-87, 223-25.

192 Stanley Elkins and Eric McKitrick, *The Age of Federalism* (New York: Oxford University Press, 1993), 425-26, 838; Chervinsky, 287-301; Stewart, 380-83, 523-24; Tagg, 251; Irving Brant, "Edmund Randolph, Not Guilty!," *William and Mary Quarterly* (April 1950), No. 2, 7:180, 182-88, 195-97.

The opening paragraphs of this essay are not the summation historians have made of Washington, in part because it would not occur to them to catalog every lapse in judgment by an administration official as that presidency's defining trait. This is so regardless of the similarities between not only the temperaments of Washington and Grant, but also what might be called the humble and apologetic parts of Washington's Farewell Address and Grant's Eighth Annual Message. Both understated their respective pre-presidential experience: Washington noted "the inferiority of my qualifications" and "experience" upon taking office, and Grant noted his lack of "any previous political training."[193] Washington admitted his "fallible judgment" and "probable . . . many errors" while adding his "good intentions" and unawareness of "intentional error."[194] Grant admitted that "[m]istakes have been made," and he added, "Failures have been errors of judgment, not of intent."[195] Washington's Farewell Address is perhaps the best remembered of his state papers, but the above passages are largely forgotten; meanwhile, Grant's last annual message has largely been forgotten except for his passages of apology.

The latter message was issued in December 1876, months after the corruption issue came to a head in the executive branch with the Babcock trial and Belknap impeachment. An honest president who set high expectations was deeply troubled by the lapses behind those and other episodes of recent memory. That regret did not depend on proof of malfeasance or moral turpitude. Less culpable mistakes that were "errors of judgment" were enough. Grant described his mistakes as occurring "oftener in the selections made of the assistants appointed to aid in carrying out the various duties of administering the Government . . . . It is impossible, where so many trusts are to be allotted, that the right parties should be chosen in every instance."[196] What Grant said next reads like an invitation to historians: "History shows that no Administration from the time of Washington to the present has been free from these mistakes. But I leave comparisons to history . . . ."[197]

Historians, however, have not been particularly interested in making such comparisons. They have not found the misdeeds of subordinates, whether real or hyped, to be a fundamental component in the assessment of presidents unless they are named Grant or Harding—not coincidentally, two chief executives historians

---

193   Richardson, 1:205, 10:4353.

194   Ibid., 1:205, 216.

195   Ibid., 10:4353-54.

196   Ibid.

197   Ibid., 10:4354.

long considered politically unsympathetic.[198] Just consider the observation of James M. Banner, who edited the 2019 updated version of a rare survey of presidential misconduct originally compiled by C. Vann Woodward during the Nixon impeachment inquiry in 1974: "To write the history of presidencies through misconduct is completely to misconstrue the nature of presidencies. Let's take Harry Truman's presidency as an example. Truman's presidency was one of the most corrupt in the twentieth century." Indeed, influence-peddling marred a host of offices in the executive branch under Truman, including a major tax fraud conspiracy involving the bribery of government officials, ultimately leading to high-profile criminal convictions. But the story for Banner—and other historians—consisted of policy issues, such as the use of the atomic bomb, the Berlin airlift, the Truman Doctrine, the Marshall Plan, and the establishment of NATO. He concluded that "if you try to write the history of the Truman administration on the grounds of the misconduct of the White House then, you're not really writing the history of the Truman administration."[199]

When the Watergate scandal brought down Richard Nixon in 1974, historians had an exemplar of actual malfeasance by a president, from his cover-up of the Watergate break-in, which included discussions about paying hush money to the burglars, to the broader abuse of power to sabotage political enemies.[200] That was corruption at an order of magnitude greater than those prior presidencies. Yet the Murray-Blessing poll of Ph.D.-holding members of college history departments in 1982 placed Nixon above both Grant and Harding, which suggests a widespread, institutionalized misunderstanding of historical facts, an inability to differentiate levels of culpability, or both.[201]

At one point, a strong ideological skew among historians against Ronald Reagan almost did him in. Of interest was bribery and related crimes in the Pentagon and the Department of Housing and Urban Development, negligence and other lapses by a number of subordinates, and most conspicuously, the covert illegal scheme orchestrated by the White House–based National Security Council

198   Ryan S. Walters, *The Jazz Age President: Defending Warren G. Harding* (Washington, D.C.: Regnery History, 2022), xix-xxi.

199   "Q&A: James Banner," C-SPAN, accessed August 31, 2022, https://www.c-span.org/video/?463504-1/qa-james-banner; Banner, 303-20; Jules Abels, *The Truman Scandals* (Chicago: Henry Regnery Company, 1956), 3-5, 311-15; Thomas A. Bailey, *Presidential Saints and Sinners* (New York: The Free Press, 1981), 225-31; Andrew J. Dunar, *The Truman Scandals and the Politics of Morality* (Columbia, MO: University of Missouri Press, 1984), 37-39, 58-77, 82, 88, 91-94, 96-120, 150-52; Jeffrey Frank, *The Trials of Harry S. Truman: The Extraordinary Presidency of an Ordinary Man, 1945–1953* (New York: Simon & Schuster, 2022), 316-24.

200   Banner, 375-84; Bailey, *Saints*, 263-67.

201   Murray & Blessing, 11, 14, 16.

and the Central Intelligence Agency to sell arms to the terrorist-supporting Iranian government and divert proceeds from the arms sales to the anti-Communist Contras in Nicaragua.[202] Amid the disclosure of the Iran-Contra affair, *American Heritage* magazine ran an article by Irwin F. Fredman that put Reagan in the same category as Grant, Harding, and Nixon, complete with a cartoon showing the four presidents falling into a hellish fiery pit.[203] Yet at that time, none other than C. Vann Woodward expressed a change of heart about Grant when asked to compare the incumbent administration with its predecessors. He wrote in a letter to another historian that "the old bench-marks of perfidy failed me totally. U.S. Grant? Boss Tweed? Black Friday? Credit Mobilier? Seward's Icebox? Grant's Santo Domingo? The Compromise of 1877? Rockefeller's trusts? Peanuts. Chickenfeed. Childsplay." He continued that "our prevailing picture of 'The Gilded Age' is preposterous, a howling anachronism. Revision, replacement, vindication, updating, call it what you will, but it is the most pressing duty facing American historians."[204] After other historians and commentators fought back with correctives on Reagan's foreign and domestic policy significance, he would later attain consistent marks in the C-SPAN poll's top ten.[205] But Woodward's latter-day epiphany regarding the "howling anachronism" of Grant's reputation was astute.

For an even starker illustration of historians' inconsistency, consider how readily they discount corrupt activity when it occurs with the participation of *the presidents themselves*, with the exception of Nixon.[206] While the arbitrary and abusive deployment of government agencies against political adversaries or others who evoke political suspicions is remembered as a consummately Nixonian brand of corruption, Franklin Roosevelt, John Kennedy, and Lyndon Johnson sanctioned such activity. This was often done through the Internal Revenue Service and under Kennedy and Johnson increasingly involved the

202 Banner, 406-12, 414-18, 421.

203 Irwin F. Fredman, "The Presidential Follies," *American Heritage* (September/October 1987), No. 6, 38:38-43.

204 Michael O'Brien, *The Letters of C. Vann Woodward* (New Haven, CT: Yale University Press, 2013), 365.

205 Alvin S. Felzenberg, "'There You Go Again': Liberal Historians and The *New York Times* Deny Ronald Reagan His Due," *Policy Review* (March/April 1997), No. 82, 51-53; Presidential Historians Survey 2021, Total Scores/Overall Rankings, C-SPAN.

206 For purposes of present discussion, twenty-first century presidents are not considered since they are too recent to have well established historical reputations.

FBI and the CIA.[207] Grant never engaged in any such misconduct. While his administration was not immune from the sort of abuse that may be endemic to law enforcement agencies that operate covertly, when such misconduct occurred in the secret service, it did not come close to the president and was followed by an atypically reformative development in the history of the executive branch—a housecleaning and restructuring.[208]

Perhaps even more telling is historians' treatment of Bill Clinton. He acted with moral turpitude, broke the law, and lied to the public in his efforts to conceal sexual misconduct with White House intern Monica Lewinsky in connection with a federal lawsuit. Whether or not his acquittal at his ensuing impeachment trial was correct, the episode reflected a level of corruption—at the presidential level—that was entirely absent from the Grant administration. Banner's volume on presidential misconduct was largely dismissive of that and other investigations of the Clinton White House it deemed partisan. It failed even to mention five cabinet members who faced independent counsel investigations and a sixth who did not face such an investigation but was asked to resign.[209] Incongruous as these omissions may seem to the many students of the Grant presidency who were told that supposedly unworthy subordinates were its main story, that selective emphasis broadly reflects how historians have approached most presidents. In the C-SPAN polls conducted since he left the White House, Clinton has been ranked steadily in the upper half of presidents and consistently above Grant, suggesting that the corruption issue has not taken any comparable toll on his reputation.[210]

The methodology behind the traditional twentieth-century assessment of the Grant presidency was a panoply of double standards: Treat the president's own integrity as a non-issue. Highlight any corruption, no matter how extravagantly defined, that can build a lurid narrative. Disregard how removed from presidential decision making, or from the executive branch altogether, actual misconduct is. Ignore whether it predated the administration or whether the administration itself

---

207 Burton W. Folsom, Jr., *New Deal or Raw Deal? How FDR's Economic Legacy Has Damaged America* (New York: Threshold Editions, 2008), 146-53, 159-64; Banner, 285-87, 376; Victor Lasky, *It Didn't Start with Watergate* (New York: Dell Publishing Co., 1977), 19-20, 42-54, 66-72, 81-93, 123-30, 145-49, 154-62, 168, 175-89, 192-95, 211-40; Lee Edwards, *Goldwater: The Man Who Made a Revolution* (Washington, D.C.: Regnery Publishing, 1995), 305-11; Robert Dallek, *Flawed Giant: Lyndon Johnson and His Times, 1961–1973* (New York: Oxford University Press, 1998), 161-64, 407-08, 576, 618-19; Bailey, *Saints*, 211, 270.

208 Charles Lane, *Freedom's Detective: The Secret Service, the Ku Klux Klan and the Man Who Masterminded America's First War on Terror* (Toronto: Hanover Square Press, 2019), 239, 242-43, 245-47.

209 Banner, 431-47; Shirley Anne Warshaw, *The Clinton Years* (New York: Facts on File, 2004), xiv, 19, 25-26, 50-52, 73-74, 115-16, 160, 197, 246-47, 254, 278.

210 Presidential Historians Survey 2021, Total Scores/Overall Rankings, C-SPAN.

rooted it out. Guilt by association is fair game. Treat innuendo like established fact. Downgrade errors in judgment to malfeasance. When Grant's subordinates went after corruption or pursued other reformative measures with his knowledge and support, detach credit from the president. When a subordinate misstepped, assign the president blame even though the conduct occurred out of presidential sight and was divorced from presidential directives. In short, layer hostile inference upon hostile inference to reach the most hostile conclusion. That is how the most reformative administration at least since that of John Quincy Adams, if not from the founding of the republic, could be reduced to C. Vann Woodward's 1957 caricature of "subordinates plaster[ing] his Administration" with "disgrace" and a cabinet of mostly "nonentities and crooks" in which "[c]orruption spread like an epidemic."[211]

The crooked edifice of past literature on the Grant presidency has begun to crumble under the weight of the recent generation of scholarship, but plenty of distortions persist. No longer can a summary of the Grant administration be presented that omits Reconstruction—or that disparages it in the style of the Dunning School. But the same summary could be expected to omit with impunity the *Alabama* claims, the *Virginius* affair, and gold resumption while it could not omit some form of the corruption narrative without seeming incomplete. To offer one last metric from C-SPAN's surveys of historians, Grant's rank in the category of "administrative skills" has lingered among the bottom ten in all four surveys conducted between 2000 and 2021.[212] Although the ethical compasses of presidents of the last century make Grant look better, not worse, the corruption narrative seems to remain embedded in historical memory. Are historians as motivated to take a fresh look at it as they are at Reconstruction? The operative dynamic might be the adage Charles Calhoun cited at the end of his study—"that stereotypes are true until proved otherwise—and then they are still true."[213]

* * *

Why should this historical corrective matter? To appreciate the American experiment in government requires civic education that identifies its pillars, whether those pillars are part of the Constitution's framework or milestones that advance freedom, equality, peace, prosperity, or human dignity generally. The recognition of particular figures as great, however imperfect the best of them were, reflects a society's

211 Woodward, "Lowest Ebb," 56, 107.

212 Presidential Historians Survey 2021, Administrative Skills, C-SPAN, accessed 31 August 2022, https://www.c-span.org/presidentsurvey2021/?category=6.

213 Calhoun, *Presidency*, 593.

judgment of its values. What does it mean to deny presidential distinction to Grant? The answer has already played out: His twentieth-century contempt-laden reputation was an embodiment of the nation's blind spots and historians' own prejudices. The legacy of slavery and Jim Crow is hotly debated nowadays, with questions often posed as to whether or how the racial caste system of the past manifests itself today. Whatever the scope of the answer, one of the most obvious enduring legacies of the Jim Crow era is its distortion of the racial equality–embracing chapter of history that that period effectively overthrew, Reconstruction. The Dunning School, like the broader Lost Cause mythology, has been rejected, but not many aspects of skewed analysis during its period of dominance that come from looking at a subject through a hostile lens.

There may remain a visceral resistance in the spirit of Justice Frankfurter to celebrating Grant's presidency for its humanitarianism—indeed, for being a high-water mark for human rights—or for bringing about a constitutional milestone. Recent studies have paved the way to change that. Biographers have become more conscious of the class-based prejudice of the elites of Grant's era that lingered in many works of history. Historians should also revise their assessments of presidents on the subject of war and peace. While they have long been apt to elevate several presidents who have gone to war for the transformative impact of their conflicts, if they fail to do the same for presidents who achieve significant benchmarks in peace—as Grant certainly did—they will miss a critical aspect of statesmanship. Not to mention providing the worst incentives to future presidents who seek history's ultimate approval. Historians should also be less dismissive of those who attained nineteenth-century economic policy goals.

Sometimes fame, with the perspective of history, does not age well. Not so in Grant's case; if any American leader deserved the accolades he received during his time, he did. Yet for all of the adulation he received during the late nineteenth century, he ultimately would be unjustly denied a place in the presidential pantheon. This should be even clearer now, one hundred fifty years after he occupied the White House, than it was to a number of generations who lived after his time. Grant's bicentennial is an occasion to break through the last vestiges of historical vilification and finally acknowledge that he belongs in America's pantheon of great presidents.

A Compensating Generosity
Chapter Twelve | *Ben Kemp*

"We must accept finite disappointment, but never lose infinite hope."
— *Martin Luther King, Jr.*[1]

Two famous historical figures toured the final home of Ulysses S. Grant, known today as Grant Cottage, in the years following his death, and each came away with a different impression. In the summer of 1889, famed women's rights advocate Susan B. Anthony stayed at the Hotel Balmoral adjacent to the Cottage on Mt. McGregor in the foothills of the Adirondack Mountains of New York. Anthony walked through the carefully preserved rooms of the Cottage that, a few years before, had housed the man she once met as president. She had a decidedly negative reaction to what she encountered, writing in her diary: "Here we saw the room where General Grant died, the invalid chair, the clothes he wore, medicine bottles, etc.—very repulsive. If the grand mementoes of his life's work were on exhibition it would be inspiring, but these ghastly reminders of his disease and death are too horrible."[2] Two years later, in 1891, a 58th birthday celebration would be held at the Balmoral for President Benjamin Harrison. After touring the Cottage, the Civil War veteran was inspired, stating:

> We are gathered here in a spot which is historic. This mountain has been fixed in the affectionate and reverent memory of all our people . . . . It has been said that a great life went out here; but great lives, like that of General Grant, do not go out. They go on. . . . [W]e will ever keep in mind his great services, and in doing so will perpetuate his great citizenship and the glory of the Nation he fought to save.[3]

---

1   Martin Luther King, Jr., *Strength to Love* (New York: Harper & Row, 1963), 83.

2   Ida Husted Harper, *The Life and Work of Susan B. Anthony*, 2 vols. (Indianapolis: The Bowen-Merrill Co., 1898), 2:653.

3   Charles Hedges, *Speeches of Benjamin Harrison* (New York: United States Book Company, 1892), 510-11.

Perhaps what makes Grant Cottage special is that both struggle and inspiration are so present and intermingled. It's a place where General Grant came to terms with the worst and best of the human experience, and it continues to provide that opportunity to all who visit.

Despite episodes of hardship and struggle during Grant's life, by the 1880s the Grant family was prosperous due in some part to the opportunities afforded to them by Grant's enduring status as an American hero. But these gains would prove susceptible to the negative aspects of human nature. Grant was extravagantly generous to and trusting of those around him. Philadelphia publisher George Childs saw a reflection of his own generous nature in his friend Grant, who "was very kind to the poor, and, in fact, to everybody, especially to widows and children of army officers."[4] Unfortunately, Grant's generosity and trusting nature would be taken advantage of numerous times during his life. The general's friends recognized his overly trusting nature and attempted to shield him from being exploited but, in the end, were unable to prevent disaster. In the spring of 1884, Ferdinand Ward, a young business partner Grant had entrusted with his financial future, betrayed him and his family. As the financial collapse unfolded, Grant admitted that "I have made it the rule of my life to trust a man long after other people gave him up. But I don't see how I can ever trust any human being again."[5] Grant's faith in humanity had been shaken to the core.

Walking with a cane, suffering the physical effects of a hip and thigh injury from the previous winter, Grant attempted to pick up the pieces of his life. As he embarked on a writing career to provide for his family, another crushing blow came that autumn in the form of a diagnosis of throat cancer. Once it became known that Grant would be writing his memoirs to provide for his family, a generous friend rose to the occasion. Author and speaker Samuel Clemens—best known to us and his own readers as Mark Twain—wanted desperately to make Grant's book a success. Clemens not only provided an impressively generous publishing contract but also became a source of encouragement to the modest author.

Grant's final battle had begun, and the struggle continued through the winter. In the spring, to avoid the oppressive summer heat of New York City, Grant and his family escaped to the cottage atop the picturesque, 1,000-foot summit of Mt. McGregor.

As Susan B. Anthony had recognized on her 1889 visit, the objects within Grant Cottage recall a tragic physical struggle, but those same objects also hold the

4   George Childs, *Recollections of General Grant* (Philadelphia; Collins Printing House, 1890), 35.

5   Charles Bracelen Flood, *Grant's Final Victory: Ulysses S. Grant's Heroic Last Year* (Cambridge, MA: Da Capo Press, 2011), 20.

Grant, seated in a wicker chair on the corner of the cottage porch, spent his mornings reading and writing. Two of his physicians, Doctors Douglas and Shrady, confer off to the side.

Grant Cottage

uplifting story of human compassion. Entering the first-floor room used as an office and editing room immediately calls attention not only to the valiant effort put forth by Grant to write his memoirs but also to the crucial assistance he received. The glass oil lamps on the editing table evoke the late nights Grant's eldest son, Frederick, and Grant's stenographer, Noble Dawson, spent as they pored over charts and books in their editing endeavor. As the clock ticked past ten o'clock in the evening, the newly installed electric lights would flicker off as the generator was shut down, and the team was forced to "burn the midnight oil" to carry on. Dawson, a Civil War veteran, was proud to serve the general in his final battle and admired the author's genuine concern for others. "Personally, the General was the most delightful and generous man I ever knew," he said. "He was always cautious in writing or talking, so as not to injure the feelings of anyone, and I remember many touching incidents of how he cut out sentences which he thought might hurt someone."[6]

Grant's bedroom—or the "sick room," as it was termed by the ever-present reporters—holds numerous reminders of his struggle. The oversized glass bottle of cocaine solution resting atop a cabinet and the Vaseline inhaler within represent a desperately ill patient but also those who tirelessly cared for him. Throat specialist Dr. John Douglas had met his future patient during the Civil War while helping coordinate the humanitarian activities of the Sanitary Commission. Grant's other physician, Dr. George Shrady, also witnessed the horrors of the war, serving at hospitals in Washington, D.C., and the war front. At a reunion of soldier's aid organizations in 1884, an emotional Grant recalled the "many things done by these agencies of mercy . . . . of service rendered, of consolations administered by the side of deathbeds; of patient, unwavering attentions to the sick; of letters written to the

6   Noble Dawson, "Grant's Last Stand," Ulysses S. Grant Homepage, accessed 6 July 2022, https://www.granthomepage.com/grantlaststand.htm.

mourning parents of noble sons."[7] The physicians and their patient shared a deep knowledge and appreciation of true suffering as well as true compassion. Grant grew attached to them in his final months, their kindness, dedication, and humor shining like a beacon through the darkness of his struggle.

The writing pads and pencil framed on the wall in the sick room of the Cottage evoke some of the most poignant moments of the general's time there. With the nearly complete loss of his voice to cancer, Grant was forced to pencil his thoughts on slips of paper. Many of these notes were saved by the recipients and recorded; some remain at the Cottage, and they provide an intimate window into the mind of the dying man. On a warm July day two weeks before his death, Grant had the opportunity to meet a generous benefactor. Charles Wood, a businessman from Troy, New York, had come to the rescue the year before when Grant was broke, sending him loans totaling $1,500 despite the fact that the two men had never met. Wood, who lost one of his two younger brothers to the Civil War, had enclosed with the first loan a note that read, "General, I owe you this for Appomattox."[8] When Wood visited Mt. McGregor, the general was in the sick room resting in the two leather easy chairs that constituted his makeshift bed—pillows behind him in one chair and his legs resting on the opposing chair. When Wood entered, an exhausted Grant handed him a slip of paper that rather poetically expressed what Wood's thoughtful act had truly represented to him: "I feel very thankful to you for the kindness you did me last summer. I am glad to say that while there is much unblushing wickedness in this world yet there is a compensating generosity and grandeur of soul. In my case I have not found that Republics are ungrateful nor are the people."[9] Wood later framed the treasured notes he received, stating that they "show, as do all the other records of the dead hero, that he was a simple, unaffected man, entirely free from overvaluation of his own work and touched by the kindly sympathy of others."[10]

One can imagine what Grant may have felt sitting in his wicker chair on the wide breezy porch of the Cottage in the summer of 1885, watching a passing stream of visitors who were filled with genuine compassion for the man who had contributed so much to their lives. It was Grant's supreme modesty that never

7   USG at the fifth annual reunion of the Christian Commission, Sanitary Commission, and Union and C.S.A. army chaplains, 2 August 1884, John Y. Simon, ed., *The Papers of Ulysses S. Grant*, 32 vols. (Carbondale, IL: Southern Illinois University Press, 1967–2012), 31:183*n*-84*n*, hereafter cited as *PUSG*.

8   Warren F. Broderick, "The President's Benefactor," in *The Best of New York Archives: Selections from the Magazine, 2001–2011* (Albany, NY: State University of New York Press, 2017), 196-98; Julia Dent Grant, *The Personal Memoirs of Julia Dent Grant*, John Y. Simon, ed. (New York: G.P. Putnam's Sons, 1975), 328.

9   *PUSG*, 31:419.

10   Broderick, 198.

allowed him to fully accept the adoration of the public, but the bitter trial seemed to change that. It was the veritable flood of generosity and sympathy, what President Lincoln so eloquently referred to as the "better angels of our nature," that helped offset the burden of Grant's struggles. Grant embraced it all wholeheartedly:

> I am thankful . . . . to see for myself the happy harmony which has so suddenly sprung up between those engaged but a few short years in deadly conflict. It has been an inestimable blessing to me to hear the kind expression towards me in person from all parts of our country; from people of all nationalities, of all religions, and of no religion; of Confederate and National troops alike; of soldiers' organizations . . . and all other soci[e]ties, embracing almost every citizen in the land. They have brought joy to my heart if they have not effected a cure.[11]

The sympathy and support arising from his former foes was especially moving for the general, a silver lining for one who had always desired unity. One heartfelt letter that particularly pleased Grant was sent to Mt. McGregor from a Confederate veteran who said he had laid down his arms at Appomattox as a boy: "I have been proud to see the nation do you honor—And now, dear Genl in this the hour of your tribulation I weep that so brave, so magnanimous a soul must suffer as you do …. [B]e assured that I am not the only ex-confederate who sends his prayers …."[12]

Shortly before his death, Grant met with Confederate veteran Simon Bolivar Buckner at the Cottage. Grant and Buckner had been classmates at West Point, and their paths had crossed at pivotal moments of their lives. Their relationship illustrated the transcendent bonds of a compassionate friendship. Grant was rapidly growing weaker but was still eager to see his old friend. The meeting was so poignant, so illustrative of his hope in harmony, that Grant would insist the notes he gave to his friend be published. One note read:

> I have witnessed since my sickness just what I have wished to see ever since the war; harmony and good feeling between the sections. I have always contended that if there had been no body left but the soldiers we would have had peace in a year. Jubel [sic] Early and [Daniel Harvey] Hill are the only two that I know of who do not seem to be satisfied on the southern side. . . . We may now well look forward to a perpetual peace at home, and a national strength . . . .[13]

11   Horace Green, *General Grant's Last Stand* (New York: Charles Scribner's Sons, 1936), 322-23.

12   A.M. Arnold to USG, 30 June 1885, *PUSG*, 31:376.

13   USG to Simon B. Buckner, 10 July 1885, ibid., 31:423-24.

Old friends who had found themselves on opposite sides of the war, Simon Bolivar Buckner and U.S. Grant met for one final reunion just weeks before Grant's death.

Puck

Grant had singled out former Confederates Early and Hill for their unwillingness to accept the results of the war and for perpetuating sectional division. Grant had proven he was willing to work with any former Confederate who was willing to accept the results of the war and help the nation move forward. As his end approached, the importance of unity came into focus, and he expressed his wish to reconcile with all, if possible, stating, "I desire the goodwill of all, whether hitherto friends or not."[14]

A small metal letterbox hangs on the east wall of the parlor of the Cottage, hidden in the shadows, representing the messages of sympathy the dying soldier and statesman received daily. Grant related to a reporter the incredible volume of correspondence he was receiving: "The public only know of but a fraction of the expressions of sympathy which I have received. . . . I receive a hundred letters in a mail and several mails a day." Incredibly touching letters came in from children with uplifting messages such as

"[W]e know what you did for us, before we were born. . . . [W]e all love you, and pray for you, with all our hearts and souls;" and "We shall remember you when the big people now living are dead. We hope your example will lead us to lead nobler lives than we would have done if we had never heard of you."[15] When told of the many souls praying for him, Grant responded, "I feel very grateful to . . . . all the good people of the Nation . . . united in wishing or praying for my improvement. I am a great sufferer all the time, but the facts I have related are a compensation for most of it."[16]

As Grant's book project neared completion, Twain came to visit his friend once more. It's easy to imagine the famous man of American letters seated comfortably on the chaise lounge in the parlor, discussing the book project with his client on a cool summer evening. Twain's efforts had been fruitful largely due to the

14　Green, 299.

15　Flood, 165-66.

16　Ibid., 207.

tremendous sympathy of the American public. An army of book agents—many of them fellow veterans helping their former commander in his time of need—were selling the general's upcoming memoir door-to-door by subscription. The early sales were impressive, and Twain was able to reassure Grant his book would be a resounding success.

A small bell in the cabinet of the sick room conjures for today's visitors worthwhile stories of figures largely overlooked because prejudice relegated them to the periphery of history books. Grant had used the small bell to ring for his two compassionate caregivers who occupied the room adjacent to him. Harrison Terrell was an African American man who had risen from enslavement to become a personal valet to the ex-president. "Faithful Harrison," as the press referred to him, had truly developed a caring friendship with Grant that surpassed that of an employee, and he provided tireless care to the end. An enema, the rubber hardened and brittle with age, also rests in the sick room cabinet—an unpleasant reminder of the extent of Grant's suffering but also of the tender care he received from his nurse, Henry McQueeney, who administered it. Grant was probably endeared to McQueeney's Irish brogue, still as thick as when he had emigrated to the United States from the Emerald Isle with his wife and children less than a decade before. Like many immigrants, McQueeney took what employment was available, even if that meant being separated from family to provide for them. McQueeney held the final lonely bedside vigil over his unconscious patient throughout Grant's final night.

The wicker chairs with faded floral cushions surrounding the folding mahogany bed in the corner of the parlor speak of the intense love and support of the Grant family for their patriarch. They had been a bedrock of support sustaining him through the hardships of life and the inspiration for his last passionate act of selfless love. On the morning of July 23, 1885, Grant's beloved wife, Julia, and their children surrounded him as he passed away peacefully in full knowledge of their undying affection. Amid the stillness of sorrow immediately after death, Fred walked to the mantle above the fireplace in the parlor and stopped the clock. The brass hands on the French blue and gold ceramic timepiece still remain frozen at that moment as a testament to the loyalty and compassion of a son.

The heavily aged floral tributes arrayed in dried immortelles that occupy the dining room of the Cottage are haunting physical reminders of the condolences and somber memorial services that spread across the nation. One piece is a pillow adorned by a sword and four stars, sent by the veterans of the Grand Army of the Republic. Grant, always supportive of and supported by his fellow veterans, wrote in his final messages to the G.A.R. that they were "engraved on my heart and I love

The parlor at Grant Cottage looks today as it did when Grant died there, in that very bed, in 1885. His wicker chair from the porch sits in the far right corner of the room.

Grant Cottage

them as my children."[17] He thanked them "for their splendid services which have resulted in giving freedom to a race, peace to a continent, and a haven to the oppressed of the world."[18] From the veteran Sam Willett, who had volunteered to stand guard on the steps of the Cottage that summer, to the many veterans who encamped on the mountain to guard the casket, grounds, and funeral train, Grant was embraced as a beloved comrade worthy of their service.

As the cannons boomed salutes from the beautiful eastern outlook near the Cottage on the misty morning of August 4, 1885, one individual who stood out from the mass of Union veterans gathering for Grant's funeral was Thomas P. Ochiltree. A Confederate veteran from Texas, Ochiltree had come to Mt. McGregor to honor a man he had known personally and admired, a man with whom he had once shared the podium in support of national progress. He stood as a representative of the veterans of the South who had supported Grant's presidential agenda to help the nation progress into a better era of harmony.

On the day of Grant's funeral, August 8, while "Taps" was being played on the bugle and Grant's remains were being placed within his brick tomb in New York City's Riverside Park, Simon Buckner and fellow Confederate general Joseph E. Johnston stood among the honorary pallbearers in a final symbolic act of respect and unity.

On the wall just across from the deathbed in the parlor of the Cottage are photographs of Joseph Drexel and his wife, Lucy. The Drexel family were good friends of the Grants and responsible for providing the Cottage for the Grant family's use. Drexel's generous decision to dedicate the home and all its contents as a memorial to the national hero began an incredible legacy of preservation that has endured for more than a century.

17　H.W. Brands, *The Man Who Saved the Union: Ulysses Grant in War and Peace* (New York: Doubleday, 2012), 630.

18　Frederick Dent Grant to John S. Kountz, *PUSG*, 31:364*n*.

The clock on the fireplace mantel in the Cottage parlor remains stopped at the time of Grant's death: 8:08 a.m.

Grant Cottage

Generosity is a bedrock quality of humanity. It's what helped sustain Grant in his final days and will allow Grant Cottage to continue inspiring individuals into the future. The objects, settings, and stories there can bring people closer to the past, but also closer to one another. Visitors to the Cottage are exposed not just to a place of suffering, but more importantly to a place that can, as it did for Grant, renew one's faith in humanity.

Human suffering can bring out the best in humanity. Grant Cottage represents an indomitable will to carry on aided by the generosity and support of others. Friends, former foes, and the public came forward when Grant needed them the most in an enduring example of how important unity, compassion, and charity are to humanity. Ulysses S. Grant had reasons to become disillusioned with humanity, but in the end, he remained resolute in his belief in the potential for good in humankind. Knowing this capacity for good, he envisioned a world where conflict was settled in tribunals instead of the bloody battlefield—a world where standing armies and navies were no longer necessary and peace reigned.[19] Despite the crushing struggle that consumed his final days, he refused to surrender his optimism for the future, as he wrote in the final lines of his memoirs:

> I feel that we are on the eve of a new era, when there is to be great harmony between the Federal and Confederate. I cannot stay to be a living witness to the correctness of this prophecy; but I feel it within me that it is to be so. The universally kind feeling expressed for me at a time when it was supposed that each day would prove my last, seemed to me the beginning of the answer to "Let us have peace."[20]

19   Speech, Philadelphia, 26 December 1879, ibid., 29:340; Second Inaugural Address, 4 March 1873, ibid., 24:62.

20   Ulysses S. Grant, *Personal Memoirs of U.S. Grant*, 2 vols. (New York: Charles L. Webster & Co. 1885–1886), 2:553.

Familiar Strangers, Unknown Kin: Sharing the Shadow of the General

Chapter Thirteen | *Ulysses Grant Dietz*

The descendants of Ulysses S. Grant have stood in his shadow ever since his quietly heroic death at Mount McGregor, New York, on July 23, 1885. I use the word "shadow" both to represent the great legacy of that gentle man, and to suggest what a gift and a burden his greatness was for his children and their heirs. Ulysses S. Grant was a hard man to live up to; his unwavering love for his family simply magnified that reality.

Who am I to write about the family of Ulysses S. Grant? Well, Ulysses S. Grant and his beloved wife Julia had four children, thirteen grandchildren, nineteen great-grandchildren, and forty-one great-great-grandchildren. I am the youngest surviving of Ulysses and Julia's forty-one great-great-grandchildren, and the only member of that generation to bear the name Ulysses. For me, the General's shadow was his name, which crept up on me and altered the course of my life.[1]

I must begin by saying categorically that Ulysses S. Grant loved his mother and father and was loved by them in kind. Jesse Root Grant was, by all accounts, a difficult father, but the sum of all I've read makes it clear that father and son cared about each other greatly, despite the significant friction that existed between them over the years. Likewise, Hannah Simpson Grant cannot be dismissed as a quiet, prim Methodist housewife. She adored her son, and her adoration was returned. Jesse gave Ulysses strength and independence, while Hannah gave him depth and compassion. These good things he carried with him into his own greatness.

Somewhat to my surprise, I also feel no doubt that Ulysses S. Grant was genuinely fond of his in-laws. Frederick Fayette Dent, frontier slaveowner and faux colonel that he was, was as much of an irritant in Ulysses S. Grant's life as his own father; but Fred Dent loved his daughter Julia, and nobody who loved her could have been Ulysses S. Grant's enemy. On the other hand, Ulysses S. Grant seems

---

1   My source for this information was not the family itself, who often know little or nothing outside their immediate lineage, but from Hugh Montgomery-Massingberd, ed., *Burke's Presidential Families of the United States of America* (London: Burke's Peerage Limited, 1981), 307-23. This valuable book has not been updated since this publication date, and thus a large number of descendants beyond my own generation have not been included.

Hannah and Jesse Grant might have stepped out of *American Gothic*. Their story, indeed, could not have been more "America."

Grant Cottage

to have had a mutual admiration society going on with Ellen Wrenshall Dent, his future mother-in-law. It was she, after all, who predicted great things for Ulysses before anyone else did. Also, we have to remember that Fred Dent junior was Ulysses' roommate at West Point and would remain a friend through the Mexican-American War and beyond. The Dents and their love-filled household taught Ulysses what it was to be openly affectionate and emotionally accessible. This, in the end, made him the kind of father he became.[2]

Ulysses and Julia Grant, married in 1848 at the Dent family's town house in Saint Louis, had four children. The first child, Frederick Dent Grant, was born at White Haven, the Dent farm outside Saint Louis, in 1850. Their second child, Ulysses S. Grant, Jr., was born at Jesse and Hannah Grant's house in Bethel, Ohio, in 1852. He took on the lifelong nickname "Buck," short for "Buckeye," because Ohio was and is known as the Buckeye State.[3] Ulysses S. Grant was deployed in the West by the time his second son was born and wouldn't see him for two years. By the time Grant resigned from the army and made his way back to Saint Louis, Fred had all but forgotten who he was, and Buck didn't know him at all. Ulysses must have felt this deeply and would do his utmost to make sure it never happened again. Ellen Wrenshall, always known as Nellie, was born in 1855 at Wish-ton-wish, a romantic gothic villa on the White Haven property. Jesse Root Grant was born in 1858 at Hardscrabble, the hewn-log house that Ulysses S. Grant built himself near the acreage

---

2   Not only did Jesse Root Grant, the General's youngest child, write with great affection about his grandfather Dent, but Nick Sacco, park ranger at White Haven, the Ulysses S. Grant National Historic Site in Saint Louis, has also talked with me about the warm relations between the Dents and young Lieutenant Grant before Julia even entered the picture. For Jesse's memoir see Jesse R. Grant, *In the Days of My Father General Grant* (New York: Harper & Brothers, 1925). See also Nick's essay in this volume.

3   A buckeye is the seed of the horse chestnut tree, commonplace all over the eastern United States. Fred Grant, his older brother, wrote that the enslaved workers at White Haven gave Buck his nickname because he was born in the Buckeye State. Frederick D. Grant, "General Grant's Home Life," *The Independent*, 29 April 1897, 49:535.

Ulysses Grant Dietz has called Fred Dent "the ancestor I've sort of denied—you know, the enslaver . . . So I was moved by how much his grandchildren loved him—more than they loved their other grandfather, Jesse, for that matter."

Library of Congress

assigned to him by his father-in-law at White Haven.

Far too much has been made of the supposed penury from which Ulysses and Julia suffered during the inter-war years when he, like many thousands of Americans at the same moment in our national history, caught up in the financial panic of 1857, struggled to make a living as a farmer. What is truly important is the fact that these years, before secession and the war, were among the happiest of his life. Being with his family and working his land were a source of unending pleasure, in spite of economic setbacks. Jesse Grant had more ready money than Colonel Dent did, and while Jesse was tight-fisted, both fathers looked out for their children and grandchildren. Ulysses and Julia's eldest and youngest sons, Fred and Jesse, wrote about their childhoods and spoke only of their father's gentleness and domesticity. The Grant children never wanted for anything and had only the happiest of memories of the supposed "hard times" before their father became famous and his shadow began to grow. Fred's son, Ulysses S. Grant III, would take great pains to point out this truth in his biography of his grandfather, published in 1969— perhaps the first such book to try to correct the falsehoods and myths that had clouded histories of Ulysses S. Grant since his death.[4]

Anyone who has ever taken a freshman psychology or sociology course at college knows something about the significance of birth order. I can see a parallel to Ulysses and Julia's family in the family in which I grew up—four children, with one sister and three brothers. I find it slightly eerie that my childhood was an echo of Buck Grant's: I was the second son, named Ulysses, born on July 22, just like Buck. Buck Grant and I even attended the same prep school, Phillips Exeter Academy, in New

---

4   Ulysses S. Grant III, *Ulysses S. Grant: Warrior and Statesman* (New York: William Morrow & Company, Inc., 1969), 102-07. My grandfather dedicated the book to his daughters, noting that his wish to "set the record straight" was for them. Ibid., 9-10.

Hampshire. People write books about this kind of family dynamic for a reason. Jesse, the oft-indulged baby of the family, wrote in his memoirs that he and his siblings each secretly believed that they were the best-loved child, and only as adults compared notes and realized that they had *all* been their parents' favorites.[5] Just because these four children were all equally loved does not, however, mean they weren't affected differently by the increasingly long shadow cast by their father. No two children raised by the same parents experience exactly the same thing. It was true in my family, and it was surely true in theirs.

Fred—my great-grandfather—was the eldest child and all through his life took on the role of the Dutiful Son. Fred, of all of Ulysses S. Grant's children, was the one who remained most in the public eye throughout his life. He kept close ties with New York society and Washington politics through his friendships with both Theodore Roosevelt and Elihu Root, who would play important roles in his life. He followed his father to West Point and, like his father, he later resigned from the army—not to be a farmer, but to take up a diplomatic post as the United States Minister to Austria-Hungary. It's worth mentioning that his standing in his West Point class of 1871 (37th in a class of 41) was far lower than his father's, something of which Fred was rather ashamed.[6] Also like his father, he returned to military service later in his life and ended up a general, serving in the Spanish-American War and in the Philippines. He ended his career as commandant of Governor's Island in New York Harbor and—again like his father—died in his early sixties.

As the oldest son, Fred was trained to be independent and strong in the same way Jesse Root Grant had taught his oldest son self-reliance and determination. Shortly before his thirteenth birthday, Fred was shot in the leg during the Vicksburg Campaign, and thus, while not actually in the army, earned a bronze plaque next to his father's in the huge Illinois memorial at the Vicksburg Battlefield. Most importantly, Fred became his father's secretary during the critical months of writing the memoirs. All four children were present when their father died, but Fred was there all along. Although he didn't get his father's name, Fred seems to have consciously modeled himself on his father, especially later in life, when his resemblance to his father was much remarked on. Like all his siblings, Fred revered his father's memory. "He ruled by love and gentleness, and so gained the love of his

---

5   Jesse R. Grant, 12.

6   Typed copies of letters Fred wrote to his wife, Ida, remain in family archives. In them, Fred talks about coasting on his name and not doing as well as he should have at West Point. He exhorts his son to be better. Ulysses S. Grant III was, in fact, sixth in his class of 1903 at West Point. Douglas MacArthur was first in that same class.

On the porch at Grant Cottage (from left): Ulysses S. "Buck" Grant Jr. (1852–1929); Julia Boggs Dent Grant (1826–1902); Ellen Wrenshall "Nellie" Grant Sartoris Jones (1855–1922); Julia Dent Grant Cantacuzene (1876–1975), daughter of Frederick & Ida Grant; (Hiram) Ulysses S. Grant (1822–1885); Ida Marie Honoré Grant (1854–1930), wife of Frederick Dent Grant; Frederick Dent Grant (1850–1912); Ulysses S. Grant III (1881–1968), son of Frederick & Ida Grant; Nellie Grant Cronan (1881–1972), daughter of Jesse & Elizabeth Grant; Elizabeth Chapman Grant (1860–1945), wife of Jesse Root Grant II; Jesse Root Grant II (1858–1934)
Library of Congress

children that we were exceedingly careful to avoid doing things that would meet with his disapproval," he recalled.[7]

In 1874, Fred married Ida Marie Honoré, daughter of a Chicago real estate developer. Ida's older sister Bertha was already married to Potter Palmer, a real estate magnate twenty-three years her senior. Ida was a striking beauty and would give Fred two children: Julia Dent Grant, born in the White House in 1876, and Ulysses S. Grant III (my grandfather), born in 1881 at the Potter Palmers' farm near Chicago.

If I had to characterize Ulysses S. Grant's second-born, Buck, in some way, I'd call him the bon vivant. He was handsome and outgoing but, according to his older brother, sensitive and easily upset. Accordingly, Ulysses S. Grant kept his namesake child away from the war. Buck followed the path of the upwardly mobile Gilded Age scion, moving from prep school to Harvard, and then to a law degree from

---

7   Frederick D. Grant, 49:535.

Columbia University. Buck practiced law and became a businessman, marrying Fannie Josephine Chaffee in 1880. Fannie was the daughter of Senator Jerome Chaffee, one of the first two senators from the newly formed state of Colorado (signed into statehood by Ulysses S. Grant, as it happens), and one of the founders of the city of Denver.

Buck was also the one who convinced his father to lend the Grant name to a new investment firm proposed by a charming young man named Ferdinand Ward. While Grant & Ward seemed to make the whole family rich for a time, its humiliating and very public collapse in 1884 bankrupted everyone and triggered the chain of events that would result in Ulysses S. Grant's desperate rush to complete a two-volume memoir while dying of throat cancer.

Fannie and Buck had a large estate in North Salem, New York, known as Merryweather Farm. This would be the center of their family life until 1893. Ulysses S. Grant would know only three of Buck and Fannie's children: Miriam, born in 1881; Chaffee, born in 1883; and Julia, born in 1885. Fannie was born in 1889, and Ulysses S. Grant IV in 1893. Fred and Ida would visit Buck and his family at Merryweather Farm before Fred took his family to Vienna for four years starting in 1889. Buck moved his family to San Diego in 1893, where he became a businessman and real estate developer, eventually building the U.S. Grant Hotel in 1910, still a landmark in the city today. Fannie, who was in fragile health for a long time, died in 1909. Four years later, Buck married a much younger widowed divorcee named America Workman Will, much to the consternation of his family. My mother recalled, as a little girl, while her parents were living in San Francisco in the early 1920s, meeting "Uncle Buck" and "Aunt America."

Nellie was undoubtedly Daddy's Princess, although I in no way mean to suggest that she was any more loved than her brothers were. It is the lot of the only girl in a family—if she's lucky—to be the apple of her father's eye. Nellie was, by all accounts, pretty and social like her mother; but she was also quiet and thoughtful like her father and her big brother Fred.

Because she was just thirteen when her parents entered the White House for eight years, Nellie really came of age at the center of national attention—and of course got to enjoy a family life more luxurious than any Grant or Dent had ever known. Her mother, as had every first lady before her, did some redecorating during President Grant's first term, and added a now-lost billiard room off the State Dining Room—a room that became the de facto Grant family room. However, it was in Ulysses S. Grant's second term that Julia got a substantial appropriation from Congress and transformed the cavernous, outdated East Room of the President's

House into a Gilded Age ballroom worthy of her fanciest new friends.[8] Julia may have imagined her beautiful teenaged daughter making her society debut in this glittering space, but she did not foresee having her wedding there. Indeed, Julia sent Nellie to England with Philadelphia friends to keep her away from inappropriate suitors in Washington, only to have her fall for Algernon Sartoris, the charming son of a renowned English opera singer, Adelaide Kemble Sartoris.[9] The 1874 White House wedding of a presidential child was splendid indeed, although President Grant, the hero who had never flinched at the specter of death, wept openly as he lost his only daughter forever.

Sartoris was also the nephew of celebrated actress Fanny Kemble and great-nephew of Sarah Siddons, the best-known English tragedienne of the Georgian era. Algernon's family were not aristocrats, but were rich, brilliant, and worldly, proud of their high-toned intellectual conversation. It's not hard to imagine that Nellie could have found herself at sea amidst the sparkling repartee of the Sartoris clan. Once Algernon, who turned out to be a heavy drinker and a philanderer, absconded back to the United States and left her with his family, she was fairly trapped, but also kindly treated. American author Henry James wrote of Nellie:

> [P]oor little Nellie Grant sits speechless on the sofa, understanding neither head nor tail of such high discourse and exciting one's compassion for her incongruous lot in life. She is as sweet and amiable (and almost as pretty) as she is uncultivated.

James was a notorious snob, and in the same way many self-important people had misunderstood her father's taciturnity as stupidity, he interpreted Nellie's silence as a lack of intelligence and culture. She didn't deserve it, and when Algernon died in 1893, followed soon after by his father, Nellie returned home and lived with her mother in Washington, D.C., for the rest of Julia's life.[10]

Despite the unhappy outcome of her marriage, Nellie did have four children, including Ulysses and Julia's first two grandsons. Sadly, the first baby, Grant Greville Edward Sartoris, born in 1875, died at less than a year old, and his American grandparents never saw him. Their second child, Algernon Edward Sartoris, born in 1877, would, after years of service in the United States Army, marry a French

---

8   See Ulysses Grant Dietz & Sam Watters, *Dream House: The White House as an American Home* (New York: Acanthus Press, 2009), 124-26.

9   Adam Badeau, *Grant in Peace: From Appomattox to Mount McGregor* (Hartford, CT: S.S. Scranton & Co., 1887), 412-13.

10   Thomas Ruys Smith, "'Poor little Nellie Grant' and the Wedding of the Century" in *American Scrap Book*, 6 March 2013, accessed 24 October 2021, http://americanscrapbook.blogspot.com/2013/03/poor-little-nellie-grant-and-marriage.html.

woman and become the patriarch of a long line of French descendants. Nellie's two daughters, Vivien May (b. 1879) and Rosemary Alice (b. 1880), would accompany her back to the United States. Both of them married but did not have children.

Nellie would request and receive her American citizenship back, an act so unprecedented for a woman married to a foreigner that it took a special act of Congress to make it happen. She remained active in Washington society after her mother died and, in 1903, was named the president of the board of Lady Managers of the Louisiana Purchase Exposition in Saint Louis.[11]

Nellie remarried in 1912, a few months after her brother Fred's death, to a widower named Frank Hatch Jones. Because the wedding took place at her summer house in Ontario, Canada, only her brother Buck was able to attend.

Jesse Root Grant, named for his father's father, was the baby of the family, a title no child wants. I think of him as the naughty boy. He was an adorable child, quick-witted and filled with humor. His best-remembered anecdote is of approaching his father upon his return from work in the leather shop in Galena one evening and challenging him to a fight. He couldn't have been much more than a toddler, and his father's response was, "I am a man of peace; but I will not be hectored by a person of your size." His father always wrestled with him and always let him win. This affectionate roughhousing left Jesse with the impression that his father was the "best battler in the world."[12] Of the four Grant siblings, Jesse knew the White House best and, only eleven when his parents moved in, would always remember it as his home during his formative years.

Jesse was also the only one of the four children to write memoirs, although his book, *In the Days of My Father General Grant,* published in 1925, was as much a series of sketches about his father as it was memories of his own life. Like his big brother Fred, Jesse went to the front with his father and witnessed history firsthand as a small child. He was with his parents at City Point in Virginia as the Confederacy was in its final death throes. He met Abraham Lincoln several times and was in the carriage with his parents on the fateful night as they traveled to the Washington train station rather than join the president and his wife at Ford's Theatre.

Jesse is also the only one of Grant's children to acknowledge experiencing slavery firsthand. The servants his mother maintained well into the Civil War were all enslaved people from his grandfather Dent's Missouri farm. Jesse remembered

11   Lillian Gray, "Nellie Grant Sartoris, Chairman Board of Lady Managers, St. Louis World's Fair," *Topeka State Journal,* 25 December 1903, 2. Interestingly, Nellie's sister-in-law's sister, Bertha Palmer, had been the president of the board of Lady Managers of the World's Columbian Exposition in Chicago in 1893.

12   Jesse R. Grant, 10-11.

the care he received as a small child, both from his mother and from the enslaved women who helped her. The irony of the wife of the Union Army commander having enslaved servants during the war her husband was fighting to end slavery can't be avoided. The fact is that Julia relied on her enslaved help to give her the freedom to manage her household in such a way as to see to her children's needs and visit her husband at the front as much as possible.[13]

Because his mother closed the grounds around the President's House and made it into a private family garden, Jesse grew up in what was, to him, simply a bigger and grander version of the homes of his playmates in Washington, D.C. In his memoirs, he remembers getting no particular deference from his neighborhood friends even when, as the president's son, he brought them to the White House grounds to play baseball. On the other hand, as the first young child to essentially grow up in the White House, he was indulged by the staff and even found himself admitted to cabinet meetings when he felt there was an issue worthy of their (and his father's) attention.[14]

Jesse left Cornell a few months short of graduating in order to accompany his parents and his brother Fred on their history-making world tour between 1877 and 1879. His own description of a ruckus at Windsor Castle is telling. In an almost diplomatic incident, Jesse threatened to leave Windsor and return to London when he was denied a place at Queen Victoria's table with his parents. Jesse, who was nineteen, describes the event as if it's all great fun, but even in his own words, he comes across as a bit of a spoiled child, used to getting his way.[15]

After a year at Columbia Law School, Jesse dropped out and became a freelance mining engineer, a position for which his Cornell studies had prepared him. In 1880, he married Elizabeth Chapman, daughter of San Francisco real estate developer William S. Chapman. Jesse and Elizabeth had two children: Nellie was born in 1881, and Chapman in 1887. Jesse and Elizabeth moved to San Diego in 1893, where they joined Buck and his family. In the early twentieth century, Elizabeth and Jesse went through a protracted and very public divorce, and Jesse married again in 1918, this time to Lillian Wilkins, a widow nearly twenty years his junior.

Jesse was also a Democrat and even ran, unsuccessfully, against William Jennings Bryan for the Democratic nomination for president in 1908. Jesse lost,

---

13   Sharra Vostral, "The Moveable Home Front," *Gateway: The Quarterly Magazine of the Missouri Historical Society* (Spring 2005), No. 4, 25:22-33.

14   Jesse R. Grant, 69-70.

15   Ibid., 223-30.

The author, Ulysses Grant Dietz, with his grandfather, Ulysses S. Grant III, on the grandfather's birthday, July 4, 1966.

Author's Collection

and Bryan lost the election by a landslide to William Howard Taft.[16]

Other than the first grandchild, Grant Sartoris, who died in infancy, all of Ulysses and Julia's remaining twelve grandchildren married, several of them more than once; but not all of them produced great-grandchildren. Ulysses S. Grant III—my grandfather—would follow his father and grandfather to West Point on the strength of a letter written in 1885 by his dying grandfather to whoever would be president when the youngest Ulysses came of age. It was President William McKinley who ultimately found the place at West Point for my grandfather.[17] In 1907, Ulysses S. Grant III married the daughter of Elihu Root, Secretary of War under William McKinley and Secretary of War and State under Theodore Roosevelt. Edith Root and young Lieutenant Grant had met at a White House reception. Sometime after his son's 1903 graduation from West Point, Fred Grant managed to get his friend Theodore Roosevelt to give his son a position on his staff. This third Ulysses would rise to become the third General Grant, serving in two world wars. He and his wife would have three daughters, thus ending the Grant surname in that line.

Ulysses S. Grant IV, my grandfather's first cousin and Buck's youngest child, would marry twice, but would have no surviving heirs to carry on the name. Thus it was Jesse's grandson, Ulysses S. Grant V, who would pass on the name to his grandson, Ulysses S. Grant VI—a third-great grandson.

Only two other descendants—so far—have borne the given name Ulysses: a great-great-grandson (myself) born to Ulysses S. Grant III's youngest daughter; and a fourth-great-grandson, Ulysse (spelled the French way) Sartoris, the first Ulysses in Nellie's family.

Oddly enough, Julia wasn't much more popular as a name among Ulysses S. Grant's descendants than his own more difficult name was. There are, to my

16   A wealth of information on Ulysses S. Grant's family can be found at the College of St. Scholastica Library, the Ulysses S. Grant Information Center: https://libguides.css.edu/usgrant/home. This is largely the work of the indefatigable Dr. Marie Krueger Kelsey, who has compiled the most complete bibliography of writings by and about Ulysses S. Grant.

17   John Y. Simon, ed., *The Papers of Ulysses S. Grant*, 32 vols. (Carbondale, IL: Southern Illinois University Press, 1967–2012), 31:336. The letter remains in the Grant family.

knowledge, eight Julias in the seven generations since the White House. Fred and Ida Grant's daughter Julia, the only descendant born in the White House, would marry a Russian prince in 1899, then bring him and their three children back to the United States after the Russian Revolution.[18] One of the princess's great-grandchildren is Julia. Buck would name one of his daughters Julia Dent Grant, and there were three more Julias in that line. Also, Ulysses S. Grant III's third daughter was Julia, my mother (1916–2014). The current youngest descendant of that name is Julia Berry, a fourth-great-granddaughter of the president and his wife, and a descendant of Fred Grant.

It feels almost arrogant for me to claim to represent all the descendants of Ulysses S. Grant and his wife, Julia. I can't, really, because I don't actually know most of them. As I mentioned, there were forty-one great-great-grandchildren of the president and his wife, of whom I am the youngest surviving member. Those descendants I do know I've met through the good offices of people outside the family. It is one of the great surprises for Grant enthusiasts that the "Grant family" doesn't hang out, doesn't have reunions, as if we formed a vast, close-knit group of cousins who actually keep in touch with each other. I wish it were so.

The truth is that all four branches of the Grant family, the descendants of Ulysses and Julia's four children, have gathered together only once in living memory. In 1998, the staff at White Haven, the Ulysses S. Grant National Historic Site outside of Saint Louis, organized a family reunion to which descendants of Fred, Buck (Ulysses, Jr.), Nellie, and Jesse all came. It remains to this day the only time I ever had the chance to meet all those distant cousins who shared the shadow of our famous common ancestor. Since that event, I have kept ties to two of those families, the descendants of Buck and the descendants of Nellie. Those third cousins and their families have become part of my extended family.

With distance from the source, the shadow of the General grows fainter. Current generations are aware of their ties to this great man, whose star only seems to get brighter these days. There are, however, a lot of other families in each of these lines of descent from Ulysses and Julia's four children. Hard as it is to believe, Ulysses S. Grant is not the most important thing in the life of his descendants. He was not all that important in my own life until, at the age of fifteen, I went to boarding school and started using my first name. All through my childhood, I had been called Grant, and few people even knew that my name was Ulysses. In

---

18   Julia Dent Grant Cantacuzène returned from Russia and published three books about her experiences under the name Princess Cantacuzène, Countess Spéransky, née Grant. She lived to the age of 99, dying in Washington, D.C., in 1975; she remained a public figure all her life. Her books are, in order of publication: *Revolutionary Days: Recollections of Romanoffs and Bolsheviki, 1914–1917* (Boston: Small, Maynard & Company, 1919); *Russian People: Revolutionary Recollections* (New York: Charles Scribner's Sons, 1920); and *My Life Here and There* (New York: Charles Scribner's Sons, 1921).

the 1950s, when I was born, being descended from Ulysses S. Grant was almost as much a stigma as it was a point of pride. Even my grandfather, for whom I was named, was glad that I was called Grant. Generations of false mythology and inaccurate history had done their work.

It was because I bore the name Ulysses and used it professionally that I was contacted in 1987—at thirty-two years old—by the managers of the General Grant National Memorial, popularly known as Grant's Tomb. I was asked to give a speech at Ulysses S. Grant's annual birthday commemoration, held every year at the Tomb on April 27. That was how the shadow of the General reached out to me and drew me in. That was how I first got involved in the great man's legacy. That was how I decided I needed to become educated on the history of this family. All of this happened because I realized I needed to live up to my name.

To circle back to a truth that has increasingly inhabited my thinking in the last few years: Each of Ulysses S. Grant's four children lived in the shadow of their great father, and each of them was unquestionably altered by the unique connection they had with their loving, famous parents. No family member since then has lived such an intensely public life as Ulysses and Julia did, and none of us has changed the world in the way our ancestor did. The perceptions formed by each of those four children were passed on to their children and to the children that followed them. Each line of descent from Ulysses S. Grant carries its own perspective on who Ulysses S. Grant was and what made him tick. Fortunately for all of Ulysses S. Grant's descendants today, there is a surfeit of information out there through which we can learn about him. All we have to do is look. The choice is ours.

Being Grant: A Perspective from the Inside Out
Chapter Fourteen | *Curt Fields*

Who *was* Ulysses Grant?

I have always had an abiding passion for history in general and the American Civil War in particular. When it occurred to me that I am the same height, build, and weight of Grant, I wanted to take advantage of those physical similarities and decided to try a first-person portrayal of him. That would provide a service to history, I thought, because I could, at the very least, show people how he really looked.

I had always been all right with Grant. I didn't have an especial liking for him and certainly not a passion for him. Like most others, I felt I knew *about* him—but I really didn't. Nor could I have known, at the beginning of my journey, what people thought of Grant, what they *thought they knew* about him, and what questions they would ask about him and his life. In portraying the general and president over the years, those questions and comments have come up consistently, both from the public during presentations and interiorly, as I have studied the man to put forth an accurate portrayal. I did not anticipate the changes that would take place within *me* in the process.

The overall perception of Grant has changed in recent years. He was enigmatic to his peers and remains so today. I would like to think out loud with you about him and my perceptions of him. As Grant said of Appomattox, "I only knew what was in my mind."[1] The same holds true here.

I would have you know I am a Grant enthusiast, *not* a Grant apologist. I have come to appreciate Grant despite his flaws, although I think those flaws have shed important light on him as a man of character. Those flaws make him more human to me, and they challenge me to know Grant better.

As of this writing in 2022, I have been portraying general and president Grant for 12 years. My first appearance as Grant was at a Fort Donelson ball in February of 2010. The crowd was pleased to have a Grant at the event and

---

1   Ulysses S. Grant, *Personal Memoirs of U.S. Grant*, 2 vols. (New York: Charles L. Webster & Co., 1885–1886), 2:492.

With hat, cigars, and calm determination, Curt Fields hits the iconic notes of U.S. Grant.

Opal Lovelace

made that feeling clear. It was then that I felt I had made the correct decision: All the study about Grant I had done over the year prior to the ball had been more than worthwhile. I had spent a lifetime reading about the Civil War, but not about Grant specifically. I quickly found out, though, that there was much more to the portrayal than simply knowing what Grant did or said. I needed to internalize the information so that when I spoke, it would appear as if I were thinking and not just parroting lines I had memorized. I also needed to have a command of the strategies and operations of the armies that Grant commanded and those he opposed.

As I began to make appearances around the country, I found that being able to answer questions added another level to knowing Grant because of the depth of familiarity required. Some inquiries could seem basic without being at all obvious, such as the question a nine-year-old in Indiana asked me: "What did Grant like for breakfast?" (That would be sliced cucumbers dipped in cold pickle brine.)

My first revelation about Grant came when I realized that it would be difficult to think of a more unlikely person to do what Grant ultimately did in American history—indeed, in world history. Never having sought fame or fortune, he ultimately lavishly received the former but never the latter.[2] Some aspects of his life are tragic because he suffered so many setbacks.

The next revelation came when I began to appreciate that he never gave up, no matter how bleak circumstances became. Through his failures in farming both in the Oregon Territory in 1852 and at White Haven in 1854–1858 (even pawning his watch to buy Christmas gifts for his children and wife) and in real estate in St. Louis through the rebuffs he received from Gen. Henry W. Halleck early in the war, Grant never gave up. He steadfastly believed in himself and was never beaten

2   Grant's wife, Julia, did receive a small fortune in book royalties from Grant's memoirs, published after his death. Julia survived her husband by seventeen years and lived a life of opulent ease during that time thanks to his literary efforts.

The outfit is different, the expression the same—
Curt Fields as President Grant.

Lena Moody

down. "Lick 'em tomorrow," he told Gen. William T. Sherman after a rough first day at Shiloh, reflecting a general attitude toward life.[3] His perseverance was a real strength.

Many people think Grant was originally from Galena, Illinois. He was actually born in Point Pleasant, Ohio, on the banks of the Ohio River, and grew up just a few miles away in Georgetown, Ohio (45 miles or so southeast of Cincinnati). He was the first of six children born to Jesse Root Grant and Hannah Simpson Grant. He did not move to Galena, Illinois, until April 1860, when Ulysses, Julia, and their four children boarded the steamer *Itasca* from St. Louis and traveled 350 miles up the Mississippi.[4] Ulysses left for the war a year later, in 1861. While maintaining a residence in Galena, he was rarely there after leaving for the war. I have frequently felt this information is only reluctantly, if at all, accepted because it seems to go too much against the truth as people "know" it.

Meanwhile, the impact of those critical, formative years he spent growing up in Georgetown get overlooked, despite their enormous value. Grant's mannerisms, attitudes, and speech—even the accent and expressions he used—all came from a town that was one of the southernmost of northern towns. He worked much of the time in Kentucky, going as far south as Louisville, and a year of his education was had in Maysville. A childhood spent in Galena would have made him a Midwesterner and a Northerner, with quite possibly different views on the issues of the day.

Another realization I came to about Grant sprang from the way his early home life determined so much about how he conducted himself as a man. His mother was distant, rarely known to smile or even talk. His father was loud, blustery, and difficult with people, with high expectations for behavior and success. His parents' personalities were poles apart, and between the two of them, it must have

---

3   Ronald C. White, *American Ulysses: A Life of Ulysses S. Grant* (New York: Random House, 2016), 219.

4   Ibid., 133.

been a difficult place for a child to grow up. This made his soft-spoken, almost too-quiet demeanor easier to understand. My point of view about Grant changed significantly because of this.

Jesse Root Grant built a tannery in the newly founded Ohio village of Georgetown and moved his family there in 1823 when Lyss (as his family commonly called him) was a year old. Jesse developed a highly successful tannery and leather business, and he also fancied himself a writer and public speaker, frequently organizing political discussions and debates in the small community. Jesse was largely self-educated, with only a few months of formal schooling, yet he was very well read and had political ambitions. He also liked to argue—a lot.

On one occasion, he and a local Georgetown teacher-cum-lawyer, Thomas Hamer, were debating the merits of a national bank. They nearly came to blows and did not speak to each other after that. Years later, when Jesse wanted Lyss to go to West Point, he had to ask then-Congressman Thomas Hamer to nominate Lyss to the United States Military Academy. Hamer graciously agreed. However, since he and Jesse had not had anything to do with each other for years, he did not actually know young Grant's name—but thought he did. He nominated "U.S. Grant," likely thinking that Lyss' mother's maiden name, Simpson, was the boy's middle name and that, since everyone called the boy "Lyss," Ulysses must be his first name (rather than Hiram). Grant was unable to have the name corrected at the Academy, and the name stuck.

"I remember Grant's first appearance among us," Sherman later recalled. "I was three years ahead of him. I remember seeing his name on the bulletin board, where all the names of the newcomers were posted. I ran my eye down the columns, and there saw 'U.S. Grant.' A lot of us began to make up names to fit the initials. One said, 'United States Grant.' Another 'Uncle Sam Grant.' A third said 'Sam Grant.' That name stuck to him."[5]

The incident shows how Grant was easygoing and did not let many things bother him, even at West Point—getting his name wrong and then, essentially, living with it. It has always made me think of Grant's apparent personal philosophy, "pick your battles."

Confusion over his name endures. The universal, and seemingly in-stone, public thinking is that Grant's middle name was Simpson. I am consistently asked about his name, and frequently, before I can address the question, am then told, with confidence, that "Simpson" was his middle name. Tradition in 1822 was to give the first male child his mother's maiden name as a middle name. That would hopefully keep her family name alive. However, family lore has it that Grant was

5   Jean Edward Smith, *Grant* (New York: Simon & Schuster, 2001), 25.

six weeks old before he was taken to a family meeting to be given a name and that his name was drawn out of a hat. The resulting given name was Hiram Ulysses Grant. The family didn't follow tradition.

If the mix-up at West Point had been appealed, another official could have corrected the name, but Grant wasn't, at the time, anxious to correct it because it would have thrown him back to the dreaded initials "H-U-G" and its resulting nickname. He had already begun signing exam papers as "U. H. Grant." Perhaps he didn't *want* to change the name. In any event, by the time he graduated, his new name had stuck, and he made no effort to correct it, then or later.[6]

In March of 1853, he wrote Julia a letter from Columbia Barracks (later Fort Vancouver) in the Washington Territory in which he explicitly addressed his middle initial. "What does the S stand for in Ulys.'s name?" he asked, referring to his second son, Ulysses S. Grant, Jr., (later called "Buck"). "[I]n mine you know it does not stand for anything!"[7]

Grant was not a physically big man. My 5'8" medium frame and weight (which match his) have frequently been challenged with the exclamations: "You can't be Grant. You aren't big enough!" When I relate the general's height and weight, I also say that two things make people seem larger than they were: pictures and history. For the most part, this suffices, and may even elicit a smile, but some are still incredulous about the truth of Grant's stature.

I was surprised to learn of Grant's sensitive nature. He loathed working in the family tannery and came to be nauseated at the sight of blood. That led to his eating meat that was burned, not merely blackened. He refused to hunt or to kill anything. He also declined to eat, as he put it, anything that walked on two legs. He had a deep, abiding love for horses and mules and would not abide mistreatment of them under any circumstances. Learning these things about him brought me to realize that he wasn't a "tough guy" at all. Perception readjustment came about again.

Grant never wanted to be a soldier. So why did his father send him to West Point? Jesse Grant knew that Lyss was not going into the family tannery/leather business. When Lyss was 16, Jesse asked him what he wanted to do with his life. His answer was to either become a riverboat man (or pilot) or a farmer. Jesse had no desire for his oldest son to work on the river, though, and had no confidence in his being a farmer. Knowing that in 1840s America, with an exploding population and westward expansion, an engineer would always be able to make a comfortable

6   For more on the mis-naming, see William Ralston Balch, *Life and Public Services of General Grant* (Philadelphia: Aetna Publishing Company, 1885), 26-28.

7   USG to Julia Dent Grant, 31 March 1853, John Y. Simon, ed., *The Papers of Ulysses S. Grant*, 32 vols. (Carbondale, IL: Southern Illinois University Press, 1967–2012), 1:298.

living, Jesse wanted Lyss to go to the only college in the country that offered a suitable education in engineering at the government's expense: West Point. Grant did not want anything to do with the military but dutifully went when the appointment, without his knowledge, was sought and gained. An irony in his going to West Point at all is that his friend and neighbor, Bart Bailey, who lived just behind the Grant home, had been asked to leave the Academy. Bailey's failure had created the opening for him.[8]

Grant swallowed hard and did what his father wanted him to, agreeing to a long-term and difficult commitment—something I think is admirable. He was tentative about going to the Academy because he felt he did not have the education necessary to succeed at West Point. His compliance with his father's wishes demonstrated that Grant had the tenacity to persevere to attain a difficult goal, even if he wasn't excited about doing so, because it was what had to be done.

Outside of the military, Grant seemed to fail at everything he tried—apparently the result of circumstances beyond his control. He seemed cursed in his work as a farmer or businessman. My perceptions of Grant's life failures changed because study of the man and his circumstances shows that his farming failures, whether in the Oregon Territory or in St. Louis, were not due to poor or foolish decisions on his part. Grant experienced a parade of bad weather, economic boom (with lower prices), economic bust (with no market to sell to), and poor health. The harder he worked, the farther behind he got until he finally went under with the weight of debt.

I marveled at all the adversity Grant suffered that seemingly would have broken a weaker-willed man. Grant pushed through, though, never doubting himself or what he was about. He certainly came across that way to his closest allies. "I believe you are as brave, patriotic, and just, as the great prototype Washington; as unselfish, kind-hearted, and honest, as a man should be," Sherman wrote to Grant on March 10, 1864; "but the chief characteristic in your nature is the simple faith in success you have always manifested, which I can liken to nothing else than the faith a Christian has in his Saviour. This faith gave you victory at Shiloh and Vicksburg."[9]

When I tell people about the setbacks Grant endured until he got into the army and the war, I see the expressions on their faces begin to change. Over time, I have come to deeply respect the man because he simply would not give up. He believed in himself and always *knew* that tomorrow would be a better day! Again: "Lick 'em tomorrow."

8   White, 22-24.

9   William T. Sherman to USG, 10 March 1864, Brooks D. Simpson and Jean V. Berlin, eds., *Sherman's Civil War: Selected Correspondence of William T. Sherman, 1860–1865* (Chapel Hill, NC: The University of North Carolina Press, 1999), 603.

It is hard to appreciate just how much Grant achieved without understanding the impact his "lean years" had on him prior to the outbreak of the Civil War. The man who would win the war and become president of the United States once peddled wood in St. Louis.

National Park Service

Another aspect of Grant that has significantly impacted me in my experience of portraying him is his alleged drinking problem. Like most people, I assumed he was a heavy drinker and maybe a drunk. Without further inquiry, I accepted the long-trumpeted image that he hit the bottle pretty hard and pretty consistently.

Almost without exception, when I have put on the uniform or the presidential suit, before an event is over, someone has made a remark or asked a question about Grant being a drunk. Sometimes it is tinged with sarcasm, but more often it is asked with genuine curiosity. I welcome the question because it gives me the opportunity to squarely address what I feel is the myth of his "legendary" drinking. I have progressed from not having an opinion when I began the portrayal to having a firm position on the matter. It was a long time coming.

I have come to feel that Grant was a man who had a problem drinking, not a problem with alcohol. A problem drinking alcohol indicates an inability to handle it and its effects on the body. A problem with alcohol indicates a need or craving for it (read: "alcoholic"). Grant said more than one drink or glass of wine would make him tipsy. Two drinks would make his gait unsteady and his speech slurred. He was a man who knew he could not handle alcohol because, with his physiology, it hit him too hard. "Virtually everyone drank, and drank quite a lot," wrote Grant biographer Jean Smith, "but in Grant's case a little liquor went a long way. His slight frame (Grant stood five feet seven inches and weighed about 135 pounds) would have limited his capacity in any event, but his metabolism was such that every drink showed."[10]

Gossip is deadly to a reputation, and Grant was no exception. During the two years when he was on the West Coast away from his wife and two babies (one of whom was born after Grant left for the Oregon Territory), reports are that he drank quite a bit. But they were second-hand and ambiguous as to his drinking habits, as well as whether it was on- versus off-duty drinking.

10   Smith, 83.

Charles G. Ellington, in his book *The Trial of U.S. Grant*, said Grant "was not a problem drinker" but "sometimes desired alcohol to relieve his loneliness. Grant did spend time in Eureka saloons, but that is not evidence of heavy drinking. Here is where community leaders met, talked about a wide variety of subjects, and expressed the civilized conviviality of that isolated place." It was only natural for Grant to be present among such company, just as it was likely that everyone's tongues wagged, loosened by alcohol.[11]

Grant scholar John Y. Simon takes it a step further:

> Separation from his wife and children for years with no prospect of acquiring the money to reunite the family, recently promoted but not likely to rise again for many years, in poor health, assigned to a small and isolated post with a commanding officer he had disliked for years, Grant had plenty of reasons to resign, and documentary evidence proves that the resignation was his own choice. If, on the Pacific Coast, he drank more than was necessary . . . the evidence is too meager and contradictory for any sound conclusion.[12]

"On one side," concludes Ellington, "we have the confusing testimony of contemporaries, along with long-standing innuendos, rumor, and shady gossip. On the other side, in addition to other contemporary testimony, we have Grant's unvarnished record—a record that has stood the test of time and has stood scrutiny for generations."[13]

To the extent the rumors were true, it is possible that Grant was self-anesthetizing his homesickness and emotional distress caused by being so far from his young family. Combined with an inability to handle alcohol and a peacetime army in which alcohol use was widespread, it's no wonder tongues wagged. The U.S. Army at that time was very small, and gossip traveled quickly.

Moreover, Grant suffered from bouts of chills and fever during his time at Fort Vancouver and subsequently at Fort Humboldt in California. He suffered from migraine headaches that would incapacitate him for days. He also had a seriously abscessed tooth that reddened and swelled his face to distortion—all of which could have easily contributed to a perception of hangover and drunkenness.

---

11   Charles G. Ellington, *The Trial of U.S. Grant: The Pacific Coast Years, 1852–1854* (Glendale, CA: The Arthur H. Clark Company, 1987), 177.

12   Ibid., 187.

13   Ibid., 187-88.

So did he resign his commission to avoid a court-martial? The story is murky, with conflicting accounts about whether or not he was drunk on duty.[14] What I must say is that I don't know. I wasn't there. That is not to take the easy way out on the matter. I acknowledge that there is a good bit of confusion, so I just I don't know. I have concluded that Grant had probably put up with all the loneliness he could tolerate and simply wanted to go home to his wife and children.

A telling factor in the matter, I think, is that he waited until he made captain of the regular army before resigning. He could have resigned at any time but held on until he had received official notice of the promotion and written the official acceptance of that rank. The calendar gives lie to the myth of being forced out of the army. The timeline is thus:

Grant arrives at Columbia Barracks (later Fort Vancouver), Oregon Territory (later Washington Territory), September 20, 1852.

- On August 9, 1853, Grant is informed by Secretary of War Jefferson Davis of his promotion to captain, effective August 5, and is ordered to Fort Humboldt, California.

- Grant arrives at Fort Humboldt, January 5, 1854.

- Grant receives his commission as captain, April 11, 1854.

- Grant writes letter of resignation on April 11, 1854, to take effect on July 31, 1854.

Plainly, Grant chose the date of his resignation and departure. Those don't seem to be the actions of a man being "run off."

Another factor that contributed to the "drunk" myth includes a very jealous officer corps—Grant's peer group—during the Civil War. Grant's career was meteoric. Over the course of the war, he rose from a colonel of volunteers in June 1861 to lieutenant general, the highest-ranking officer in the Union army since George Washington, in March 1864. Some officers remembered tales of his drinking in the old army out in the Northwest. Jealous wags recirculated old hearsays. Obviously, the stain stuck to Grant.

Any careful scrutiny of this issue must include his behavior for the rest of his life, after his return from the West Coast. He didn't drink to excess when he was with his family—he had no need to. The loneliness was gone, and he was gainfully occupied in his life as a farmer. His later life also gave lie to the accusations of being a drunk. During his presidency, as he navigated Reconstruction, political enemies north and south again resurrected the old tales in an attempt to soil Grant's

14   Ibid., 177-78.

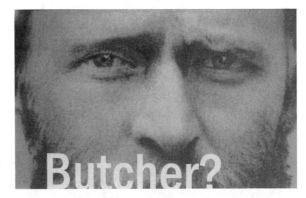

A provocative exhibit at Ulysses S. Grant National Historic Site questions the myths and misconceptions about Grant, offering evidence to suggest most Grant myths are more fiction than fact.

National Park Service

reputation. However, there are plenty of examples of Grant taking an occasional drink during the frequent social events he attended, and there is no evidence of his ever being drunk again.

Another tarnish on Grant's reputation is that he was characterized as a butcher for the last year of the war. I don't think he was. He knew that the way to defeat Gen. Robert E. Lee was to give the Confederates no rest and continually engage them. That constant engagement ran up the casualty numbers quickly. However, Grant felt that the higher losses from intense combat in the short term would be preferable to the greater numbers of deaths from drawn-out combat over time, which included soldiers succumbing to cholera, measles, smallpox, dysentery, and all of the other maladies of camp life. Knowing the sound thinking behind the military tactics does not ease the horror of those incredibly high numbers. However, Grant was not a butcher, reckless with his men. He was sensitive to the mounting casualty lists, but he knew what it took to win.

He also knew that was why President Abraham Lincoln had brought him to the Eastern theater in the first place: to engage Lee and end the war as soon as possible. Pinning Lee in Virginia would prevent the Army of Northern Virginia from joining the other Confederate armies.[15] Grant hoped Lee would give him battle in the open, but Lee declined to engage him that way, and Grant agonized over the war stretching out longer and longer yet.

Grant had his faults and failures. We could compile a list, but a few deserve mention in particular: Was he surprised at Shiloh? Of course he was. At both Vicksburg and Cold Harbor, he made second assaults he later said he regretted. His General Orders No. 11, issued in anger, expelling the Jews from his military district in 1862, was horrendous, and he paid for it the rest of his life.[16] Although he was

15   Think, for instance, of James Longstreet's First Corps slipping off to help the Confederate Army of Tennessee at the battle of Chickamauga in September 1863.

16   Grant later recognized the order deserved censure and apologized for it. Jonathan D. Sarna, *When General Grant Expelled the Jews*, (New York: Schocken, 2012), xi, xiii, 118, 141.

Grant left West Point a middling student. By the time Fields returned for the dedication of a Grant statue in 2019, the Point recognized Grant as one of its greatest achievers.

U.S. Army

mild-mannered, it was, indeed, possible to get on Grant's bad side and stay there. Conversely, he was sometimes personally loyal to a fault.

As I said earlier, I am a Grant enthusiast, not a Grant apologist. I am frequently asked if I have difficulty keeping my personality out of my portrayal of Grant—how much is Grant and how much is me? The reality is that I don't have to make any effort to keep myself out of the presentation. His was such a distinctive personality that my own never comes into play when bringing him to the public. His statements and writings were clear; his actions were definitive. His memoirs and letters, the rich body of work about him by contemporaries, and the excellent latter-day scholarship by outstanding authors are all more than enough to put him forth as his peers saw him. The difficulty is not what to say, but rather, what not to say without running a presentation too long.

Grant was a man who, like most people, I *thought* I knew. I didn't. Reading about him and what he did during the war was informative. Reading what people who didn't like him had to say was illuminating. Reading what he had to say was interesting. He learned from his mistakes and seldom made the same one a second time. He was cool under fire and tremendous pressure. He had a strong sense of humor that isn't brought out much in writings about him. He was a devoted, trusting friend and was scrupulously honest. He consistently demonstrated a military sense of space and time, what needed to be done, where it needed to be done, and who should do it. As I have studied him, I have come to genuinely like him. I didn't expect that. His contemporaries would have described him as "an upright man." In today's language, he would be "a good guy." I certainly think he was, and I am pleased to present him to the public whenever possible. I like to think he would be pleased, too.

The Odyssey of Grant's Tomb Through the Ages
Chapter Fifteen | *Frank J. Scaturro*

In 1886, New York's legislature expressed that Grant's Tomb should be "a suitable monument," a "sacred trust" that would receive "perpetual care." There, "the remembrance of the events in which General Grant took so important a part may be cherished," and "his virtues and the services which he rendered to his whole country may be held in reverence."[1] These words appeared in a law incorporating the Grant Monument Association (GMA), the organization charged with constructing and administering Grant's final resting place. Five years later, GMA treasurer Horace L. Hotchkiss told members of the legislature, "The Memorial . . . will last as long as the American Republic. It will be built for all time. Its situation will be second to no other monumental structure in the world."[2]

Such sentiments reflected the stratospheric esteem in which Ulysses S. Grant was held across the nation. At the time of his death in 1885, Grant was widely considered the equal of George Washington and Abraham Lincoln. It was not by happenstance that his funeral in New York City was witnessed by as many as 1.5 million people, making it the largest gathering in the history of the North American continent up to that time.[3] Nor is it happenstance that Grant is entombed in the largest mausoleum in the Western Hemisphere. The massive monument, designed by architect John H. Duncan and constructed with a granite exterior and a marble interior, rises 150 feet above the ground and 280 feet above the banks of the Hudson River. Its 90-foot-square lower section, adorned with Doric columns, is surmounted by a circular drum, surrounded by an Ionic colonnade, with a stepped pyramidal top. The monument's neoclassical design includes a number of relief sculptures, among them allegorical figures probably representing Victory and Peace flanking

1   An Act to Incorporate the Grant Monument Association, ch. 7, 1886 N.Y. Laws 14.

2   Horace L. Hotchkiss, Address given to the New York State Assembly, Manhattan Historic Sites Archive, National Park Service, accessed 10 August 2022, http://www.mhsarchive.org/item. aspx?rID=GEGR%20%20%20%20%20622.0037&db=objects&dir=CR%20GEGR&collid=GEGR. COLLECT.003&page=0.

3   Charles Bracelen Flood, *Grant's Final Victory: Ulysses S. Grant's Heroic Last Year* (Cambridge, MA: Da Capo Press, 2011), 246.

A program consisting of 16 pages, with an ornamental paper cover, outlined the day's planned events for the Tomb's dedication. Note the figure atop the Tomb, drawn in as an anticipated final component to be added at some point after the dedication. The statue was never installed.

National Park Service, Manhattan Historic Sites Archive

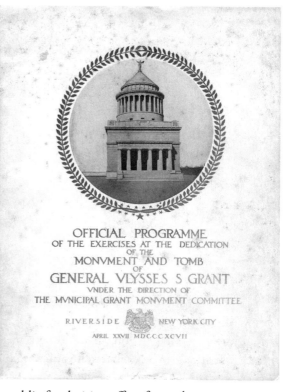

OFFICIAL PROGRAMME
OF THE EXERCISES AT THE DEDICATION
OF THE
MONVMENT AND TOMB
OF
GENERAL VLYSSES S GRANT
VNDER THE DIRECTION OF
THE MVNICIPAL GRANT MONVMENT COMMITTEE

RIVERSIDE   NEW YORK CITY
APRIL XXVII MDCCCXCVII

the Tomb's epitaph, "Let us have peace." Those words were taken from Grant's letter accepting his 1868 nomination for president by the Republican National Convention.[4] The GMA had raised (with accrued interest) $600,000 from an estimated 90,000 donors for this undertaking, the largest public fundraising effort for such a purpose up to that time.[5]

The dedication of the monument would not occur until nearly 12 years after Grant's death, on April 27, 1897, which was the 75th anniversary of his birth. Yet the dedication exercises brought 50,000 to 55,000 marchers, and an estimated one million spectators crowded New York's streets—remarkable considering how quickly the departed typically recede from memory over that span of time.[6] During its initial years of planning and overseeing Grant's Tomb, the GMA could claim former and future presidents, cabinet members, diplomats, governors, mayors,

4   Overview: Building Design, Grant Monument Association, accessed 10 August 2022, https:// grantstomb.org/overview/#BuildingDesign, hereafter cited as GMA, Building Design. The Garfield Memorial in Cleveland, Ohio, which is President James A. Garfield's final resting place, rises to 180 feet but does not surpass Grant's Tomb in volume. Ibid.

5   David M. Kahn, General Grant National Memorial Historical Resource Study, National Park Service, January 1980, accessed 10 August 2022, https://web.archive.org/web/20170222222332/https:// www.nps.gov/gegr/learn/education/upload/Kahn-Historic-Resource-Study-1980.pdf, 2, 113.

6   Ibid., 140.

At the time of its dedication, Grant's Tomb rose high above the clear landscape, unblocked from view by other structures. Throngs of people attended the ceremony.

Library of Congress

business leaders, and publishers among its trustees and supporters.[7] Grant's death had been mourned by both former Confederates and former slaves—and indeed across every stratum of American society. This dynamic was visible not only in the widely reported Union and Confederate veterans among the marchers at his funeral and on dedication day, but also in a variety of individual tributes: African Americans crediting Grant with helping to set them free; emotional visits to the Tomb by former battlefield foes; Chief Joseph of the Nez Percé riding at the head of the dedication parade with its grand marshal, Gen. Grenville Dodge; and the annual journeys to the Tomb on the anniversary of Grant's funeral by his last surviving pallbearer, Rabbi Edward B.M. Browne, who placed wreaths for decades after the event.[8]

7   Ibid., 29, 38, 103; Louis L. Picone, *Grant's Tomb: The Epic Death of Ulysses S. Grant and the Making of an American Pantheon* (New York: Arcade Publishing, 2021), 80-81, 102-03, 163, 175-76, 270-71.

8   Picone, 46-48, 66-71, 179, 193-94; "Beauregard at Grant's Tomb," *Switchmen's Journal* (December 1886), No. 8, 1:352; Jonathan D. Sarna, *When General Grant Expelled the Jews* (New York: Schocken, 2012), 144; *New York Times*, 9 August 1913.

Grant's Tomb, stately, as the 1800s
rolled into a new century.

New York State Archives

In its early history, Grant's Tomb was internationally renowned, even surpassing the Statue of Liberty in visitors until World War I and maintaining high visitation levels through the 1920s.[9] The site accordingly was a focal point for notable events. Prominent examples included Wilbur Wright's historic 1909 flight, witnessed by a million people, from Governor's Island to the Statue of Liberty to Grant's Tomb; and on "Suffrage Day" in 1914, when the monument was the gathering place for hundreds of demonstrators pushing for women's right to vote. During World War I, the Tomb was decorated with the colors of allied nations when their foreign delegations were in town.[10] The monument had a place in American life comparable to that of the famous monuments to Washington and Lincoln on Washington's National Mall in later years.

Yet the monument would fade out of public consciousness over the years that followed. This trend tracked the diminution of Grant's standing in historical memory during the first half of the twentieth century, particularly after the disappearance of Grant's contemporaries who had firsthand memories of his career. For the rest of their lives, Civil War veterans and others who experienced the nation's bloodiest conflict retained vivid impressions of its associated sacrifices and challenges. For successfully taking on the formidable challenges of military leadership, Grant invited the greatest appreciation. When his Tomb was dedicated, his wartime service was more prominent in the public mind than his presidency.[11]

Interestingly, however, the monument's original relief sculptures did not emphasize the earlier over the later component of Grant's public career, and during his long dedication ceremony oration, the GMA's president, Gen. Horace Porter,

9   Picone, 195, 197; Joan Waugh, *U.S. Grant: American Hero, American Myth* (Chapel Hill, NC: University of North Carolina Press, 2009), 262.

10   Picone, 196.

11   "Grant Day," *Harper's Weekly*, 1 May 1897, No. 2106, 41:431.

actually devoted more words to the White House years than to the Civil War years.[12] Even though Grant's military career had been groundbreaking enough to impress observers who paid little attention to his political career, there were already ominous developments for Grant's reputation in play as of 1897. Perhaps most conspicuous was the collapse of Reconstruction and repudiation of much of the associated legal architecture of equal rights that Grant had helped to build. Less than a year before the dedication, the Supreme Court had decided the case of *Plessy v. Ferguson*, which upheld state-imposed racial segregation in railroads. When he was president, Grant had secured a Civil Rights Act that prohibited segregation in transportation and accommodations. With the emergence of Jim Crow in the South, the nation seemed to be ironically burying part of President Grant's legacy just as it was entombing his physical remains.

Sure enough, the Myth of the Lost Cause and the related Dunning School's condemnation of Reconstruction during the twentieth century would shape generations of history books. Grant's generalship was routinely disparaged next to that of lionized Confederates, and his presidency was mercilessly trashed, with historians compounding their hostility to Reconstruction with additional layers of political bias.[13] Despite substantial population growth, the Tomb's visitation decreased noticeably from the annual attendance of its early years, which regularly exceeded half a million. It plummeted during the Great Depression, dipping below 100,000 in 1933, before increasing to about 300,000 by the 1950s.[14] For many, Grant's Tomb became more closely associated with the catchphrase, "Who's buried in Grant's Tomb?"—the joke question popularized by Groucho Marx while hosting *You Bet Your Life*—than with its architecture or its principal occupant's story.[15]

By mid-century, the GMA was suffering a declining membership and aging leadership and lacked the resources to care for the site.[16] The organization's trustees, therefore, decided to turn the site over to the National Park Service (NPS), which took over in 1959 following the passage of authorizing legislation the prior year. Such a move is typically viewed as the successful conclusion of a historic

12   *New York Times*, 28 April 1897. Busts of five of Grant's lieutenants during the war and reliquary room murals depicting maps marking Civil War battles were installed during the 1930s. Mosaic murals depicting Grant's victories at Vicksburg, Chattanooga, and Appomattox were installed during the 1960s. But these features memorializing Grant's military career were not part of the 1897 construction. GMA, Building Design.

13   These trends are explored in greater detail in essays in this volume by Gary W. Gallagher in Chapter Seven and by me in Chapter Eleven.

14   Kahn, 147-48, 162-63; Picone, 191, 195, 197, 199, 206, 210, 220.

15   Picone, 214-15.

16   Kahn, 175, 186; Picone, 210.

preservation story, and Grant's Tomb's acquisition by the federal government was no exception.[17] That perception was only natural. The National Park Service Organic Act, after all, requires that agency to "conserve" the features of its parks and monuments "and to provide for the enjoyment of the same in such manner and by such means as will leave them unimpaired for the enjoyment of future generations."[18] Yet the Tomb's transfer presaged its darkest chapter.

A hint of the trouble that lay ahead had already been evidenced when NPS officials were studying the prospects of making Grant's Tomb into a national park. The national park system is, of course, better known for components like Yellowstone or Yosemite that preserve natural resources. It did less conspicuously include historic sites, but it had not previously included a mausoleum.[19] The 1958 authorizing legislation had designated the monument as the General Grant National Memorial, a name that had never previously been used for the site. While there was nothing inherently derogatory in using the title "General" rather than the highest position Grant had held during his public career—it was common during his time for military titles to continue to be used after soldiers had gone on to civilian positions—here it reflected the then-dominant mindset that his presidency left little to be commemorated. And as innately innocuous as the national memorial designation was, NPS officials had an obtuse conception of memorials and failed to appreciate the Tomb on its own terms. A 1956 report following an NPS team's preliminary inspection expressed dissatisfaction that it seemed to be "only a tomb." It concluded, "There should be additional development to give the visitor a more pointed feeling that this structure is a memorial." Shortly afterward, the NPS regional director went so far as to write to the national director that the "relocation of and subordination of the sarcophagi" would be "essential to accomplish" the transformation from a tomb to a memorial.[20] That thankfully was never pursued. But an NPS historian's report soon after the Tomb's transfer in 1959 still presumed that developing the site meant "a shift of emphasis from the mortuary to the interpretive."[21] After all, he reasoned, the NPS was "not administering Grant's Tomb but General Grant National Memorial."[22]

So, the agency was hampered from the outset by a lack of appreciation of both the history of the man and the nature of his final resting place. A decade

17   Kahn, 178-79; Picone, 211-12.

18   39 Stat. 535.

19   Picone, 211.

20   Kahn, 176-78.

21   Ibid., 180.

22   Ibid., 181.

later, the NPS adopted an unfortunate plan under which, among other destructive alterations, the agency obliterated the features of the Tomb's two reliquary rooms. In the center of each room was an elaborate bronze trophy case, likely designed by Duncan himself, which held Civil War battle flags. NPS employees destroyed them with sledgehammers, and the flags were shipped off to storage. Elaborate murals by Dean Fausett, which had been added during the 1930s, were now painted over in raspberry and blue paint in the east and west reliquary rooms, respectively. Photo exhibits were installed in their place. The murals, according to an employee on site at the time, "were just beautiful, and in perfect condition except for a little surface dirt."[23] One room of photos was dedicated to Grant's military career, the other to the balance of Grant's life. The latter included only a few photos relating to Grant's presidency and, for the most part, ignored his political accomplishments. A larger panel summarized his presidency as "clouded by disgrace and dishonesty," a quote apparently taken from the *World Book Encyclopedia*'s article on Grant by William B. Hesseltine.[24] The photo captions were incoherently organized and hard to read, with inaccuracies that included a picture of someone else misidentified as Grant. In addition to the damage done by these changes, which were implemented between 1969 and 1970, invaluable features of the archival collection inherited by the NPS, including drawings submitted in the competition for Grant's Tomb and information regarding original contributors to the monument, were either disposed of intentionally or otherwise lost during the agency's early years in charge.[25]

The most alarming trend at Grant's Tomb, however, was desecration. Instances of vandalism had been recorded earlier in the monument's history. That vulnerability coincided with the lack of police protection, which at one time was provided on a round-the-clock basis but did not last.[26] Starting in the 1960s, a new chapter of rampant desecration of the monument tracked a crime wave and social revolution that included a marked decline in patriotism and respect for history in general.[27] Annual visitation to the monument plummeted from 253,000 in 1965—the end of the Civil War centennial—to 120,000 in 1966. Between the 1970s and early 1990s, it was much lower, often less than half the 1966 level.[28] At Grant's 150th

23   Ibid., 189-90.

24   William B. Hesseltine, "Grant, Ulysses S.," in *World Book Encyclopedia* (Chicago: Field Enterprises Educational Corporation, 1967), 8:304.

25   Decline & Preservation: Mismanagement, Grant Monument Association, accessed 10 August 2022, https://grantstomb.org/restoration-preservation/#Mismanagement; Kahn, 194-95.

26   Kahn, 148-49, 162-63.

27   Picone, 213, 220-21.

28   Annual Park Recreation Visits, General Grant NMEM, National Park Service, accessed 10 August 2022, https://irma.nps.gov/STATS/Reports/Park/GEGR, hereafter cited as NPS, Annual Visits.

birthday ceremony in 1972, West Point's 40-member band outnumbered the audience.[29]

That same year, the NPS launched a new project, ostensibly to mark the centennial of the establishment of Yellowstone as the first national park during Grant's presidency: It installed mosaic benches around the monument under the rationale that the benches would improve community residents' connection to the site and therefore decrease graffiti vandalism. The project did nothing of the kind, and it is mystifying that the NPS could think of no theme from Grant's rich public career to connect residents to the Tomb. The subject matter of the abstract, multi-colored, serpentine benches had almost nothing to do with Grant and so starkly clashed with the Tomb's neoclassical architecture as to visually disparage what it was supposed to enhance. This is not an innate criticism of the benches themselves. They were influenced by the Catalan Modernist architect Antoni Gaudí, whose whimsical designs make wonderful additions to recreational parks, still visible in his home city of Barcelona. But at a presidential tomb, as Ulysses S. Grant Association president Ralph G. Newman observed, "It's like having a roller-coaster ride running up and down the Lincoln Memorial." Additionally, when it implemented the construction of the mosaics, as with its unfortunate alterations of the reliquary rooms a couple of years earlier, the NPS made no effort to comply with the National Historic Preservation Act of 1966.[30]

Those years and the two decades that followed were the Tomb's nadir. The monument was routinely marred by graffiti. Drug and alcohol use at the site were also rampant. The Tomb was used as a bathroom and shelter by the homeless at night, leaving a lingering urine stench around the entrance throughout the day. I witnessed these trends on an extensive basis during my time volunteering at Grant's Tomb during the early 1990s when I was a student at nearby Columbia University. On occasion, I also encountered at the site the use of explosives, periodically employed to blow the beaks off the Tomb's granite eagles flanking the front stairs (the NPS had a supply of replacement beaks); damaged or stolen exhibit panels; apparent prostitution; slaughtered chickens, evidently as part of an animal sacrifice ritual; and damage to the structure itself. Inappropriate recreational activities like sunbathing and skating on the Tomb were common, as was littering, punctuated by a garbage pail found hoisted atop a flagpole one morning. It was difficult to think of a form of disrespectful activity that did not occur at Grant's Tomb. And this was in addition to the basic maintenance needs that went unaddressed, including discoloration and

29   "Band Outnumbers Spectators at Celebration Here of Grant's Birthday," *New York Times*, 28 April 1972, 82.

30   Kahn, 190-93; Picone, 221-24; "Skirmish at Grant's Tomb Over Benches," *New York Times*, 23 July 1979, B3.

water damage in the dome, cracking throughout the granite plaza in front of the monument, and the long-abandoned restroom facilities in the overlook pavilion across the street.[31]

It was futile trying to appeal to the NPS from within the system to correct these problems. Those with supervisory authority not only failed to act but also told staff not to disclose what we observed. No doubt the agency suffered from a lack of funds to meet its mandate as custodians of this national park, but those who were put in immediate charge of the site were unmotivated to remedy even simple issues; a typical example was the failure to replace a photo stolen from an exhibit panel even after a coworker found the replacement photo sitting in the office.

Sadly, by that time, the degradation of Grant's Tomb, whether by misguided official decisions or by vandals, had become normalized as a component of urban decay—at least among some of the few local observers who paid any mind to the monument.[32] Architecturally, the monument had long suffered from the disparagement of classically designed buildings after World War II as a new International Style became the standard against which the critics and the New York press judged buildings.[33] Even a relatively sympathetic *New York Times* commentary in 1977 by August Heckscher, a former commissioner of the New York City Parks Department, stated with a marked lack of enthusiasm that "[t]he living generation is bound to support" Grant's Tomb "as it would an aged and slightly zany parent."[34]

The diminishing of Grant's historical reputation was an even more momentous blow to the monument. The eighteenth president was essentially downgraded so far from his former stature that a mausoleum of such grandeur no longer seemed to fit him. The problem was not that vandals were reading the Dunning School, but the vast distortions of Grant's story during the twentieth century helped diminish the resources and the will within the system to maintain and safeguard his final resting place. By contrast, the Lincoln and Jefferson Memorials in Washington, D.C., similarly classical masterpieces, suffered no comparable turn for the worse. Those monuments to American icons were built during the nadir of Grant's reputation,

---

31   Frank Scaturro, "A President Dishonored," *Nineteenth Century* (1994), No. 2, 14:5-7; Decline & Preservation: Desecration, Grant Monument Association, accessed 10 August 2022, https://grantstomb.org/restoration-preservation/#Desecration.

32   Picone, 221, 227-28.

33   Kahn, 192-93.

34   August Heckscher, "Design Notebook: A Fond Look Back at Evocations of the City's Patriotic Spirit," *New York Times*, 11 August 1977, 51.

Vandals spray-painted the walls of the Tomb and urinated in the corners near the entrance. Drug paraphernalia was often littered across the floor in addition to the surrounding stone plaza.

National Park Service

and Grant's Tomb's appropriations from Congress were a minute fraction of the funding they received.[35]

Yet, with broad exposure of the Tomb's deplorable condition, which occurred between 1993 and 1994, it soon became clear that Americans were not willing to accept desecration and neglect at the final resting place of a national hero. Even at the height of their influence, Lost Cause–inspired diatribes had never transformed Grant into a villain in the public mind, and by the 1990s, his military star had been rising for more than a generation, to the point that it became common to regard him as the greatest military leader ever produced by the United States. The more severe excoriation of Grant's presidency took longer to reverse, but that substantial upswing would begin during the 1990s. My essay in Chapter Eleven of this volume explores this trend and the reasons Grant should be remembered as a great president. Even without specific knowledge of the emerging history, Americans took offense to the notion that a president's tomb would be treated like a sewer. The news media presented this situation as a disgrace without slouching toward normalizing it as inevitable, as some past commentary had.

As the issue became public, Congress responded. The monument's operational budget, although still a fraction of the amount that went to the presidential

---

35   U.S. Congress, House, Subcommittee on the Department of the Interior and Related Agencies, *Department of the Interior and Related Agencies Appropriations for 1994: Hearings before a Subcommittee of the Committee on Appropriations, Part 1*, 103rd Cong., 1st Sess., 1993, 1223, 1227.

memorials in Washington, more than quadrupled.[36] With support from Grant's descendants, a new GMA was incorporated in 1994 as a successor to the original organization, which had dissolved in 1965. The new GMA has served as an outlet for citizen support. The NPS installed nighttime security and adopted procedures to keep the Tomb off limits during those hours in which it had been most vulnerable to desecration. In 1995, the agency completed a restoration of the reliquary rooms, recovering the murals by Dean Fausett that had been painted over and reproducing the destroyed bronze trophy cases, which now housed battle flag replicas. On Grant's birthday that year, Fausett, then an octogenarian, was on hand to witness the rededication of his work. For that and broader restoration to be completed by the monument's centennial on Grant's birthday in 1997, Congress appropriated more than $2 million. This included the cleaning of graffiti, application of graffiti barrier coating, repair of the roof and accompanying water damage in the dome, a cleaning of the Tomb from top to bottom, and replacement of the deteriorating granite plaza in front of the Tomb. A parade up Riverside Drive preceded the 1997 rededication ceremony, which had thousands in attendance, and newspapers announced the renovations with headlines such as the *New York Daily News*' "New Life for Old Tomb."[37]

Additional restoration awaited the twenty-first century. The overlook pavilion across the street from the Tomb, which for decades lingered in a serious state of disrepair, was renovated and reopened in 2011 as a visitor center. Its new interior included a gift shop, a presentation room, two single-user restrooms, and additional office space for the NPS.[38] The plaza north of the Tomb, which includes a fenced-in plaque in Chinese and English along with memorial trees planted by order of Chinese viceroy Li Hung Chang in 1897 at the site of Grant's temporary tomb, sits on park land owned by New York City, which for years appropriated almost nothing to maintain it. It had badly deteriorated walkways and a stairway that was unusable. In 2018, nearly a quarter century after the GMA first called

---

36   Ibid.; U.S. Congress, House, Subcommittee on the Department of the Interior and Related Agencies, *Department of the Interior and Related Agencies Appropriations for 1995: Hearings before a Subcommittee of the Committee on Appropriations, Part 1*, 103rd Cong., 2nd Sess., 1994, 1450, 1454.

37   Decline & Preservation: Restoration, Grant Monument Association, accessed 10 August 2022, https://grantstomb.org/restoration-preservation/#Restoration, hereafter cited as GMA, Restoration; Kahn, 186-87; U.S. Congress, House, Subcommittee on the Department of the Interior and Related Agencies, *Department of the Interior and Related Agencies Appropriations for 1998: Hearings before a Subcommittee of the Committee on Appropriations, Part 1*, 105th Cong., 1st Sess., 1997, 1083; *New York Daily News*, 26 April 1997, 13.

38   GMA, Restoration; Decline & Preservation: Opening the Overlook Pavilion, Grant Monument Association, accessed 10 August 2022, https://grantstomb.org/restoration-preservation/#OpeningtheOverlookPavilion.

Exhibit space in the visitor center includes a number of Grant-related artifacts: a Grant 63rd birthday book, the memoirs, a cornerstone laying ticket, a ticket to a performance that raised money for the Tomb, and a picture of the sarcophagus.

National Park Service

for its restoration, the city finally replaced them.[39] The federal government actually owns only the .76 acre of land on which the mausoleum sits out to its nearby retaining walls, and the GMA's position is that surrounding city-owned land should be transferred to the NPS so that the actual boundaries of the national park align with the common-sense boundaries of the site associated with Grant's Tomb.[40]

The quarter century that followed the centennial also saw significant improvements in educational and ceremonial activities at the Tomb. The abstract mosaic benches would remain, but not the illusion that such a distraction could convey the monument's true meaning to visitors. Instead, Grant's historical revival was incorporated into site programming, as was an enhanced commemorative schedule. Grant's birthday used to be the only regularly observed anniversary at the site. But in recent years, the anniversary of Grant's death; the birth and death anniversaries of his wife Julia, who is interred next to her husband; and special anniversaries of battles and presidential achievements have been added to the mix. A 2015 program marking the 150th anniversary of Gen. Robert E. Lee's surrender to Grant at Appomattox would have resonated with those who witnessed the Tomb's centennial program fifty years earlier. In 2020, a wreath laying and

39   Current & Future Projects: Land Transfer, Grant Monument Association, accessed 10 August 2022, https://grantstomb.org/current-future-projects/#LandTransfer.

40   This and the changing of the name of the site from General Grant National Memorial to the more familiar and historical Grant's Tomb National Monument were components of legislation introduced in Congress during the 1990s. The Grant's Tomb National Monument Act, as the legislation was known, was last introduced in 1997 as H.R. 546 in the House of Representatives and S. 155 in the Senate. The GMA still advocates these goals and requested members of Congress to introduce similar legislation in 2019. See An appeal to elected officials on behalf of Grant's Tomb, Grant Monument Association, 28 March 2019, accessed 10 August 2022, https://grantstomb.org/appeal-to-elected-officials, hereafter cited as GMA appeal to elected officials.

presentation commemorated the 150th anniversary of the ratification of the Fifteenth Amendment, which prohibited racial discrimination in voting; that program would have seemed a novelty during the years in which Grant's presidency was treated with disdain. Such an event would have eluded the 1970s-vintage conception of Grant's final resting place as fading from relevance and dependent upon the sympathy shown to "an aged and slightly zany parent." Today, it is that supposedly sophisticated and modernist view that has aged poorly. Grant's legacy has emerged as more fresh, more relevant than the dismissiveness of generations of critics whose own insight into the age of Grant was limited. Today, Grant's public career emerges as a towering benchmark in advancing liberty, equality, peace, and human dignity.

Grant's Tomb is not the only site with a story arc that reflects the Grant renaissance. The fates of several Grant sites illustrate the contrasts over changing times. Grant's "summer White House" in Long Branch, New Jersey, was demolished in 1963.[41] During the 1980s, Grant's home in Saint Louis, White Haven, was threatened by private development, and New York State had plans to close the cottage on Mount McGregor where Grant died. Concerned citizens saved both. White Haven became a national park, the Ulysses S. Grant National Historic Site, pursuant to a law enacted in 1989, the same year that the Friends of the Ulysses S. Grant Cottage was formed to operate Grant's final home.[42] The latter site was designated as a national historic landmark in 2021.[43] Yet another Grant site, the house in Detroit where Ulysses and Julia lived between 1849 and 1850, was relocated in 2020 from the Michigan State Fairgrounds, where it had been closed to the public for years, to Detroit's Eastern Market, where it is undergoing rehabilitation in preparation for reopening to the public.[44] Nowadays, the demolition or closure of Grant's homes is widely considered unacceptable. Even the site of the Long Branch cottage that did not survive received a historic marker installed by the GMA as part of the Grant bicentennial observance.

41   Jerry Carino, "In Long Branch, a President Slept Here—a Lot," *Asbury Park Press*, 29 August 2016, A5.

42   Ulysses S. Grant and White Haven: A Timeline, National Park Service, accessed 10 August 2022, https://www.nps.gov/articles/000/ulysses-s-grant-and-white-haven-a-timeline.htm; Grant Cottage History, Ulysses S. Grant Cottage National Historic Landmark, accessed 10 August 2022, https://www.grantcottage.org/the-cottage-and-its-site. Two of the essays in this volume, by Nick Sacco in Chapter Three and by Ben Kemp in Chapter Twelve, come from the talented staffs of these historic sites.

43   "Grant Cottage State Historic Site Gains Federal National Landmark Status," New York State Office of Parks, Recreation and Historic Preservation press release, 21 January 2021, accessed 10 August 2022, https://parks.ny.gov/newsroom/press-releases/release.aspx?r=1622.

44   The Project, Julia & Ulysses S. Grant House, Michigan History Center, accessed 10 August 2022, https://www.michigan.gov/mhc/museums/granthouse/project-history.

At the most famous of all Grant sites, the GMA in the twenty-first century enjoys a collaborative relationship with the NPS in the development of programs. This is a dramatic improvement from the acrimonious dynamic of the 1990s at Grant's Tomb. But any properly functioning historic site depends on multiple components, and the absence of any one of them can spell trouble. During the 35-day federal government shutdown between December 2018 and January 2019, Grant's Tomb was without security, and surely enough, it suffered a graffiti attack. It was a reminder that the need for security measures implemented during the 1990s has not and will not disappear; that public officials who control the government's purse strings have an ongoing obligation to provide sufficient resources for preservation; and that as historic preservation goes, there is no substitute for eternal vigilance on the part of concerned citizens, no matter what protective laws are on the books.

As commendable as the NPS's recent improvements at the monument have been, some perspective is in order: Grant's Tomb began its restoration story so far behind the curve that dramatic improvements were necessary simply to bring the site up to the minimum standards our country should demand of such a national treasure. Public awareness of the monument has improved, but there remains much room for growth. At more than 126,000, visitation to the Tomb in 1997 was the highest it had been since 1965. Since then, the site would often but not usually surpass 100,000 in annual visits.[45] The passage of time still brings basic maintenance needs such as stone plaza and stairway deterioration and water damage to the roof. These problems are not as severe as they once were, but they still require attention that is too often delayed for a matter of years.[46] With few exceptions, historic urban national parks that are not within the line of vision of federal lawmakers in Washington have tended to be stepchildren of the national park system that receive less attention. Even a measure like the Great American Outdoors Act of 2020, one of the most important national park funding laws of the past half century, created a multi-billion-dollar fund that so far has not brought any proceeds to Grant's Tomb.

There remains on a grander scale unfinished work at the site, old and new. When the monument was dedicated, two principal features were still missing: a crowning figure for the summit of the building, which consists of an empty pedestal, and an equestrian statue of Grant. In his dedication day address in 1897, Horace Porter referred to the crowning figure as a goal to be reached in the near

---

45   NPS, Annual Visits.

46   GMA appeal to elected officials.

Grant knew the choice of his final resting place would be of great public interest. Despite some dark times for the Tomb, interest remains—and continues to grow.

Chris Mackowski

future. A finial was even drawn onto the photo of Grant's Tomb on the cover of the official dedication ceremony program, but it never materialized.[47]

An equestrian statue was similarly part of early designs—initially conceived to be placed on the monument's front steps but projected under later GMA plans to go into the plaza in front of the monument.[48] The idea remained popular among those involved with the transfer of the Tomb to the NPS, and the agency in 1959 authorized the GMA to raise money for an equestrian statue. Not surprisingly, during those waning years for the monument, sufficient funds were not forthcoming.[49] Grant's Tomb's architectural trajectory has paralleled Grant's trajectory in the history books, and completing the monument would be a fitting part of the ongoing Grant renaissance.

47   Kahn, 152-53.

48   Ibid., 76, 153, 157-58, 161, 172.

49   Ibid., 181-83.

As ceremonies for Grant's bicentennial birthday demonstrated, Grant's Tomb again exudes the majesty its designers intended, worthy of the man—and his wife—entombed there.

Albert Trotman

Not among the earlier plans for the monument, but no less an important component of its future, would be a visitor center that does justice to Grant's story. Public knowledge of that story is nowhere near what it was at the turn of the twentieth century, and visitors to the site deserve more than a cursory introduction to Grant. The overlook pavilion currently serving as a visitor center is better described as a makeshift visitor center, with two single-user restrooms, a gift shop, and a presentation room crammed into a relatively small area once dedicated entirely to restrooms. In the dual-purpose presentation room, both Grant's biography and the story of the Tomb are condensed into six exhibit panels along the walls, with 40 chairs squeezed in. The Tomb should have a separate, spacious facility on site that can put to optimal use the advances in presentational technology and availability of artifacts in order to leave visitors of all ages with an appreciation for Grant's rich life and legacy.

Surely the nation that was saved by his achievements can afford the modest expenditure it would take to educate visitors to the site about a story that too few Americans know. We should build it. We should tell Grant's story. We should invite visitors to be inspired by it, just as Grant's contemporaries were when they constructed this grandest of American mausoleums. Those contemporaries are long gone, but that inspiration, like the monument itself, endures, waiting to be shared with us and with future generations for ages to come.

U.S. Grant: An Appreciation
Epilogue | *Jack Kemp*

Excerpt from an Address to the Civil War Institute at Gettysburg College—June 29, 2001

It is time for us to restore Grant and to help fix him in the constellation of stars in which he deserves to be. When one looks at the whole life and career of Grant—not just as a general, but as a citizen, as a father, as a husband, as a president, and in retired life—one cannot, with a clear lens, see Grant as anything but a truly great man, deserving of our respect, admiration, and gratitude.

From his humble beginnings as the son of a leather tanner, Grant became Lincoln's comrade in arms as a savior of the Union and our nation. As I said here eleven years ago,". . . Slavery was an abomination, a hideous stain defiling the nation's soul; it could only be cleansed by a baptism of fire in civil war." President Lincoln and General Grant presided over that baptism. A man who graduated in the middle of his class at West Point led the nation in her toughest hour. . . .

I'm struck by his utter lack of guile, his complete magnanimity, his humility, and the total absence of racism of any kind in a century rife with hatred of blacks, persecution of Indians, and fear of immigrants. . . .

[W]hile Grant had, until recently, been ranked in "the bottom ten" of our nation's presidents, I would argue Grant should more appropriately be ranked in the top ten, along with Washington, Lincoln, Roosevelt and Reagan . . . .

During his presidency, as Professor [Jean Edward] Smith notes, America "crept [on] the world stage, almost" without notice. He treated Indians as individuals saying in his first inaugural: "I will favor any course toward them [the Indians] which tends to their . . . ultimate citizenship." As the abolitionist writer Wendell Phillips said, "Thank God for [Grant,] whose first word was for the Negro and the second for the Indian."

Grant made himself synonymous with the 15th Amendment—he believed the rights of the freed blacks could only ultimately be secured through the right to vote. After the 15th Amendment's passage, William Lloyd Garrison remarked, "this wonderful, quiet, sudden transformation of four million human beings" moved them "from . . . the auction-block to the ballot box." So monumental an amendment was the 15th that the American Anti-Slavery Society disbanded; they saw their work as done. . . .

Many historians say Grant was a man of few words and then, when words came, that they were not words to be admired. But if you read his annual messages to Congress, you will not read a man of few words. And if you want to know about how well his words were crafted, I think the person to defer to is Mark Twain, who lobbied Grant to allow him to publish his memoirs. And when you read those memoirs, you will see a very gifted writer—they are a treasure of history. And Grant wrote them, determined to complete them, while dying from an excruciatingly painful form of esophageal cancer that withered and wrecked his body. The inner strength he summoned while dying—and knowing he was dying—to finish his memoirs is a story of courage and valor under fire, as honorable and noble as any battle he fought on the battlefield. . . .

The first Republican platform called slavery a "relic of barbarism." The platform on which Lincoln was elected integrated the Declaration of Independence into the party. Lincoln gave life to the words of the Declaration, and by opposing slavery, he ended it. Grant picked up Lincoln's flag and ushered in voting rights for blacks and a free economy. *Enterprise and freedom; strength and liberty.* Those were the watchwords of our nation's Founding. *Limit the ends of government, do not limit the ends of man.* That was the political philosophy of our Founding. It took an Abraham Lincoln and a Ulysses S. Grant to make those words real. In so doing, they taught us all what true statesmanship is. It is humility tempered by a moral sense. It is strength when needed and gentleness when forgiveness is wrought by peace. In sum, it is magnanimity in victory and the prayer that the victory will come from a just cause. Ulysses S. Grant represented and lived this creed.

Contributors

Charles W. Calhoun, a specialist in the history of the United States from 1865 to 1900, is the author of, most recently, *The Presidency of Ulysses S. Grant*. He is Thomas Harriot Distinguished Professor of History emeritus at East Carolina University and past president of the Society for Historians of the Gilded Age and Progressive Era. A former fellow of the National Endowment for the Humanities, he has written six books and edited four others.

Ulysses Grant Dietz grew up in Syracuse, New York. He studied French at Yale, and was trained to be a museum curator in the Winterthur Program in American Material Culture. A curator at the Newark Museum for thirty-seven years before he retired, Ulysses is a great-great grandson of Ulysses S. Grant. His late mother, Julia, was the president's last surviving great-grandchild, youngest daughter of Ulysses S. Grant III and granddaughter of the president's eldest son, Frederick. He serves on the board of directors of the Ulysses S. Grant Association.

Alvin S. Felzenberg is a presidential historian, political commentator, and former public official. He holds a Ph.D. in Politics from Princeton University and has lectured at the University of Pennsylvania, Yale, Princeton, Johns Hopkins and George Washington Universities. In 2006, Felzenberg was a Fellow at the Institute of Politics at the John F. Kennedy School of Government at Harvard. Felzenberg has served in two presidential administrations and as official spokesman for the 9-11 Commission. He is author of *A Man and His Presidents: The Political Odyssey of William F. Buckley, Jr.*, *The Leaders We Deserved (and a Few We Didn't): Rethinking the Presidential Rating Game*, and *Governor Tom Kean: From the New Jersey Statehouse to the 9-11 Commission*.

Curt Fields has had a strong interest in the Civil War since he was about 12 years old. That interest led him, ultimately, to portray General Grant in first-person. In "being" General and President Grant, he developed a deep respect for the complex man that Grant was—a man who has, regrettably, been shunted into the shadows of history. In the 21st century, Curt has been a police officer and hostage negotiator; a high school teacher and later a principal; and a university instructor. In 2022, he was elected to the board of directors of the Ulysses S. Grant Association. He lives in Collierville, Tennessee, a suburb of Memphis.

Gary W. Gallagher is the John L. Nau III Professor of History emeritus at the University of Virginia. He has published widely on the era of the Civil War, most recently *The Enduring Civil War: Reflections on the Great American Crisis* and *Civil War Witnesses and Their Books: New Perspectives on Iconic Works* (co-edited with Stephen Cushman).

Ben Kemp was born and raised in the Saratoga region of New York State. He is a living historian, speaker, and researcher who has been featured by C-SPAN, PBS, the History Channel, and the National Park Service. Kemp has been a staff member at Grant Cottage Historic Site since 2014 and is the current Operations Manager.

Jack Kemp was a professional quarterback who learned the value of leadership, teamwork, equality and competition; a member of the U.S. House of Representatives (1971–1989) who knew the power of ideas, human capital, and opportunity; and Secretary of Housing and Urban Development (1989–1993) and 1996 Republican vice presidential candidate who spoke passionately of the power of free markets and free people. His work appears in this volume courtesy of the Jack Kemp Foundation.

Chris Mackowski is the editor-in-chief and co-founder of Emerging Civil War, and the managing editor of the Emerging Civil War Series (Savas Beatie). He is a writing professor in the Jandoli School of Communication at St. Bonaventure University, where he also serves as the associate dean for undergraduate programs, and the historian-in-residence at Stevenson Ridge, a historic property on the Spotsylvania Court House battlefield.

John F. Marszalek graduated from Canisius College and The University of Notre Dame, where he earned his Ph.D. He joined the History Department of Gannon University in 1968 and Mississippi State University in the fall of 1973. Mississippi State University named him a William L. Giles Distinguished Professor in 1994, and in 2008, he became executive director of the Ulysses S. Grant Association and Presidential Library, retiring from that position in the spring of 2022. He has written 15 books, more than 300 articles, and many book reviews. His most famous book is *Sherman: A Soldier's Passion for Order* published by The Free Press in 1993. He is considered an expert on William T. Sherman and U.S. Grant, completing the 30-plus-volume series on the papers of Ulysses S. Grant and the recent annotated version of the Grant's *Personal Memoirs*. He is presently completing *The Sherman Memoirs* for Harvard University Press.

Nick Sacco is a park ranger with the National Park Service at Ulysses S. Grant National Historic Site. He regularly gives tours of White Haven, the childhood home of Julia Dent Grant and the place where Ulysses and Julia first began their relationship. He also designs education programs and interpretive exhibits for the park. Nick published an article with the *Journal of the Civil War Era* in 2019 about Grant's relationship with slavery. He holds a master's degree in history from IUPUI.

Frank J. Scaturro Frank J. Scaturro is an attorney and the author of *President Grant Reconsidered* (1998) and The *Supreme Court's Retreat from Reconstruction* (2000). He is the president of the Grant Monument Association, which is dedicated to the preservation of Grant's Tomb. He previously served as counsel for the Constitution for the Senate Judiciary Committee and as special counsel to the House Select Investigative Panel. He now serves as vice-president and senior counsel of JCN.

Ryan P. Semmes is professor and director of research at the Ulysses S. Grant Presidential Library at Mississippi State University. He has been on the faculty at Mississippi State University since 2007 and has worked with the Ulysses S. Grant Presidential Library since 2009. Ryan's research focuses on the connections between foreign and domestic policy and the nature of citizenship during the Reconstruction era.

Timothy B. Smith teaches history at the University of Tennessee at Martin. He is the author or editor of more than twenty books, including *Shiloh: Conquer or Perish* and *The Real Horse Soldiers: Benjamin Grierson's Epic 1863 Raid through Civil War Mississippi*. He is currently writing a five-volume history of the Vicksburg Campaign and is under contract to produce a new examination of Albert Sidney Johnston's command in the Western theater.

Joan Waugh, professor emerita of the UCLA History Department, researches and writes on the American Civil War, Reconstruction, and Gilded Age eras. Waugh has published many essays and books on Civil War topics, including *U.S. Grant: American Hero, American Myth* and *The American War: A History of the Civil War Era*, co-authored with Gary W. Gallagher. Waugh's current projects include an exploration of the nature of U.S. Grant's surrender policy during the Civil War.

Ronald C. White is the author of two *New York Times* bestselling presidential biographies: *American Ulysses: A Life of Ulysses S. Grant* and *A. Lincoln: A Biography*. He has also written *Lincoln's Greatest Speech: The Second Inaugural*, a *New York Times* Notable Book; *The Eloquent President: A Portrait of Lincoln Through His Words*; and *Lincoln in Private: What His Most Personal Reflections Tell Us About Our Greatest President*, recipient of the 2021 Barondess/Lincoln Award. He received a Ph.D. from Princeton University.

Frank J. Williams served as chief justice of the Supreme Court of Rhode Island between 2001 and 2008. He is the author or editor of more than twenty books, including *Judging Lincoln; The Emancipation Proclamation: Three Views*; and *Lincoln as Hero*. Williams is currently writing *Grant as Hero*. Among the leadership roles he assumed for several historical organizations and initiatives, from 1990 to 2022, he served as president of the Ulysses S. Grant Association. In 2017, he donated one of the nation's largest private Lincoln collections to form The Frank and Virginia Williams Collection of Lincolniana at Mississippi State University, which is housed next to the Ulysses S. Grant Presidential Library.

Index

Cities are listed as subheads under the state where each is located. For instance, find "Richmond" as a subhead under "Virginia." Battlefield features are listed as subheads under the battlefields where they're located. For instance, find "Devil's Den" as a subhead under "Gettysburg battlefield."

Grant at 200

is a joint collaboration between
The Ulysses S. Grant Association and
The Grant Monument Association.

The Ulysses S. Grant Association

https://www.usgrantlibrary.org/usga

The mission of the Ulysses S. Grant Association is to conduct research into the life of Ulysses S. Grant and preserve the knowledge of his importance in American history.

• We edit and publish Grant's writings both in hardcover and digital format.

• We acquire and preserve artifacts and memorabilia from Grant's lifetime and make them available to scholars and the public.

• We conduct teacher and student institutes and classes, and organize lectures and symposia.

• We maintain the Ulysses S. Grant Presidential Library as the major repository of information about Ulysses S. Grant and his era.

The Grant Monument Association

https://grantstomb.org/

The GMA remains the primary outlet for citizen support for Grant's Tomb. The GMA's mission:

• To commemorate and perpetuate the accomplishments of Ulysses S. Grant and Julia Dent Grant and their memory.

• To undertake educational activities and ceremonies as they pertain to President Grant's service to his country.

• To cooperate with public and private parties to insure the repair, maintenance and upgrading of Grant's Tomb in New York City.

• To raise funds to accomplish the foregoing purposes.